The Angel and the Cad

GERALDINE ROBERTS is an historian and writer who
lives in East London. In 2010 she decided to follow her life-long
passion for history and attained an MA with Distinction from
Queen Mary University of London. *The Angel and the Cad*
is her first book.

GERALDINE ROBERTS

The Angel and the Cad

LOVE, LOSS AND SCANDAL IN REGENCY ENGLAND

PAN BOOKS

For Greg

First published 2015 by Macmillan

First published in paperback 2016 by Pan Books
an imprint of Pan Macmillan
20 New Wharf Road, London N1 9RR
Associated companies throughout the world
www.panmacmillan.com

ISBN 978-1-4472-8352-2

1 3 5 7 9 8 6 4 2

A CIP catalogue record for this book is available from the British Library.

Printed and bound by CPI Group (UK) Ltd, Croydon, CR0 4YY

Visit www.panmacmillan.com to read more about all our books
and to buy them. You will also find features, author interviews and
news of any author events, and you can sign up for e-newsletters
so that you're always first to hear about our new releases.

Contents

Contents

Contents

Catherine's Family: Part 1

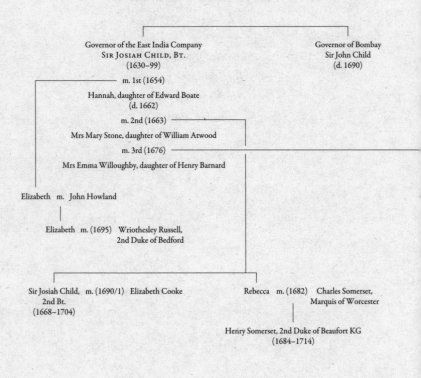

Governor of the East India Company
SIR JOSIAH CHILD, BT.
(1630–99)

Governor of Bombay
Sir John Child
(d. 1690)

m. 1st (1654)
Hannah, daughter of Edward Boate
(d. 1662)

m. 2nd (1663)
Mrs Mary Stone, daughter of William Atwood

m. 3rd (1676)
Mrs Emma Willoughby, daughter of Henry Barnard

Elizabeth   m.   John Howland

Elizabeth   m. (1695)   Wriothesley Russell,
2nd Duke of Bedford

Sir Josiah Child,   m. (1690/1)   Elizabeth Cooke
2nd Bt.
(1668–1704)

Rebecca   m. (1682)   Charles Somerset,
Marquis of Worcester

Henry Somerset, 2nd Duke of Beaufort KG
(1684–1714)

Richard Child
(later Tylney)
(1711–34)
Viscount Castlemaine

SIR JOHN CHILD
(later Tylney)
(1712–84)
4th Bt. & 2nd Earl Tylney
(Died unmarried in Naples
Titles became extinct)

Josiah Child ('Joe')   m.   Henrietta Knight
(d. 1760)

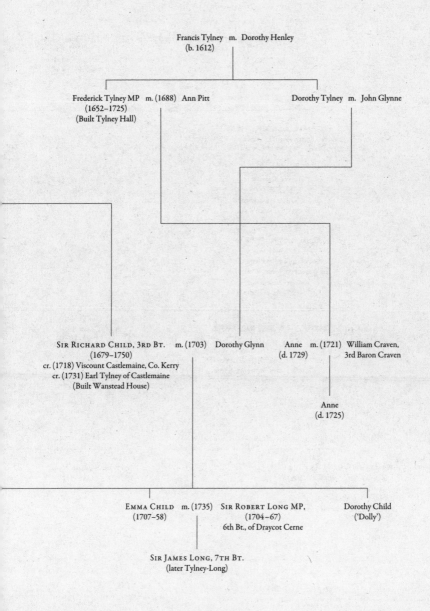

Francis Tylney m. Dorothy Henley
(b. 1612)

Frederick Tylney MP m. (1688) Ann Pitt
(1652–1725)
(Built Tylney Hall)

Dorothy Tylney m. John Glynne

SIR RICHARD CHILD, 3RD BT. m. (1703) Dorothy Glynn
(1679–1750)
cr. (1718) Viscount Castlemaine, Co. Kerry
cr. (1731) Earl Tylney of Castlemaine
(Built Wanstead House)

Anne m. (1721) William Craven,
(d. 1729)   3rd Baron Craven

Anne
(d. 1725)

EMMA CHILD m. (1735) SIR ROBERT LONG MP,
(1707–58)   (1704–67)
                     6th Bt., of Draycot Cerne

Dorothy Child
('Dolly')

SIR JAMES LONG, 7TH BT.
(later Tylney-Long)

SIR ROBERT LONG MP, 6TH BT.   m. (1735)   Lady Emma Child
(1704–67)   (1707–58)
of Wanstead House
and Tylney Hall

SIR JAMES LONG MP, 7TH BT.
(Tylney-Long by Royal Licence from 1775)
(1737–94)

m. 1st (1775)

Harriot Bouverie
(d. 1777)
dau. of Viscount Folkestone
of Longford Castle, Wilts.

m. 2nd (1785)

Catherine Sidney Windsor
(1755–1823)
dau. of the Earl of Plymouth
of Warmstry House, Worcester

CATHERINE m. (1812)   William Wellesley-Pole   Dorothy
(b. 1789)   (1788–1857)   (1792–1872)
nephew of the Duke of Wellington
Viscount Wellesley from 1842
4th Earl of Mornington from 1845

WILLIAM RICHARD ARTHUR   James Fitzroy Henry
POLE TYLNEY LONG WELLESLEY   (1815–51)
(1813–63)
Viscount Wellesley from 1845
5th Earl of Mornington from 1857

Catherine's Family: Part 2

Charles Long (of Grittleton)   m. (1777)   Hannah Phipps   Dorothy   Emma
      (d. 1783)   of Heywood House

Emma   Sir James Tylney-Long, 8th Bt.
(1793–1877)   (1794–1805)

Victoria Catherine Mary
(1818–97)

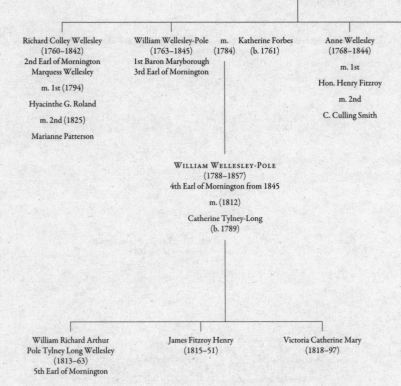

Garret Wesley
(1735–81)
2nd Baron Mornington
1st Earl of Mornington

m.

Lady Anne Hill
(1741–1831)
dau. of Arthur Hill,
Viscount Dungannon

Richard Colley Wellesley
(1760–1842)
2nd Earl of Mornington
Marquess Wellesley

m. 1st (1794)

Hyacinthe G. Roland

m. 2nd (1825)

Marianne Patterson

William Wellesley-Pole
(1763–1845)
1st Baron Maryborough
3rd Earl of Mornington

m.

Katherine Forbes
(1784)   (b. 1761)

Anne Wellesley
(1768–1844)

m. 1st

Hon. Henry Fitzroy

m. 2nd

C. Culling Smith

WILLIAM WELLESLEY-POLE
(1788–1857)
4th Earl of Mornington from 1845

m. (1812)

Catherine Tylney-Long
(b. 1789)

William Richard Arthur
Pole Tylney Long Wellesley
(1813–63)
5th Earl of Mornington

James Fitzroy Henry
(1815–51)

Victoria Catherine Mary
(1818–97)

The Wellesley Family

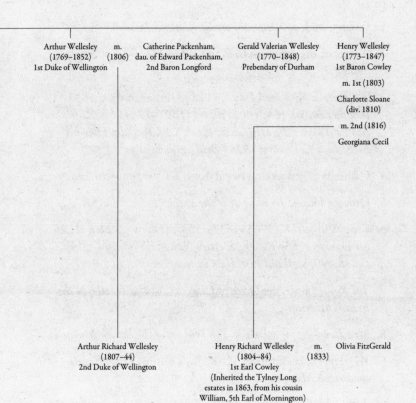

Arthur Wellesley   m.   Catherine Packenham,   Gerald Valerian Wellesley   Henry Wellesley
(1769–1852)   (1806)   dau. of Edward Packenham,   (1770–1848)   (1773–1847)
1st Duke of Wellington   2nd Baron Longford   Prebendary of Durham   1st Baron Cowley

m. 1st (1803)

Charlotte Sloane
(div. 1810)

m. 2nd (1816)

Georgiana Cecil

Arthur Richard Wellesley   Henry Richard Wellesley   m.   Olivia FitzGerald
(1807–44)   (1804–84)   (1833)
2nd Duke of Wellington   1st Earl Cowley
(Inherited the Tylney Long
estates in 1863, from his cousin
William, 5th Earl of Mornington)

List of Illustrations

Notes on the Text

The spelling of Catherine's surname varies in newspapers, but has been standardized to the correct version, Tylney (as opposed to Tilney).

All quotations are cited in the references at the end of the book, but a few have been standardized and updated to modern English for the ease of understanding and clarity.

Money plays a huge part in Catherine's story, but conversions over time are notoriously difficult. The Bank of England currency converter bases its calculations on average inflation of two per cent per year, estimating that £100 in 1810 is equivalent to around £7,000 in 2010 (i.e. multiply by 70). Very conservatively speaking, therefore, the Bank of England calculates that Catherine's annual income of £40,000 would convert to around £2,500,000 today. This method is unreliable, however, because certain costs have soared disproportionately, such as house prices and rents. This is highlighted by the fact that in 1825, Catherine's husband bought a detached villa in Hall Place (now Hall Gate), set in two acres adjoining Regent's Park, for £6,000. Using the Bank of England converter, this villa would be worth around £320,000 in the early twenty-first century, when in reality a property like this would now fetch tens of millions of pounds. These soaring values must also factor into the equation, because Catherine's assets were largely tied to land and property. So, in effect, accurate monetary comparison is unfeasible and Catherine was far richer than the Bank of England conversion rates imply.

Throughout this book, I multiply by 100 to provide rough twenty-first-century equivalents. Even this, I believe, is conservative when calculating Catherine's income.

Introduction

❧

I first came across Catherine in a nineteenth-century newspaper, which summarized the remarkable twists and turns of her life. Eager to learn more, I scoured the Internet hoping to find a book or biography, but apart from a few sketchy outlines there was very little information about her. For some reason Catherine stayed with me, and I mentioned the article to my husband, telling him that it would make a terrific story for someone to write about. I am not usually superstitious, but it seemed like fate when I discovered a box of Catherine's correspondence lying undocumented at Redbridge Archives. I was immediately gripped by her letters, which are disarmingly candid and deeply moving. After reading through them I felt a compelling urge to tell her story.

In the main, Catherine has been portrayed as a feeble character. Kilvert's diaries state that she was 'weak and foolish'; letters to Lord Eldon suggest that she was dim and dull; while Octavia Barry repeatedly refers to her as 'sad . . . sorrowful . . . pathetic'. This one-dimensional view has prevailed, even though all these previous publications were written in the nineteenth century, when it was considered proper for women to be acquiescent. Barry, in particular, endeavoured to portray Catherine in a sympathetic light by painting her as a saint, while deliberately avoiding all mention of the uproar she caused. When I began to scratch beneath the surface of this story, a very different image of Catherine emerged. Primary materials revealed that she was a vivacious, forthright, highly accomplished woman who painted landscapes, composed music and managed a huge household with efficiency. Her two most defining traits were her unwavering sweetness and courage.

Although Catherine wrote hundreds of letters during her lifetime, very few survive among her private papers at Redbridge

Archives. Much of her correspondence was destroyed in a fire, which may have been started deliberately to protect her privacy. Owing to this, when I first started researching, there were huge gaps in my timeline, literally twenty years of Catherine's life with no personal information to go on. The task of piecing together her story was daunting, but I was spurred on by my husband, Greg, who was researching a closely related subject. Over the subsequent ten years, our quest for clues extended to archives the length and breadth of Britain, from Southampton to Aberdeen, plus resources in Ireland and the USA.

My journey of discovery has focused on Catherine and her influence in Regency high society. I have been enthralled by the glamour and excitement of her life: the fashions and festivities, the scandal and gossip. As a popular celebrity, she was constantly in the news, which meant that contemporary newspapers provided much insight into the details of her life. The Hiram Stead Collection of Wanstead House material, held at Newham Heritage and Archives, has been an invaluable resource as it comprises a miscellany of newspaper and magazine clippings from a wide range of contemporary publications, some of which no longer exist elsewhere since sections of the British Library were bombed during World War II. Useful information was also gleaned from diaries, memoirs, fashion magazines and auction catalogues. But it has been particularly difficult to get to grips with finances due to the lack of primary source information. Much of the surviving fiscal documentation is riddled with inconsistencies, which means that the full picture cannot be definitively established.

The Angel and the Cad began its life as my MA dissertation, which explored the influence of newspapers in Regency England and the growth of celebrity culture. Newsmen of the day employed all kinds of literary devices to influence the public and capture their imagination. Reports about Catherine were filled with satire, tragedy and melodrama – her life unfolded in the press rather like the chapters of a highly wrought novel. Owing to this, contemporary newspapers provided the perfect framework for this book, enabling the story to unfurl rather as it did at the time.

Although newspapers were rich in detail about events and occurrences, they did little to shed light on Catherine's thoughts and feelings. In the early stages of my research, she remained a shadowy figure, compelling but elusive, and I needed to find primary source material that would flesh out her character. When my breakthrough eventually came, it was definitely worth the wait. Some years into her marriage, Catherine was embroiled in a scandal that resulted in a high-profile court case, which shocked the British public and resonated for many years. Discovering the trial transcript was a major step forward, particularly as the affidavits are so vividly descriptive. They include testimonies from many eye-witnesses, including the butler, tutor, close relatives and friends. Statements from the long-suffering valet are often comical, while accounts from the family physician are very powerful because he was Catherine's confidante. Doctor Bulkeley observed many shocking scenes, and his descriptions are so graphic that I felt I was actually there watching the drama unfold.

I have been extremely fortunate to have had such wonderful material to work with. Regency gossip columns endeavoured to captivate the general public and their style of reporting remains accessible to a modern mainstream audience. In addition, the educated classes actively engaged in social networking, exchanging gossip through letters and notes. Letter writing was an art form and they rejoiced in the written word, entertaining friends with a droll turn of phrase or amusing anecdote. They delighted in the latest scandal, offering up snippets of gossip or describing acquaintances in acid detail. Extracts taken from letters, diaries and affidavits have greatly enriched this book, and I am indebted to the real-life characters that have added such colour and flavour.

The main purpose of this book is to tell Catherine's story, but the narrative opens a window into the Regency period, broadly defined as 1811–30.[1] It spanned a crucial time, from the aftermath of the French Revolution to the eve of the first Reform Act, when people were questioning traditional customs, morals and beliefs. Conflict in Europe erupted in the 1790s and the Napoleonic Wars raged until 1815. Throughout this period, Grand Tours and other excursions to the continent were unfeasible. Paris was out of bounds to those searching for the latest trends, as was Italy for architecture and opera. For the better part of two decades, English society looked inwards for culture and inspiration. As a result, the Regency period was a seminal era of innovation and ingenuity, a time when ideas and ideals were changing rapidly.

The social structure did not fit neatly into a three-class model of nobility, bourgeoisie and proletariat. Each class in society had at least three tiers. Contemporary statistician Patrick Colquhoun produced a detailed assessment of annual incomes for 1812.[2] Working-class innkeepers and publicans scraped a living on £100; labourers were malnourished on £48; while the 1.5 million paupers suffered real want, barely surviving on just £10. In the middle ranks, size and profitability of businesses varied considerably. Eminent bankers and merchants could expect to earn around £2,600, judges £400, surveyors £300, while tailors, clergymen and military officers could live fairly comfortably on around £150. At the very top end of society the landed gentry was broken down as follows: 516 peers of the realm earned around £10,000, baronets £3,500, knights and squires £2,000. The royal princes made approximately £18,000. This puts into context Catherine's extraordinary wealth – in 1812 her income was £40,000 – confirming that she was at the very top of the pile.

Culturally, for those in high society, the Regency was an exciting time filled with glamour and decadence. It was the 'Age of Elegance', when matters of taste and refinement were paramount and the English were bursting with creativity, wit and accomplishment. It was the world of Romantic poets and artists such as Byron, Shelley, Keats, Wordsworth, Turner and Constable. All classes of society were raucous, delighting in the many satires and cartoons in circulation. The public at large took an interest in public affairs, and daily news bulletins could be heard and discussed in alehouses, inns, coffee shops and lecture rooms. Advances in information technology, such as the introduction of the steam-powered printing press, meant that daily news reached a wider audience than ever before. These developments saw London emerging as the first truly modern metropolis with booming consumerism, a buoyant fashion industry, mass media and celebrity culture.

Politically, there was instability because the ruling elite had too much supremacy. The nation's power and wealth was controlled by around 350 families out of a population of eighteen million, and they largely commanded trade and industry, while also determining the laws of the land. The gap between rich and poor was vast: more than seventy-five per cent of the population lived in squalor and suffered biting hardship, while a small minority lived in splendour. The system was unjust, but it was difficult to alter the status quo because just two per cent of adults had the power to vote – eligibility was restricted to men with property and money. Anti-government propaganda spilt onto the streets through newspapers, ballads, posters and cartoons, with appeals for parliamentary reform. Domestic issues took a back seat during the Napoleonic Wars, but after the Battle of Waterloo, in 1815, the working classes grew increasingly militant and were close to rebellion.

Women were also becoming more vocal about their rights and the time was ripe for change. Catherine's celebrity status attracted media scrutiny on an unprecedented scale and as the twists and turns of her life unfolded in the press, the British public were shaken to the core. Her story highlighted some of the key issues of the time, resulting in nationwide reflection and debate about moral standards. Rather than being weak and foolish, as historians have suggested, Catherine was a woman of her time constrained by the laws and conventions of the society in which she lived. As a prominent public figure, she played a part in bringing about important changes that continue to resonate in modern multicultural Britain today. I hope that Catherine will finally gain the recognition she deserves.

Prologue

～❦～

LONDON 1825

Late in the evening on 7 July, there was an unexpected caller at Catherine's house in Clarges Street, Piccadilly. The door knocker tapped loudly and the under-butler opened up to a surly ruffian dressed in a shabby brown stuff coat with coarse trousers. His face was in shadow, obscured by a black chip hat and bushy black beard. The red handkerchief tied round his neck completed a look designed to inspire great alarm and terror. When the thug tried to push past him, the under-butler succeeded in blocking his path, stalling him for a short time.[1]

Just across the hallway, Catherine sat in the drawing room with her two sisters, chatting quietly as she picked at her needlepoint. By now she was living in seclusion from all public society, constantly in fear that the man at her door would come looking for her, intent on wreaking revenge.[2] Many sleepless nights had been spent imagining the worst. Most of all, Catherine was petrified that he would snatch her children and hold them to ransom. It was even possible that he would hire an armed gang to assist in the kidnap. After months of living on her nerves, there was something about the knock and tone of voice in the hallway that made the ever-vigilant Catherine uneasy. As realization dawned on her, she rose quickly from her armchair and said, 'Hush, that knock on the door and that voice is very familiar. I am convinced that it must be [*him*].'[3]

'That cannot be!' remarked Dora.

Nevertheless, Catherine was sure that he had come. Retreating quickly into the back parlour, she had just left the room when the intruder burst in. 'Where is Catherine?' he demanded. When Dora and Emma did not answer, he smashed his fist into a side table and repeated, 'Where is Catherine?' His demeanour was frightening, but the sisters refused to cooperate. Rushing up the stairs, the ruffian stormed from room to room searching for the children. Crashing about, he slammed doors and overturned furniture before realizing that he was wasting his time – the children were not there.

During the commotion, Catherine had wasted no time in gathering up Victoria, and she slipped quietly down the backstairs with her precious daughter cradled in her arms. The servants were at supper when she hurried in, begging them to help her. Terrified that her tormentor would find her child, she was in a state of great agitation and a ferocious spasm gripped her chest. Although she was bent over double with pain, she took control of the situation and had the foresight to dispatch a footman to summon officers of the police from Marlborough Street.

With all the noise and confusion above stairs, Catherine had no idea how many intruders were rampaging through her house, possibly brandishing weapons. She made a snap decision to flee. Clutching her daughter tightly, she escaped through the back door. Under the cover of darkness, she cautiously felt her way along the deserted yard until she came to the stable block. Crouching down in the shadows, shielding her child, she was overwhelmed with fear as all kinds of scenarios played out in her head. Eventually she heard the rumble of a carriage and saw that the lights were heading towards her. Catherine knew that her fate rested on a knife-edge; she could only pray that the carriage would contain her rescuer, not her pursuer.

PART ONE

COURTSHIP

'The suitors were innumerable.
She received offers right and left.'

Lady Charlotte Bury

1. The Richest Heiress in the Kingdom

৵৵

1811

No one who had ever seen Catherine Tylney Long during her infancy could have imagined the sensation she would arouse. An unremarkable child, she grew up quietly in the provinces in a world immortalized by Jane Austen's novels. Her situation was similar to that of Elizabeth Bennet in *Pride and Prejudice*; although her father was wealthy, Catherine and her two sisters were very much the poor relations as the entire family fortune was set aside for a male relative, in accordance with custom.[1] All this changed overnight when a quirk of fate transformed her life and she became 'the richest heiress in the Kingdom'.[2] This was just the start of a remarkable story, which ignited a media frenzy that kept the nation enthralled for over two decades as the twists and turns of her life were serialized in the press. Catherine captured the hearts of the public because fame and fortune did not turn her head; in fact she remained so unpretentious and sweet-natured that she became known as 'the angel'.

By portraying Catherine as 'the angel', the media implied that she was the perfect woman. Virtue and goodness were her primary attributes, but Catherine also possessed numerous other qualities that were universally admired. She was intelligent, accomplished, self-assured and benevolent. The ideal modern woman was not cloyingly virtuous, but was closer to the character of Elizabeth Bennet in *Pride and Prejudice*. Austen herself remarked that Elizabeth was 'as delightful a creature as ever appeared in print',[3] and she has remained one of the most endearing characters in British literature. Although Elizabeth was respectable, it was her pluck, her arch remarks and stubborn refusal to marry a man she did not love that made her so captivating. Similarly, Catherine was a spirited woman with a playful sense of humour that endeared her to almost everyone she met. She was popular with the public because they admired her virtue, as well as her spark.

Catherine's coming of age portrait shows a beautifully groomed woman with a graceful swanlike neck and gentle gaze.[4] The artist captures the essence of her character in her expression, which is open, amiable and direct. A demure hairstyle and absence of jewellery or adornment indicates her lack of ostentation. Her modesty was such that the only hint of her immense wealth was the luxurious fur draped across her shoulders.

Born on 2 October 1789, Catherine was the eldest child of Sir James Tylney Long, seventh Baronet (1736–94),[5] and Lady Catherine Sydney Windsor.[6] The Longs had lived at Draycot in Wiltshire since the early fifteenth century when the clothier Robert Long purchased the picturesque estate, comprised of over 3,000 acres. For most of his life, Catherine's father was an unassuming country squire, renowned throughout Wiltshire for his charitable work. As Knight of the Shire, Sir James represented the county in Parliament, nominally a Tory but often voting with the opposition.[7] A bachelor for most of his life, he married at the age of forty, to Lady Harriet Bouverie, who died less than two years later. Although his first marriage was short-lived, Sir James formed long-lasting ties with Harriet's relations – the Earls of Shaftesbury and Radnor – two Whig families who would later become instrumental in the fight for social reform.[8] Undoubtedly, these associations reinforced Sir James's progressive ideals as he worked to support his local community, taking a personal interest in the welfare of the workers on his estate.

Sir James was affluent, owning around 10,000 acres of land spread over four counties, which yielded approximately £10,000 per annum in rents. He became enormously wealthy, however, when he inherited a vast fortune from his uncle, in 1785. The Tylney legacy comprised of around 10,000 acres in Essex, 2,500 acres in Hampshire, several stately homes plus sums held in stocks and bonds. Perfectly content with life in Wiltshire, Sir James had no desire to leave his ancestral home and move into one of the palatial mansions he now owned. However, he felt it was his duty to produce heirs to the Tylney estate. In 1785, he married Lady Catherine Sydney Windsor, a charitable, deeply religious woman. A memoir by a close family friend records their happy marriage and philanthropic work: 'Their tastes and feelings were the same. Sir James was a generous promoter of public and private charities . . . Volumes might be filled in describing his benevolence.'[9] Schools were set up in three of the parishes surrounding Draycot. The poor, old and infirm received food, clothing and winter fuel.[10] In effect, an early system of welfare state existed at Draycot, funded entirely by the generosity of the Tylney Long family.

Much to the couple's delight, three daughters were born in quick succession: Catherine in 1789, Dora in 1792 and Emma in 1793. Happy as they were, however, Lady Catherine was almost forty and they did not have a male heir. A precious son eluded them until the ninth year of their marriage when James finally arrived, in September 1794. By now, Sir James was in poor health, seized by an illness that baffled his doctors and agonized his wife as she watched him suffer. After deteriorating alarmingly quickly, he died in November 1794, aged fifty-eight, leaving his wife inconsolable with grief and in charge of four young children. Five-year-old Catherine was the only child old enough to recognize the nature of the loss, and she missed her father dreadfully.

Although the family was exceptionally wealthy, the custom of primogeniture determined that the eldest male inherit everything. Catherine's infant brother assumed the grand title of Sir James Tylney Long, eighth Baronet, becoming sole heir to the entire family fortune. To ensure there could be no misappropriation of funds, the late Sir James had ensured that all money was tied up in trusts and managed by professional advisors until his heir came of age. His son was made a Ward of Court in Chancery and inventories of the houses were made, in 1795, to ensure that his inheritance was preserved. Liberal provisions were made for the widow: Lady Catherine had a jointure of £5,000, a further £500 in pin money, a lifetime residency at Draycot House and other benefits.[11] This enabled the family to live very comfortably.

Lady Catherine lived quietly for many years, socializing with a small group of close friends and devoting herself to raising her children.[12] She found solace in religion and philanthropy, instilling her daughters with Christian principles. Catherine, Dora and Emma often accompanied their mother on charitable missions, taking food baskets to the sick or handing out prizes in the local schools sponsored by family trusts.[13] As a result, the girls grew up with a strong sense of benevolence and humility. As one neighbour recalled, 'They were a blessing . . . working for the poor, visiting them in their cottages, as divested of all pride, as if fortune had never smiled upon them.'[14]

Catherine's best friends and constant companions were her sisters. Tutored at home, the girls spent their mornings in lessons and afternoons walking on the estate or calling on neighbours. Sir James had the foresight to bequeath portions of £15,000 to each of his three daughters, which they would receive when they married, or reached the age of twenty-one, whichever occurred first. These funds would set them up in comfortable homes and enable them to attract respectable middle-class husbands from within the ranks of enterprise or from the professions, such as a manufacturer, retailer, doctor, lawyer or clergyman. Marrying well was a task that preoccupied both sexes; men commonly believed that a comfortable home, with a capable wife generating warmth and conviviality, was the perfect platform for happiness and social success.[15] To achieve this ideal, from an early age Catherine learned the practical skills needed to become the mistress of a genteel household, such as managing servants, juggling accounts and entertaining guests. To improve her social graces, she learned to play the piano and to dance, and received sufficient education to make her a pleasant companion who was able to cultivate polite conversation on topics such as music, art and literature.

More than anything, the three sisters doted on their little brother, with his ready smile and sunny disposition. James had been a delicate infant, but although his strength improved considerably, his mother and sisters remained fussy and over-protective, discouraging him from riding horses, climbing trees or participating in any boyish activity that held potential to cause him harm. Whenever the weather was even the slightest bit overcast, the children were encouraged to play inside and the long corridors at Draycot rang with their laughter as they ran up and down. The family physician believed that James was too pampered and advised that his health would benefit from fresh air, exercise and the regular routine of boarding school. Bowing to pressure, Lady Catherine reluctantly agreed that her son could leave home. But tragedy struck just a few months later, when eleven-year-old James contracted an illness at school and died suddenly, in 1805. The exact cause remains a mystery, but was possibly the result of exposure after he swam in a lake. Needless to say, Lady Catherine blamed herself for acting against her better judgement and sending her child away. The end of James's short life closed an important chapter in the family's history – because baronetcies can only pass along the male line, the family title became extinct.

With no surviving males in her immediate family, destiny took a dramatic turn for sixteen-year-old Catherine and she became heiress to one of the largest fortunes in Britain. On coming of age she would receive around 23,000 acres of land spread over six counties, several stately homes and an annual income rumoured to be £80,000, although £40,000 was a more realistic figure.[16]

The magnitude of the legacy left to Catherine can be attributed to the meteoric rise of one remarkable man. The Tylney family made their money in the seventeenth century through the East India Company's merchant shipping, thanks to the vision and entrepreneurial skills of Josiah Child (1631–1699). He rose from relatively humble origins to become one of the richest men in Britain.[17] Starting out as a brewer in his early teens, his business grew rapidly after he secured a contract to supply beer and other services to the navy. Aged nineteen, he transported goods from Plymouth to Lisbon for the parliamentary fleet, gaining invaluable experience in trade and commerce. By 1659, he was provisioning East India Company ships, gaining a licence a few years later to embark on private ventures to India. Substantial profits were reinvested into new businesses, including a brewery in New Hampshire and a sugar cane plantation in Jamaica, where he manufactured rum. However, Child had shrewdly determined that trade with India would be the most lucrative. Investing heavily in the East India Company, he became their largest shareholder, as well as their Governor. It was the optimum time to gain control as the company started to diversify, importing chintz for household fabric, fine muslin for dresses, spices, silk and porcelain. The East India Company thrived and prospered under his direction, becoming the greatest merchant shipping company in the world, dominating the oceans and monopolizing trade between England and the Far East. As a pioneer of foreign commerce, Child wrote several important books about economics. *A New Discourse in Trade*, published in 1668, became the rulebook for companies involved in free trade. Acquiring the title of baronet in 1678, Sir Josiah Child was by now one of the wealthiest men in Britain. The extent of his fortune can be gauged by the fact that in 2007 the *Sunday Times* listed him in the top one hundred of the wealthiest Britons since 1066.[18]

Josiah's gritty determination spilt over into his private life and he actively courted social advancement. Marrying advantageously three times, he also ensured that his five surviving children married into some of the highest families of the nobility. When his daughter Rebecca Child married Charles Somerset (1660–98), heir to the Duke of Beaufort, her dowry was reputed to be an enormous £25,000. It proved to be money well spent, however, as Sir Josiah's grandson Henry Somerset became the second Duke of Beaufort,[19] while his granddaughter Elizabeth went on to become the Duchess of Bedford, wife of the second Duke of Bedford and the mother of Lord John Russell, fourth Duke of Bedford.[20]

Having secured a lineage steeped with aristocratic blood, Sir Josiah wanted to establish an ancestral home that would reflect his newfound wealth and status. In 1673, he paid £11,500 for the manor of Wanstead in Essex, a scenic estate comprised of rolling hills, forests and lakes, with the River Roding flowing through it. Located seven miles north-east of the City of London, it was an ancient seat with strong royal associations, having been the hunting lodge of Henry VIII and a favourite retreat of Elizabeth I. Wanstead was central to Josiah's aspirations, the crowning glory of his success. Samuel Pepys recorded that it was 'a fine seat, but an old ancient house'.[21] Leaving the house intact, Josiah concentrated his efforts on landscaping the gardens, planting avenues of trees at 'prodigious cost'.[22] Vistas of walnuts and sweet chestnuts fanned out westwards from the house, augmented by ornamental lakes and landscaped features. In his final years, Josiah devoted most of his time and energy to his gardens, fashioning an ornamental lake (later known as the octagonal Basin) and personally supervising the planting of an avenue of elms around it to create a magnificent approach towards the house. Fittingly, when he passed away in his seventieth year he was laid to rest in the family crypt at St Mary's Church on his estate close to the elms he had so lovingly planted.

Twenty-four-year-old Sir Richard Child inherited his father's fortune and title in 1704. He boosted his wealth even further by marrying an heiress and acquring the vast Tylney estates in Hampshire from his wife's family. On being raised to the peerage, he adopted his wife's surname and became the first Earl Tylney.[23] Wealth and status encouraged him to fulfil his father's aspirations for Wanstead. The old Tudor mansion was crumbling, so Earl Tylney decided to knock it down and construct a new house on the same site. The building of magnificent Wanstead House would prove to be his greatest triumph. At the turn of the eighteenth century, British architecture was dominated by the Baroque splendour of buildings such as Blenheim Palace, which was being built in highly decorative style with lavish use of curves and embellishment. In 1712, Earl Tylney bravely broke with tradition, commissioning the relatively unknown Colen Campbell to draw up plans for a private mansion that would rival the royal palaces.[24]

Campbell's scheme for Wanstead was the first of its kind in Britain, reflecting a change in taste to simpler, more understated, classical Palladian architecture. Built in the finest Portland stone, the frontage of Wanstead House was 260 feet across and 70 feet deep. Clean lines and symmetry perfectly offset the stately central portico with six Corinthian columns. This was architecturally significant, the earliest recorded use of a temple feature in domestic design in England.[25] Exquisitely hand-crafted features provided decoration, such as the bas-relief crowning the portico, ornately carved with the Tylney crest, a spread eagle clutching a snake. The building alone was reputed to cost £100,000, with an equal amount spent on the gardens.[26]

After spending a fortune on the house and grounds, William Kent was hired to create equally magnificent interiors.[27] William Hogarth's painting *Assembly at Wanstead House* (c. 1730) shows Earl Tylney seated in the ballroom surrounded by his family. It also captures the splendour of Kent's staterooms: the sumptuous furnishings, ornate gilding and richly painted ceiling frescos. A gold spread eagle crowned the marble chimney piece, a reference to the family crest. This was a common theme throughout the house, with majestic spread eagles standing proudly in every room, forming the centrepiece on gilt chandeliers, table legs, silverware and fireguards.[28] Wanstead was a pleasure palace designed for display and entertainment, with boating lakes, hunting grounds, garden rooms, banqueting halls, assembly rooms and the only purpose-built ballroom in any private house in England. Whenever nobility visited Wanstead, they were left in no doubt that they were guests of one of the richest families in England.

When John Tylney inherited his father's title and estates in 1750, he became known as 'the bachelor Earl Tylney'. A flamboyant character, the bachelor earl lived decadently and dangerously at Wanstead, where his homosexual activities were an open secret. After being discovered in flagrante delicto with a male servant,[29] he fled to Italy in 1768, settling in Naples where he devoted his time to acquiring treasures for Wanstead. He purchased antique furniture, paintings by Casali and Rembrandt, plus the crowning glory of his collection – three ancient bronze statues recovered from the ruins of Herculaneum.[30] While he was living in exile, Wanstead House and Park were kept in a constant state of readiness, but almost two decades passed and the magnificent Palladian palace lay unoccupied. During this time, the pleasure grounds became a tourist attraction, a popular spot for day trippers, delighting visitors and 'travellers from all parts of the world'.[31] Set amidst such spectacular gardens, Wanstead House was considered to be one of the finest seats in the realm and was described by many as the English Versailles.[32]

When the Earl died a bachelor in 1784, his estates passed on to his nephew, Sir James Tylney Long – Catherine's father. Wanstead House would remain vacant for another two decades while the family continued to live in Wiltshire. After the French Revolution, royal tenants moved in; the Prince de Condé and other exiled members of the House of Bourbon rented the house from 1802 to 1810, and during this period Wanstead witnessed a renaissance as a venue for aristocratic gatherings and entertainment.[33] But the magnificent mansion was lying in wait for Catherine. On coming of age, she would take possession and start preparing the house for all the glittering events – and shocking scandals – that would follow.

2. *In Training*

✥

1805–10

Catherine had mixed feelings when she became heiress to the vast Tylney Long fortune, in 1805. The death of her beloved brother cast a long shadow over her life and her good fortune would always be tinged with sadness. One of her earliest poems was a lament for James, which included a line expressing her quandary simply and artlessly: 'Oh most beautiful benefactor, thou hast given me more than I could ask or think.'[1] In deference to James, she felt a responsibility to make the very best of her life. Despite this sudden change in her circumstance, Catherine's entire inheritance remained tied up in trust until she came of age. While she could petition the trustees for funds in times of emergency, money was only released at their discretion and they tended to keep a tight rein. This did not trouble her, because she preferred to live quietly while she mourned her young brother. During this period Lady Catherine was devastated; she lay in bed unable to encounter even the closest of friends. Before too long, however, she realized that her surviving children were grieving and in need of her comfort, so she roused herself as best she could for their sakes.[2]

One year after James's death, in October 1806, Catherine became even wealthier when she inherited the estate of her uncle, Mr Long, which was worth more than £200,000 (around twenty million pounds today). Newspapers reported that even before this unexpected windfall, Miss Tylney Long had been 'the richest heiress in the British dominions'.[3] The heiress was a novelty because family estates normally passed along the male line, so it was highly unusual for a woman to inherit such vast sums. Luckily, her father had been an enlightened, progressive man who chose to bequeath his fortune to his daughter rather than some distant male relative. But inheriting enormous wealth changed Catherine's prospects entirely. No longer destined to be the wife of a middle-class doctor or clergyman, she would mix within the highest echelons of society, live in one of the most palatial mansions in the kingdom and have her pick of suitors from aristocratic and royal circles.

Catherine had become the nation's most talked about young woman.[4] Much more was now expected of her on all levels: intellectual, social and sartorial. In view of this, it was decided that she should finish her education in the metropolis, with its stimulating and fashionable environment, and where 'masters of superior abilities' could be found.[5] The heiress was not shown any special favour by her mother, who lavished the same amount of care on all of her daughters, believing that whatever was good for Catherine was also appropriate for Dora and Emma. The whole family travelled to London and moved into a stylish town house in Grosvenor Square, which they rented from a family member (possibly an elderly aunt named Dora Long). The change of scenery benefited them all, allowing them to escape from the ghosts at Draycot. The three sisters remained close as they continued their schooling together, sharing tutors, lessons and confidences.

As the eldest, seventeen-year-old Catherine enjoyed a little more freedom than her sisters, although she kept a very low profile, mainly attending functions held by close friends and family. She made her first public appearance on 19 March 1807, at a ball hosted by Mrs Spencer Stanhope, a neighbour in Grosvenor Square.[6] Catherine also went to stay with her maternal aunt, Lady Sarah de Crespigny, whose husband owned Champion Lodge in Camberwell, just south of London. The house was a popular venue for cultural gatherings, particularly as it was also home to Lady Mary Champion de Crespigny, Lady Sarah's mother-in-law, who was a renowned patron of the arts, especially promoting women writers. She was well qualified for this role, being a prolific diarist and occasional poet, as well as published author of a novel and a conduct book.[7] Catherine was often present at her aunt's dinner parties where guests included à la mode writers, composers and artists such as David Cox or Alfred Edward Chalon, who would paint Catherine's coming-of-age portrait.[8] Lively, thought-provoking conversation flowed around the table, inspiring Catherine to embark on a rigorous course of self-improvement. This was the start of her asserting her independence, as she began to pursue her own interests, hiring the most eminent teachers and immersing herself in music, art and literature. The renowned David Cox instructed her in drawing and painting watercolours;[9] she learned to perform classical concertos on the piano, to compose music and to play the harpsichord and harp.[10] But Catherine also enjoyed more carefree amusements, practising pirouettes or entertaining her sisters with renditions of lively reels or her favourite waltzes. Dancing was one of her greatest joys and she often scribbled down dance steps on her sheet music, and practised the moves with Dora and Emma.[11] Voltaire was on her reading list, but Catherine preferred popular fiction, devouring romantic novels that reflected and reinforced her belief that true love was the greatest source of happiness.[12]

Over the next four years the Tylney Long ladies moved between London and Wiltshire, renting the house in Grosvenor Square each season and retiring to Draycot over the winter months. Whenever Catherine was back at Draycot she made a point of visiting Dr John Barry, a close friend of her parents, and a man she trusted implicitly. Much of the correspondence that passed between them was of such a sensitive nature that he would add a postscript, 'this letter should be destroyed'.[13] Dr Barry was like a benevolent uncle and Catherine often sought his guidance. Acquiring knowledge of business had become a primary aim of hers, and although she already possessed a good understanding of accounts, there was much more to learn. The advice she received from Dr Barry made a lasting impression on her character. Having watched her grow up, he knew that she was too obliging, which did not bode well for the future as people would take advantage of her good nature. Begging letters were already a daily feature of her life, and various cousins were constantly tapping her for funds. Barry gave Catherine a piece of excellent advice: 'NO . . . is a small monosyllable . . . which may be used to very great advantage.'[14] He also insisted that it was not necessary to explain or justify a decision, simply to say 'no' as politely as possible.[15] This technique worked well for Catherine and over the following years she would employ it graciously, never arguing or being unpleasant, but standing her ground.

Dealing with troublesome family members was very different from handling her estate managers and trustees. It was highly unusual for women to be involved in the cut and thrust of business, particularly on such a large scale. With no standard to follow, Catherine developed her own style of management. With her coming of age looming, she had requested information about her finances, but the trustees were obstructive and she was increasingly at odds with them. Needing a strategy, she turned to Dr Barry, who yet again provided brilliant advice: 'Establish that character of *a lady of business* . . . be resolute – be firm.' Even at this early stage, Catherine realized that it was imperative to create the right impression because, being in the public eye, her actions would be scrutinized. Barry reassured her that a professional approach would gain her respect, insisting, 'There may be those who cast reflections upon the vulgarity of it . . . but the more valuable part of society will *ever applaud it.*'[16]

Embracing Dr Barry's advice, Catherine tackled her trustees with more confidence, calmly reminding them that the following year, *they* would be accountable to *her*.[17] This bold approach was hugely successful; the information she requested was forthcoming. By confronting her trustees and advisors, Catherine was at odds with the custom of the time, because women were conditioned to yield to the judgements of men. But she had watched her mother bow to pressure with disastrous consequence – the tragedy involving James made her more inclined to question the opinion of her advisors and to trust her own instincts.

Dora and Emma were in awe of Catherine's boldness, which resulted in them following her lead and becoming more self-assured. This was apparent whenever the ladies attended mass at Draycot Cerne, where the stone church was perishing in winter. Sitting in the freezing cold for two or three hours was very unpleasant, but luckily the family pews were towards the rear of the church, tucked inside a small alcove and well concealed from the prying gaze. Catherine used this to her advantage. Drawing the curtains across, she would instruct her footman to swaddle them in blankets and open a bottle or two of wine, strictly for medicinal purposes, of course. The alcohol certainly helped to fortify the sisters and ease the tedium of lengthy sermons.

Catherine was growing so confident that she even secured a large advance from her trustees to commence refurbishments at Wanstead. More than anything, she was thrilled at the prospect of living in the magnificent house. Wasting no time, she served notice on her royal tenants and instructed her estate manager to organize a workforce to spruce up her new residence. As she wandered through the staterooms surveying work in progress, the aspirations, hopes and dreams of generations of ancestors rested heavily on her shoulders. The family portraits hung in the Salon and Sir Josiah Child stared out at her imperiously, with ambition burning in his eyes. It was perfectly clear to Catherine that it was her duty to marry as high as possible, to form a powerful alliance and add value to her inheritance. Next to Sir Josiah was Hogarth's painting of Sir Richard surrounded by his large family, reminding Catherine of her responsibility to produce heirs to secure the lineage. Only the bachelor Earl Tylney appeared to promote more romantic ideals; gazing at her kindly, he seemed to advocate – follow your heart.

When Catherine came of age on 2 October 1810, she took full control of the vast Tylney Long fortune.

It was customary to mark the succession of an heir, and because Catherine had just inherited one of the largest fortunes in the kingdom, the celebrations needed to be suitably spectacular. Festivities at Draycot lasted a whole week, as London's finest arrived in carriages to attend the sumptuous dinners and balls. Local people were accustomed to sharing special occasions with the generous Long family, and Catherine arranged a fete especially for them. Around 5,000 workers converged on the estate from surrounding farms, schools and parishes to enjoy the hospitality. They were entertained with a fair in the gardens that included horse racing and other amusements. Food was laid out on long tables, beer tents served a profusion of strong ale, and a fine ox was roasted whole and distributed among the crowd. In the evening, the pleasure grounds were lit with variegated lamps and there was dancing in the great barn. Much hilarity ensued and the evening concluded with a grand display of fireworks that did much credit to its famous orchestrator, Mr Invetto.[18] Needless to say, the cost was enormous, particularly as Catherine had employed some of London's foremost caterers; Mr Gunter's bill for confectionery alone was £508 6s 6d (around £50,000).[19] The week of celebrations was so memorable that locals were still talking about it over sixty years later.[20]

Twenty-one-year-old Catherine had grown into a spirited and forthright woman, well equipped for her launch into fashionable society. She had learned many valuable lessons. Her self-assurance was bolstered by Dr Barry, who encouraged her to make her own decisions and to stand her ground. Lady Mary Champion de Crespigny was another magnificent role model, backing female writers and demonstrating that women could be strong and influential.

With the world at her feet, Catherine's bags were packed and she prepared to head for London. Of course, she had visited the capital many times before, but this occasion was different because she was now an exceptionally wealthy woman, on a determined mission to find a husband. She was excited at the prospect of being out at glamorous parties every evening, laughing, dancing and flirting. But there would also be a lot of pressure because a lady was expected to secure a suitable husband in her first season – it was a mark of success. Although Catherine was well aware of her duty to marry advantageously, she was also a thoroughly modern woman with informed opinions and romantic ideals. More than anything, Catherine was searching for passion and true love.

3. London

꧁❦꧂

1811

Arriving in town with money to burn must have been wildly exciting for twenty-one-year-old Catherine. At the time, London was the epicentre of the British Empire and the world's largest, wealthiest, most vibrant city. In many respects, the hustle and bustle of the capital was much like today, with teeming pavements, busy shops, noisy taverns, crowded coffee houses, theatres, exhibitions, parks, pleasure gardens and newspaper hawkers hollering the headlines of the day. When Parliament was in session, the ruling elite lived in town houses near Westminster, from where they controlled government, trade, industry, commerce and culture through patronage of the arts. The nation's power and wealth were concentrated within just 350 families out of the country's eighteen million inhabitants, and it was from within this tight-knit circle that Catherine was expected to find a husband.

Catherine and her family moved back into their rented town house in Grosvenor Square, quickly settling into the familiar surroundings. Spread over five floors, the house was luxuriously furnished, with tall windows overlooking the street and park beyond. Most importantly, the location was Mayfair – the most stylish part of town – perfect for launching young ladies into fashionable society. By now the Tylney Longs were well acquainted with many of their neighbours, including Mrs Thompson, Mrs Richards, Mrs Knox, Mrs Spencer Stanhope and their various debutante daughters. The young ladies paid calls on each other or took a stroll in the central gardens outside their houses.

Emma and Dora were eighteen and nineteen years old respectively, meaning all three Tylney Long sisters had officially come out in search of husbands. London society was exclusive; only the fortunate few could break into aristocratic circles. The capital's glitterati lived in splendid style with their mansions in St James's, entertaining each other by hosting lavish events in their own homes. Entrance to these select parties was by invitation only, which kept undesirables out and the family lineage secure. But Catherine was guaranteed approval in the highest circles because she was the catch of the decade, boasting one of the highest incomes in Britain.

Wealth was not her only asset; Catherine had blossomed into a renowned beauty, with considerable grace and poise.[1] Standing at around five feet tall, her dainty frame gave the impression of a 'pleasing fairy creature', but she was also sensuous with luscious curves that earned her the nickname 'pocket Venus'.[2] Her allure owed as much to manner as to features; refreshingly sincere and warm-hearted, she exuded naturalness and good nature. She was a popular lady and had many friends. One of her most endearing qualities was her delicious sense of humour, which was mildly teasing. Catherine was always 'gay and happy', laughing easily and often.[3]

Newspapers announced Catherine's arrival, while 'the country rang with the fame of Miss Tylney Long, her beauty, her accomplishments, and her immense fortune'.[4] Invitations flooded in, and members of the public jostled to catch a glimpse of her. Although Catherine had spent four years preparing for her debut, working hard with her various tutors, she was astonished to be the object of such intense scrutiny, which she found both daunting and thrilling. She was thoroughly enjoying all the fun and excitement, savouring the heady days and nights spent in a dazzling whirl of dinners and balls, open-air concerts, garden parties and river cruises. With so many occasions to attend, mornings were often devoted to shopping, but she happily stood for hours as she was pinned and fitted for an entire new wardrobe. Fashion that season was influenced by Thomas Hope's *Costume of the Ancients*, which had been published the previous year.[5] Catherine opted for evening gowns that were light and romantic, like those worn in ancient Egypt or Greece, draped in shimmering silks and satin. This simple, elegant empire line suited her perfectly, moulding her voluptuous curves tantalizingly before falling away in soft folds.

Whenever Catherine was out in company she was surrounded by a swarm of admirers vying for her attention. Everybody wanted to see her, so she was always put on display and chosen for the ensemble that marked the opening of a ball. Eight to sixteen couples would take to the floor and perform for the gathered crowd. Graceful Catherine loved dancing, so she was in her element, with one onlooker observing that 'as a butterfly among the flowers, she seemed to tread on air'.[6] Unsurprisingly, the exquisite heiress was soon inundated with marriage proposals. Newspapers recorded, 'The suitors were innumerable. She received offers right and left . . . it was droll to see admirers about her carriage, as the guards do about the King's'.[7] Besieged with tributes and declarations of love, the ceaseless adulation may have turned the head of a more conceited woman, but Catherine somehow managed to keep her feet firmly on the ground.

Even though she was in high demand, Catherine remained closest to her sisters and they went everywhere together, chaperoned mainly by their elegant aunt Lady Sarah de Crespigny. Naturally, there was always much to discuss and gossip about: who was the handsomest man at the ball, which lady was the best dressed, who had behaved badly. Catherine drew the most attention by far, but Dora and Emma did not appear to resent this in the slightest. They adored Catherine, they were in awe of everything she had accomplished and were thrilled to be the ones sharing her secrets. Back home at Grosvenor Square, the girls often sat huddled together, giggling uncontrollably as they read out extracts from 'tender love epistles' sent to Catherine.[8] 'Oh thou fair maiden, guardian of my heart and soul,' read one. The poems were even more ludicrous. One admirer sent a lock of hair, 'cut from my tender pate, Oh place it on your bosom fair, I then shall learn my fate'.[9] There were a great many suitors for them to laugh over, particularly as all three sisters by now boasted an array of dubious followers.

The public were similarly entertained by the courtship proceedings. Catherine lived in a raucous society that relished satire. People were amused that many of the gentlemen pursuing the lovely heiress were highly unsuitable middle-aged men, who clung to the flamboyant style of the eighteenth century, wearing bright colours, frilled shirts and high-heeled shoes. One such specimen was the eccentric Robert Coates, the son of a wealthy diamond merchant, who had sailed from his native Antigua in search of adventure.[10] His dearest ambition was to perform Shakespeare on stage, but as Mr Pryse Lockhart Gordon politely pointed out, 'He did not always *stick to the author's text*.'[11] In his defence, Coates replied, 'Ay . . . but I think I have *improved* upon it.'[12] The Creole grandee launched his career at the Theatre Royal in Bath, where he appeared as Romeo in a spangled costume of his own design. The audience convulsed with laughter as he invented dramatic scenes and dialogue of his own, although this performance took place 'without any loss of life, since nothing heavier than an orange peel was thrown on this occasion'.[13] 'Romeo Coates', as he was thereafter nicknamed, became famous for all the wrong reasons as people of rank and fashion packed into theatres to watch his dire performances. Much to Catherine's mortification, Romeo Coates fell madly in love with her and was keen to accommodate her every whim. He followed her about day and night, reciting sonnets in celebration of her beauty and generally driving her to distraction. Too good-natured to humiliate him in public, Catherine sent him away on errands and enjoyed some devilment at his expense. 'When she would not drink the water without some delicacy to banish the iron taste, it was he who stood by with a box of vanilla-rusks. When he shaved his great mustachio, it was at her caprice.'[14]

Another dubious admirer was the self-styled 'Baron' Ferdinand de Geramb. Having served as a mercenary in various foreign armies, the Austrian came to London as a guest of the government, intending to enlist 24,000 Croatians in the British army. Caricaturists were amused at the splendid sight of the Baron, with his colossal pointed mustachios, garishly overdressed in a red military coat emblazoned with pure gold braids and buttons. Catherine was horrified to receive attention from such an unsavoury character, particularly as it was rumoured that the Baron was a double-agent, working for Napoleon. He was eventually deported on suspicion of espionage.

Fortunately for Catherine, her suitors also included an impressive collection of fine young bucks. To name just a few, there were Lords Killeen and Kilworth, plus Fredrick Foster, son of the infamous Lady Elizabeth Foster, who boasted that Catherine had 'secretly determined in favour of him'.[15] Numerous eligible gentlemen went out of their way to gain access to her, preying on her friends for an introduction. Thomas Champneys was a close friend who Catherine found hilarious.[16] He sent her many entertaining letters and on one occasion wrote recommending Lady Payton's twenty-year-old son. Reporting tongue-in-cheek, he stated that handsome Mr Bradshaw was 'a beau garcon of *Modern Days* . . . temper particularly good, hair well-dressed, pumps well-fitted, coat well-cut, cravat accurately tied'.[17] The playful side of Catherine's nature was apparent as he felt able to gently tease and include sexual innuendo, assuring that Bradshaw would not disappoint with his 'snuff box *remarkably large*'.[18]

Relishing every moment, Catherine was vibrant and flirtatious, 'bestowing smiles liberally'.[19] While gentlemen clamoured for her attention, she became the object of jealousy and criticism for many queens of the social scene. Manners played a major role in society, as exhibited by the many conduct books that were in circulation. Those in the haughtiest circles advocated that young women should possess submissiveness and delicacy. Owing to this, Lady Charlotte Bury called Catherine 'an ill-born mushroom',[20] a sentiment echoed by a small minority. They believed that Catherine lacked refinement because she was too candid, self-assured and friendly, contending that it was vulgar for a woman to be involved in business. By the same token, Catherine did not subscribe to the malice that permeated some of the more urbane cliques: the false delicacy, duplicity and stinging one-liners that rolled readily from the tongue. Instead, Catherine was a straightforward, sweet-natured woman, which was why the vast majority of people found her to be refreshing and 'bewitching'.[21]

Catherine was the talk of the town; gossip columns continued to speculate wildly as every fortune-hunter in the British Isles wooed her.[22] She remained unfazed by all the attention. Even when the glare of publicity was intense, she did not crumble under pressure, always conducting herself with dignity, laughing at the absurd rumours circulating about her courtship.

The contest for Catherine's hand continued, but no one man emerged from the pack until the night of the Prince's Ball.

4. The Prince's Ball

Catherine had been propelled into a dazzling world filled with glamour, gaiety and decadence, but she made her debut into fashionable society at a time of major political upheaval in England. George III had been suffering from a long, cruel illness and when he finally relapsed into madness, Parliament reluctantly passed the Regency Bill decreeing that the king's eldest son, George, should assume power. The bill came into effect on 11 February 1811, heralding the start of the Regency, one of the most formative and exciting periods in English history.

The newly appointed Prince Regent was a notorious spendthrift, renowned for ostentation, gambling and keeping mistresses. Many within the aristocracy followed his lead, spending lavishly on fashion and entertainment. From the outset, the Prince Regent set the moral tone for the era with his Grand Summer Fete at Carlton House on 19 June 1811. There could be no official coronation while George III was alive, so invitations ostensibly suggested that the fete was in honour of the French royal family, who were living in exile in England having been deposed by Napoleon. In reality, the prince simply wanted to host a spectacular celebration to inaugurate his appointment as Prince Regent.

More than 2,000 invitations were sent, and the fashionable world was in rapture as everyone prepared for the royal extravaganza. Pawnbrokers lent out diamonds for the night at eleven per cent interest,[1] while seamstresses worked round the clock to ensure that the queen bees of society would be suitably attired. Elaborate court dress was required: lavishly decorative, complete with trains and headdresses. Catherine chose an elegant gown of white satin, richly appliquéd and trimmed with silver, topped with a headdress of pearls and feathers.[2]

On the day of the fete, Catherine and her sisters set off for the palace in good time. Guests were invited for nine o'clock, but by eight the approach to Carlton House was jammed with equipages that formed a solid block all the way back to the top of St James's Street. Liveried footmen regulated the traffic, permitting six carriages onto the courtyard at one time. Catherine watched with anticipation as wave after wave of the *beau monde* alighted, dressed in their finest clothes and jewellery. Ladies wore mainly white gowns of satins, silks or lace ornamented with silver. Gentlemen appeared in formal court dress or military and naval uniforms.

Nerves and excitement consumed Catherine as she entered the Grand Grecian Hall and joined the line of guests waiting to be presented to the host. The Prince Regent liked to create an air of fantasy, so the hall was hung with billowing drapery to give the illusion of a Bedouin tent, complete with exotic ornamental shrubs. Catherine and her party had plenty of time to admire their surroundings as they shuffled past a row of Yeomen of the Guard, all standing to attention. As she approached the top of the queue, dainty Catherine glimpsed the forty-eight-year-old Prince Regent looking suitably resplendent in a field marshal's red coat, well-corseted to contain his bulk and sparkling with extra gold braids and buttons. When she finally stood before the imposing figure of His Royal Highness, Catherine was completely awestruck as she dropped into a graceful curtsey.

Formalities completed, Catherine was escorted outside where the fantasy continued. She stood spellbound, gazing around the gardens that were illuminated by thousands of variegated lights.[3] It was like a vision of heaven, creating an illusion that guests were floating among the stars. Trellises had been erected to form supper galleries, with tables and chairs brought in to seat 2,000. Festooned with flowers, the galleries had large mirrors in place of walls, reflecting lights that 'gleamed like stars through the foliage'.[4] Fine wine flowed as hundreds of footmen, dressed in smart blue and gold livery, weaved among tables replenishing glasses. As Catherine sat sipping champagne, she felt intoxicated by the heady sensations of the evening: the sweet scent of roses and geraniums, the melodious strains of a band wafting from a distant corner, and the profusion of flickering lights casting a glow of enchantment over the proceedings.

As the buzz of conversation grew increasingly raucous, Catherine began to relax and enjoy herself. Dinner was served on 2,000 matching silver plates; there were hot and cold soups, and a variety of roast meats, followed by exotic fresh fruits such as peaches, pineapples and grapes lovingly cultivated in hothouses. Dancing in the gardens began after supper, in four huge marquees pitched on the lawns. Bands of Guards, in full state uniform, performed throughout the night. Danced off her feet by a relentless stream of admirers, Catherine did not leave the party until dawn. The Prince Regent was a legendary host, but the fete was an exceptionally extravagant affair even by his standards. It was typical of him to spend so recklessly when he was already deeply in debt – the fete cost an enormous £120,000 (around twelve million pounds today).[5] Divided between 2,000 guests, the price worked out at £60 a head, an obscene amount of money, particularly when considering that most families in England survived on just £50 a year.

In late Georgian England, the gulf between rich and poor was vast. While the aristocracy and the gentry enjoyed all the comforts that money could buy, the majority of the population was on the brink of starvation.[6] The Prince Regent was in a position to exert his considerable political influence to help the underprivileged. Instead, his Regency remained a time of biting poverty and hardship for around seventy-five per cent of the population.[7] The working classes were severely malnourished, lived in squalor and suffered real want. Desperate with hunger, men resorted to stealing to feed their children despite the fact that the penalty was usually death by hanging. The law had no compassion and numerous people were sent to the gallows for petty theft, leaving behind helpless young families to fend for themselves as best they could.

Social commentators did not have much of a forum for debate due to government censorship of the press. At the start of the French Revolution, newspaper criticism of the British Establishment was seen as a potent threat to the status quo. During what became known as his 'winter of terror', Prime Minister William Pitt suspended Habeas Corpus (1794) and passed the Treason and Sedition Act (1795). From the 1790s until the 1820s, the government used censorship and imprisonment to silence its critics. Even as late as 1849, the investigative journalist Henry Mayhew faced litigation after writing a series of articles for the *Morning Chronicle*, outlining the gruesome living conditions in London's slums. In one article he described how people were forced to drink and bathe in murky river water contaminated by cesspools, slaughterhouses and noxious waste from factories. Mayhew recorded:

> The sun shone upon a narrow strip of water . . . we gazed in horror, we saw drains and sewers emptying their filthy contents into it . . . In this wretched place we were taken to a house where an infant lay dead of cholera. We asked if they really did drink the water? The answer was, "they were obliged to".[8]

In his voluminous survey, Mayhew encountered endless scenes of abject poverty and suffering among the labouring poor of London. He lamented, 'I could not have believed that there were human beings toiling so long and gaining so little, and starving so silently and heroically.'[9]

London was a city divided. To the west stood an elegant enclave of Georgian squares and spacious town houses to accommodate the well-fed middle classes. In stark contrast, the east was overrun with warrens of unsanitary slums, housing starving people blunted to feelings of ordinary misery.

Caricature was hugely influential during the Regency because illustrations were more ambivalent than text, making them difficult to repress. Political caricaturists James Gillray (1757–1815) and George Cruikshank (1792–1878) were among those who highlighted the struggles of the working class, using satire as a powerful rhetorical tool to expose the grave social and moral issues of the time.[10] The Prince Regent was a favourite target because he was considered to epitomize the excesses that blighted the era.

Print-shop windows provided Londoners with a colourful, theatrical, urban space, a place of shared laughter for all classes in society.[11] City workers routinely stopped to view the gratis exhibitions; doctors, lawyers, rat-catchers and chimney sweeps all crowded round, eager to discover the latest antics of their Regent and others in the public eye. Unsurprisingly, the Regency fete provided ample ammunition to lambast the prince for his extravagance. In *Merry Making on the Regent's Birthday*,[12] Cruikshank showed him flirting with his bosomy mistress while two men in the background hang from the scaffold at Newgate. Pitiful wives and orphans stand outside begging for a pardon, but His Royal Highness is too busy enjoying himself to worry; in fact, he is so unconcerned, his dancing foot crushes the petition for mercy. Packed with detail, when this caricature appeared in print-shop windows the message was clear to everyone, including the illiterate.

At the start of the Regency, most among the privileged classes did little to alleviate the devastating poverty. Dripping with jewels, guests at the fete made no apology for their good fortune. Despite her philanthropic upbringing, there can be little doubt that Catherine thoroughly enjoyed the dazzling entertainment at Carlton House that evening, without stopping to dwell on the state of the nation. It would be hard not to. Surrounded by an unrelenting throng of admirers, her immediate concern was to find a husband and on that magical night at Carlton House a worthy competitor entered the fray. The Duke of Clarence, younger brother of the Prince Regent, was enthralled by her and the advantages she presented. Gushing with compliments, Clarence noted that Catherine was 'lovely, beautiful and bewitching'.[13] Staying close by her side, he paid such marked attention that it was clear he intended to deliver a proposal of marriage.

At the time the Duke of Clarence was fourth in line to the throne; Catherine was aware that if she married him, her children would be royalty, potentially even the future king or queen of England.

5. A Lady of Business

❧

JULY 1811

London was the hub of a buoyant press industry; gossip columns fed the growing fascination with human-interest stories, particularly those of well-known figures with glamorous lifestyles. Catherine's rags-to-riches fairy tale captured the public imagination, providing the nostalgia and glamour they craved. Catherine was their real-life Cinderella: sweet-natured and deserving, liberated from a dreary existence, transformed by fine clothes and carriages. There was even a magnificent castle at Wanstead awaiting her. To complete the fantasy, a prince had appeared on the scene to sweep her off her feet.

Shortly after the Regency fete, the Duke of Clarence stated his intentions by opening negotiations with Catherine's aunt, Lady Sarah de Crespigny, who happened to be a friend of his. The family was delighted; it appeared that Catherine had made a brilliant match. Surely it was every young woman's fantasy to marry a prince? Regrettably, the fairy tale had one vital flaw: this particular royal was the antithesis of love's young dream. The Duke of Clarence was a portly, florid man, with a complexion and girth that bore witness to his weakness for good food and wine. Having spent much of his youth in the navy, he was at times bawdy and uncouth, with a weather-beaten face that made him look even older than his forty-six years. Added to this, he was openly living with his mistress of twenty years, Mrs Jordan, a famous actress on the London stage and the mother of his ten illegitimate children, aged between five and seventeen years old.

From Catherine's perspective, it was certainly flattering to be courted by royalty, but this fat old man with considerable baggage was far from ideal. Renowned for their derisive humour, the Great British public followed the courtship with amused interest, rejoicing in the folly of the Duke of Clarence and other suitors as they published poems or fought duels to impress the heiress. Glossy pictures of Catherine appeared in magazines, captured by some of the most celebrated caricaturists of the time. George Cruikshank's *Worshippers at Wanstead* appeared as a frontispiece for the *Scourge* in December 1811,[1] showing Catherine seated on a throne with a motley group paying homage at her feet.

Aside from intense personal pressures, Catherine was saddled with mammoth commercial responsibilities. She embraced her role as 'a lady of business' immediately upon coming of age, taking charge of her affairs and instructing her solicitor to conduct a full audit of her assets. As part of this exercise, she insisted that up-to-date maps of all her estates should be prepared, covering the entire 23,000 acres, including the various tenancies and holdings. The sheer scale of the task involved must have been daunting, but Catherine was determined to rise to the challenge, demonstrating that she was a capable, organized woman.[2]

Keeping track of her finances was another onerous task. There were letters from Messrs Hazard & Co. regarding transfer of stock, plus a huge backlog of unpaid debts that had amassed over the seventeen-year period since her father's death. Systematically working her way through piles of papers, she agreed to settle some bills, while querying others by writing in the margins, 'I should wish to have all this account explained.'[3] Catherine was a shrewd business woman, who drove a hard bargain. When her estate manager, Mr Bullock, presented her with a bill, she haggled a deal and knocked down his price from £1,290 to £1,000, a considerable saving.[4]

During this process, Catherine discovered that her mother had built up debts, running to thousands of pounds, which was surprising because ample financial provisions had been made for her. It appeared that Lady Catherine had given away substantial sums to people in need and various family members, plus there had been considerable outlay in relation to Dora and Emma's coming out.

Catherine settled these debts without further ado, particularly as her kind-hearted mother had been driven by the need to provide for others. But an even more shocking revelation surfaced: it transpired that Lady Catherine harboured a dark secret of a scandalous nature, and she was being blackmailed by a man threatening to 'do his worst' and make the story public.[5] To save her mother's reputation, Catherine dealt with the blackmailer herself; after receiving various assurances, she paid the man a substantial bribe of £1,000, which put an end to the matter.[6] All related paperwork was burned, so the precise nature of Lady Catherine's indiscretion is unknown, although it seems most likely that she had a lover who decided to cash in. In terms of romance, Lady Catherine was restricted. Remarrying was probably not an option because she would have lost her entitlements. Her husband's will specified that she could receive pin money and other benefits 'so long as she shall continue to be my widow'.[7]

Blackmail is a sordid business, but Catherine acted discreetly and efficiently, showing that she was worldly and open-minded. Furthermore, she did not judge her mother, and Dr Barry was full of praise for her 'truly filial affection to a mistaken parent'.[8]

Wanstead was a pet project for Catherine. She had set her heart on living there as soon as she married and consequently supervised the refurbishments closely. Almost a century had passed since the first Earl Tylney built the house, so specialist artisans were employed to revive the interiors, the chipped paintwork and faded gilding. Whenever she was away, Mr Bullock wrote with updates: 'Painting the upper storey has been much the most troublesome and tedious, on account of the ceiling and other carved work.'[9] Concerning the Great Hall, he reported, 'I have not suffered them to do anything . . . until you see it again.'[10] Looming two storeys above the Great Hall was an ornately gilded ceiling, framing a fresco painted by William Kent depicting scenes of *Morning, Noon, Evening and Night*. Restoring this work of art involved delicate workmanship, but Catherine sought specialist advice and sent strict instructions on how to proceed. Mr Bullock wrote back immediately, assuring her that 'no time will be lost, in getting it completed'.[11]

The formal gardens were in disrepair. Locals had grown accustomed to driving their carts through the gardens, causing damage, and it quickly became clear that one of her priorities was to stop trespassers and secure the parkland around the house. Catherine also became involved in a dispute with the Duke de Bourbon, her former tenant, who persisted in keeping his hounds nearby at Woodford and then turning up regularly at Wanstead with large hunting parties, damaging the gardens and distressing the pheasants that the gamekeeper was trying to raise. It must have taken courage for a single lady to confront a member of the French royal family, but having already politely written to him on several occasions, Catherine was not afraid to take the matter further and instruct her legal advisors. Her solicitor agreed that very strong measures were required, 'as not only your property, but even your domestic comforts are thus assailed, and the whole neighbourhood are very warm in their complaints of the trespass committed by the Duke and his hounds'.[12] True to form, Catherine remained courteous but resolute until the duke was shamed into sending an apology along with assurances that it would not happen again.[13]

Privacy and personal security were also concerns. Due to her celebrity status, Catherine was pursued by newsmen eager for a story and fanatics trying to catch a glimpse of her, as well as undesirables issuing death threats. Owing to this, she decided that she would not renew the leases on certain holdings adjoining the park, as she did not want tenants living within close proximity of the main house. The Lake House was a particularly delightful structure located on a small island at the centre of the lake, previously used as a banqueting hall by the first Earl Tylney. Having rented the property for many years, Mr McClean hotly objected when Catherine served him notice. In response, she was firm but fair, granting a short extension, offering alternative accommodation, but insisting that he vacate the Lake House within one year.[14] Similar notices were served to the tenants at Blake Hall and Highlands House, followed by equally loud protests, which were dealt with as before. Catherine disliked confrontation, but she had become adept at standing her ground to achieve her goals and set her affairs in order.

Since coming of age, Catherine had demonstrated that she was a force to be reckoned with, asserting her authority in no uncertain terms. Although she coped admirably, it was daunting for her to conduct such hard-edged business in a male-dominated world and the burden of responsibility sat heavily on her shoulders. She wished for a husband by her side, supporting, advising and sharing the load.

Refurbishments at Wanstead House were progressing well enough for Catherine to host a 'splendid *déjeune*' on Wednesday 10 July 1811, a fete lasting all day and night with dancing and entertainment continuing into the early hours.[15] It was an opportunity to prove herself to her new London circle and to show off her magnificent home. Guests began arriving at two o'clock, carriages rattling through the stone gateposts just when the house and gardens were at their most glorious, bathed in afternoon sunlight. Entering the park, visitors admired the aspect of the house in the distance, standing on high ground with lawns sloping gently down to the octagonal lake. The approach provided delights at every turn: Sir Josiah's stately avenue of elms, the steeple of St Mary's Church and perfectly manicured gardens. Alighting on the elevated terrace, London's finest gazed in awe at their surroundings: the elegant sweep of the house, the majestic portico with soaring Corinthian columns, plus the beautiful prospect of the river with lakes, walks and wildernesses beyond. As Catherine stood in the portico greeting her guests, radiantly beautiful, framed by the backdrop of her magnificent Palladian palace, it was easy to see why her allure might be overwhelming.

The Royal Dukes of Clarence, Cumberland and Cambridge arrived at about four o'clock, and dancing commenced soon after on temporary platforms erected on the lawns. German waltzes graced one platform, while Mr Gow's famous orchestra played reels in a tent some distance away and the Duke of York's military band entertained in another area. Those who did not wish to dance promenaded through the pleasure grounds or took a guided tour of the house, passing through twenty staterooms sumptuously furnished with paintings and artwork. *Déjeune* was served around six o'clock, with Catherine seated in the Great Hall amongst her most distinguished guests. No expense was spared, with food provided by London's most renowned caterer:

> The company sat down, to partake of the delicacies of the season, provided by Mr Gunter, the celebrated confectioner . . . At the banquet there were seven hundred and eighty-two dishes of roast and boiled; and five hundred baskets of fruit . . . Soups – turtle, vegetable and pea. Roasts – venison, pheasants, chicken, lamb, veal. Boiled – tongue, ham, prawns, lobsters and crayfish. To this it may be added, jellies, ice-creams, *chantellias*, and whip cream, crepes, pastries, [etc.].[16]

Dancing recommenced in the ballroom and went on until two o'clock in the morning, when a second banquet was served, equally as costly as the first, and guests did not disperse until dawn. Newspapers reported over the course of several days, as snippets of gossip emerged. On 14 July, the *Morning Post* highlighted the frenzy surrounding Catherine, describing how villagers attempted to catch a glimpse of the proceedings: 'A strong party of the police preserved order . . . upwards of *ten thousand people* . . . were standing over every barrier, and up every tree to gratify a more eager curiosity than we ever before witnessed on any similar occasion.' On 15 July, the *Morning Post* reported that the fete excited such interest in the fashionable world that there were more than six hundred gate-crashes. Some turned up claiming to be related to dukes, while others 'that had invitations, brought three and four persons with them, and as they were of titled distinction, Lady Catherine knew not how to refuse them'.[17] As a result, the food was adequate but not plentiful because around 1,200 people sat down for the banquet, instead of the expected 550.

In many respects the purpose of the *déjeune* was to display everything Catherine had to offer, including her personal attributes. Newspapers recorded, 'The ball was led off with a new and very lively tune, composed by the rich and accomplished heiress.'[18] Catherine's composition was a simple but sweet piano piece, known simply as 'Miss Tylney Long's Waltz'. It became one of the most popular melodies of 1812, with the accompanying quadrille danced in ballrooms across the country.[19] Exhibiting considerable social skills, Catherine demonstrated that she was a talented musician, a graceful dancer and a charming hostess with a lively sense of humour. Highly gifted and possessing many fine qualities, Catherine was captivating; many men were genuinely in love with her. The *déjeune* revealed that she was competent, well able to manage a large house and organize an event of this scale. It was clear that she would be an asset to any man, even one as high ranking as a prince.

The press were in awe of Catherine and everything she had accomplished in such a short space of time. Her *déjeune* was such a triumph that the *Morning Post* declared, 'we have beheld nothing which will bear comparison with it'.[20] Just as Dr Barry had predicted, the better part of society was applauding. Catherine had become a perfect role model for ladies of business, and women in general. Catherine was an enthralling woman, vivacious in company, but politely determined in business. She was a beguiling combination of sweetness and courage, delicacy and drive. She wanted a husband who would love and cherish her, who would share her hopes and aspirations and would work alongside her to carve their niche in society. Believing that he was the best man for the job, the Duke of Clarence issued another proposal, also reminding everyone that he was the 'first unmarried man in the kingdom'.[21] Catherine could be queen, and Wanstead would make a perfect royal palace. Catherine's family actively encouraged the match; her mother, her aunt Lady de Crespigny and her uncle Henry Windsor all tried to persuade the heiress to acknowledge the duke as her suitor.

Much to everyone's alarm, however, it was becoming apparent that Catherine had set her sights elsewhere. William Wellesley Pole possessed the dashing good looks of an archetypal romantic hero, with dark wavy hair, piercing blue eyes and a dazzling smile. Naturally, he was a charmer and highly unsuitable on many levels, but Catherine was completely smitten.

6. The Finest Young Dandy

❧

1811

Always sharply dressed, impeccably groomed and pleasantly perfumed, twenty-three-year-old William Wellesley Pole was a dandy, one of a new breed of English gentlemen who took pride in being elegant, cultured and witty. In terms of his style and incredible good looks, he was peerless. *La Boudoir* labelled him, 'the finest young dandy to grace the streets of St James', and years later when they crowned Count D'Orsay the 'First Man of Fashion', they qualified it by saying, 'but he would not have gained that distinction at the time when [Mr Wellesley Pole] was seen about town'.[1] William was known as Mr Pole, a nickname that he embraced as it suited his raffish image. Although he was not particularly wealthy, he was very well connected being the nephew of Wellington, the great military general.[2] At the age of sixteen, William had been sent to work abroad and over the following five years he was engaged in military and diplomatic service. He had been secretary to the embassy at Constantinople, fought heroically in the Peninsular War, and worked at the embassies in Vienna, Copenhagen, Lisbon and Cadiz. It was unusual for a young gentleman to be so widely travelled, because revolution and war in Europe had put a stop on Grand Tours. William was one of the few who had immersed himself in other cultures, gaining sophistication far beyond his years.

William was urbane; he loved London and was pleased to be home. The area he frequented around St James's was a hotspot for male leisure, an exclusive urban playground filled with gentlemen's clubs and select menswear boutiques, where he spent lavishly. As an avid follower of fashion, he was greatly influenced by his close friend George 'Beau' Brummell, the undisputed leader of the dandies. With the dawn of the nineteenth century, Beau Brummell had led a revolution in fashion, advocating that gentlemen's attire should not be showy; true elegance depended on low-key simplicity. Perfectly cut, his coats were made of plain dark cloth, offset by a pristine white shirt and crisp white cravat. The dandies adopted this sober style, parading around London in dark tailcoats and glossy top hats. Male grooming was another of Brummell's innovations and William too was fastidious about cleanliness; he washed, shaved and preened every day, unlike many other men who continued to mask body odour with heavy perfume. Manners were essential; a dandy was well bred and poised. Wit was also a prerequisite and William was a charming companion at dinners, entertaining with well-rehearsed anecdotes and droll stories. Additionally, he danced exceptionally well, making him a welcome guest at any party.

Catherine had first met William at a gathering the previous year, shortly after he had returned from his travels. She was instantly drawn to his easy good nature and amused by his witty conservation, which was seasoned with tales about his time abroad. Catherine longed to travel and William's stories intrigued her. She was further impressed by his performances in the ballroom; William had learned to waltz beautifully in Vienna and his dancing was unparalleled in London society. Whenever there was a display at the start of a ball, Catherine contrived to be his partner. Waltzing can be exquisitely sensual; swept up in his arms, she felt as if she was floating on air, the headiness heightened by the delicious scent of him. The attraction was intense. Catherine confided to her sisters that she was captivated by his 'fascinating manners'.[3]

Young gentlemen usually cultivated their favourite pastime to a very high standard and the nation was littered with fine musicians, painters and writers. Macho and thrill-seeking, William was a sportsman. A renowned horseman, he had performed equestrian feats for the crowds at Catherine's coming-of-age celebrations.[4] He could ride at full gallop, grip his mount with his thighs and then swoop down to pluck a handkerchief from the floor. Since arriving back from Constantinople, he had been teaching his friends a new equestrian sport called 'polo', which young Mr Pole claimed was named after him.[5] This might indeed have been the case, as he certainly popularized polo in England while serving in the cavalry. Society was highly impressed that he was such a 'capital polo player',[6] and also an innovator, bringing back new ideas from his travels. To add even further to his allure, William possessed a strong athletic physique that paid testimony to many hours spent on the sports field. Who could blame Catherine for being so captivated?

Parading in the city parklands was another amusement enjoyed by the dandies. Rotten Row, in Hyde Park, was like an outdoor salon where fashionables went to see and be seen, dressed in their finest clothes or driving a swanky new carriage. William enjoyed riding there, showing off his glossy chestnut stallion and his horsemanship. There was a ritual of 'greeting and not greeting, doffing hats or "cutting" those out of favour'.[7] Brummell is credited with perfecting the 'cut'; he would 'assume that calm but wandering gaze, which veers, as if unconsciously, round the proscribed individual'.[8] This was the ultimate social snub, and nobody wanted to be on the receiving end of a 'cut', especially as it was often dealt very publicly.

On the surface William was a typical dandy: well dressed, witty and entertaining. But dandyism was not simply about appearance; it was also an ethos, an expression of distaste for the excesses of the previous generation and of empathy with the new mood of democracy. There were many paradoxes. The dandies spoke of low-key restraint but then spent copiously and gambled. Manners were paramount but they were often impolite, possessing the haughtiness that Catherine had encountered from some quarters, the caustic wit and tendency to belittle others.[9] As a result there were countless contradictions and dandies could not be neatly categorized – they were individual.

For William, the most pertinent part of being a dandy was the style and image. He approved of the fashion, but did not necessarily subscribe to some of the attitudes, such as the inherent snobbery. There were times when he was conceited and arrogant, but in the main he was a genial man who was happy to converse or play sport with everyone regardless of their wealth or standing. Catherine admired his unaffectedness, particularly as it complemented her own down-to-earth nature.

Catherine craved pleasure and excitement, which was why she found dashing and daring Mr Pole so appealing. It was clear to everyone that she adored him, but although he had proposed on several occasions she was still undecided. Catherine was no fool; William had a rakish reputation and needed to prove that he was a changed man, steadfast in his devotion to her. In the meantime, she could not resist a little mischievous teasing to keep him on his toes. Whenever she chatted with one of her simpering suitors, she was lively and flirtatious, beaming at all the lavish compliments. She found the excessive flattery exquisitely ludicrous, and William's obvious discomfort made it even more entertaining for her. One observer remarked that William endured 'many an uneasy quarter of an hour when she bestows smiles elsewhere . . . It amuses *her*. But it puts *him* in agony.'[10]

Catherine was clearly in love, but her family and friends were unimpressed by young Mr Pole. Aside from the fact that he was penniless, with dubious prospects and a dreadful reputation, they suspected his interest was purely financial. Most of them believed that she would be better off with someone steady and reliable. Lady Darnley summed up the general feeling when she declared, 'Mr Pole . . . is very ill-conducted and, I believe, not a very wise young man.'[11] Other onlookers considered him a scoundrel who indulged quite openly in improper behaviour. One objectionable pursuit was his waltzing, which in Regency terms was akin to dirty dancing in the eyes of some. Fearing the nation's morals were being undermined, *The Times* published a report condemning 'the indecent foreign dance called the Waltz . . . the voluptuous intertwining of limbs . . . is far removed from the modest reserve . . . distinctive of English females'.[12] Broad-minded Catherine was undeterred by all the protests and continued to delight in waltzing.

William was also criticized for his frivolous lifestyle. While visiting London, Mirza Khan, the Persian ambassador, observed that the dandies 'do nothing all day but write letters or walk about town twirling their watch-chains, and their evenings are spent at the theatre or at parties, dancing in shoes too small for them in order to impress the ladies'.[13] An Irish student studying in London wrote an equally scathing account, accurately mirroring William's daily routine. He noted that the first act of each day occurred at noon, with a careful examination of the papers.[14] After visiting his stables to inspect horses and chat with the grooms, he was out in his curricle parading the parks, visiting his mistress, then making for Tattersall's, a key venue for horse dealing. The late afternoon was set aside for visiting print shops, hoping to see himself in the latest satirical caricatures, which gave him 'a little celebrity'.[15] Following this, plans were drawn for the evening over a beer and sandwiches in a local hostelry, and he would return home to dress. Dinner was at seven, the opera or theatre at ten, and the night finished at a club or gaming house.

A renowned Lothario, there were rumours linking William with various women including someone named Mathilda, but he assured Catherine that his days of womanizing were over. Family and friends of the heiress remained wary. One of their biggest objections was that William could never stay out of trouble for long. In August he became embroiled in a very public scandal that led to him being issued with a challenge. The resulting duel was folly of the highest order; aside from the fact that it was illegal, there was a possibility that one man would die and the other hang for murder.

The duel was fought on a trivial pretext, but in reality it was the culmination of intense rivalry over the heiress, highlighting the extent of the frenzy surrounding her. Seventeen-year-old Lord Kilworth was a strong contender for Catherine's affections, so there was already trouble brewing between him and William. Mounting tensions exploded after a satire appeared in the press, mocking William's pursuit of Catherine:

> *With the tumult of Waltzing and wild Irish reels,*
> *A prime dancer I'm sure to get at her . . .*
> *But by Jesus I vow, by my own precious self,*
> *That a Wellesley shall win her and wear her!*[16]

Annoyed by the slur, William was further riled when Kilworth laughed about the skit in public. A petty row erupted and Kilworth felt compelled to issue a challenge.

Gossip columns revelled in the unfolding melodrama, publishing correspondence that passed between the rivals. The letters were leaked by William in an attempt to vindicate himself by showing that he was not the aggressor:[17]

Lord Kilworth to Mr Pole, Thursday evening 8 August
Sir – Not deeming [your] answer sufficiently satisfactory . . . I must request a further explanation, or a total disavowal of the words you used at Lady Hawarden's.

Mr Pole to Lord Kilworth, a quarter to twelve, 29 Conduit Street, 8 August
My Lord – Your letter has afforded me extreme surprise . . . I conceive that in that conversation your Lordship was the aggressor . . . if your Lordship is resolved to quarrel with me, and to throw me the glove, I have only most reluctantly to accept of it.

Lord Kilworth to Mr Pole, Friday morning – approx 12.30 a.m.
Sir – Your long and unsatisfactory answer . . . compels me to demand a meeting with you, on Wimbledon Common, at six o'clock in the morning.

Mr Pole to Lord Kilworth, Conduit Street, two o'clock a.m. Friday
My Lord – . . . I shall do myself the honour of accepting your Lordship's invitation to Wimbledon Common, at half past six tomorrow morning.

Luckily for William, his second in the duel was Colonel Merrick Shawe, a loyal family friend with years of diplomatic experience. Accompanying William to Wimbledon Common, Shawe successfully performed the foremost duty of a second: mediating persuasively to ensure that the duel was resolved before shots were fired. On 14 August, both seconds published a joint statement in the press confirming: 'Everything was amicably adjusted in the most honourable manner. It did not appear to the seconds that any apology was necessary, nor was any made.'[18]

Unfortunately, this was not the end of the matter; a further bout of verbal sparring prompted Kilworth to issue another challenge. A second duel took place at Fulham Fields on 15 August, and on this occasion shots were exchanged. Kilworth fired first and missed. William was a sportsman and a deadly shot, but he showed mercy and 'fired his pistol in the air'.[19]

The duel was typical of William's stubborn and reckless nature; he would rather risk his life than apologize for causing offence. The story delighted the media for several weeks, and there were many veiled quips about a lovely heiress that had driven two admirers to desperation, causing them to behave like common highwaymen, brandishing pistols and firing off shots. Catherine was horrified by the whole episode and furious with William for many reasons: rash behaviour, publishing private letters and making her the object of public scandal. Could she really marry a man who was so thoughtless? Although he called at her home several times, she refused to see him. He sent notes, which she ignored. He visited the opera and all the other places she frequented, only to discover that she had left London without saying goodbye to him. Worse still, Catherine would not be returning for several months. It appeared that William had been unceremoniously dumped. Desolate, he sent her a plea from the heart: 'You may but justly suppose my dearest Miss Long how wretched and unhappy I must feel, at the idea . . . I have caused you the least pain . . . I cannot describe to you how wretched this business has made me.'[20]

Parliament was in recess, the season was over, and the nobility retreated to their homes in the country to escape the heat and stench of London. Catherine joined her mother, sisters and aunt, who were already comfortably settled in a house on the seafront at the fashionable resort of Broadstairs, Kent. Catherine's mother and Lady de Crespigny were delighted that William was seriously out of favour. They seized the opportunity, trying their utmost to persuade the heiress to accept the Duke of Clarence, who had taken the trouble to rent a house close by, just to be near her. After all the recent upset, Catherine was at a low point, with her resolve wavering. Succumbing to pressure, she agreed to walk out in public with Clarence. Although this was not an affirmative, it was a promising development for the royal suitor.

7. The Royal Lover

AUTUMN 1811

With his main rival sidelined, the Duke of Clarence felt confident that Catherine would agree to marry him eventually. Negotiations continued with Catherine's aunt, Lady de Crespigny, who pointed out that no self-respecting woman would accept a marriage proposal from a man who was still living openly with his mistress! By now the duke had 'convinced himself that he loved Miss Long as well as desired her fortune', and he was prepared to go to extraordinary lengths to capture her affection.[1] Early in October, he returned home and ended his twenty-year relationship with Mrs Jordan. Then he removed all his belongings from the family home, so that the separation became public and official.

With Mrs Jordan callously disposed of, Clarence was free to pursue Catherine with renewed vigour, and he invited the Tylney Long sisters to grand balls and intimate supper parties. Lady Catherine was delighted that her family were part of the elite royal inner circle and was particularly enamoured with the prospect of having royal grandchildren. As she had been happily married to a man twenty years her senior, Lady Catherine hoped that her daughter would look favourably on the duke's proposal.

Throughout the following four weeks, the duke inundated Lady de Crespigny with letters, pouring out his hopes. Early on he gushed, 'I really flatter myself that the lovely little nice angel does not positively hate me. I walk with her and of course never leave her . . . her dear little eyes sparkled with pleasure at many things I said.'[2] The sparkle he detected may well have been Catherine's eyes glazing over. The old duke dominated her attention, getting drunk and divulging excruciatingly dull stories about his exploits in the navy.

Over the course of one week, Clarence pursued Catherine relentlessly, declaring his love constantly, proposing marriage at least half a dozen times and referring to her as 'the charmer of my heart and soul'.[3] She remained unfailing polite, but the duke drove her to distraction. Whenever he tried to 'venture the topic of love', she cut him short saying, 'I must ever respect you as the Prince'.[4]

Eventually, with her customary degree of candour, Catherine felt compelled to speak her mind. The duke reported back to Lady de Crespigny: 'Miss Long has already expressed to me she considers my attention too pointed, in consequence of which, since last Monday, I have not seen her.'[5]

Leaks to the press were commonplace. Private details of the courtship found their way into the public domain, which was why press reports and caricatures contained such accurate information. On 1 November 1811, the *Morning Chronicle* mocked Clarence's zealous pursuit of Catherine, reporting that he wooed her 'with the magnificence and ardour of an English tar (sailor)'. Newspapers were fed intimate details about Clarence by close friends of his jilted mistress,[6] and Peter Pindar's illustrated poem, 'The Royal Lover', was particularly close to the mark.[7] It showed the blundering duke proposing on one knee. His foolish expression and Catherine's wagging finger accurately depicted the sentiments revealed in private letters.

With Clarence dominating her time, Catherine was growing increasingly despondent. Luckily, William was about to come to her rescue. The renowned Wellesley charm concealed a grittily determined nature. Refusing to be beaten, he saddled up his steed, galloped to Broadstairs and pleaded for forgiveness. Relieved to see him, Catherine relented immediately. The Duke of Clarence was perturbed, complaining to Lady de Crespigny, 'This morning I found Miss Long walking with her mother and Emma followed by Pole.'[8]

At the ball that evening, Clarence extracted a promise from Lady Catherine that her daughter would dance only with him.

When William tried to cut in, the duke jigged on, telling him very civilly, 'I would not give her up to any man.'[9] Imagine poor Catherine's predicament, having to dance all night with the odious old duke, his overweight body damp with sweat, his breath stale with tobacco. Eventually the heiress made the classic excuse, 'that she had hurt her foot', and sat out the dancing.[10]

Clarence always used heavenly imagery when describing Catherine. Sensing his chances slipping away, his desperation was evident as he appealed to Lady de Crespigny: 'The bewitching Catherine looked not mortal but divine. Do try to persuade this dear and lovely angel to think more favourably of me. I really deserve her.'[11]

It takes bravery to stand firm against your family, to defy all their hopes and expectations. The pressure was immense and poor Catherine was in a quandary. She was aware that marriage to the Duke of Clarence would raise her clan to great heights – the Tylneys could be the future kings and queens of England. But when she looked up into his fleshy, lined face her resolve vanished. Perhaps she might have succumbed if she was not already in love with another man, but she had admitted to her sisters that her 'heart was won' by William, who was constantly in her thoughts.[12] Should she sacrifice the man she adored for the prestige of becoming royalty?

Intrigued by Catherine's predicament, the public debated her dilemma and even more cartoons appeared. William's surname had lewd connotations, which the press found irresistible, and satirists claimed that Catherine found it 'impossible to resist such a Pole'. They continued in this vein with the caricature *Miss Long-ing for a Pole*,[13] which showed William standing proud, clutching an impressively 'Long Pole', calf muscles rippling, with the watering can and rake alluding to him sowing wild oats. In contrast, the paunchy duke looked unappealing with his mistress and ten children clamouring in the background. Catherine stood between them, her skirt filled with gold coins and her hand reaching out towards William.

Revelling in the company of her debonair young suitor, Catherine's good humour returned. The physical attraction and sexual tension was evident. There was no more flirting with other men, because she was deeply in love with William, who 'was always at her elbow' or by her side. Everyone at Broadstairs could tell that the young couple shared a great deal in common; they were always gay and happy in each other's company, laughing and joking, engaging in playful banter. But their relationship ran much deeper: William was one of the few people Catherine confided in. Celebrity can be lonely, never knowing who to trust, and it was a relief for her to be able to let down her guard and truly be herself. Discussing their hopes and dreams for the future, the couple talked earnestly at great length and seemed to share profound understanding.

But still, Lady Catherine would not consent to the match and Catherine was equally resolute in refusing to accept the Duke of Clarence. At the end of October Catherine celebrated her twenty-second birthday and shortly afterwards the whole family returned to their home at Draycot to settle in for the winter. It was an unsatisfactory situation, because the season was over and Catherine had still not settled on a husband. Legally, she did not need parental consent as she was over the age of twenty-one. However, she was a respectful, dutiful daughter who would not get married without her mother's blessing.

When they parted, the Duke of Clarence had asked Catherine to write to him, but William could not face the whole winter without his sweetheart. He drove to Wiltshire and stayed in lodgings near Draycot, bribing servants to assist as the courtship carried on clandestinely. The frisson created by these forbidden trysts was deliciously thrilling, hardening the lovers' resolve and passion. William was exemplary in the role of romantic hero, as one diarist recalled:[14]

> Wellesley used to drive his Tilbury down to the Langley Brewery, leave it there, and then hide himself in the sunk fence in front of this house . . . When he had watched Lady Catherine drive across the common into Chippenham with her four or six long-tailed black horses, he would run down

to the Brewery, get into his Tilbury, and gallop over to Draycot, where he saw Miss Long by the connivance of the servants.

Rules of propriety demanded that unmarried women were
chaperoned at all times, so it was highly unusual for Catherine to
entertain a man alone. Sneaking her lover into the house was risqué;
it paid testament to the strength of her desire for William. Under
normal circumstances these illicit meetings would probably have
ruined her reputation, but enormous wealth made her immune –
nothing could damage her marriage prospects. Although it is
unlikely that she would have risked full intercourse, some form of
sexual dalliance probably took place. For the era, Catherine's behaviour was brazen, revealing the bold and daring side to her nature.

On one occasion William happened to be at Draycot House
when a man broke in, hoping to ambush Catherine. A fanatical
stalker named Mr Scott had been harassing the heiress for eighteen
months, bombarding her with declarations of love and insisting 'it
was ordained that they should be matched . . . only he would make
her happy'.[15] When this did not have the desired effect, Scott took
up residence nearby, attempting to force his way into the family
home on countless occasions and regularly waylaying Catherine's
carriage.[16] The Tylney Long ladies had grown so fearful that they
had hired guards for protection and were prisoners in their own
home. The local magistrate could not persuade Scott to desist, so
William gallantly sprang into action. Galloping on horseback all
the way to London, he returned some days later with Townsend, a
Bow Street officer, who threatened to take Scott into custody for
breach of the peace. This had the desired effect; after some hesita-
tion, Scott ordered a chaise and left town.

Once again, *The Times* and *Morning Chronicle* followed the unfolding melodrama gleefully and a few days later another cartoon
appeared in print shops. 'Townsend the umpire of love' showed
William sheltering behind the Bow Street officer as he fended
off the stalker.[17] The caricature also likened Catherine and
William's courtship to one of the greatest love stories of all time,
showing them as star-crossed lovers forced apart by disapproving

families. Portrayed as Juliet on the balcony, Catherine cries out to her Romeo, 'Risk not thy precious life my Love.' Her passion for William was clear for all to see.

William came from a powerful family and the Wellesleys exerted influence over Lady Catherine. 'Lady Wellington in particular [was] most active,'[18] especially after William saved the life of her little boy. The incident occurred in Broadstairs while the family was away from home, without access to the trusted family physician. When the child became seriously ill, William acted quickly by saddling up his horse, locating a reliable physician and driving him to the house. Lady Wellington applauded William's heroism all over town, stating that 'the boy would certainly have died if William had not by his extraordinary exertions brought Doctor Mayo at the moment he did'.[19]

Broadstairs had been abuzz with the story of William's heroism and even Lady Catherine began to thaw. Despite her misgivings, she eventually consented to the match because her daughter's happiness was paramount. Catherine was a romantic young woman, completely infatuated with William. Who could blame her, after he had played the part of romantic hero so brilliantly, even galloping up on horseback to woo her! To add to the allure, he was witty, handsome, a risk taker and a cad – 'the combination was irresistible'.[20]

Speculation finally over, newspapers announced the engagement in November 1811: 'Miss Tylney Long, confessedly the richest heiress in Europe, after having been besieged by Dukes, Marquesses, and Earls, English, Scotch, and Irish, is said to be about to surrender to a Subaltern of the enterprising corps of Wellesley.'[21] The fashionable world was shocked by her decision. Catherine had challenged the conventions of her time, fighting for the right to marry for love rather than status. She gave up a great deal for William and only time would tell if she had made the right choice. William was the man she picked, for better or for worse – despite knowing the truth about his past.

Gallant in defeat, Clarence sent Catherine a fond message through Lady de Crespigny: 'The Duke Of Clarence asked me to say he hopes you have taken a marriage that will ensure the happiness you so deserve and that you have and always will have his best wishes.'[22] At the time, Catherine could not have anticipated that her decision would have major significance, affecting the very course of British history. In 1830, the Duke of Clarence was crowned William IV. If Catherine had married him she would have become Queen of England and her children would have ascended to the throne. Instead, William IV died without producing any legitimate heirs and his niece was crowned Queen Victoria.

8. A Dynamic Family

❧

Despite his reckless ways, William's pedigree could not have been finer. His grandfather was Garrett Wesley, an Anglo-Irish politician and composer, who was awarded the title Earl of Mornington in 1760, in recognition of his musical and philanthropic achievements. William's father and uncles were extraordinary men with remarkable drive and ambition, rising from obscurity to become the most powerful political family in England.

William's uncle Richard was the eldest of the five brilliant brothers, and the self-proclaimed head of the family. Aged twenty-one, he had inherited the family title and property, along with crippling debts. Working tirelessly to support his younger siblings, he managed his run-down estates and boosted finances by taking a low-ranking position in the Irish Parliament. He was a brilliant, charismatic politician with a talent for oration and his rise through the Irish government was swift. Transferring to the English Parliament in 1788, he became MP for Windsor, changing the family surname from Wesley to the more anglicized Wellesley. Despite his burgeoning political career, Richard continued to take his responsibilities as head of the family seriously, scraping together funds to educate his three youngest brothers at Eton. It was a struggle, particularly as he had a young family of his own to support – five illegitimate children by Hyacinth Roland, his feisty French mistress who had been an actress at the Palais Royal. They eventually married in 1794, despite his mother's disapproval.

Richard's big career break came in 1797, when he was appointed Governor of Madras, and Governor-General of Bengal. In this role, he skilfully negotiated various treaties with defeated Indian rulers, which enabled Britain to gain tens of millions of pounds in trade. While the ethics surrounding the British Empire are now considered to be dubious, there was no doubt that Richard's contribution to his own government was monumental. His achievements were recognized when he was awarded the title Marquess Wellesley in 1799. But success had come at great personal cost. On returning to England in 1805, Richard discovered that eight years of separation had destroyed his marriage, and his children barely knew him. To make matters worse, it seemed the governor-general had grown too powerful in India and his peers treated him with jealousy and suspicion. There was no job for Richard in government. Instead of reaping rewards, he was faced with redundancy and estranged from his family. Having spent his entire life working hard, trying to do the right thing, it was too much to bear and Richard went off the rails. During four long years in the wilderness, he spent his time drinking and whoring. But by the end of 1809, there was immense unrest in England, and Parliament recalled the talented Marquess Wellesley – Richard was appointed foreign secretary.

In contrast to the ambitious Richard, William's uncle Arthur had been considered the 'dunce' of the family. His mother removed him from Eton, and he was sent to the Royal Academy of Equitation in Angers, where he learned military skills. On returning to London he took up a lowly position in the 76th Regiment at an income of £300 per annum. A taste for carousing meant that his career remained undistinguished, until he joined Richard in India in 1797, where the powerful governor-general advanced the prospects of his younger brother. Working diligently, Arthur made the most of his opportunities, quickly becoming renowned for his military skills and earning promotion to the rank of general. The dynamic Wellesley brothers were a powerful combination; Arthur's astute military tactics enabled his brother to reign supreme in India. Together they worked tremendously hard for seven years to expand the Empire in India. Their success was extremely lucrative for Britain, as the increase in trade added millions of pounds in revenue to the ravaged economy. Arthur was so successful in his military campaigns, he amassed a fortune of £40,000, as grateful sultans showered him with prize money, and he was eventually awarded the title Lord Wellington. Returning home with status and wealth, the thirty-seven-year-old military hero could have had his pick of women, but he was badgered into marrying his old flame, Kitty Pakenham. On the day of the wedding, Wellington had a terrible shock. Kitty had suffered smallpox in his absence, an illness that scarred her both mentally and physically, leaving her pock-marked, withdrawn and almost blind. 'He had been warned. But the sight of his faded, thirty-four-year-old bride was a shock all the same.'[1] Many years later, Arthur decided he had been 'a fool' to proceed with the wedding, being 'not in the least in love with her', but the principled gentleman went ahead and honoured his commitment, marrying Kitty in Dublin in 1806.[2]

Eclipsed by his two brilliant brothers, William Wellesley Pole (William's father) was nevertheless hugely successful in his own right.[3] Fiercely independent, he left Eton when he was fifteen years old to earn his living in the navy. A lucky break gave him prosperity at a young age, when he inherited an estate in Ireland from his cousin, William Pole of Ballyfin. In recognition of this bequest, he adopted his uncle's surname, signing his letters W. W. Pole. As a result, his family referred to him as 'Mr Pole', a name he liked because it suited his unpretentious nature and differentiated him from his brothers. In 1782, nineteen-year-old Mr Pole gave up his career at sea to marry Katherine Mary Forbes, a renowned beauty with a whimsical sense of humour. Wealthy and well connected, Katherine was the daughter of Admiral Forbes, and the granddaughter of the third Earl of Granard and the third Earl of Essex. The fact that young Mr Pole was welcomed into such esteemed circles paid testament to his character and charm. He adored his wife and they would remain devoted to each other throughout their married life. Mr Pole was a talented politician, serving as MP for Trim before transferring to the British Parliament in January 1790. Working his way steadily through the ranks, he served as Secretary to the Admiralty from 1807 until 1809, when he was appointed Chief Secretary for Ireland. While his brothers sought fortune and glory abroad, he chose to stay behind with his wife and children. Plain old Mr Pole was the unassuming, steady influence in the family, but he was shrewd with money. By 1810, he had acquired a smart town house in Savile Row and an idyllic mansion in leafy Blackheath, plus the large estate in Ireland.

Gerald and Henry, the two youngest brothers, were both married to daughters of the first Earl Cadogan. Henry Wellesley became famous for his troubled marriage rather than his distinguished diplomatic career. His wife, Lady Charlotte Cadogan, caused a sensation when she eloped with Lord Paget, abandoning her husband and four small children. Gerald Wellesley was a religious minister whose wife, Lady Emily Cadogan, followed in her sister's footsteps, deserting Reverend Wellesley in 1815, and causing such scandal that it prevented Gerald's progress in the Church.

The Wellesley brothers were ambitious, diligent, honourable men, with mesmerizing charm. They made the most of their opportunities, excelling at everything they did. Unfortunately, with the exception of Mr Pole, the one thing that seemed to elude them was matrimonial harmony.

William Wellesley Pole was born in London on 22 June 1788, at a time when his parents were experiencing such pecuniary difficulties that he shared his baptismal ceremony with the daughter of a local shopkeeper.[4] With the Irish estates heavily mortgaged, the family had moved to London so that Mr Pole could pursue a career in the government. Opportunities were scarce and he told friends that he 'would be glad to be employed without any salary at all than remain idle'.[5] Various jobs were found for him, some at the Admiralty courtesy of his father-in-law, although these were not always paid positions. Throughout the 1790s, Mr and Mrs Pole struggled financially, living in rented rooms in Hanover Square with their young family – a son and three daughters. While Mr Pole beavered away at government administration, Mrs Pole championed her own causes, helping young women in distress by teaching them a trade. Lessons were held at her home, where she personally taught sewing skills for seamstresses. There were also classes in cooking and housekeeping.

In many respects, William's upbringing was similar to Catherine's, as he came from a loving home with exemplary parents that upheld the principles of hard work and benevolence. William was the second child and his greatest ally was his elder sister Mary, who could always be relied upon to cover up his mischief. He liked to play practical jokes, particularly on the young women who attended his mother's classes, but he met his match when Betsey Allis locked him in a cupboard one afternoon.[6] William neglected his studies, and whenever his tutor reprimanded him for indolence he would reply, 'What use is there in poring over books, [and] writing like a fat citizen's clerk?'[7] His father sent him away to be educated by Reverend Gilly, at Hawkedon Parsonage, near Bury St Edmunds, in the hope that the tranquil rural location would have a calming effect. Instead William discovered new delights in the bed of a local seamstress. He also made a string of rash purchases and accumulated debts with local tradesmen. Despairing Reverend Gilly reported to Mr Pole, 'I was just in time to stop the order of a pair of pistols . . . Indeed such indiscretion is scarcely to be credited'.[8] Although young William believed he was savvy, he was easily hoodwinked by traders who sold him goods at inflated prices. He was the complete opposite of sensible Catherine, who was busy educating herself at the age of sixteen, learning to bargain and barter as she prepared herself for her role as a lady of business.

By the time he was sixteen years old, William was already a hell-raiser, deeply in debt and 'apathetic about everything except drink, horses and women'.[9] A portrait of him at this age shows that he was a typical Wellesley with luxurious dark wavy hair, a narrow jaw and aquiline nose.[10] A curved humorous mouth, coupled with smiling eyes, imparted a permanent air of geniality. His eyes were particularly compelling, a brilliant shade of blue with thick black lashes, what the Irish call 'blue eyes put in with dirty fingers'. Deep-set and heavily lidded, they held a seductive, languorous quality. William spent his days hunting or playing sport, while evenings were reserved for lounging around town with his dandy friends, carousing into the early hours. He spent copiously; unpaid bills for clothes

and horses mounted up so alarmingly that only his father's intervention saved him from debtors' prison. A diplomatic posting was
swiftly arranged by his family, which seemed the perfect solution to
improve his mind and keep him out of trouble. On 8 August 1804,
sixteen-year-old William set sail from Harwich, and over the following five years he would work as an attaché at British embassies
in Austria, Turkey, Denmark, Portugal and Spain. This résumé was
not as impressive as it sounded; William never stayed anywhere
very long because he caused too much trouble. Blundering from
one crisis to another, he wreaked havoc as he made his way across
Europe.

Initially, the powerful Wellesley family had called in favours
to secure William a plum job, working as an attaché to the British
ambassador, Charles Arbuthnot. The first stop was Vienna, an easy
posting because Arbuthnot's entourage were to provide temporary
cover for six months. The sociable nature of his new job seemed to
suit William. Diplomats were usually cultured men, but William
was still young and inexperienced. He managed to conceal his lack
of knowledge admirably, memorizing choice quotes from Shakespeare and other literary works so that he always had a fund of
ingenious remarks at hand when dining out. Vienna was the home
of the waltz, and the impeccable young dandy quickly became the
charm of the town, learning to dance beautifully and displaying his
wit at lavish embassy functions.

On quitting Austria, Arbuthnot's party travelled through
Greece, arriving in Constantinople (now Istanbul) in June 1805.
Constantinople was of strategic importance to world trade as it
sat at the gateway to India and the Far East. The British economy
depended on merchant shipping, and in war-torn Europe it was
essential to preserve diplomatic relations with Turkey (or the Ottoman Empire as it was officially known). William was aware that he
would be performing an important role. Constantinople was an
exotic metropolis filled with all manner of diversions including
colourful bazaars, glittering mosques and lewd floorshows. Much
to his delight, he discovered that amusements were more salacious
than anywhere in Europe. For many young men, travel abroad was

a time for reckless adventure; outrageous sexual fantasies were acted out in steamy bathhouses and brothels. Notorious for his exploits, William was a highly sexed man renowned for his prowess. No doubt he honed his craft in Constantinople, where nimble whores taught him tricks he never believed possible. This was also where he became addicted to the equestrian sport that became known as polo.

Despite all the distractions, William performed well at his job, shadowing the British ambassador and learning a great deal about running an embassy. Everything ran smoothly until Charles Arbuthnot's wife died during childbirth. The ambassador was so grief-stricken he was unable to get out of bed or attend to any of his duties. Arbuthnot's breakdown occurred at a sensitive time when hostilities had broken out between Russia and Turkey over the provinces of Moldovia and Wallachia. The situation required delicate handling and William dealt with the complicated dispatches to Parliament, conducting all political negotiations between Britain and Turkey. His diligence was rewarded when he was appointed Secretary to the Embassy in December 1806, but his acclaim was short-lived. Just one month after his promotion, William became involved with two scheming Russian princesses, who flattered and manipulated the gullible young diplomat, persuading him that he had the authority to intervene in the war between Turkey and Russia. Puffed up with self-importance, William barged in on the Turkish foreign minister, flung himself on the sofa, threw up his legs and delivered a note: 'If the princes of Wallachia and Moldovia are not reinstated, an English fleet of twenty sail shall come and burn down Constantinople – I'll be damned if they shan't.' An order was given to this effect, and Pole galloped within half an hour to the nearby town of Buyuckdere and entered crying 'Victory'.[11]

In effect, William had declared war on Turkey without the knowledge or consent of the British government. The Turks retaliated by announcing that if the Royal Navy fired just one shot, all English subjects in Constantinople would be seized as hostages. They would suffer imprisonment, death and 'the most severe torture that malice could invent'.[12] As a result, the British embassy in

Pera had to be abandoned, and Charles Arbuthnot and his staff escaped just in time to avoid an angry mob that burned and looted the building. Merchant residents were forced to flee for their lives, leaving behind their homes and possessions. Fortunately the *Endymion* was in the port and British subjects scrambled on board, sailing away under a barrage of cannon fire.

Thanks to William's diplomacy efforts, Britain was now at war with Turkey. Under his instructions, a diminished fleet of twelve ships launched a feeble attack on Constantinople, but were soon forced to limp away with heavy losses. The situation was resolved fairly rapidly at the mutual interest of both parties. But when news of the debacle reached England, the public were outraged that the Royal Navy had been humiliated so soon after their glorious victory at Trafalgar. The British ambassador faced an enquiry in the House of Commons and was held responsible – ultimately he had been in charge and should have been more watchful of William. It was the end of Charles Arbuthnot's diplomatic career, but luckily for William, his family somehow kept his name out of the press, shipping him off to Copenhagen until the outcry had died down. Ironically, newspapers even applauded William for his 'very great abilities as Secretary to the British Embassy to the Ottoman Porte'. The powerful Wellesleys had orchestrated a family cover-up on a major scale.[13]

Shortly after the fiasco in Turkey, Mr Pole decided that his son would benefit from the discipline of a military career. Wellington was about to sail to the Peninsula as Napoleon was running riot through Europe. French armies had already achieved supremacy over forces in Austria, Prussia and Russia, and in 1808 Napoleon moved 100,000 troops into Spain, deposing the monarchy and placing his brother Joseph Bonaparte on the throne. Following this, he swept across the border to capture Portugal. Britain alone had survived the onslaught, having defeated Napoleon's fleet at Trafalgar in 1805. Nevertheless, Napoleon's forces posed a constant threat and needed to be stopped. Wellington knew that he was entrusted with a vital task. It was with great reluctance, therefore, that he agreed to employ impetuous William as one of his personal aides. Wellington's aides-de-camp were a handpicked group of trustworthy young men who lived with him in his head-quarters, soothing his worries and carrying sensitive messages on his behalf. On this campaign his closest assistants included the ever-dependable Lord Burghersh and Lord Fitzroy Somerset.

Setting sail for Portugal in July 1808, Wellington was pleasantly surprised by his nephew, who had proved very useful sourcing horses and other supplies. William had also kept the troops entertained while they were waiting for fair winds, teaching the cavalry polo, which boosted morale, improved equestrian skills and kept both horses and soldiers fit. William's first experience of war was at the Battle of Roliça on 17 August 1808, where he played a key role by riding bravely among the battalions, relaying orders and messages between the British generals, as musket fire whistled past his head. Dispatches paid tribute to his bravery, but he did not have time to revel in glory because the French counter-attacked at Vimeiro just a few days later. It was another resounding victory for the British, and again the newspapers singled out William for praise.[14]

William was a hero, but his acclaim was once more short-lived, due to his insubordinate and audacious behaviour. It was a crucial time as British troops were about to seize control of Lisbon and Wellington did not have the time nor inclination to humour his petulant nephew. William was indiscreet and insolent, blatantly disobeying orders from his superiors. He even went absent without leave for several days after borrowing money from colleagues. Wellington wrote to Mr Pole to inform him of the situation, describing how William's attitude was causing friction in the camp. With unfailing honesty, Wellington provided a coherent assessment of William's behaviour and character, telling Mr Pole,

> He is lamentably ignorant and idle; and yet upon some occasions he does not want for sense and sharpness . . . he talks incessantly [on topics not] judiciously chosen . . . he will never be upon a par with the rest of society till he shall have educated himself.[15]

William was dismissed from the army, his military career lasting just three months. When Lisbon was liberated, Wellington deposited his nephew at the British embassy and marched on without him. Instead of finding himself in disgrace, however, William lived in the lap of luxury. Wellington had freed the city, so everyone treated his nephew like a hero. Once more, William's powerful family ensured that the truth of the matter was suppressed. Official reports focused on William's bravery, with glowing articles appearing in newspapers describing how he 'greatly distinguished himself by the good conduct, activity and courage, throughout the whole campaign'.[16]

From Lisbon, William was shunted to the embassy at Cadiz where his uncle Richard, Marquess Wellesley was working as British ambassador to the Spanish junta. Richard appeared to be a good influence, and William remained in Cadiz for over one year without too much incident. There was one small transgression, however, when he was reprimanded for masquerading around town 'rigged out for show in a coat of his father's – the uniform of a Captain General!'[17] For several weeks, he had enjoyed the celebrity of a senior officer as he paraded about accepting gifts and homage from Spanish grandees, grateful to the brave men fighting to liberate their country. He was eventually caught and disciplined after causing embarrassment at an official function aboard HMS *Donegal*.

After five years in exile, William's family hoped that he was finally tame enough to be allowed back into polite society. When Richard, Marquess Wellesley was recalled to England, as foreign secretary, he offered William a job on his staff, presenting him with yet another golden opportunity. Richard wrote home to Mr Pole, 'William is very diligent and I think you will find him improved. I have no doubt that he will listen to my advice. I shall bring him home with me.'[18]

When twenty-one-year-old William arrived back in London early in 1810, his family were filled with renewed optimism regarding his future prospects, believing he was ready to buckle down to a career in politics. In private letters they had referred to William as 'rash, lamentably ignorant, idle, ungrateful and indiscreet'. But they also described his 'generosity, gallant behaviour and thoroughly good heart'. Only time would tell which of these characteristics would prevail, but it certainly seemed that William was a lovable rogue with many endearing qualities. As this was the man Catherine was about to marry, everyone hoped that his wild days were over.

9. *Engagement*

◈

William and Catherine were eager to marry quickly. Weddings often took place within weeks of the engagement, and the excited young couple planned to marry before Christmas. Ordinary folk usually got married in church, where it was necessary to publish banns on three successive Sundays. This was intended to alert the community, so that any irregularity could be exposed prior to the marriage. People of high rank often gained exemption from the process, and their wedding ceremonies tended to be conducted in the privacy of their stately homes, after purchasing a 'special licence'. As a result, rumours abounded in the press about when and where the forthcoming marriage would take place. The most likely venue seemed to be Apsley House, Marquess Wellesley's magnificent residence in Mayfair, or perhaps Mr Pole's town house in Savile Row.

As soon as the engagement was announced, dozens of letters of congratulations poured in from William's family and friends. Writing from Houghton Hall, Lord Cholmondeley captured the general feeling of jubilation when he wrote, 'Hurrah, Hurrah. Rejoiced I am dearest William. I am proud that my friend has so well succeeded. All here delighted I can inform you.'[1] There was no doubt in anyone's mind that William had won a great prize. All three of his sisters sent letters expressing their delight, while his mother could barely contain her euphoria when she wrote:

> The more I reflect on the astounding good fortune you have had, the more delighted I am. For in my sober reflection, I lay aside the brilliancy of it, but I consider her good sense, her

grand conduct, her affection and duty to her mother, her charity, and her religious disposition the foundation of all without which, she should not be in my eyes, as great an acquisition to our family as I expect she will prove.[2]

Although Mrs Pole doted on William, she was also a realist well aware of his reckless nature. Underlining for emphasis, she ended her note with a caution: 'She is a very pretty likeable creature, and if ever you make her unhappy *I shall hate you my dear!*'[3]

In contrast, the response from Catherine's side was subdued. Bartholomew Bouverie was among those who voiced serious concerns to her face, and others sent anonymous letters with ominous predictions:

> Is it possible that the amiable, the virtuous and good Miss Long is going to bestow her hand upon that reptile Pole? Your fortune Madam is a worldly accident, which any of us may possess. But that endowments such as yours, such a heart and such a temper, should be enjoyed by this peevish, vain, self-sufficient profligate young gentleman is not to be endured by anyone who ever had the pleasure of knowing you. He will break your heart, be assured.[4]

For some strange reason, Catherine held on to these warnings, although she did not heed the advice. She was too deeply in love with William to care about what others thought.

Although the young lovers were keen to marry immediately, Catherine's family insisted on waiting until a pre-nuptial marriage settlement was in place. Catherine lived in a male-dominated society; the law of the time decreed that a woman's entire assets automatically passed to her husband when she married. A husband gained absolute control of everything: his wife's property, including clothing and jewellery, her earnings and even her children. This was why Catherine's family considered it imperative to protect her interests with a marriage settlement, which was common practice among the propertied class.

The terms of the settlement were partly controlled by previous family wills, but much was left to Catherine's discretion, with one advisor telling her, 'The arrangements . . . must be entirely governed by your own feelings and judgement as they concern the dispensation of [your] property.'[5] Sensible Catherine enlisted the help of Bartholomew Bouverie, the family member most forceful about safeguarding her interests. He was an astute negotiator, and a member of the renowned Shaftesbury family, so he was the perfect advocate to negotiate a fair deal. As William was heir to his father's estates in Ireland, along with mansions in Savile Row and Blackheath, Bouverie suggested that he should bring his own inheritance to the table. William refused, claiming they were his father's assets not his own. During these mediations, Bouverie found William to be a slippery character with barely 'a squeeze of cordiality'.[6] Once again he warned Catherine about his misgivings regarding her choice of husband, but she was determined to proceed.

Negotiations dragged on into January, and as one newspaper recorded, 'The rolls of parchment employed in preparing the marriage articles, conveyances, and other deeds . . . are sufficiently numerous and bulky to load a cart.'[7] By February, William was desperate to get married, and he wrote to Catherine with growing impatience, 'My Dearest Love, we should have done all this business ourselves.'[8] The couple had an unusually long time to wait, but this also gave them the opportunity to prepare for their big day. Catherine had plenty of time to design a special wedding outfit, while William set about purchasing gifts and other luxury items to present to his bride. They were both stylish and innovative, and what started out as fairly moderate plans quickly escalated into what would be a momentous moment in the history of the English wedding.[9]

Finally, after four solid months of negotiations, the pre-nuptial marriage settlement was in place. Catherine's assets included around 23,000 acres of land and six stately homes, which were divided up between the couple. Catherine granted William a lifetime interest in the Tylney legacy, which included the family seat at Wanstead House:

Landed estates assigned to William	acres
Wanstead House & the greater Wanstead Estate, Essex	1,830
Rochford Hall Estate, SE Essex	1,961
Felstead, Halstead and North Essex Estate	3,760
Roydon Hall Estate, Herts and High Ongar and Fyfield, Essex	2,598
Tylney Hall, Hampshire	2,500
Total	*12,649*

William now had direct control of more than half of Catherine's estates, for the term of his lifetime only. The 'life interest' clause meant that he was entitled to all the rents and income from the estates, but he did not have the power to sell.[10] Catherine retained rights to the Long estates, including the family seat at Draycot:[11]

Landed estates assigned to Catherine	acres
Draycot and Seagry Houses, Wiltshire	4,000
Athelhampton Manor and land in Dorset	1,700
Land at Kirby Hill, Cundall with Leckby etc., N. Yorkshire	4,400
Land at Higham Park, Northants	600
Total	*10,700*

In theory, Catherine still had control of approximately half her estates. Although she was the legal owner of this property, however, the law stipulated that a husband was entitled to his wife's earnings. This meant that William was perfectly at liberty to seize *all* her rents and income. To prevent this happening, it was determined that Catherine would receive £11,000 in pin money every year, which would be raised by the trustees managing the rents and paid direct to her, into a separate bank account entirely for her own use.[12] A clause specified that William was not permitted to 'inter-meddle therewith'.[13] This would allow Catherine some independence and protect her in the event of a separation. Every quarter the trustees would account as follows: Catherine would be paid one quarter of her pin money; instalments on annuities would be settled and William would receive all remaining rents of around £25,000.

The terms of the marriage settlement also specified that Catherine was not permitted to be a joint party to any loan agreements entered into by her husband, nor was she 'subject to his debts or engagements'.[14] This was to protect her against any liabilities that William might accrue.

William was delighted with the settlement and, despite some misgivings, Catherine's advisors were ultimately pleased with the deal. Even if William managed to squander or gamble away the vast fortune, Catherine was protected because she could not be held liable for his debts and, furthermore, she had a substantial independent income of £11,000. Most importantly, William was not permitted to dispose of any land. The advisors firmly believed the agreement was watertight, and that they had done everything they could to preserve the Tylney Long legacy for future generations.

One of Catherine's most endearing qualities was her generosity and compulsion to help others; she regularly donated to numerous trusts and charities. In recent years, she had been a guardian angel to her family, repaying her mother's debts and shielding her when she was being blackmailed. It had become clear that her sisters needed money to enable them to live comfortably. As she would receive £11,000 in pin money each year, Catherine decided that she could afford to support them. Keeping £7,500 for herself, she provided annuities of £2,000 to Dora and £1,500 to Emma, who were enormously grateful to receive a regular income.[15] A separate arrangement allowed Lady Catherine to continue living in the family home at Draycot House for the duration of her life, after which the property reverted to Catherine in accordance with her father's will.

Catherine was also generous to ageing members of her staff at Draycot, sending them into retirement with handsome pensions, and the loyal old nursemaid who had tended her through her infancy was particularly well provided for. These parting gifts were bittersweet, as many of them had watched Catherine grow up and they loved her like a daughter. The old footman, Mr Porte, was warm in expressing his gratitude when he wrote, 'My pen cannot express all my feelings, for though I have not the honour to reckon you amongst *my children*; I do love you very much indeed.'[16]

By now, Catherine knew all about William's past. He had confessed much of it himself, but she had also heard the rumours and received numerous anonymous letters.[17] She knew all about his exploits in Europe, plus other indiscretions of a more personal nature. On first returning to England, he had cohabited with a seamstress in Ipswich, followed by a liaison with woman called Mathilda. He had also accumulated debts, spending lavishly on clothes and raucous nights out. To his great credit, William did not deny the accusations, but was open and honest with her, repenting his mistakes and providing many reassurances. His sincerity was disarming, only serving to make Catherine feel closer to him, to love him even more. Furthermore, recent experience had taught her that no one was perfect; even her saintly mother had been indiscreet. Catherine knew about William's faults and she was entering into the marriage with her eyes wide open.

William had wonderful parents; even before the marriage they adored Catherine and they would grow to love her like a daughter. Mr Pole believed that Catherine was the ideal match for his reckless son, because she was 'the best and most sensible woman in the world'.[18] From the very beginning, Mr Pole was candid, telling

Catherine, 'William has always been a most affectionate and dutiful son, and has ever (avoided all his follies, and you know there have been many), shown a most excellent heart. I trust he bids fair to be a good husband.'[19] He was well aware that Catherine knew all about William's recklessness, but she loved him anyway, because he was so good-natured, attentive and loving.

Mr Pole finished his letter by saying, 'All my family will receive you as a sort of Guardian Angel to us.'[20]

10. A Celebrity Wedding

❧

Breaking with tradition among the elite, William and Catherine's wedding ceremony took place at St James's, Piccadilly, on 14 March 1812. On arriving at the church, the Marquess of Wellesley handed the bride down from her carriage and led her to the altar.[1] Filled with her hopes and dreams for the future, Catherine radiated happiness as she floated down the aisle.

Everyone was impressed by the bride's stunning wedding garments, which exuded glamour. Catherine wore a pelisse of white satin, open at the front to reveal an exquisite gown underneath, made from delicate Brussels point lace. The pelisse was elaborately trimmed with swansdown, with a luxurious sweep of soft white feathers swishing at her ankles. On her head she wore a chic bonnet made from satin and lace, and ornamented with two ostrich feathers and a long lace veil.[2] The bridegroom looked equally stylish in top hat and tails, which comprised of 'a plain blue coat with yellow buttons, a white waistcoat, buff breeches, and white silk stockings'.[3]

London newspapers were quick to report on the events of the big day. On 17 March 1812, the *Morning Chronicle* supplied titbits of gossip, remarking on the prodigious cost of Catherine's outfit: 'The Lady looked very pretty and interesting . . . The dress cost 700 guineas, the bonnet 150, and the veil 200.' The total outlay for this ensemble was more than the average labourer earned in twenty years, demonstrating precisely why marriage ceremonies were usually low-key. Details of Catherine's extraordinary generosity in regards to the marriage settlement also emerged as the *Morning Chronicle* outlined the bequests she had made to her sisters and how 'every domestic in the family has been liberally provided for; they all have had annuities settled upon them for life'.

White weddings were a relatively new trend reserved for the rich and fashionable. Most women simply got married in their best gown, regardless of the colour. Details of Catherine's outfit caused a sensation and made the white wedding dress desirable at all levels of society. From this moment onwards, brides increasingly wore white as a symbol of romantic love and purity.[4]

Proud of his sense of style, William had taken the utmost care with the arrangements, ensuring that everything was perfectly coordinated. He had commissioned a swanky new carriage, emblazoned with 'the united arms of the Wellesley and Tylney families ... It was a singularly elegant chariot, painted a bright yellow and highly emblazoned, drawn by four beautiful Arabian grey horses, attended by two postilions with superbly embroidered jackets in brown and gold.'[5]

The church service did not proceed entirely smoothly, however, because William somehow overlooked the most important detail. Much to the amusement of the press, proceedings at the altar came to an abrupt halt because the bridegroom had forgotten to purchase a wedding ring. One newspaper recorded that 'a messenger was in consequence dispatched to Mr Brown, a jeweller, in Piccadilly, opposite the Church, who immediately attended with an assortment, and then the ceremony proceeded without further interruption'.[6]

One thing William did get right was the stunning diamond jewellery he chose for his wife as a wedding gift. The necklace was a superb row of thirty diamonds of unparalleled size and brilliance – the stone at the centre was one of the rarest yellow diamonds ever seen.[7] As the *Hull Packet* verified, the necklace was of 'first water and magnitude that cannot be matched in England, and probably not in Europe'.[8] The set included a magnificent tiara and a pair of drop earrings, purchased at the enormous cost of 25,000 guineas. Apart from the diamonds, Catherine's trousseau was a treasure trove of jewels, containing matching sets of necklaces, bracelets and earrings made from precious stones. Newspapers published descriptions of the hoard: her rubies were exceptionally large and rich in colour; her emeralds were tastefully set and truly elegant;

her amethysts were as rich and fine as could be procured; and her pearls were unique in colour and lustre.[9] The *Lancashire Gazette* reported that the emerald set was particularly extraordinary, containing 'the largest emerald ever seen . . . imported from the East Indies, it was one of the most valuable stones of [Tipu] Saib's crown'.[10] One of the casualties of Wellington's Indian campaign was Tipu Sultan of Mysore, so the jewel from his crown was probably a spoil of war. Whenever Catherine wore the trophy it would be a talking point, serving as a powerful reminder of the valour and might of the Wellesley family.

All Catherine's jewels were fit for a queen, but the dazzling diamonds were easily her favourite and they became her trademark, silently proclaiming her enormous wealth. The total cost of the jewellery was estimated at £50,000,[11] and everyone complimented Mr Wellesley on his style and taste. Only the most cynical gossiped about the fact that the £50,000 had not come out of William's purse.

When the ceremony was over, Catherine linked arms with her dashing husband, impatient to leave the gathering. They left through a back doorway, to avoid the eager curiosity of the crowd that had assembled outside. This was a rare treat for the public – a high-society marriage taking place in church – and they were keen to catch a glimpse of the action. As the bells rang, the happy couple held hands and raced out of the church, emerging in Jermyn Street, where their smart new equipage awaited. William lifted his bride into the carriage and ordered the coachman to hurry on. The newlyweds drove off at great speed, laughing with delight as they headed for their honeymoon in Blackheath.[12]

The wedding captured the public imagination: the bride's white wedding dress, the groom's top hat and tails, the church ceremony and the fine carriage to transport the newlyweds. Perhaps this formula had been used before, but never with such pomp or publicity. It was a defining moment in the history of the British wedding, establishing a blueprint that remains popular today.

*

Mr and Mrs Long Wellesley became the celebrity couple of their era, setting the trends that others followed. As individuals they were newsworthy, but as a couple they were even more compelling. The public were curious to read the next chapter in their story, to discover what would happen to their sweet Cinderella now that she had married a thrill-seeking libertine. Before the wedding, William had changed his name by Royal Licence to something suitably impressive – William Pole Tylney Long Wellesley. Officially, his wife became Mrs Catherine Pole Tylney Long Wellesley, although the press would use variations. With the Wellesley family riding high, it was beneficial to emphasize this connection so the newly-weds called themselves Mr and Mrs Long Wellesley.

The cult of celebrity was a relatively new phenomenon and blossomed as the media increasingly developed the means to broadcast the minutiae of private lives. The era was a time of tremendous innovation, when advances in technology such as mechanized paper-making (1803) and the steam-powered press (1814) enabled low-cost, high-speed dissemination of images and the printed word. This mass production resulted in daily newspapers reaching a wider audience than ever before. No longer confined to single-page broadsides, reporters could comment at length on society gossip, providing daily updates to tantalize the public. Scandal sold well, which meant that publishers paid handsomely for scurrilous information about people in the public eye. Gossip had become a tradeable commodity.

With this explosion in information technology and mass media around the time of their wedding, William and Catherine were perfectly placed to become the first ever 'celebrity couple'. They excited the public interest on an unprecedented scale – people wanted to read about them simply because they were attractive, glamorous and innovative. Famous for being famous, carefully branded and packaged for consumption, the public fed on delicious titbits about their private lives.

Private letters reveal that the press printed surprisingly accurate accounts about the couple. This was probably because William craved publicity to such an extent that he kept the media supplied with news by leaking information about himself, or inviting journalists to his parties so they could report in colourful detail. This was unusual for the time, as many of his contemporaries were deeply suspicious of newsmen. William quickly learned how to harness the power of the press to his own advantage, becoming one of the first to dedicatedly manipulate the media for his own ends. But he would later discover the impossibility of keeping control when the public become involved in private concerns.

Fascination with the Long Wellesleys continued in the weeks after the wedding; even when there was nothing in particular to report, the press could not resist writing about them. The *Morning Chronicle* followed them most enthusiastically and regularly featured the pair in a daily gossip column entitled 'Mirror of Fashion'. Shortly after the marriage, the *Morning Chronicle* published a thinly veiled skit of the wedding. This article tickled Catherine's sense of humour sufficiently for her to cut it out to keep among her private papers:

> It is with great satisfaction, we can at length announce the long expected nuptials of Mr William Simpson Soames Wilkins and Miss Soames Simpson. The ceremony took place at St Giles in the Fields. At eight o'clock, the procession approached the church by Hog lane, in order to avoid the crowd assembled ... [The Bride] was handed from the Hackney coach (No 254) by Mr Soames, who led her into the vestry. She was simply dressed in a flowered gingham, with a belcher handkerchief carelessly tied over her shoulders.[13]

Lampooning William for his ridiculously long surname, the article goes on to mock him for his blunder with the wedding ring:

> On Mr Wilkins approaching the altar, it was discovered that he had forgotten to put on any small-clothes, and a friend was dispatched to a neighbouring shop in Monmouth Street, from which a pair were quickly procured, and the ceremony proceeded.[14]

With countless reports and caricatures of the couple in circulation, they became household names, instantly recognizable to the public. Newspapers such as the *Hull Packet* and *Manchester Iris* picked up the stories from the London press, reprinting extracts and spreading their fame throughout England. As the *Lancashire Gazette* pointed out, their courtship had 'created more fashionable conversation and conjecture than any marriage project that has been on the *tapis* for many years'.[15]

The ironies of courtship were of great amusement to the Regency public, as the runaway success of Jane Austen's novels demonstrated. Newsmen were not alone in exploiting Catherine – Jane Austen herself also capitalized on her popularity. The author was busy making major revisions to several of her manuscripts at precisely the time Catherine was constantly in the news. Owing to the widespread obsession with the famous heiress, Austen changed the name of her heroine in *Northanger Abbey* from Susan to Catherine. Her many devoted readers would have made the connection instantly, especially with the other main character being called Tilney. The name Catherine invoked a more vividly real debutante for the reader, a modern woman with celebrity associations whose image appeared widely in the media. At the conclusion of the novel 'the bells rang and everybody smiled' as Catherine Tilney finally got her happy ending, calling to mind the recent social spectacle of the Long Wellesleys' marriage.[16] The similarities between Catherine and her fictional counterpart are striking: in *Northanger Abbey*, Catherine Morland is a naive parson's daughter plucked from a sheltered existence in Wiltshire and thrust into the predatory marriage market at Bath. Her charm lies in the naturalness and sweetness of her nature, her loyalty to her family and her lack of guile or mercenary instincts as she determines to marry for love not status.

Just like her namesake, Catherine had learned many valuable lessons. Since coming of age, she had matured into a capable and confident woman, with a mischievous sense of humour. It seemed that she was well equipped to deal with the challenges of married life, including the ability to handle a man as raffish as William.

He, too, seemed a reformed character, ready to settle down and take on responsibility. As the bells tolled for the newlyweds, Colonel Merrick Shawe rightly commented that Mr and Mrs Long Wellesley had 'as fair a chance of happiness as any [couple] in England'.[17]

PART TWO

WEDDED BLISS

'Upwards of 500 of the first rank and fashion sat down to a most splendid supper . . . The table was covered with every variety and delicacy that the season affords.'

Chelmsford Chronicle, August 1816

11. Lord of the Manor

❧

1812

William and Catherine spent their wedding night at Mr Pole's house in Blackheath, where they passed a few idyllic days getting used to each other. Their marriage had taken place just as the pace of London's fashionable season was picking up. As the weeks slipped by, Mr and Mrs Long Wellesley were much in demand, out late every night as society hostesses competed to stage the most talked-about event of the year. They attended breakfasts, suppers, balls, masquerades, soirées, concerts, routs and levees. Theatres were full every evening as audiences enjoyed performances from the ever-popular Kemble and Mrs Jordan (the Duke of Clarence's former mistress).

By June, the season was in full swing and entertainment could move outdoors, with river cruises and garden parties. Carefree Catherine thoroughly enjoyed the social whirl that summer. For the first time she was able to revel in the pleasures of high society without the pressures of courtship. Now a respectable married woman with a husband to escort her about town, she was at liberty to get tipsy on champagne and enjoy everything on offer. Catherine was the belle of the ball with her stylish gowns and wonderful waltzing. One of the most delightful evenings was the Lord Mayor's Grand Turtle Feast at Kew. After supper, his Lordship's party climbed aboard the stately City Barge for a scenic cruise along the river. Two other boats sailed alongside carrying an orchestra of wind instruments, singers and performers. Sipping champagne, serenaded by soothing strains, Catherine watched the sun set over London.

When the party returned to Kew, the band set up on the lawns and dancing continued until dawn.[1]

Vauxhall Gardens held open-air concerts and themed fetes throughout the summer with supper served in booths near the Grove. The Duke of Cambridge's masquerade ball was a particularly spectacular affair: avenues were lit up with exotic Chinese lanterns as minstrels, fire-eaters and acrobats strolled around entertaining guests, with a thrilling firework display to finish off the proceedings. Attending the most select gatherings, the captivating Mr and Mrs Long Wellesley were mentioned in newspapers alongside dukes and royalty. Singling them out for attention, the *Morning Chronicle* reported that they attended an intimate music party at Countess Cholmondeley's house in Piccadilly, where their Royal Highnesses the Prince Regent and Duke of Cumberland were also present.[2] William and Catherine moved in the most exclusive circles, mixing among aristocracy who had theatres fitted up in their homes, or the Duke of York's band at their disposal to entertain during supper. When it was their turn to entertain, they needed to come up with something equally impressive to amuse guests – and they did not disappoint.

Wanstead House now belonged to William. Thoroughly relishing his role as lord of the manor, he masterfully took charge. William believed that his most defining quality was his sense of style, and he intended to make his home the talk of the town. Guests would judge his hosting skills by the table he kept, so one of his first tasks was to hire a top-class chef along with cooks to assist. In many houses, platters were left on the table for guests to help themselves, but William could not tolerate this inelegant scramble for food. At his parties, only the highest standards prevailed and dinner was a spectacle, served with flair. Footmen at Wanstead were trained in silver service, drilled under the steely eye of the butler until they could serve from a heavy silver platter without dropping even one single pea. Waiting staff had to be pleasing to the eye, as well as efficient, so William dressed them in smart new liveries of Wellesley blue. Fastidious about cleanliness, a washhouse and laundry was set up specifically to clean and press staff uniforms. William did not want the smell of body odour to overpower his wonderful food. The wine cellars at Wanstead would become renowned, and William's close friend Colonel Merrick Shawe helped with restocking. A connoisseur of good food and fine vintages, Shawe steered William in the right direction, helping him to track down crates of rarest Madeira, sherry and claret.[3]

William loved dancing and, as he entertained so frequently, it is likely that he kept a band of musicians permanently employed at Wanstead. Always on hand to perform at suppers or balls, they filled the house with music, often playing just for William's pleasure as he worked, dressed or coached Catherine in waltzing.

Driving fast horses was another of William's greatest pleasures, so he enlarged the stables to accommodate his growing number of thoroughbreds. (In modern terms, he owned a fleet of top-of-the-range classic and sports cars – Aston Martin, Porsche, Ferrari, Lamborghini, Rolls-Royce and Bentley.) Apart from the four Arabian greys that drew his carriage, he treated himself to a chestnut stallion that was fearless over fences and could outrun any horse in the neighbourhood. He also purchased a number of racehorses, which were his pride and joy, and hired grooms to care for them, polishing their coats until they gleamed.[4]

Kennel men cared for a pack of staghounds that William kept 'in a style of princely magnificence', feeding them on huge hunks of meat.[5] These dogs were not foxhounds, but a rare breed of old-fashioned staghounds, bred and trained to be exceptionally fast. Wealthy men, including George III, permitted themselves the luxury of acquiring one or two pairs of these pedigree dogs, but William was the only man in England to own an entire pack.[6]

With political ambitions to cultivate, William thought it prudent to own a home close to Westminster, so he purchased a smart town house at No. 43 Dover Street. The Long Wellesleys often spent several nights there during the week, as it was close to all the fashionable shops and parties. From William's perspective, it was important to be seen in all the right places and the Long Wellesley carriage was easily recognizable, emblazoned as it was with their coat of arms, the Arabian greys wearing eye-catching headdresses of tall blue plumes. To complete the look, two footmen flanked the carriage, riding postilion, standing smartly to attention in liveries of Wellesley blue.[7] These burly guards were not simply for decoration; they provided protection when the Long Wellesleys were out, escorting them around, carrying parcels while they shopped and grandly knocking on doors when they paid calls.

The theatre was one of the best places to see and be seen. The Theatre Royal on Drury Lane had been rebuilt after burning down and was due to re-open in November. Fitted out in the height of style, there were fourteen private boxes for sale. Anxious to secure the best seats, William approached his friend Richard Sheridan, who was manager of the theatre. True to form, he managed to secure the most expensive box, situated on the lower circle directly opposite the stage, at the enormous cost of £5,250 for a twenty-one-year lease.[8]

William also undertook minor refurbishments to the Lake House at Wanstead. Although Catherine had been adamant that she did not want tenants living within the boundaries of the park, for reasons unknown William agreed to lease the idyllic Lake House to Colonel Paterson and his family. The colonel had served under Wellington in India, so William may well have let the property as a favour to his uncle. Whatever his reasons, Wanstead now belonged to William for the course of his lifetime and Catherine was happy to allow him free rein.

Managing the estate was like running a large business. The parish of Wanstead had a population of around 900, and many of these people relied on William for their livelihood. There were the tenant farmers who leased parcels of land, plus those William employed. Forty-six domestic servants ran the household while outside scores of estate workers tended the stables, pleasure grounds, kitchen gardens, fruit groves and hothouses. Outbuildings included a laundry, brewhouse, slaughterhouse, dairy, forge and a water mill providing running water to the house, which contained a three-barrel pump engine worked by horses.[9] Employees included grooms, stable lads, kennel men, gardeners, farmers, carpenters, gamekeepers, deer-keepers, mole-catchers, brewers, slaughter men and laundresses.

Many staff changes took place at Wanstead in the months after the wedding. On the death of Dr Glasse, Rector of St Mary's Church in Wanstead, William awarded the post to his childhood mentor, the Reverend William Gilly. It was an extremely prestigious position for Gilly and he remained eternally grateful. From William's perspective, it was useful to have the local rector as an ally. Various staff members were fired, including the loyal caretaker Appleton, who had forty years of service. While the bachelor Earl Tylney had resided abroad, Appleton had served as the house tour guide, proudly showing guests around and verifying the provenance of furniture and artefacts. With his unsurpassed knowledge of the house and contents, the caretaker was undoubtedly a huge asset, but the new owner was determined to adopt a fresh regime. Within a short space of time, many of the people Catherine trusted were replaced and Wanstead House was filled with William's allies.

Enjoying adulation from his peers, William intended to make his mark at Wanstead House by setting trends and taking entertainment to a new level. It was his ambition to become the most celebrated and influential man in the county of Essex.

12. Tenderly She Loved Him

❦

1812

Having chosen love over status, Catherine started married life 'under the very happiest auspices'.[1] One can only imagine what went on behind the closed doors of the marital bedchamber, but William was a man of renowned prowess. Whatever techniques he employed certainly put a glow in Catherine's cheeks and a twinkle in her eye. Close friends noticed 'how tenderly she loved him',[2] while her rapt expression made it clear to everyone that the couple 'lived together on very affectionate terms'.[3]

Sparkling as brightly as the diamonds that adorned her throat, Catherine looked 'singularly beautiful' and blissfully happy.[4] She was now one of the most fashionable women in London. Her new lady's maid was an accomplished hairstylist with a keen eye for fashion, ensuring that her mistress always looked immaculate, with curls piled informally on her head during the day and more elaborate styles reserved for the evening. Good grooming gave Catherine a permanently glossy sheen. Her flawless creamy complexion was like a blank canvas and, with the help of a little paint, her lady's maid could transform her into a masterpiece. At Queen Charlotte's birthday celebrations, newspapers singled out Catherine for praise, describing her outfit as 'a profusion of diamonds, draperies of white and silver . . . headdress blue and white ostrich feathers. This dress was singularly beautiful.'[5] At another function Catherine dazzled in 'white satin richly embroidered with plumes of gold, studded with silver . . . headdress feathers and diamonds'.[6] Stylish, feathered and bejewelled, Catherine had come a long way since her coming-of-age portrait.

Georgiana, Duchess of Devonshire, had been the 'Empress of Fashion',[7] but since her death in 1806, newspapers had been searching for a new leading lady to brighten up the society pages. Catherine was proving a worthy replacement, particularly since her wedding outfit had caused such a sensation. When the ensemble was put on display by her robe-maker, ladies flocked to the shop, queuing round the block for hours to get a close look.[8] Fashion magazines agreed that the breathtaking outfit 'excelled, in costliness and beauty, the celebrated one worn by Lady Morpeth at the time of her marriage, which was exhibited for a fortnight at least by her mother, [Georgiana] the late Duchess of Devonshire'.[9] Catherine's use of swansdown was a particularly popular innovation, copied widely the following winter. In November 1812, *The Lady's Magazine* commented on the influx of swansdown trimmings on satin pelisses, velvet cloaks, hats, bonnets, and on evening dresses 'round the bosom and sleeves'. In Hull, a milliner boasted of his fine selection of dress hats from London, most notably 'the Tylney Long'.[10]

Catherine had blossomed into the nation's foremost female celebrity and fashion icon. The fact that she chose to exhibit her wedding dress suggests that she was aware of her influence, and that she actively courted fame. Being a leader of style was high maintenance, particularly in an era that was dubbed the 'Age of Elegance'. Catherine often changed her outfit several times a day before embarking on daytime calls, walks in the park, shopping trips or supper engagements. An even stricter dress code applied for evening wear, with semi-formal dinner dresses or formal ballgowns required, richly embellished and made from shimmering silks and satins. Catherine spent so much money on clothes that dressmakers competed for the privilege of calling on her at home with their latest designs or bolts of rare material. Mrs Thomas's establishment in Chancery Lane was typical of the places she frequented when shopping in London. The front shop was fitted with counters tempting customers to purchase material, buttons, ribbons, silver lamé and all types of trimmings. The discreet back rooms were reserved exclusively for ladies with serious amounts of money to spend. Pretty apprentices paraded in front of clients, modelling a variety of the latest fashions, while Mrs Thomas was on hand to suggest variations, a different colour or finer fabric perhaps.

Ultimately, it was up to the woman herself to create a unique look that would make her stand out from the crowd. In keeping with the fashion of the time, Catherine's style was understated elegance, wearing beautifully cut gowns that rippled and flowed, while sculpting and skimming her curves in all the right places. Although she favoured simple white fabric, her evening gowns were often delicately embroidered with threads spun from real gold or silver, making her distinctive in the midst of a gathering as she shimmered iridescent in the candlelight. Dressed all in white, this approach focused attention on her glittering necklace and tiara; an explosion of diamonds that made Catherine appear like a celestial vision. This cemented her public image as an angel, all virtue and goodness.

Although it was important for a woman in Catherine's position to look good, she did not lead a frivolous, idle existence. Marriage was a partnership; wives in the upper ranks of society played a crucial role and were often instrumental in their husbands' advancement. Wellington summarized this perfectly, declaring that the primary duty of a wife was to 'raise her husband in the eyes of the world'.[11] Catherine supported William's social and political aspirations by hosting dazzling events at Wanstead House. Mr and Mrs Long Wellesley were a good team. Although William had ultimate control at Wanstead, Catherine was responsible for the day-to-day running of the household, a mammoth task considering the sheer size of the mansion. Managing the army of forty-six indoor servants with calm efficiency, Catherine quickly earned the regard and respect of her new staff. Whenever she entertained on a large scale, hundreds of invitations had to be sent, innovative menus compiled, top-class performers hired and furniture rearranged to suit the gathering. The latter task was not as simple as it may sound, because Wanstead House was like a museum, stuffed full of family heirlooms, antiques and artwork, which Catherine had to catalogue to keep track of. In many respects she was like a curator overseeing her collection. In modern terms, she ran the equivalent of a marketing department and corporate entertainments business in order to promote her husband.

Catherine must have been doing a good job as William's rising status in society was endorsed by an official royal visit. As heads of the military, the Dukes of York and Cambridge visited Wanstead Park to inspect the three regiments of East India Volunteers. Following the military parade, Catherine hosted an intimate banquet for forty guests. A feast was served in the Salon at four o'clock, while singers and musicians entertained. The dukes quit the gathering at nine o'clock, leaving the Long Wellesleys to enjoy the rest of the evening with their closest friends, including Catherine's mother and sisters.[12]

Although Catherine played a major role in running the household, her husband took overall charge of the finances. As owner of Wanstead House, William had complete control of the marital home, and he also received all the rents from the estates. Under the terms of the marriage settlement, Catherine was entitled to receive her £11,000 pin money (£7,500 after deductions), but everything else went to William. In keeping with the common practice of the time, Catherine deferred to William's judgement in all major decisions. As the era's vast number of books and articles on the topic demonstrate, it was a wife's duty to submit to her husband. In 1808, a popular magazine urged married women not to 'overlook the word OBEY'.[13] This dictate was not as oppressive as it may seem, because men usually wished for marital harmony and a happy wife. In fact, behind closed doors wily wives learned how to bargain or cajole until they got their own way. In the main, during the Regency, upper-class marriage was a bond of mutual respect, embodying warmth and tenderness. Catherine, the respectful daughter, became an equally devoted wife. She loved and trusted her husband and was content to concede to his wishes.

Whenever Catherine had a spare moment, she enjoyed walking in the gardens, taking long scenic strolls. Despite its proximity to London, Wanstead was very much a rural location with the house set amid 300 acres of parkland. The pleasure grounds had originally been laid out in a formal style by the celebrated George London, but had been modified by the bachelor Earl Tylney to create the more natural landscape advocated by Lancelot 'Capability' Brown. Winding avenues led through woodland arranged with statues telling stories from mythology; there were follies, temples and a boathouse in the form of a curious grotto. Catherine relished the peace and tranquillity of her gardens, which were designed to create theatre and drama, surprising and delighting at every turn. The spectacular landscaping could be viewed from the upper floor of the house, and from the rear staterooms Catherine could see the gardens stretching out before her in a continuous panorama. A grass terrace walk almost as wide as the house ran in a straight line down to the River Roding, and the formal gardens contrasted perfectly with the surrounding wilderness, linked seamlessly by meandering walks that led to clearings, bowers or forest gardens.

Four months after the wedding, Catherine's happiness became complete. On 16 July 1812, the *Morning Chronicle* announced, 'Mrs Wellesley Long Pole, to the great joy of that family, is reported to be in the family way.' Catherine walked about in a state of pure joy and wonder, stroking her still flat stomach, trying to absorb the notion that William's child was growing inside her. By now the unrelenting social whirl of the London season was winding down, allowing her some leisure time to pause and reflect on her good fortune. Catherine woke up each morning to a symphony of bird-song, with views of mist rising from the lake and fresh scents from her gardens that were now in full bloom. Having returned to the house in Grosvenor Square for the season, Lady Catherine, Dora and Emma were frequent visitors at Wanstead that summer, accompanying Catherine on strolls in the gardens and sharing her joy over the pregnancy. There was a great deal to talk about since nineteen-year-old Emma had fallen in love with an Irishman named Mr Burke; she was hoping to settle down and start her own family. Excitedly, the sisters discussed how wonderful it would be when they were all mothers, the cousins always playing together and growing up to be great friends.

The women took pleasure in attending Sunday Mass together at St Mary's Church, which stood near the octagonal Basin, about a hundred yards from Wanstead House. The architecture complemented the main building, with a classical portico at the front, supported by four soaring Doric columns, plus a clock tower and cupola at the west end supported by eight Ionic columns. The local community expected to see the lady of the manor in church and enjoyed participating in a little pomp. Catherine dutifully obliged, following a tradition laid down by her ancestors, who were now buried in the family vault beneath the church. Whenever she attended mass, a footman would be waiting in the porch, a cushion in his hand to convey her prayer book.[14] As she entered the church, the congregation would rise as a mark of respect, and she would walk up the aisle to the altar, where the family's box pews were prominently positioned beneath a huge marble statue of Sir Josiah Child. Catherine attended church regularly as was a requirement of the time, an obligation for all respectable ladies and gentlemen. She had much to be thankful for. She loved her husband passionately, she was thrilled with life at Wanstead and she looked forward to giving birth to her first child. It seemed that she had finally found perfect happiness.

13. Member of Parliament

❦

On 11 May 1812, the Prime Minister and Chancellor of the Exchequer Spencer Perceval was assassinated in the lobby of the House of Commons. Uncertainty and unrest followed, particularly as the economy was already in disarray: Britain was at war and the army was in retreat due to lack of supplies; there was poverty and misery at home; George III was too ill to rule; and the government had fallen apart. Ministers agreed that the country needed a strong efficient leader and Marquess Wellesley seemed the obvious choice. On 1 June 1812, the Prince Regent summoned Richard to Carlton House and authorized him to form a government. With his uncle poised to become the next prime minister, William wanted to be in a position where he could capitalize on his success. Ideally, he wanted a seat in Parliament as this could lead to a top job in government. He enlisted the help of his most loyal and long-suffering friend, Colonel Merrick Shawe, who could be relied upon whenever there was a problem to be fixed. Discreet enquiries were made and Shawe located a pocket borough that could be acquired at a reasonable price. William paid a brief visit to the constituency, greased a few palms and was duly elected Member of Parliament for St Ives.

Catherine certainly seemed to be having a positive effect on William because he embraced his new career with a passion. He spent many evenings in Westminster, working tirelessly to help his uncle form a coalition. It was a difficult task because the Regent had insisted on a bi-partisan ministry at a time when Whigs and Tories had no desire to share power. William took this role seriously, reading political literature and pamphlets to educate himself. The gentlemen's clubs of St James's were like an extension of Parliament, with many political alliances forged over leisurely dinners or port and cigars. This type of sociable environment suited William perfectly, and he became adept at debating politics with some of the keenest minds in the country. He forged some strong alliances during this period including his rather unlikely friendship with the famous playwright and Whig politician Richard Sheridan.[1] With his elegant attire and acid wit, Sheridan was renowned for his rousing speeches in the House of Commons. Although he was old enough to be William's grandfather, Sheridan enjoyed the hospitality at Wanstead House, where the two men often sat up late into the night drinking port, discussing politics and setting the world to rights.[2] Coming from a Conservative family, William found Sheridan's liberal views enlightening and he subsequently stood for Parliament as an Independent candidate. For William, the ideal man would have the poise and elegance of Brummell, while possessing the blithe wit and genius of Sheridan.

William worked hard, hoping to prove himself, and also to reap huge rewards for his endeavours. As Governor-General of Bengal, Richard, Marquess Wellesley had used his influence to bring his brothers up in his wake. In a society steeped in patronage, William fully expected to be promoted to a top job very soon. Richard seemed set to fulfil his life-long ambition, but suspicion and bad luck were to foil him yet again as a devious plot had been forged to damage his reputation. Just before Spencer Perceval's assassination, Richard had written a damning statement, criticizing him. He never intended to publish the report, but his enemies leaked the document after the prime minister's death. The timing was terrible for Richard, as his statement caused great offence to the whole of Parliament and shocked the public. No member of Perceval's government would support him after that and his rival, Lord Liverpool, became prime minister. Once more, Richard fell dramatically from grace. False accusations had kept him out of office after his Indian campaign, and now misunderstandings held him back yet again. Tarnished by association, Mr Pole lost his job as chief secretary to

Ireland. William knew that he could no longer rely on his uncle Richard for a leg-up in his career. Although he was MP for St Ives, his canvassing around Westminster had come to nothing and there was no job for him in Lord Liverpool's new government.

Fortuitously for William, another uncle was about to make his name. In the Peninsular War, Wellington had led forces that had helped to liberate Portugal. Now his army was sweeping through Spain, winning every battle. On 22 July, Wellington gained an important victory at Salamanca, which opened up the road to liberate Madrid. Recognized as a military commander of unequalled genius, he was awarded the title Marquess Wellington and given a grant of £100,000 towards establishing a country seat in England. Victory celebrations after Salamanca were riotous and lasted for three days. On the second night, Richard, Marquess Wellesley was driving around the West End admiring the illuminations when he was recognized and cheered in Whitehall. Richard stopped and made a short speech on behalf of his brother. Deprived of the hero Wellington, who was still abroad, a drunken mob settled for the next best thing. They dragged Richard from his carriage, held him aloft and paraded him about London against his will. The slender little man was carried off to St Paul's, marched around the West End and finally dumped unceremoniously outside his home at Apsley House. Apart from anything else, the experience must have been a little galling as a few weeks earlier Richard had been poised to become prime minister, and now it was his sibling who was the toast of Westminster. It seemed possible that Arthur might outstrip his achievements and fame. Richard had a narrow escape, as the crowd was still relatively good-humoured when they whisked him away. But social unrest was a feature of the time and, after the illuminations were turned off, the mob became violent. They smashed windows, shot off firearms and hurled fireballs in protest at the biting poverty and hardship that affected the vast majority.

More than anything, William wanted renown. But MP for St Ives was not a prominent position – it was a pocket borough with little sway in Parliament. Eager to assert his standing in other ways, he worked hard to establish himself as the most influential man in the county of Essex by becoming actively involved with the local community and reviving some of the old traditions. He sponsored the Chelmsford races and local Florist Feast, where he contributed burgundy, champagne and claret of the highest quality from his well-stocked wine cellar.[3] A daring horseman, renowned for his speed and dexterity, he became famous for his hunts, where local squires regularly enjoyed his hospitality. William would provide extravagant breakfasts at the Eagle Inn, where everyone ate and drank at his expense. In fact, his hunting parties became so legendary, *Baily's Monthly Magazine of Sports & Pastimes* (now *Horse & Hound*) was still reminiscing about them seventy years later. On 1 January 1880, they recalled that William was 'one of the jolliest fellows imaginable . . . scattering sovereigns to the countrymen in the hunting field, as readily as other liberal sportsmen would give shillings or sixpences'. On another occasion, they described how William always looked dapper on the hunting field: his hat jauntily set to one side, boots highly polished, waistcoat spotlessly white and his cravat perfectly tied with a flourish.[4] Never compromising on style, he refused to wear a conventional scarlet hunting coat, opting instead for 'a ribbed jacket of soft toned grey'.[5]

William hosted the famous Epping Hunt in 1813, traditionally held at the Roebuck Inn in Buckhurst Hill on Easter Monday. When the first Earl Tylney resided at Wanstead, the Epping Hunt had been a grand event, often attended by the Lord Mayor.[6] Hospitality tents supplied food and drink, bands played music and the day was usually 'concluded with a Ball Alfresco'.[7] Nobody had sponsored the event since the bachelor Earl Tylney had fled abroad, so the Epping Hunt had gradually degenerated into a rough affair dubbed 'The Cockney Hunt', 'attended by barbers, bakers and even bruisers'.[8] East Enders arrived in droves by 'carts, buggies, dillies, dray-horses and Hackney-coaches'.[9] Accidents were inevitable and numerous; in 1785 eight young persons ended up in hospital at St Bart's and a Mr Humphries fatally broke his neck when riding under a tree.[10]

Determined to restore the Epping Hunt to its former glory, William ensured that an uncommonly large contingent of the aristocracy turned out, filling the stables until they overflowed with stately carriages. As it was a fine spring day, Catherine arrived in her open cabriolet drawn by the four Arabian greys, flanked by two postilions. A group of her female friends gathered round in their carriages, comfortably seated on plush upholstery, ready for the proceedings. Straddling their thoroughbreds, riders waited in anticipation. Everyone watched as the host made an entrance, cantering up on his glossy chestnut stallion. A deer was released and given a head start, while barking bloodhounds were restrained on leads. The hunters gave chase for two hours, but despite the calibre of the field, the deer was eventually lost.[11] A sumptuous feast was waiting at Wanstead House for nobles and gentry. For the locals, tents were set up to provide food and strong ale, all paid for by William.[12] People cheered, raising their tankards as the generous host withdrew from the gathering. Mounting his horse in one fluid motion, William threw a handful of sovereigns into the air, which scattered amongst the crowd like confetti. As he rode away, people scrambled about in the dust grappling for the gold left in his wake.

Catherine surrounded herself with creative, forward-thinking people and her close friends included Caroline, Lady Scott, who would go on to publish three novels,[13] and Lady Sarah Spencer, who would become Lady Lyttelton the following year, on marrying the Whig politician, William Lyttelton. While William was busy with parliamentary duties, she mixed with her own circle in town, calling on her friends or taking a carriage ride through Hyde Park. Morning or afternoon tea was a female ritual enjoyed in polite drawing rooms across England, and it gave women the opportunity to catch up on the latest gossip or talk about their concerns. In bluestocking circles the conversation was often intellectual, revolving around philosophical thought and the politics of the day, particularly women's issues. Although Catherine read widely and enjoyed stimulating discussion, she tended to mix in less serious circles. Her sense of humour was whimsical, and during her years at Grosvenor Square she became friendly with comical Thomas Champneys, a married man in his early forties, who was a close friend of the Lytteltons, Mrs Richards and other members of her clique. Well known for his love of disguise, Catherine first met him at her neighbour's masque where he appeared heavily made-up and dressed as the fictitious Lady Belinda Blossom.[14] Much to her amusement, he stayed in character all evening, gossiping with the ladies, flirting with the men and fluttering his eyelashes over the top of his fan. More recently he had arrived at Mrs Dawson's masquerade with a group of friends all dressed as inimitable barristers, loaded down by briefs.[15] Descending like a flock of crows, they proceeded to ask embarrassing questions and cross-examine guests. The party had taken place amidst the frenzy of Catherine's courtship, so it seems likely that Mr Champneys placed her in the dock to enquire about whom she would marry, calling on witnesses to pass an opinion. He had a penchant for sexual innuendo and his antics were frowned on in some circles, but Catherine found him hilarious and, in response, he enjoyed her adulation.

Catherine was popular, with many appealing qualities that endeared her to both men and women. She mixed in enlightened circles, inspired by her altruistic family that included visionaries such as the seventh Earl of Shaftesbury and Lord John Russell, who would be instrumental in the fight for social reform. Perhaps always searching for a father figure, she often seemed to form strong bonds with gentlemen twenty years her senior. A particular friend was the poet and politician Sir George Dallas, who would become one of her closest confidants, advising her on personal affairs as well as business.

Whenever she was back at Wanstead, she mixed with ladies from the surrounding neighbourhood, going for carriage rides in the countryside, taking afternoon tea or hosting informal soirées in the intimacy of her private drawing room. She had become very friendly with Ann Rushout, who had recently inherited a nearby estate, Wanstead Grove, comprising sixty acres. The eldest daughter of the first Lord Northwick, Miss Rushout was an artist, traveller and diarist, sharing many interests with Catherine. As they were both modern women conducting business in a man's world, they almost certainly had many fruitful discussions on the subject. Miss Rushout was a bluestocking, with radical opinions. A poem pasted into her commonplace book (or scrapbook) expressed her views on marriage:

> *Then shun oh! shun that wretched state,*
> *And all the fawning flatterers hate.*
> *Value yourselves & men despise,*
> *You must be proud if you'll be wise.*[16]

By contrast, Catherine was a romantic who believed that love and marriage provided the greatest source of happiness. The ladies probably had many interesting debates, setting out their different views on the subject. Miss Rushout never married, possibly because she was unwilling to give up her property and independence. During their discussions, however, Catherine gained valuable insight into the early stirrings of proto-feminist thinking, and she would always remember one important piece of advice – 'value yourself'.

14. Joy and Pain

❧

1813

During the first summer of her marriage, Catherine had been blissfully happy and particularly delighted at the prospect of becoming a mother. But the harsh winter that followed was made even bleaker when she suffered a miscarriage and lost her precious baby. Elegant soirées with blazing fires did little to relieve the aching emptiness she felt inside as she shuffled about the house suffocated with sorrow. In this depressed state, she did not notice the first buds of spring until she threw back her curtains one morning to find that the gardens had bloomed overnight. Walking around the pleasure grounds helped her to regain her strength and lift her spirits. One of her favourite spots was the shaded bluebell wood, with its wild natural beauty and tranquillity. Strolling through forests freshly washed with rain, she breathed in the therapeutic, woody scent of pines and sweet chestnuts. Soothed by the whisper of a breeze stirring the rushes, she listened for the gentle ripple of herons landing on the lake. Signs of new life were all around: young lambs frolicked in her fields, birds laid their eggs and fragile blossoms magically appeared on barren trees. Finding hope in this rebirth, she prayed that it would not be too long before she was graced with a child.

William was attentive during this difficult period, devoting time to his wife. Sharing their hopes for the future, he fuelled her desire to travel with stories of his time abroad. They talked about visiting colourful bazaars and balmy beaches or taking in the sights on a Grand Tour of Italy. But, more than anything, the couple longed for an heir and this common purpose brought them closer together. Catherine loved William deeply and she desperately wanted to bear his child.

Another situation troubling Catherine was the fact that a bitter argument had erupted between William and her family over money. The dispute had started early in 1813, after her sisters began to press William for the £15,000 bequeathed to each of them under the terms of their father's will. As Dora was almost twenty-one, her portion was owed shortly, and Emma had requested her money because she was betrothed to Mr Burke and needed funds to establish a home of her own. First Lady Catherine wrote to William and then, on 7 January 1813, Dora sent another reminder, stating, 'I shall be very much obliged to you if you will now take measures for the payment of that part of my fortune, £15,000.'[1]

When William replied four days later, he insisted the delay was not his fault, claiming, 'I have left it entirely with your professional person [Mr Bicknell] to point out the most eligible mode in which he conceived your portion might be offered you.'[2] Clearly affronted by Dora's tone, William launched into a sanctimonious tirade:

> I venture to suggest, that such letters, as those of yours and Lady Catherine never were before written to a man of charac- ter. The unfortunate mode in which you have chosen to wage your claim upon me, is one which no person of business, integ- rity, or knowledge of the world, would ever have resorted to and one which has no parallel in the history of polite society. Your letters have *seriously offended your sister*.[3]

Full of bluster, William's letter was unnecessarily pompous and hostile, stating that Dora had no 'integrity' or knowledge of 'polite society'. William was in the habit of complaining that Catherine's family were uncouth and, as a result, many people genuinely believed that Dora and Emma were ignorant, insipid creatures. However, Dora's letters to William refute this and she would later prove to be a formidable adversary. Unfazed by his bullying tactics, her reply was short with a hint of sarcasm:

I am much obliged to you for your letter, but must trouble you once more to observe that Mr Bicknell was fully empowered by me to negotiate the business alluded to with any professional people whom you might appoint. Pray forgive my boring you thus.[4]

A stalemate developed, with Catherine stuck in the middle. William was withholding Emma's money because he did not approve of Mr Burke and insisted that he would arrange a more suitable match to a man with better prospects. He was also annoyed that the ladies were griping about money after Catherine had provided them with such generous annuities, paying £2,000 to Dora and £1,500 to Emma. The main excuse that he gave to his wife, however, was that their finances were in such disarray, and Catherine knew this to be true.

During the first year of his marriage, William had worked hard to make sense of the accounts. With hundreds of small tenancies and holdings spread across six counties, it was difficult to keep track. Working his way through estate ledger books, William scrawled comments in the margins: 'This amount is not very large … Where are these accounts? … This is all perfectly unacceptable.'[5] According to William, a great deal of money remained unaccounted for, causing him to suspect that the trustees had mismanaged the estates, while systematically taking large cuts for themselves. Nothing was ever proven, but it gave William the perfect excuse to get rid of the old advisors and bring in his own people.

Another problem William encountered was the fact that Catherine's inheritance was not as large as he had expected. Although Sir Josiah Child had been fabulously wealthy, his son, the first Earl Tylney, had lost a fortune in the South Sea Bubble, while the bachelor Earl Tylney had depleted funds further by spending lavishly. Added to this, rents were in arrears because tenants were struggling to turn over profits. Nevertheless, William's rent roll was in the region of £40,000 – a vast sum. But before any money was paid to him, the trustees settled the various annuities: £7,500 to Catherine, £2,500 to Dora, £1,500 to Emma and around £5,000 to Lady

Catherine. After these deductions William was entitled to draw the balance, which left him with a personal income of around £25,000. When he had paid off the huge backlog of debts accumulated since Sir James's death, William barely broke even in his first year.[6]

Cajoling his wife, William explained that there had been many one-off expenses since their marriage, which meant that he would not be able to settle with her sisters until the following year. Dora and Emma accepted the situation for the time being.

However, financial pressures did not stop William spending copiously on himself. Shortly after their first wedding anniversary, he presented Catherine with a novel trinket: a brooch in the design of a bee, intricately worked and made up entirely of precious stones. Newspapers were impressed by the ingenuity: 'The wings of the bee are extended, and upon touching a spring they open, and discover one of the smallest watches that was perhaps ever seen.'[7] With her huge hoard of jewels, another expensive bauble was the last thing that Catherine needed, but the brooch became a talking point just as William intended, bolstering the image he wanted to create.

In return, Catherine presented William with a gift even more precious. Much to everyone's delight, she was pregnant again. However, because Catherine was so dainty, there were concerns that she would never be able to carry a baby full-term and so the joy was somewhat subdued. Added to this was the sobering statistic that around one in twelve women died through childbirth.[8] William was well aware that if his wife expired without producing an heir, her share in the estates would automatically pass to her sister Dora. Naturally, it was a stressful time for everyone concerned.

Catherine had planned to deliver her child in London, under top medical supervision, but she was caught unawares when she went into labour much earlier than expected. Riding out from Wanstead to fetch assistance, William was in a dreadful panic because his wife had become violently ill and it promised to be a difficult birth.[9] So much could go wrong. In an age without pain relief, antiseptic, antibiotics or the efficient use of forceps or caesarean section, labour was a protracted, excruciating ordeal. Even if the child was safely delivered, unsanitary practices meant that mother and baby were at risk of dying of a fever or infection in childbed. Given her diminutive size, Catherine was susceptible to one of the most common and agonizing problems, the unborn child becoming obstructed by the head. She knew that if this happened a choice would have to be made to save either the mother or the child. Even then there were no guarantees. Furthermore, if the baby became trapped and died it was possible that it would have to be 'torn apart within her and removed in pieces'.[10] Not surprisingly, Catherine was terrified as she wondered what the next forty-eight hours would bring.

The press always held Catherine in great esteem. Breathing a sigh of relief, newspapers proudly announced, 'Mrs Long Wellesley was safely delivered of a son and heir, at Wanstead House, on Thursday (7 October), at a quarter past three o'clock. Mrs Wellesley and the child are both doing extremely well.'[11]

In stark contrast, the same report lampooned William by stating, 'Wellesley Long Pole, on riding to town for the accoucheur to attend his Lady, was so overjoyed at finding him at home, that he forgot where he left his horse.'[12] William did not receive deference in the press and satirists could not resist referring to him as Mr Long Pole. This nickname had many connotations: it questioned his ability to stay loyal to Catherine, while suggesting that he was cocky, and also a 'big dick' (or dickhead). Perhaps they had a point, because some of his comments were decidedly inappropriate, as indicated by a letter he sent announcing the birth of his first child. 'My dearest Mother,' he wrote, 'the younger gentleman has my eyes and nose but Mrs Wellesley's mouth, and that he has a lock of black hair . . . For my part I think it an ugly little wretch, but Mrs Wellesley makes a great to-do about it.'[13]

William Richard Arthur was born on 6 October 1813. Catherine's life changed completely when her son was born and she spent hours sitting beside his crib just watching him, marvelling at the perfection of his tiny toes and fingers, stroking his soft skin, breathing in the sweet milky scent of him. She was amazed by how much her sleeping child looked like her beloved William; soft dark curls tousled on his forehead, thick eyelashes curling on perfect creamy cheeks and sweet rosebud lips. Wealthy women often relinquished care to wet-nurses, but Catherine stayed heavily involved. On visiting Wanstead two weeks after the birth, William's sister Emily commented that Catherine was 'looking as well as possible and walking about the room with her baby in her arms'.[14] Catherine had longed for a baby, but nothing had prepared her for the intense, overwhelming love she felt for her child.

15. A Consumer Society

❧

1813

William always maintained that while his wife had brought money to the marriage, his contribution was even more valuable – he supplied the style. With the huge quantities of money at his disposal he had become even more elegant and dazzling. In the early nineteenth century the British fashion industry was booming. Fashion had been revolutionised by William's friend Beau Brummell, who became a prominent member of London society after inheriting £30,000 in 1799. Around this time, tailoring was growing popular among the wealthy due to an increasing desire to project a sense of identity through individualist styling. Menswear shops and boutiques sprang up around the area of St James's to cater to the new trends. Frequenting tailors such as Schweitzer and Davidson on Cork Street, Brummell experimented with new designs and cloths, choosing finely woven wool for his coats and introducing 'fish darts'.[1] The three-seam kite back created the shape of the idealized classical torso, widest at the shoulders and tapering to the waist. Working closely with the tailor Jonathan Meyer on Conduit Street, Brummell replaced his knee-length breeches with full-length trousers, worn with a loop that hooked under the heel to keep the line straight and neat.[2] Made from figure-hugging material such as doeskin or chamois leather, his trousers accentuated the male crotch, again evoking the classical nudity that influenced the era. With such cutting-edge fashions, Brummell is credited with creating the definitive style of the English gentleman – the tailored suit, a look that has endured worldwide for generations.

By 1813, thirty-five-year-old Brummell was in decline, having grown jowly and paunchy. Gone were the days when he was the chief exponent of his own fashion ideals and he increasingly relied on a coterie of dandy followers to exhibit his style. Of these, William was the most glorious. He had the ideal physique to model the tapering, cut-away jackets that emphasized his broad shoulders and trim waist. Lightweight, skin-tight trousers flaunted his muscular thighs and shapely calves, while revealing precisely why he was nicknamed Mr Long Pole. Whenever William was in the company of an attractive female, his appreciation was evident! One society hostess later lamented the passing of this fashion because 'one could always tell what a young man was thinking'.[3]

Delectable and daring, William's celebrity status had made him a sex symbol and women would continue to swoon in his presence for many years to come. Bearing more than a passing resemblance to the fastidious Mr Darcy in the recently published *Pride and Prejudice*, William epitomized male desirability. The many assemblies held at Wanstead became a venue where young debutantes arrived eager to catch a glimpse of him, and he did not disappoint. Watching him waltz in tantalizingly tight breeches that left little to the imagination, women marvelled at his performance in the ballroom while pondering his renowned talents in the bedroom.

Needless to say, William's bespoke Savile Row suits were extremely burdensome on the pocket. But his clothes were a relatively minor expense compared to the amounts he was about to lavish at Wanstead.

Previous owners had left their mark at Wanstead. Having secured a male heir to maintain the family line, William felt it was time he put his stamp on the house by transforming the interiors with his exceptional sense of style. Spending copiously on refurbishments was very much the trend of the time. By the end of the eighteenth century, Georgian London had emerged as the first truly modern metropolis, obsessed with commodities, fashion, mass media and celebrity. Consumerism had been booming for decades. Affluence had encouraged men like the bachelor Earl Tylney to purchase simply for the joy of it: household furnishings, carriages, clothes, wines, books and paintings. Exotic silks were imported from the Far East, exquisite hand-painted china from Dresden and the latest fashions from Paris. The upsurge in disposable income extended to the middle classes, the factory owners and merchants, the artisans and tenant farmers, who were keen to emulate their social superiors. Unprecedented amounts were spent, stimulating a new economy that was not just materialistic but also included intellectual pursuits and leisure activities. The explosion in print culture played an important role in this new consumerism, with retailers such as Chippendale using illustrated brochures to promote their products, while advertising columns in newspapers enticed people to buy a wide range of goods and services.

One of the greatest spendthrifts of his time, William intended to lavish enormous amounts on Wanstead House. In the hundred years that had elapsed since the mansion was first built, the profound architectural significance of Wanstead House had become apparent. Preliminary plans had been drawn up in 1713, and these designs took prominence in Colen Campbell's *Vitruvius Britannicus*, first published in 1715. By this time, the shell of Wanstead House was already standing, within close proximity of London, and people flocked there in droves to view the property.[4] It was the new model for gracious modern living, providing comfortable family accommodation on the ground floor, with splendid staterooms above. The magnificently understated Wanstead House was the ideal advertisement for Palladian architecture, inspiring similar designs at Chiswick House, Wentworth Woodhouse and Houghton Hall. Most notably, it influenced the design of the White House in Washington DC, where an exact copy of the portico at Wanstead was reproduced for the official residence of the president of the United States.

Undoubtedly, the first Earl Tylney had been tremendously astute in commissioning the first privately owned house in this style. Wanstead House was an architecturally significant building that had led the way in the Palladian revival in Britain. It appealed

to the changing taste for elegant simplicity and, during the ensuing property boom, large swathes of London were constructed in
Palladian design. Wanstead House had helped to revolutionize
Georgian architecture, transforming the landscape of eighteenth-
century Britain by inspiring the elegant squares and sweeping
terraces that came to epitomize the era.[5]

In terms of style, the house could not have been in better hands
than those of William Long Wellesley. Still decorated in the
fashion of one hundred years earlier, the house required complete
renovation and William set about the task sympathetically and
lovingly. As usual, gossip columns were quick to report: 'Mr Wellesley Long Pole, they say, is fitting up Wanstead House in a style
of magnificence exceeding even Carlton House.'[6] By comparing
Wanstead to Carlton House, newspapers subtly suggested that he
was furnishing his home like a palace, a slight jibe at William's
excessive lifestyle.

A floor plan of the principal state floor showed how the
assembly rooms at Wanstead were perfectly proportioned and
laid out in an interconnecting circuit, forming one huge space for
entertainment.[7] The Great Hall led into the Salon, and then on to
the Drawing Room, Music Room, Ante Room, Ballroom, Billiard
Room, Reading Room and Library. Earl Tylney's ambition had
been to create a pleasure palace and with this in mind Wanstead
House boasted the first ballroom in any private house in England.
Unique in design, the Ballroom extended the full length of the
building with tall windows along three walls, providing panoramic
views of the gardens. Although this idea had been copied many
times since it was first built, William was in his element, gratified
to have a seventy-foot ballroom along with eight other rooms set
aside specifically for amusement. Thanks to Colen Campbell's
wonderful architectural design, William did not need to make any
structural changes to the harmonious conformity.

When William first arrived at Wanstead House, he found crates
of treasures shipped from the continent by the bachelor Earl
Tylney, who had often purchased items indiscriminately on a whim.
As he had lived abroad in the latter decades of his life, nobody had

lavished any time on arrangement and the exquisite furniture was scattered about the house at random. Superb serpent-shaped card tables stood next to oriental ebony cabinets or beside rare Persian ottomans. There was already an abundance of furniture, but William could not resist purchasing some exquisite pieces of French buhl, available in the aftermath of the French Revolution.[8] His particular favourite was a splendid rosewood and buhl library table, which he commandeered for his own private rooms.

William set about the task of reorganizing and rearranging, giving each room a theme. The Great Hall was the showpiece of the house, with classical bronze statues posing proudly on plinths, while Kent's painted ceiling was illuminated by two massive cut-glass chandeliers with gilded spread eagles as their centrepiece. The Salon had an exotic oriental flavour, with ebony-framed sofas and chairs inlaid with ivory, plus a colourful six-leaf Japanese screen hand-painted with landscapes. Parisian clocks ticked in the Grand Drawing Room, which was filled with William's prized antique French buhl. Mahogany and gilt prevailed in the Grand Dining Room, with its thirty-foot-long dining table plus two circular extensions for each end.[9]

Although the furniture was magnificent, William was not satisfied with the results. The curtains and carpets were old, and some of the sofas were covered in mismatched materials. He decided that the only way to create a stylish uniform effect would be to reupholster all the soft furnishing in matching fabrics. William chose a rich colour scheme of crimson and gold for the principal floor. This meant that when all the interconnecting doors were open, there would be no clash of colour from one room to the next. Newspapers approved of his choice, commenting, 'The whole of the interior will present one uniform blaze of crimson and burnished gold.'[10] The only exception to this scheme were the rooms at the front, which required sober masculine hues. The Library, Reading Room and Billiard Room would have green Genoa velvet.

A team of decorators arrived to hang silk wall coverings in all the staterooms. At least 500 yards of velvet were required to make around forty pairs of curtains, all bordered with three rows of gold lace and finished with Turkish silk tassels. Axminster provided over a thousand square feet of bespoke silk carpets, bordered with gold and woven with the Long Wellesley family crest at the corners.[11] Dozens of plush Grecian-scroll back and end sofas were regilded and reupholstered in matching crimson fabric complete with gold trimmings. In the Ballroom alone, nine sofas were restored, as were the many stools and chairs.

Intrigued newspapers speculated about the costs:

> The furniture is of surprising magnificence, the carpets and hangings alone having cost £60,000. The family arms of Tylney and Wellesley are embroidered on all the carpets, the material of which is silk. The walls, as well as the windows, are hung with the richest Genoa velvet, with three borders of gold lace, at three guineas and a half per yard.[12]

The £60,000 (six million pounds) spent on soft furnishings seems exorbitant, but it was probably a fair estimate taking into account the quality of the materials. Spun with real gold, the trimmings were so intricate it would have taken a lace-maker four hours to produce one square inch. At least three thousand yards of this lace was needed for edging the curtains, plus whatever was required for the sofas and chairs. William was a perfectionist, insisting on three rows of gold lace on the curtains to match the three rows of gilding around the door frames. In total harmony with the architecture, the burnished gold threads on borders accentuated the intricate gilt mouldings that adorned the staterooms.

Just like his predecessors, William put his own mark on the house. As he promised, Wanstead House was made even grander by virtue of his superb sense of style. Both the public and high society were intrigued and on tenterhooks for their first glimpse of the Long Wellesley palace.

16. Festivities at Wanstead House

‿❦❧‿

1814

Curious about the new interiors at Wanstead, the public appetite was whetted when newspapers announced that Mr Long Wellesley would be hosting a grand fete at Wanstead in June 1814, to mark the baptism of his infant son.[1] The christening of an heir was a momentous occasion, and the celebration would be all the more spectacular because it coincided with the triumphant return of Wellington, victorious from the Peninsular War. His army had liberated Spain after driving the French back across the Pyrenees. When Napoleon finally surrendered himself, he was imprisoned on the island of Elba, and the whole of England rejoiced. On 3 May 1814, Arthur Wellesley was awarded the title Duke of Wellington, in recognition of his success. The long and expensive war was finally over, and the working classes hoped that now the starvation and hardship they had endured for many years were finally coming to an end.

William was highly gratified to have a national hero in the family. There could not have been a more opportune moment for him to show off his newly refurbished home while at the same time exhibiting his powerful family connections. Wellington's tremendous success was good for the entire Wellesley clan, and with the family back in favour, a top job was found for William's father. Mr Pole had been striving away in the background of government for many years, and his contribution was finally acknowledged when he was awarded the prestigious position of Master of the Mint, which included a seat in the Cabinet. With rewards for the Wellesley family being handed out, William hoped there would be something in it for him.

On returning to England at the end of June 1814, the Duke of Wellington received standing ovations wherever he went and victory celebrations were held in his honour at Vauxhall Gardens and other public parks. Keen to maximize his own celebrity, William made sure to be seen in public with his famous uncle as often as possible. Just days after Wellington arrived back in London, William took him out for the evening. Rumours abounded that the conquering hero would be present at the opera on Saturday night and crowds flocked to the Drury Lane Theatre. William's private box was festooned with garlands of laurel, keeping alive expectations of an appearance throughout the performance of *Artimidoro*. In the middle of the ballet, the audience noticed that the noble duke had surreptitiously slipped into the theatre and was sitting in the box. The whole assembly rose and burst into cheers of welcome. The orchestra struck up 'See, the Conquering Hero Comes' and was drowned out by singing from a thousand voices. His Grace modestly kept back, but William pushed up against him, jostling him into the limelight. Standing shoulder to shoulder with his uncle, William waved to the crowd and soaked up the adulation. The torrent of applause continued for several minutes, as Wellington bowed respectfully to the company. He was genuinely moved by their enthusiasm, but when the ovation showed no signs of abating he stepped back into the shadow. After some time the ballet was permitted to go on, but the ripple of excitement stayed in the theatre for the rest of the evening.[2]

William's association with Wellington gave him access to the highest circles in Europe. The grand fete at Wanstead was to take place on 29 June 1814, but the planned baptism was sidelined in favour of a lavish celebration honouring the Duke of Wellington, thus ensuring that royalty and dignitaries from across Europe would feel obliged to attend. Wanstead House had been a hive of activity for a full nine months. Dozens of gardeners planted beds of brightly coloured blooms, decorators hung new wall coverings, velvet curtains appeared on the windows and Axminster sent a procession of carriages loaded down with thick rolls of silk carpets. Days before the fete, fresh produce was gathered from around the estate, the culmination of many months of planning and hard work. Lambs, pigs, cows and deer were slaughtered, farm labourers filed through the kitchens wheeling great barrows of fresh vegetables, gardeners carried in exotic fruit lovingly cultivated in the hothouses, and florists made up tasteful displays for the tables.

On the day of the fete, the interconnecting doors of the assembly rooms were thrown open, so that guests could appreciate the perfectly coordinated décor. Wanstead House had reached the height of perfection: Sir Josiah's gardens were in full bloom; Sir Richard's Palladian palace was tastefully renovated; Sir John's priceless art collection was out on display. William, too, was looking exceptionally elegant. Sartorially astute, he set a new trend that evening by wearing a tailcoat with black silk lapels perfectly offset by an 'ample tie of black silk . . . he was the embodied perfection of a man of fashion'.[3] It was the first time a black tie appeared in society, but the style was so striking it became instantly famous.[4] Even Brummell approved, conceding that this innovation was suitably elegant and restrained. The black tie has remained the ultimate in gentlemen's formal evening wear ever since.

Around six o'clock a procession of state carriages made their way to Wanstead House, conveying the Duke of Wellington, the Prince Regent, the Duke of York and the Prussian Princes Frederick-William and Henry.[5] As carriages rattled through the stone gateposts, blazing torches flamed along the driveway, creating theatre and illuminating the stately avenue of elms when dusk fell. William had organized the event down to the finest detail, borrowing chefs, cooks, waiters and stable hands from his friends and neighbours. Liveried footmen directed the incoming carriages in a clockwise direction around the lake. After guests alighted at the front steps, their carriages and coachmen were led away to nearby stables, to be fed and watered in preparation for their journey home.

A military band played in the portico while William and Catherine stood in the Great Hall proudly presenting the Duke of Wellington to the guests waiting in line. When everyone had assembled, the infant William Richard Arthur Pole Tylney Long

Wellesley was christened, swaddled in a regal green and gold damask table cover that had been seized by Wellington from Joseph Bonaparte's carriage.[6] The Iron Duke presented the trophy to Catherine, who promised to preserve the cloth for future generations, as a symbol of Wellesley valour. An altar was set up against the rear wall of the Ballroom and a respectful silence fell over the proceedings as Reverend William Gilly performed the rite. Throughout the entire ceremony, the Duke of Wellington cradled the child in his arms, 'beaming with benevolence, and free from every trace of the cares of war or politics . . . a subject worthy of the pencil of the finest painter'.[7]

Supper tables were laid for 150 guests, all seated in the Great Hall surrounded by ancient statues, sparkling chandeliers and a display of rare gold plate.[8] The top table was on a raised platform, where the most distinguished guests were enthroned on ebony dining chairs once owned by Elizabeth I. When supper was served, a hundred footmen paraded into the Great Hall, each carrying a silver platter at shoulder height. Fine wine was brought up from the well-stocked cellars with suitable vintages to accompany each course. The food was of such quality and abundance that Frances, Lady Shelley, remarked, 'It was the most magnificent banquet I ever saw.'[9] After everyone had raised their glasses to the king's health, the Prince Regent made a neat speech proposing a toast to the Duke of Wellington. Smiling broadly, the Iron Duke rose to reply, although he seemed to regard all the pageantry and the honours of that day as nonsense and fun.

Around 200 more guests arrived later that evening for the Grand Ball.[10] Wellington opened the proceedings by dancing a polonaise, promenading his partner around the Ballroom with a long line of couples gliding behind him in order of rank. The Prussian General Blücher joined in and danced a German country dance, skipping down the middle of the room with William's sister, Lady Burghersh, on his arm. Old Platoff, Hetman of the Cossacks, then performed his own national dance, which involved 'stamping his feet like a horse and nodding his head. The whole thing was exquisitely ludicrous and the Duke could not help joining in the laughter.'[11] Festivities did not break up until eight in the morning, when forty close friends and family sat down to an intimate breakfast in the Small Oak Dining Room.

The event was a triumph for William but it was only a trial run. Two years later, on 14 August 1816, he would host a fete on an even grander scale. On this occasion supper tables were laid for 550 guests, with 150 seated in the Great Hall, 200 in the adjoining Salon and 200 in the Grand Dining Room. One newspaper recorded:

> Upwards of 500 of the first rank and fashion sat down to a most splendid supper . . . The table was covered with every variety and delicacy that the season affords . . . interspersed with temples, pyramids, and other ornamental devices, richly wrought in the highest style of taste on silver wire-work. The dessert was truly splendid, and the fruits of the most exquisite kind, with every possible variety.[12]

After this supper, 600 more guests arrived for the Grand Ball. 'Three bands of music played waltzes, cotillions, and country dances, and went merrily round after supper, in various rooms, during the whole night.'[13] At the height of the party, around 1,100 revellers were inside the house, dancing and feasting. It was 'universally allowed that a more splendid entertainment had never been witnessed, except the first grand fete given by the Prince Regent at Carlton House'.[14] Entertaining on this scale was usually reserved for royalty. The *Examiner* compared William's extravagance to the court of Henry VIII, remarking, 'The private hospitalities of England, however celebrated, furnish no precedent, in expense, variety, and extent, since the days of Cardinal Wolsey.'[15]

Following the fete in 1814, William and Catherine's most intimate circle stayed on at Wanstead for a few nights to participate in a house party. The English elite were relentless in their pursuit of pleasure, but they often found gratification in its most rarefied and refined forms. Full of creativity, many spent their leisure time cultivating their favourite pastime to an extremely high standard.

There were accomplished poets such as Byron and Shelley, along-side many talented musicians, singers, composers, playwrights, artists and painters. Owing to this, house parties were imaginative affairs, with the character varying from house to house depending on the interests of the hosts. Undeniably, these gatherings also provided guests with the ideal opportunity to sneak about and indulge in illicit sexual exploits. Devonshire House, the town house of the fifth Duke of Devonshire, was 'the setting of so many intrigues' as well as the place for serious political discussion.[16]

It had become fashionable for the aristocracy to have little theatres in their homes, where famous actors or singers performed alongside family members eager to display their talent. The Priory, for example, country seat of the Abercorns, was renowned for amateur dramatics, engaging guests in full-scale theatrical produc-tions.[17] Everyone got involved in some capacity, writing scenes and sketches, playing piano or painting scenery. Various professionals were recruited to oversee the proceedings, including the famous painter Thomas Lawrence for the stage sets and Mrs John Kemble to coach the actors.[18] The middle classes also had a taste for the theatre and boasted the likes of Keats, Wordsworth, Coleridge and Blake among their ranks. In *Mansfield Park*, Jane Austen illustrates the bourgeois fascination for amateur theatricals when her charac-ters stage the scandalous play *Lovers' Vows*. Austen successfully captures the hilarity and sexual thrill that play-acting evokes, dem-onstrating why it was such a popular activity and perfectly suited to house parties.

As an accomplished sportsman, William's greatest passions were horses and carousing. His house parties would have been high-spirited affairs, which revolved around hunting, fine dining, music and dancing. There were plenty of other diversions for guests as the pleasure grounds at Wanstead boasted boating lakes, scenic walks and follies such as the Temple, which was perfect for open-air concerts. Indoors, there was the Billiards Room, Music Room and well-stocked Library. With so many options at his disposal, William undoubtedly had many novel amusements planned.

No records exist to tell us definitively who attended this particular house party at Wanstead. However, as all three of William's sisters were in the process of moving abroad, the gathering was probably to allow the family to spend quality time together before they emigrated. The sisters were known in society as 'The Three Graces', and renowned for their beauty and vivacity. Priscilla, Lady Burghersh, was relocating to Florence where her husband would become the Envoy Extraordinary and Minister Plenipotentiary. Emily, Lady Fitzroy Somerset was heading to Paris, as her husband was to become Private Secretary to Wellington. Mary Bagot would be settling furthest away as her husband, Charles Bagot, was appointed Envoy Extraordinary and Minister Plenipotentiary to the United States (where he would become famous as the man who defined the border between British North America, now Canada, and the United States). In fact, it was possibly the last time all the siblings were together under one roof.

Visiting Wanstead was like staying at an opulent boutique hotel. Vases bursting with fresh flowers scented all the rooms. Luxurious toiletries stood beside the washstands: thick towels, china dishes of perfumed soaps, bottles of expensive French scents, plus trays of brushes and other grooming utensils.[19] On the state floor, there were four magnificent bedchambers with adjoining en suites. The most exquisite of these was the Blue Damask Suite overlooking the front gardens and lake. A massive four-poster dominated the bedroom, six feet wide and sixteen feet high, with an elaborately carved oak frame. The dressing area contained a particularly beautiful French buhl armoire, inlaid with elaborate gilt and tortoiseshell mouldings and friezes of arabesque design, together with a matching dressing table and escritoire. The adjoining Blue Damask Dressing Room was fitted up with wardrobes, full-length cheval mirrors and a bidet, as well as a washstand with china basins and ewers.

Dinner on the first evening would have been a relaxed affair, as the assembled party knew each other intimately. Guest speakers were invited to keep discussions interesting, while the addition of one or two raconteurs, such as Sheridan or Beau Brummell, provided amusement. Following the meal it was customary for guests to entertain each other by singing or playing instruments. Lord Burghersh was a talented musician well up to the task and Catherine was one of the ladies present who played piano beautifully. Wanstead House had an exquisite music room fitted out for this purpose, complete with Catherine's grand piano, harpsichord and harp. The merriment would have continued late into the night with games of charades and card tables laid out for those who wished to play a few hands of faro.

Some aristocratic houses were like gambling dens, where the stakes set at card tables were so high, guests left parties thousands of pounds poorer. Even the well-heeled Duchess of Devonshire described how sickened she felt by her gambling losses, confessing to debts so large they almost bankrupted her. She wrote, 'I never had the courage to own it . . . I have kept absolute ruin to myself scarcely off.'[20] Brummell, too, had mixed fortunes at gambling. In 1813, he had reputedly won £26,000 at one card game and a further £30,000 from betting on horse races.[21] But in the following year, losses spiralled out of control, leaving him deeply in debt and reliant on the benevolence of his friends. Guests at Wanstead were safe from this fate, however, because – contrary to popular belief – William was not a gambler. Later in life he successfully sued the *Sunday Times* after they printed an article stating that he had lost huge amounts at the gaming tables.[22] During the libel action, William told the court that he had 'never lost by gaming, any sum amounting to £500, or that he ever won above £50, or ever played for more than £20'.[23] In response, the *Sunday Times* could produce no evidence of William's gambling because his name did not appear in any betting books. As a result, the newspaper was forced to retract the statement and print an apology.[24]

William had a highly competitive nature and he enjoyed winning simply for the sport. Rather than gambling, he would place a bet on his own abilities, challenging his friends to a race on horseback or a shooting match, for a stake of no more than £20. During the house party he would certainly have organized one of his legendary hunting parties, resplendent with pomp and pageantry, inviting local gentry along to make up the numbers. For those guests who did not bring their own mounts, William had a stable full of thoroughbreds at their disposal. A hunt breakfast would have followed, washed down with generous quantities of alcohol.

While the men were out hunting, Catherine and the other ladies would have started their day in a more leisurely fashion with a breakfast tray in bed. After this they were free to explore the pleasure grounds, strolling together along the tree-lined vista to the finger of water, where pleasure boats bobbed invitingly. If the weather was fine, lunch may well have been served outdoors on the lawns, with tables and chairs set up under awnings to protect them from the sun. Enjoying each other's company, the gathering was an opportunity for William's sisters to get to know Catherine. They found her refreshingly genuine and unspoilt. Whereas their brother enjoyed being the centre of attention, Catherine excelled at making others feel special by putting them at ease and encouraging *them* to talk. Mary would later remark that Catherine was 'an angel . . . all virtues and excellencies'.[25] Gossiping among themselves, the sisters were pleased to observe that William seemed to have given up his flirtations, to settle down very happily with his wife.[26] Emily declared that William was 'in high delight', stating that she was gratified to see him expressing 'proper feeling' towards Catherine.[27]

William was keen to impress his sisters and show them how far he had come since his reckless teenage years. Growing up, he had been closest to Mary, often confiding his misdeeds to her. After one incident Mary had written to him, 'I have not mentioned your letter to Mamma, for I think it would almost *kill her*!'[28] Spending time with his siblings, William took them on a behind-the-scenes tour of the house. Visitors to Wanstead were familiar with the rooms on the principal state floor, but very few were granted access to the family apartments on the ground floor. William's private sanctuary was a particularly impressive set of rooms. His study was bright and airy with views of the gardens spilling in through three generously sized windows. The particularly splendid French buhl library table formed the centrepiece, inlaid with an intricate design in pure gold. Flamboyant purple morocco sofa and chairs provided an artistic splash of colour, offsetting the rich golden browns of the

furniture and velvet curtains. No doubt the sisters raised an eye-
brow at the sight of two huge rosewood bookcases stuffed full of
William's political literature and legal reference books – not bad
for someone who had never particularly enjoyed reading. The
adjoining rooms testified to their brother's obsession with grooming and preening. His bedchamber was comfortably furnished with
solid, masculine, mahogany furniture. His dressing room contained
an innovation not often seen in England – a large marble bath
plumbed in with hot and cold running water. Numerous brushes
and grooming utensils were displayed on a cabinet, with nine
bottles of scent lined up neatly beside the washstand. The three
sisters were cheered by all the positive changes they detected in
William. He was clearly in his element, thoroughly relishing his
role as lord of the manor. They were also impressed by his resolve
to educate himself for a career in politics, and heartened by his
devotion to his wife. William seemed to have settled very happily
into married life. As for Catherine, the sisters noted that she was
completely smitten with William. Emily remarked, 'She devours
him with her eyes, and she is desperately in love.' [29]

Life at Wanstead, however, was not all fun and games for William.
One cold morning in March 1813 he came close to being murdered
on his own doorstep. Running the estate was arduous and there
were many contentious issues to deal with. Despite possessing
an inherently genial nature, William could be an argumentative
man who refused to back down on certain matters. Natural stub-
bornness was compounded by the fact that, as a man of wealth
and privilege, he was accustomed to getting his own way. Over the
course of his lifetime he was involved in an inordinate amount
of disputes and litigation. During the first months of his marriage
he became embroiled in a disagreement with his neighbours, and
local people eventually took him to court after he blocked access
to Wanstead Park by locking the gates and digging trenches to
stop trespassers. Tensions were high as locals argued that the park
had been an important recreational facility for many centuries;

1. Josiah Child, Catherine's great-great-grandfather, was Governor of the East India Company. He was a shrewd businessman who rose from obscurity to become one of the richest men in seventeenth-century Britain.

2. A view of the approach to Wanstead House (c. 1815), picturing the octagonal Basin and the avenue of elms installed by Josiah Child.

3. *Assembly at Wanstead House*, by William Hogarth, shows Richard Child and his family gathered in the ballroom c. 1730. The painting captures the opulence of William Kent's staterooms: the luxurious furnishings, striking ceiling frescos and ornate gilding.

4. Catherine aged around twenty-one, in an engraving after Alfred Edward Chalon.

5. Draycot House, Wiltshire, Catherine's childhood home, pictured here c. 1900.

6. The Duke of Clarence became William IV in 1830. If Catherine had married him the course of British history might well have been altered.

7. *The Royal Lover* lampoons the Duke of Clarence for his relentless pursuit of Catherine. His back is turned away from a picture of his mistress and in his sights is a map of Catherine's estates.

8. *Miss Long-ing for a Pole* is loaded with innuendo. William looks virile as he clutches an impressively 'long pole', providing a striking contrast to the ungainly Duke of Clarence. Catherine's preference is clear as her hand reaches towards William.

9. *Worshippers at Wanstead* by George Cruikshank ridicules the frenzy surrounding Catherine. From left to right: William duels with Lord Kilworth; Romeo Coates has a cock crowing on his head; Lord Skeffington recites a love poem; Mrs Jordan is emptying a chamber pot over the Duke of Clarence; Baron de Geramb is being bribed by Napoleon.

10. Arthur Wellesley,
Duke of Wellington, painted by
Sir Thomas Lawrence c.1815.

11. William's father,
William Wellesley Pole,
c. 1814.

12. By the time he was
sixteen, William was
a stylish young man.
This miniature was
painted at Vienna
in 1804.

13. Wanstead House was the first private residence in Britain to be constructed in the Palladian design. It was a hugely influential building, providing a blueprint for the elegant Georgian squares and terraces that came to epitomize the era.

14. Knyff and Kip's views of Wanstead (c. 1710) show the spectacular landscaping of the 'English Versailles'.

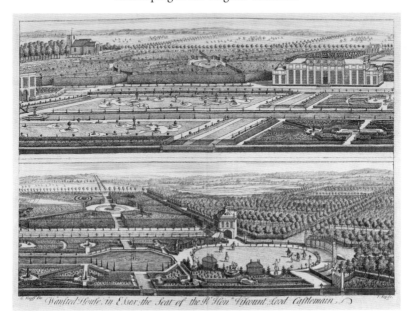

Wanstead House in Essex, the Seat of the R.t Hon.ble Viscount Lord Castlemain.

15. The Epping Hunt was traditionally held at the Roebuck in Buckhurst Hill on Easter Monday. As a keen sportsman, William spent an enormous amount of money on reviving this event.

16. Drury Lane Theatre was a place to see and be seen. William had the best view in the house as his private box was on the lowest tier, facing the stage.

a sanctuary where working folk could escape for an hour or two, to take a scenic stroll or enjoy a family picnic.

On 12 March 1813, a total of thirty-two locals appeared to give evidence at the trial *The King v Long Wellesley*, held at Chelmsford Assizes. A carriage driver from the Red Lion in Ilford declared that Wanstead Park was his favoured destination when taking clients for pleasure rides, a magistrate recalled playing in the grounds since the age of four and a Whitechapel undertaker liked to divert his funeral cortèges through the park to give the dead 'a final turn around the parish'.[30] No one disputed Long Wellesley's legal ownership of the land; their concern was that he had meddled with tradition by refusing unrestricted entry. The presiding judge agreed and directed the jury to rule in favour of the local community. Following the trial, William built Blake Hall Road to redirect traffic around the estate. Farmers ignored the new thoroughfare and continued to drive their hefty carts, laden with produce, right through the gardens. Eventually, in 1817, William used his position as an MP to overturn the court order by a private Act of Parliament. Generous in victory, he granted the public access to his pleasure grounds on Saturdays, but from then onwards the park was strictly out of bounds to all commercial traffic.

William's fight to close the park was not due to simple possessiveness; he desperately needed to safeguard his family. Having received various threats, he believed that they were in real danger from fanatics, or criminals hoping to extort money. This fear was exacerbated after he was attacked on his doorstep by an early-morning caller at Wanstead House. Visibly deranged, the man lunged at William with a large carving knife; only the strength and bravery of attending servants prevented a tragedy. It transpired that the assailant was Catherine's stalker, Mr Scott, who had continually besieged her house and waylaid her carriage at Draycot. He had recently escaped from a Norwich madhouse. On the morning of 12 March 1813, William appeared at Walthamstow magistrates to give evidence against Scott, who was remanded to Barking Bridewell prison.[31] The incident made William even more determined to keep people off his land: to protect his property, to preserve his privacy and to safeguard his family.

The family's increasing need for privacy and personal security highlighted the challenges facing those caught up in the developing celebrity culture. William had his wife's wholehearted support in closing Wanstead Park. Catherine sincerely hoped that this would be the last that they saw of the madman Scott and others like him, but she would continue to encounter threats and danger from various quarters.

17. Waterloo

After three years of blissful domesticity and relatively good behaviour, William was beginning to feel restless. He missed the impulsiveness of his bachelor life, the freedom that came with living abroad and the wild sexual adventures. Keen to get away, he had been petitioning Wellington for a commission in the army, hoping to attain some glory in the final throes of the Napoleonic Wars, but no position had been offered. This made him resentful, particularly since his brothers-in-law had all been awarded top diplomatic postings. William did not stop to consider how he had squandered his own opportunities. Now that the Congress of Vienna was imminent, he badgered his uncle yet again, and Wellington eventually agreed that he could attend the conference as one of eighty British aides.

With Napoleon in captivity, the four victorious powers met at the Congress of Vienna to redraw the political map of Europe. The Duke of Wellington was Britain's representative, arriving at the conference on 3 February 1815, when talks began in earnest. Vienna was packed full of influential sovereigns, leaders and dignitaries. Rather than making the most of this chance to gain recognition in the diplomatic arena, William chose to concentrate his efforts on developing other talents. Congress members indulged in so many glittering events, Prince de Ligne quipped, 'the Congress dances, but does not progress'. Vienna was the home of the waltz, and William could not resist the lavish parties or the stylish foreign women. Ladies flocked around the Duke of Wellington's handsome nephew and William needed no encouragement to stay out every night, carousing into the early hours. It was to his great disappointment, therefore, when the Congress of Vienna broke up after Napoleon escaped from Elba on 1 March 1815. Wellington returned to the battlefield and William was sent back to Wanstead.

Within three weeks, Napoleon reached Paris as allied forces scrambled to regroup. Under the command of Wellington, an ill-equipped and inexperienced British army struggled to mobilize troops, particularly as many Peninsular veterans were now engaged in the war against the USA. Correctly guessing where Napoleon would strike next, Wellington's troops were ready and waiting when the French army invaded Belgium on 15 June 1815.

Before the battle of Waterloo, William's mother travelled to Brussels to be near her family, who were entrenched at the front line with Wellington. Mrs Pole particularly wanted to be with her heavily pregnant daughter, Lady Fitzroy Somerset. Emily adored her husband, and she feared the worst after a premonition that his luck had finally run out.

Imminent danger did not deter the lively entertainment in Brussels and the Duchess of Richmond's ball was a grand affair. Handsome young officers dressed in red military jackets drank heartily and twirled their wives around the dance floor. The party broke up dramatically in the early hours when a messenger arrived calling the troops into battle. Cries spread through the crowd as women kissed their husbands goodbye, possibly for the last time. As the officers were already wearing uniform, many went straight from the ballroom to the battleground.

When the sound of firing started, Mrs Pole took Emily to the park, hoping to distract her attention. 'They sat on a bench with a Frenchwoman who said to them "*Mon Dieu, Mesdames, n'entendez vous pas le canon?*"' (My God, ladies, do you not hear the cannon?)[1] Shortly afterwards the wounded began to arrive and Emily howled pitifully when she spotted her husband's bloody body lying in a cart. Her knees buckled and Mrs Pole just managed to stop her keeling over by grabbing her under the arms. Then the body moved as Fitzroy struggled to sit up. The dinner coat he had worn the previous evening was soaked with his own blood. Emily ran to him, expecting the worst, but he managed to smile at her through his pain and tears. He had lost an arm.

Emily accompanied her wounded spouse to the makeshift infirmary while Mrs Pole waited in the park for news of her favourite brother-in-law, the Duke of Wellington. She waited all day. Darkness had fallen when Henry Percy, aide-de-camp, arrived to confirm the battle was won following the timely arrival of allied reinforcements led by the Prussian General Blücher. Henry Percy had last seen Wellington leading a fearless charge straight through the French lines. Surviving the first assault, the Iron Duke had doubled back, ploughing through enemy ranks from behind. Percy felt sure His Grace 'must have been taken when he got amongst the French'.[2] Mrs Pole never gave up hope. She went to the duke's lodgings and got down on her hands and knees to pray for his return. Dawn was breaking when she heard a rumble of excitement, followed by loud cheers. Rushing to the window, she saw a small group of cavalrymen approaching. Among them was the unmistakable silhouette of Wellington, wearing his famous blue cape and mounted astride Copenhagen, his powerful chestnut charger. Progress was slow, as the horses drooped with weariness. When Wellington finally dismounted, he reached up to embrace the loyal creature that had carried him safely through battle. Copenhagen had been taken to the limits of endurance, witnessing too much carnage. The stallion bridled, backing away stubbornly. Then he reared up, lifting one mighty hoof to cuff his master. The waiting crowd gasped with horror. Wellington had survived the battle, but now it seemed that a blow from his horse would crush his skull. The brave general did not even flinch; standing stock-still, he faced his faithful friend. Crumbling, Copenhagen dropped his head wearily while Wellington stepped forward to whisper soothing words.

When the duke went up to his rooms, Mrs Pole was waiting. She flung her arms round his neck and thanked God he was safe. Holding him at arm's length, she looked him up and down, amazed he had escaped without a scratch. Having heard of Wellington's bravery, Mrs Pole firmly believed that only divine intervention could have spared him. Reading her thoughts, Wellington confirmed, 'The finger of God was upon me all day – nothing else could have saved me.'[3] Exhausted, the duke sat down heavily on his bed. For many nights he had barely slept as he meticulously planned his strategy for the battle. When Mrs Pole congratulated him on his victory, the duke put his face between his hands to hide his tears. 'Oh! Do not congratulate me – I have lost all my dearest friends.'[4]

Mrs Pole let him weep for a while, then gently removed his boots and lifted his legs onto the bed. When he was lying down, she undid his coat, pulled a blanket over him and took the gloves from his hands. Holding the gloves to her face, she smelled gunpowder and death. Crying with relief, she slipped his gloves into her bag to cherish for posterity.

The next day Wellington dressed in plain clothes, filled a curricle with supplies and rode back out to the battlefield. Some of the wounded British soldiers had been taken away to the infirmary, but many still lay in agony on the blood-soaked ground. Also, as Napoleon's army had retreated, there was no one to help the injured French soldiers. 'The French lay as if they had been mowed down in a row without any interval.'[5] It was such a distressing sight, Wellington wept as he walked among the wounded and dying, administering brandy from a holster to English and French alike, while speaking words of comfort to dying men. A young Frenchman reared himself up from a pile of dead bodies and the duke went over to him. The man had a broken leg, but was not wounded in any other way. Having fortified him with alcohol, Wellington spoke in fluent French, promising that he would send some conveyance to carry him off. He apologized for it not having been done sooner, on account of the number of his own men that required assistance.[6]

Wellington's astute military strategy had defeated Napoleon, but he felt unable to celebrate his victory when so many men were lost. With the exception of Henry Percy, all his personal staff were dead or wounded. Casualties had been heavy on both sides: around 17,000 British, 7,000 Prussians and 26,000 French.[7]

Speaking to Lady Shelley shortly afterwards, his eyes glistening with tears, Wellington said sadly, 'I hope to God . . . that I have fought my last battle.'[8]

Having defeated Napoleon at Waterloo, exhausted troops marched for three days before they crossed the border into France, heading for Paris. A man of great integrity, Wellington took pains to ensure that his army respected French soil. Soldiers were ordered to march in single file through the cornfields so that crops would not be destroyed and special guards were appointed to flog every man found looting or loitering behind his regiment. Nevertheless, Wellington was unable to prevent the Prussians from seeking reprisals; they committed rape and murder on a savage scale. '"England has never been overrun by French armies," one of them explained, "or you would act as we do. The French acted a cruel part in Prussia . . . they taught us a lesson we are now come to France to put into practice."'[9]

Waterloo was a defining moment in the history of Europe. Tired of all the bloodshed, Wellington was keen to secure peace. An armistice was signed on 3 July and shortly afterwards a king was back on the throne of France.

Restoration of the Bourbon monarchy was unpopular in many quarters. Over the following years, with peace in Europe fragile, Wellington remained in France to act as an intermediary between the main powers. Considerable diplomatic skill was required and very few men would have been equal to the task, but the Iron Duke commanded so much respect that he was able to maintain concord. As ambassador to the French court, Wellington became hugely powerful, living in Paris where he became the object of universal veneration, with honours heaped upon him from every quarter. Wellington was a hero in Portugal and Spain, as he had led forces that liberated both countries. The tsar of Russia named him 'Conqueror of Waterloo'. The king of the Netherlands awarded him the title 'Prince of Waterloo', along with chivalric orders of knighthood from Russia and other European states. This international acclaim gave Wellington more power and influence in Europe than any other Briton has ever achieved.[10]

William was proud to be a Wellesley; it was a defining part of his identity. He believed that his uncle's phenomenal renown elevated the status of the entire family, which in turn gave him certain rights and special privileges. As a result, William was gradually becoming even more overbearing and cocksure. Unfortunately, this was to have adverse repercussions for Catherine, as his attitude towards her grew increasingly cavalier.

18. Money Wars

❧

1815

While Wellington was at war on the continent, Catherine had her own battles to fight. Money is often a cause for argument between couples and the Long Wellesleys were no exception. Whenever they disagreed, Catherine employed a reliable tactic suggested by Dr Barry: 'be solitary for a few minutes . . . adapt your words . . . leave your closet and show the reasonableness of your determination'.[1] Although Catherine used this measured approach to great advantage in her business dealings, it did not work with her husband, because he never accepted 'no' for an answer. William's methods were vividly portrayed by Lady Wellington, who called him an 'insufferable puppy', tail-wagging and yapping at the heels until he got his way.[2] There were usually three stages to this process. First he would try to win over Catherine with a charm offensive, coaxing and cajoling to get his own way. If this did not work, he would grow petulant and peevish, hoping his bad mood would persuade her to back down. In the final phase he could become fairly menacing.

By 1815, tensions were high between the couple. William's excessive lifestyle had taken a toll on finances. Catherine had no way to curb his spending because he went all over town buying goods on credit and accumulating debts. In addition, he had even commandeered her £7,500 pin money. During the first year of their marriage William suggested to her, 'as we have but one common interest, we ought to have but one common purse'.[3] Catherine later confided to a friend that she agreed to this proposal 'in the honour and affection' of her husband.[4] She provided the necessary consent to her administrator, confirming that her pin money could be paid direct to William. It made sense to her at the time, as he was paying all the bills, but now she regretted giving up her financial independence. She had the power to renege at any time and reclaim her income, but this would merely inflame the situation and cause an even bigger rift in the marriage.

To exacerbate the situation further, the Long Wellesleys had quite different views on how their money should be spent. William lavished huge sums on carriages and thoroughbreds, entertainment and furnishings. Feeling great sympathy for the poor, Catherine's attitude was very different. Although she had no power at Wanstead, she owned the estates in Wiltshire and held sway over the running of Draycot. Much to William's annoyance, she continued to fund the many charitable trusts established by her father, supplying bread and coal to the poor, sponsoring schools in four parishes near Draycot, while also paying generous pensions to former members of her staff.[5] Apart from this, various tenants at Draycot had fallen into arrears with their rents, but as she knew many of them personally Catherine could not bear to send them to the workhouse, where families would be separated into different lodgings. Rather than evict them, she decided to reduce some rents at Draycot by twenty per cent. As William pointed out, this was not good business; but even though she usually deferred to him, she would not budge on this particular subject. A mother herself, she refused to stand by and watch parents be separated from their young children. William didn't share her empathy. Although he spent copious amounts on trying to impress his wealthy friends, he cared little for the poor. The hospitality he provided to the local community in the first year of his marriage had long since dried up. He had even lost interest in the Epping Hunt, and although people continued to gather at the Roebuck on Easter Monday, 'neither stag nor hounds were forthcoming'.[6]

The main bone of contention between the couple, however, was the fact that William still had not settled the £15,000 portions due to Dora and Emma. By now their inheritances were long overdue, but William showed no inclination to pay up. Emma was considered the prettiest of the three sisters, with a sunny temperament

that ensured she always had a string of admirers vying for her attention. Despite all the interest, Emma remained true to her heart,
and after three years of courtship she longed to marry Mr Burke.
Without her inheritance, however, she could not afford to leave
the security of her mother's home. But William continued to with-
hold Emma's portion, insisting Burke was not good enough for her
because he was penniless, with a dubious reputation. The irony of
these objections was obviously lost on him.

If Emma was the handsomest sister, Dora was certainly the
most forceful. She was the one who set about tackling William,
pointing out that if he had spent a little less freely on swags and
tassels, he would easily have been in a position to pay over their
entitlement. In all honesty, settling the Miss Longs' inheritance
during the first year of the marriage should not have been an issue
for William, particularly considering the vast sums he had lavished
on himself. Catherine's wedding jewels alone had cost £50,000, far
in excess of the amount owed to Dora and Emma.

William claimed that money had been misappropriated from
the estates, but it was commonly acknowledged that Catherine's
bank balance had been in excess of £300,000 (thirty million
pounds) at the time of her marriage.[7] This was made up of the
substantial £200,000 windfall she inherited from her uncle, plus
sixteen years of accumulated rents yielding around £40,000 per
annum with very little outlay. Was it possible that William could
have run through that amount of money in three years? Whenever
Catherine asked questions, William was reassuring, pointing out
that they had many one-off expenses and their finances would
level out. But this was not going to happen while he continued to
spend so recklessly.

Three years had passed since Dora and Emma had first requested
their portions, and there was still no sign of the funds. In fact,
William had changed the boundaries of the dispute considerably,
stating that the sisters were not due *any* money. Slippery as ever, he
claimed that Dora and Emma had agreed to waive their rights to
the £15,000 in return for the annuities of £2,000 and £1,500 that
Catherine had settled on them at the time of the wedding. When

solicitors asked for proof, he had to admit, 'no deeds to that effect appear to have been executed', although he continued to maintain that there had been a verbal agreement.[8] William was so sanctimonious and persuasive that Catherine began to doubt her own understanding of the situation. By the time he had finished pontificating, Catherine did not know what to believe.

Regardless of William's opinion, the Miss Longs were fully entitled to receive the portions set aside in their father's will. Eventually Dora called upon one of her powerful relations to mediate, the sixth Earl of Shaftesbury. The earl was a fair-minded man who carried much sway and William had previously agreed to abide by his decision. Shaftesbury's cousin, Bartholomew Bouverie, had been party to the marriage settlement, so he was in a position to confirm categorically that Emma and Dora had never agreed to sign away their inheritance. William was subsequently ordered to pay the amounts owed to them.[9] When William still did not honour the payments, the family feud continued to fester.

The full extent of the discord was unknown to Catherine, because her sisters kept her out of the negotiations. William discouraged his wife from visiting Draycot, while making it clear to Lady Catherine, Dora and Emma that they were not welcome in his home. On one occasion, he even sent the ladies away when they called at Wanstead, and Catherine was not told about the incident. The sisters endeavoured to remain on the right side of William to keep the peace. They adored their older sister and went out of their way to protect her feelings. Despite their best intentions, Catherine sensed the deepening alienation within the family and she found it very distressing.

Catherine did not actively participate in the London season of 1815, for she was pregnant once more, with a baby due in August. She spent much of her time at Wanstead, mixing with the ladies in her neighbourhood, nursing her precious little bump and trying not to dwell on the disharmony in her marriage. After all the excitement at the Congress of Vienna, William derived no pleasure from mixing in the same tight circle every night, meeting up with his married friends and making polite conversation with their wives.

There was no fun in that, no game, no chase. For him, womanizing was a recreational sport, entirely separate from his domestic life. By the time he was in his mid-thirties, he claimed to have bedded 'a thousand and three women'.[10] Perhaps the number was exaggerated, but this statement suggests that William was notching up conquests throughout his marriage. In order to accommodate this prolific sex drive, his staff probably included a number of obliging housemaids willing to indulge their master.[11]

William was also disposed to going out on the prowl, picking up and sampling all kinds of women. Left to his own devices, he began to spend more evenings in town, skulking about like a tomcat and seeking sexual adventure in his former bachelor haunts. His box at the Drury Lane Theatre provided an informal source of amusement as he did not need to worry about inviting guests or compiling menus. He could simply turn up, sit in his box and the entertainment came to him. High-class courtesans and actresses used the opera as an opportunity to meet rich patrons, so the theatre was a good place to socialize with females excluded from respectable drawing rooms. Providing colourful company, these women visited William in his box to chat and flirt. If they amused him sufficiently he took them to a late-night supper club after the show. The Clarendon was reputedly the smartest of all the London hotels, but William preferred Grillion's as it was less formal and more suited for the company he was keeping. Many of the people he associated with were not wealthy, but William thought nothing of buying supper for twenty people if it benefited his own enjoyment. Grillion's charged around £3 a plate, with champagne and claret at around one guinea a bottle, which meant that William's bill at the end of a night out could regularly be in excess of £100. Nevertheless, he continued flashing money to impress his new friends.

One of his most frequent companions on his London jaunts was the wealthy banker Douglas Kinnaird, a member of the Drury Lane Theatre group. Kinnaird was close friends with Lord Byron and John Cam Hobhouse, who had both spent time with William in Cadiz in 1809, when they were adventuring on the continent.

Byron and Hobhouse were not enamoured with William, but as he was on the periphery of their circle, they tolerated his company on occasion. Famously libertarian, Byron was among those who admired Napoleon for his endeavours in bringing down the tyrannical French monarchy, while launching a new era of freedom and justice. Though all members of the circle did not necessarily share Byron's enthusiasm for Napoleon, they were all Whigs, firmly in favour of social justice and parliamentary reform.

The Wellesleys were staunch Conservatives, but mixing with Sheridan and other prominent Whigs led William to harbour the self-delusion that he was a liberal-minded visionary. Elected to Parliament as an Independent candidate, unaligned to any one party, the ambivalence suited William as he could tailor his politics to suit the company he was keeping. After all, it was difficult to be truly intimate with a person who did not share your principles.

In reality, William's thinking was far removed from Whig ideology. This much was clear from his complete lack of social responsibility or compassion for the poor. Rather conveniently, his philosophy was simply that some men are born rich while others are born poor, and that is what God intended. One example of William's obstinate lack of understanding was his attitude toward poachers. With so many families desperate with hunger, petty crime was on the rise. However, because poachers stole the odd rabbit or pheasant from his estate, William felt perfectly justified in setting lethal mantraps to kill or maim them. Pouncing on the story, newspapers raised the question, 'man traps and spring guns have been set in the forest coppices of Mr William Pole Tylney Long Wellesley . . . can any law justify the setting of engines of destruction in woods and coppices . . . and public paths?'[12]

With Catherine out of circulation for much of the season, rumours abounded about a growing rift in the Long Wellesleys' marriage. William's infidelities were an open secret among his set and, as everybody loved to gossip, the news spread quickly. There were also stories about William's secret trysts inside the old boathouse at

Wanstead. Hidden away from the prying eyes of servants, the isolated boathouse Grotto was the perfect setting for romantic encounters. It had been built by the bachelor Earl Tylney in the 1760s, a mysterious cave-like structure nestled on the banks of a lake, with curious interiors that added to the air of surrealism.[13] The lower level resembled an ancient cavern with glistening stalactites dropping from the ceiling. A tessellated staircase led to the upper chamber, a magically romantic room that had craggy walls with holes gouged into them to create candleholders. Flames flickered randomly at different levels, casting shadows and lighting up the domed ceiling, glittering with its mosaic of coloured glass, pieces of mirror, crystals, pebbles, shells and semi-precious stones. Stained-glass windows radiated a rainbow of jewel colours, adding even further to the dreamlike effect.[14]

The curious Grotto was famous throughout England and visitors streamed in to view it whenever the park was open. Rumours about William's amorous adventures simply added to the appeal. It was suggested that he entertained all kinds of women there: housemaids, milkmaids and even the occasional married lady or duchess. The encounter would start with a short boat ride along the finger of water towards the shadowy Grotto cocooned by lofty chestnuts and weeping willows. Navigating the boat through the arched doorway, William would lead his paramour up the stairs and into the candlelit upper chamber for a night of passion. As these stories gained momentum, they took a more sinister turn, and there was speculation that William used the secluded boathouse as a prison, to incarcerate his wife.[15] The prospect of solitary confinement would certainly have made Catherine more amenable to his demands.

Regency society was resolutely male dominated and according to the law a husband had absolute power over his wife. He even had control of her body: he could use her sexually whenever he desired; he could beat her (within reason); he could lock her up if she defied him in any way. As head of the household, some men felt it their moral duty to keep their wives in check and were not averse to using violence or incarceration to achieve the desired effect. In most circles, however, this type of behaviour was not tolerated. Convention demanded that a man treat his wife with kindness and respect. William was not a violent man and he did not settle marital disputes with blows or beatings. Even in the midst of their quarrels about money, it is difficult to imagine that he would actually have resorted to shutting his wife away. Nobody in his circle would have stood for it: not his parents, his friends, nor most of all Catherine. Furthermore, there is no evidence to support the allegations, no references in letters or diaries. These rumours, however, exposed the level of power a husband could legally wield over his wife, serving as a reminder to Catherine that William had many stratagems at his disposal, if he were that way inclined.

All summer, William continued to flit between Dover Street and Wanstead. When he was at home with Catherine, he was aloof and distant. Determinedly loyal, she made excuses for him, attributing his surliness to the pressures of business. She was especially vulnerable at this point in the marriage, heavily pregnant, with serious concerns that she might not survive the birth. Terrified by the precariousness of her own mortality, she would have loved nothing more than the comfort of her mother and sisters, but William still barred them from Wanstead. Instead of offering reassurance at this difficult time, William presented Catherine with a document to sign – a will. If his wife were to die, William would no longer enjoy full control of the finances because her share in the estates would automatically become tied up in trust for their young son. In view of this, William insisted that Catherine bequeath him a lump sum of £50,000 in the event of her death.[16]

Naturally, Catherine was reluctant to comply. As things stood, if she died William would retain around half her fortune. Quite rightly, the other half was set aside for her son and Catherine was wary about signing away any part of this inheritance. Calmly taking the document, Catherine told William that she needed to take advice from Bartholomew Bouverie. Persistent as ever, William badgered and bullied her, insisting that time was of the essence as something might happen to her any day now. This was hardly a reassuring sentiment. Catherine managed to stall William for a few days but he was relentless, hurling accusations that she did not trust him. Finally, one afternoon, he issued an ultimatum. Dressed in his riding clothes, he left the document on her writing desk and insisted that it had to be signed by the time he returned from his exercise. Bowing under the pressure, Catherine signed the new will on 1 July 1815.[17] Their relationship was precarious, and William's power over Catherine was only increasing.

19. The Dishonest Cleric and Other Anecdotes

❦

1817

Much to everyone's relief, Catherine safely delivered a second son: James Fitzroy Henry was born on 12 August 1815. In the months after his birth, strolling through Wanstead Park helped Catherine regain her strength and put the bloom back into her cheeks. Delighted with her new baby, she spent her days in the nursery watching over James and playing with Will, who had grown into a lively toddler. She was not too distracted, however, to notice that the sparkle was fading from her marriage. Longing to return to the intimacy they had once shared, Catherine reached out to her husband. William also wanted his marriage to work. As he watched his gentle wife nurse their newborn son, he was filled with tenderness, and resolved to treat Catherine with more affection in future.

William was a complex character, a man of many contradictions. On dismissing him from the army, Wellington had summed him up perfectly, remarking, 'He is the most extraordinary person altogether I have ever seen. There is a mixture of steadiness and extreme levity, of sense and folly in his composition such as I have never met with in any other instance.'[1] Everybody has shortcomings. Even Mr Darcy, the most compelling romantic hero of all time, was often proud and haughty, 'continually giving offense', as demonstrated at the ball in Meryton.[2] Similarly, while William was often thoughtless, he could also be big-hearted.

Baily's Monthly Magazine of Sports & Pastimes was one of the publications that focused on the more positive aspects of William's character. On 1 March 1893, it published an anecdote about his fascination with breeding horses. It was widely known that William's collection of thoroughbreds was his pride and joy. Highly polished with gleaming coats, they were the fastest horses in the county. On one occasion, he spent a huge amount on a colt whose parents were both prize-winning racehorses. Despite its lightning speed, the young horse had such a feisty temperament that nobody could control him. Expert horsemen travelled from far and wide to try to break him in, but nobody could master the horse until a man named Smith came forward. When the hounds met at Glen Gorse, Smith suffered no less than eight tosses over fences before the colt submitted to him.

By the time he dismounted, a love affair had blossomed and the horse followed Smith, nuzzling the back of his hot neck. William saw hunger in the man's eyes, recognizing that this talented jockey would never be able to afford a mount of this calibre. In a gesture of extreme generosity, William handed the reins to Smith and said, 'Here, take him.'

Shocked, Smith insisted, 'I could not accept, sir.'

'Nonsense! You are the only man in England equal to this colt, so you shall have him.'

Delighted, Smith took the horse, and named him 'The Gift'. They became an unbeatable combination; the jockey won many cash prizes, finding fame and fortune on his feisty stallion. Smith was so successful he went on to found a school teaching horsemanship. This gesture was typical of William's impulsive generosity.

William was also witty, and had an amusing turn of phrase. This yarn, told in his own words, shows why people found him so charming and entertaining:

A postilion was once driving me at a furious rate down a hill near Bradford. His horses and him sustained a dreadful look-ing fall; the fellow bellowed and howled immoderately, swore his bones were all broken . . . I and my servant assisted in car-rying him into a public house. The stage-coachman, who knew his man, insisted on stripping the postilion stark naked, which, with much difficulty, and howling, was accomplished. No sooner was the postilion quite naked than the coachman applied the lash of his whip to his naked body. The fellow, till the whip was applied, was all aches, pains, broken bones, and immoveable; but upon this application he became as blythe as a lark, begged to dress himself, and we proceeded on our journey, myself enjoying considerably the profit I derived from the cunning of the two fellows, for I was about to give all the money about me to the postilion.[3]

In its publication dated October 1863, *Baily's Magazine of Sport* featured another interesting story showcasing William's compassion and generosity. Mr Long Wellesley had many hangers-on, including a sporting young cleric with a smoothly shaved head. The priest often joined William's hunting parties and his family were constant guests at Wanstead House. He was one of the friends for whom William always had an open hand and the clergyman regularly received substantial handouts of £500.

Early one morning, William was in his dressing room at Wanstead when a post-chaise arrived bearing the confidential clerk of his bankers. Requesting an urgent interview, the clerk was shown into William's private office where he produced a cheque. Folded over to reveal only the written name, the man asked, 'Sir, I am desired to ascertain whether it is your signature on this cheque?'

'No,' said William, studying it carefully, 'it is certainly not my writing. However, let me examine the body of the cheque, just to make sure.'

'Pardon me, sir,' replied the clerk, quickly putting away the paper. 'I am instructed peremptorily to ask the question only, and not to show any part of the cheque except the appended signature.'

That evening, another carriage arrived at Wanstead and the wife of the cleric, in a state of distraction, rushed unceremoniously into William's private apartment. She got down on her knees and begged for pity and mercy for her husband. Pressed for immediate payment of a large sum, he had forged a cheque for £800, and signed it William Long Wellesley. The money was paid, but after a suspicion had arisen, a bank clerk was dispatched to check its authenticity.

Forgery was a capital crime, so quite rightly the cleric's wife was inconsolable. William did his best to calm her down by assuring her that no harm would come to her husband, if he could prevent it. As it was a Saturday evening, the woman feared that nothing could be done until the bank opened on the Monday. At the crack of dawn the next day, however, William headed for London as fast as four post horses could convey him. He knocked up the bank clerk, who always passed Sundays in solitary devotion on the bank premises.

William insisted that the official open up the vault where the cheque was deposited for safekeeping. This was in defiance of all rules, but William refused to be denied. Once the forged cheque was obtained, William ordered the clerk to accompany him to the banker's house, which was situated ten miles to the west of London.

'What can be the matter, Mr Long Wellesley?' asked the surprised banker when William appeared on his doorstep.

'Nothing very material. It is simply the matter of this cheque,' said William, holding up the paper for the millionaire banker to inspect.

'Ah! Indeed! It is a sad – a shocking business! So well connected, with a wife and family too. What is the world coming to, and what will it say? The authorities have already been apprised of the circumstances, and we shall require your presence tomorrow, I believe.'

'Now listen. I declare before your clerk, as witness, and you as my banker, that this is my very own signature,' said William.

'You are an extraordinary man, Mr Long Wellesley. Do you really mean what you say?' enquired the astonished banker.

'I repeat that this cheque is properly signed. I ask that you honour it. Ensure that it is duly paid,' insisted William.

'You are the only man in England who would take this line. It is not good for business!'

'That's my affair!' William replied to the unsympathetic banker, who possibly would have felt justified at having a man hanged simply for overdrawing his bank account.

On returning from stag hunting on Monday, William found the grateful clergyman waiting for him. He was red-faced, with beads of perspiration glistening on his shining bald head. Overcome by emotion, the man flung himself onto his knees, expressing his gratitude while choking back tears.

'There, none of that nonsense,' said William. 'Take a glass of sherry, steady your nerves and stay to dinner.'

'That is impossible,' said the astonished cleric.

'But you must, and you shall,' insisted William. 'I have a party coming. There are rumours circulating, but if you stay and dine with me all gossip will cease.'

The cleric stayed to dine at Wanstead. His host was in jocular form, entertaining his guests with amusing tales. Furthermore, William remained discreet; he never mentioned the incident again, to the clergyman or anyone else. William's humour, generosity and often extraordinary compassion were such that many people were captivated by him – and none more so than Catherine.

20. The Bastard

࿔

1817

Five years into their marriage, Catherine had learned that William could be a genial, generous husband – as long as he got his own way. She resolved not to ask too many questions about his spending, and in return he was at his most attentive. Catherine still enjoyed nights out on the town with her husband, attending dinners and balls, but her priorities had changed since her marriage, and her two young boys were her main concern. Owing to this, she did not always accompany William when he stayed over at their town house in Dover Street for a few nights, particularly if he was busy with parliamentary duties. But their marriage was mostly harmonious, and they were getting along much better since Catherine had yielded over money issues. When they were alone together William was pleasant company, entertaining her with amusing stories and soothing her with tenderness.

William found the season of 1817 subdued following the departure of many of London's most colourful characters. Richard Sheridan had died the previous year, Beau Brummell was in Calais avoiding his creditors, and Lord Byron had fled abroad to escape scandal. With the Drury Lane Theatre set sadly depleted, the friendship between William and Douglas Kinnaird blossomed. According to his closest companions, Kinnaird was a 'kind and benevolent' man who always stood by his friends.[1] His loyalty was evident that summer as he endeavoured to solve William's financial problems, while also planning a trip abroad to offer support to Byron.

The one thing that Kinnaird treasured most in the entire world was his long-term mistress, Maria Kepple. Although the bewitching actress and singer was not actually married to the banker, they had lived happily together for almost a decade and so everyone called her 'Mrs Kinnaird'. She was not welcome in polite circles, but this did not seem to bother her and she was perfectly happy to host intimate gatherings at home in Clarges Street, Piccadilly. As an actress and singer, entertaining was second nature and her conversation was amusing and candid, with a hard-nosed, cynical edge. Well able to indulge in scathing banter, her cultivated guests quickly discovered that the captivating, dark-haired beauty was not a woman to trifle with. Kinnaird was so besotted, Byron could not resist remarking, 'Nobody keeps their piece nine years now-a-days – except Douglas K.'[2]

Conversation at Mrs Kinnaird's table was not stifled by the strict rules of propriety. Lively political debates and salacious gossip were the order of the day, especially when the likes of Hobhouse or Thomas Moore were present. On one particular evening, gossip was rife as guests made shocking revelations about mutual acquaintances. Trying to impress the company, William dropped hints about a cover-up at the Treasury involving the former foreign secretary, George Canning. Pressed on the matter by Hobhouse, William revealed that a dispatch from Portugal had been burned because it did not reflect well on the foreign secretary. Furthermore, it had been William's job to précis a false report, altering the facts to Canning's advantage.[3] Exposing the foreign secretary in this way was a dreadful betrayal of trust, particularly as Canning was a close friend of Richard, Marquess Wellesley. William had not learned from previous blunders and remained as indiscreet as ever.

Having visited Constantinople with Byron in 1810, Hobhouse had heard first-hand reports of William's astounding folly in declaring war on Turkey. When the matter came up over dinner, William remained genial and good-natured. Always seeking approval from his peers, he invited Hobhouse to Wanstead, saying jovially, 'I hope you will find me a better country gentleman, than an ambassador.'[4]

Later that evening William retreated into another room to discuss his finances. Kinnaird was a huge support, giving William sound advice and trying to find ways of reducing the 'vicious interest' he was paying on loans.[5] Having made discreet enquiries about selling Catherine's diamonds, Kinnaird advised him that the jewellery would not fetch even a fraction of the true value because the market was so depressed. This was disappointing news for William but, ever the optimist, he felt confident that there would be an upturn in the economy very soon.

In August 1817, Kinnaird and Hobhouse travelled abroad to visit Byron. With Parliament in recess, William spent more time with his family. For Catherine, staying at Wanstead while William worked in town was a convenient arrangement. If she were in London, she would be obliged to make calls and entertain guests. Instead, she could devote time to her two boys, now aged four and two, taking pleasure in the fresh air and green pastures of the estate. Catherine enjoyed the best of both worlds, spending quality time with her children, but also going into town when the occasion demanded. Whenever William came home, he was attentive and, by the end of August, Catherine was pregnant again.

Early in 1818, Maria Kinnaird gave birth to a baby boy. Friends called on her at home, bearing gifts of congratulation, but Hobhouse was among those who remained resolutely unimpressed. In his view, something was clearly amiss and he referred to the newborn as 'the bastard'.[6] Maria vehemently denied any wrongdoing and despite his misgivings Kinnaird desperately wanted to believe her. Nevertheless, the dates simply did not add up; Kinnaird calculated that the child had been conceived while he was away in Brighton. Late in February, Hobhouse rode up to London to dine with friends and he found Kinnaird in a state of torment. The two men walked up and down St James's Street in the early hours, while the banker poured out his sorrow. The prospect of losing his mistress was breaking his heart, but she had abused his generosity and made a fool of him. When Kinnaird eventually determined to separate from his mistress, Hobhouse was sceptical, recording in his journal, 'I foresaw he would *not* but still thought it my duty to advise him in the affirmative.'[7]

Much to everyone's surprise, Kinnaird demonstrated remarkable resolve by ordering his mistress to pack her bags and leave
with the baby. Even the usually scathing Byron felt saddened,
lamenting Kinnaird's loss, acknowledging, 'she made your house
very pleasant'.[8] Writing from exile, Byron commented, 'Poor Maria!
... I understand that you have provided for her in the handsomest
manner which is in your nature and does not surprise me.'[9] Nevertheless, without the protection of Kinnaird, Maria found herself
shunned by society. Her only hope for security in the long term
was to seek acknowledgement from the father of her child – a man
of great wealth. When this was not forthcoming, she wrote to his
wife.

Henry Bicknell was a young man of great honour and integrity.
Aged just thirteen when he entered service at Wanstead in 1812, he
rose quickly through the ranks, earning the distinction of becoming
the youngest butler in England.[10] Nothing escaped his steely eye
and he was privy to the Long Wellesleys' darkest secrets. Bicknell
knew all about William's liaison with Mrs Kinnaird because he had
been in attendance, standing with the coachman outside the house
in Clarges Street.[11] Over the years, Bicknell had remained fiercely
loyal to Catherine, doing everything in his power to protect his
sweet mistress. It was with much trepidation, therefore, that he
delivered the letter that would shatter her world.

Devastated by her husband's betrayal, Catherine was not the
type of woman who could look the other way. At the turn of the
nineteenth century, infidelity was rife in some upper-class circles, as
demonstrated by the fifth Duke of Devonshire's ménage à trois, and
Lady Caroline Lamb's well-publicized affair with Lord Byron, conducted with the knowledge of her mother-in-law, Lady Melbourne
(who in turn had been mistress to the Prince Regent). Catherine,
however, was not part of this scandal-ridden world; she had been
brought up with strict Methodist beliefs, aspiring to the romantic
ideals of domesticity portrayed by Jane Austen. Post Waterloo, the
brittleness and sardonic wit that had been so fashionable was giving

way to a softer approach. In many respects, Catherine embodied the ideal of femininity of the time; she was small and curvy, and there was softness in her looks and her manner. Her nature was charitable and kind, patient and giving. The values Catherine cherished were, by now, foreshadowing the Victorian age.

A forthright woman, Catherine confronted her husband with Maria Kinnaird's letter. William confessed that he was the father of her baby but insisted that while he felt it his duty to provide some financial assistance, he wanted no contact with the child or the mother. William genuinely wanted to save his marriage. Having recently witnessed the downfall of close family and friends, he did not want to become the next casualty. His uncle Richard, Marquess Wellesley was bankrupt and homeless. Lord Byron had been forced to flee abroad in 1816, following the most sensational scandal of the decade. The poet's downfall had been sudden: one moment he was the toast of London, the next he was an outcast. William resolved to learn from the mistakes of others. But Catherine was not inclined to forgive him just yet.

Although Catherine was furious, she wanted their marriage to work. Despite William's frailties, she still loved his gentleness and strength, his tall stories and practical jokes, the fun and excitement he injected into her life. Most importantly, he was the father of her children and she craved a harmonious family life. Nevertheless, she insisted that William should show remorse, and promise to reform his conduct so that this situation would never occur again.

In elite circles, it was not uncommon for men to father illegitimate children, but attitudes and practices varied considerably. Men often provided some form of maintenance. Others took it a step further, raising the child in the family home, passing it off as a servant or orphaned relative. There were also those who ignored the problem completely. But, ultimately, the appropriate course of action was almost always determined by the man. With regards to William's illegitimate child, however, it was Catherine who took charge.

Handling Maria Kinnaird was not straightforward, particularly as there was no precedent. Numerous instructional books offered guidance for tricky situations such as 'rejecting a gentleman's address' or 'requesting a loan of money', but rather unhelpfully there was no section entitled 'confronting your husband's mistress'.[12] It was an era when women did not take control. In fact, the advice would probably have been '*do not* meddle in your husband's affairs'. But Catherine was a resourceful woman, well accustomed to standing up for herself. Driving a hard bargain, she made it clear that she would support the child, but only if she got something in return. After some negotiation, Catherine undertook to provide maintenance of £500 per annum, strictly on the understanding that Maria Kinnaird did not reside within fifty miles of Wanstead House. If she broke this condition, or had any further contact with William, the agreement would become void and she would get nothing. This did not deter Maria, who continued to live nearby, possibly in the hope that William would return. Catherine kept a close eye on the situation and eventually sent orders that Mrs Kinnaird should move to France.[13] It was only after she complied with these terms that she received an annuity of £500.[14] These funds were paid directly from Catherine's personal allowance, reducing her pin money from £7,500 to £7,000. The whole business was distressing for Catherine, but more than anything she wanted to preserve her marriage, particularly now that she was pregnant with her third child.

William was determined to win back the affections of his wife. Over the previous two years, he had learned lessons from observing the changing fortunes of his two famous uncles. The decline of Richard, Marquess Wellesley had started when he left his wife to pursue a life of debauchery. Within the space of a few years, he was deeply in debt and the family estates in Dublin were sold at auction. After this, he still owed an enormous £183,000. By August 1816, the situation had deteriorated even further and bailiffs stormed his home determined to seize assets, including his cherished trophies from India. Apsley House was the ultimate symbol of the governor-general's achievements, filled with prizes and mementoes from grateful sultans. Mr Lightfoot, the solicitor, quickly stepped in to buy off the bailiffs, but the situation was desperate. Richard had no option but to sell Apsley House along with his most treasured possessions.

In contrast, in the years following Waterloo, Wellington had soared to great heights. When the duke heard about his brother's financial distress, he believed it would be easier for Richard if Apsley House stayed in the family, so he stepped in and bought the mansion for £42,000. It was a generous gesture, and Richard made a good profit on the £16,000 he had paid seven years previously.[15] In many respects, however, it was extremely painful for the eldest brother to step aside once again to make way for Arthur. Richard watched helplessly as all his trophies from India were stripped away and replaced with Wellington's spoils.

Apsley House is a famous landmark, nicknamed 'Number 1 London', and standing in a prestigious position overlooking Rotten Row in Hyde Park. When William visited in 1818, he was hugely impressed by the renovations that were underway as Wellington prepared to transform his home into a 'Waterloo Palace', fit for a national hero. The house itself was not as large or magnificent as Wanstead, but the contents were splendid, full of prizes that money could not buy. On the vast mahogany dinner table stood a magnificent twenty-six-foot-long centrepiece, cast from silver and displaying dancing figures and joyful cherubs, presented by the grateful Portuguese. The Prussians had spent two years crafting a 400-piece dinner service, each plate a masterpiece, exquisitely hand painted with different battle scenes. From the king of France came an Egyptian service, while the tsar of Russia had presented Wellington with a diamond-hilted sword. William was awed by the display cabinets heaving with silver plate, medals and jewel-encrusted swords awarded by the sultans of India and the sovereigns of Europe. The crowning glory of the collection was a ten-foot-tall marble statue of Napoleon, in the nude, standing proudly in the entrance hall. The splendid sculpture had been commissioned by Napoleon himself, to adorn his own residence, but the British government bought the trophy from the Louvre for 66,000 francs and presented it to Wellington.

Walking through the staterooms at Apsley House, William was confronted with the evidence of Arthur's tremendous achievements. Not only was he the nation's hero, he was worshipped throughout Europe. Apsley House was in the process of being transformed into a Wellington Museum, which would open to the public one day, so that future generations could view all the magnificent tributes.[16] Arthur Wellesley had earned his place in history. Inspired by what he saw, William wanted some form of glory for himself, a career that would raise his profile and earn him merit and distinction.

Back at Wanstead House, Catherine tried not to dwell on the past, for the sake of her unborn baby. On his best behaviour, William tried his hardest to please his wife, assuring her that he had taken steps to raise a mortgage in order to pay over the portions owed to her sisters. Desperate for money, he had applied for a huge loan of £60,000, specifying that funds were needed 'without delay'.[17] His solicitor advised that substantial surety would be needed, 'the whole of the estate at Rochford', comprising around 2,000 acres.[18] Accruing debt is never ideal, but Catherine was relieved to hear that the family dispute over money would soon be settled. Offers of marriage were still pouring in for Emma, with John Fremantle emerging as one of her most ardent admirers along with the Portuguese Mons de Sauveur. Writing to his uncle, Fremantle said that William was actively encouraging him because he 'was anxious to get me or any other Englishman, fearing she might fancy this Portuguese'.[19] For more than a year Fremantle pursued Emma without success, because she remained steadfast in her love for Burke.[20] Eventually Fremantle told his uncle that he had the opportunity to marry a wealthy widow. He went on to say, 'but I can't help regretting my little Long, in short I am in the agonies of the Damned'.[21]

By now, William was almost thirty years old, and he had come to realize the advantages of forging a successful career in the public eye. Supposedly in another gesture to gratify his wife, he announced that he would be standing for election in Catherine's home county. Her father had nurtured strong ties with his local community and it was traditional for a member of the Long family to represent Wiltshire in Parliament. In February 1818, William published a statement in the newspapers addressed to the Noblemen, Gentlemen, Clergy & Freeholders in the County of Wiltshire, stating his 'anxious desire' to stand for representation of Wiltshire.[22] In an attempt to drum up support, he claimed that his motive was to restore the honour to the House of Draycot and the ancient Long family of which he was now a member.

William's battle to be elected MP for Wiltshire in 1818 was to become one of the most notorious contests in England. Embarking on a campaign of violence, blackmail and intimidation, he would demonstrate just how corrupt the voting system could be. His antics were outrageous: hilarious and appalling at the same time. This was denoted by his opening gambit, when he assured the voting public, 'Gentlemen, you will not find me, throughout this contest, a hot-headed, hair-brained Irishman, but a cool, honest, warm-hearted Englishman.'[23]

21. Cock of the Walk

❧

1818

In 1818, the vast majority of the population did not have the power to vote. Women were automatically disenfranchised, while eligibility for men was determined by property and wealth. Overall, just two per cent of adults qualified to vote. Many thought the government to be 'the greatest perfection of fraud and corruption'.[1] Despite impassioned speeches about liberty and the Rights of Freeborn Englishmen, there had been no reform of Parliament and representation remained hugely disproportionate. Some constituencies, known as 'rotten boroughs', had only a handful of voters, while other large cities that had sprung up during the industrial revolution such as Leeds, Manchester and Birmingham did not have any representatives in Parliament. In effect, the innovative manufacturing class had no voice in government. As a consequence, nineteenth-century England could not claim to be a fully functioning democracy.

The imbalance did not end there. William was part of a culture that was largely blind to many forms of discrimination: sexual inequity was taken for granted; religious intolerance meant that Roman Catholics were not permitted to sit in Parliament; and racial condescension was a prevailing social attitude. It was without irony, therefore, that William made derisory comments about his Irish roots, while continually insisting, 'I am an Englishman born and bred.'[2]

Domestic issues had taken a back seat during the Napoleonic Wars, but now the time was ripe for change. It was the ideal moment for William to make a mark in politics. With parliamentary elections looming, he could have kept his seat as MP for St Ives for the price of a small bribe. The constituency was a pocket borough in the control of a Mr Hulse, who requested a 'donation' of just £500. Merrick Shawe set up a dinner appointment to clinch the deal and sat waiting with Hulse for hours, a nice bottle of Sauterne chilling on ice, but William failed to turn up for the meeting. This slight proved to be a serious error of judgement, particularly as Hulse had made a 300-mile journey from Cornwall. He went away disgruntled, without his money, and William lost his seat in Parliament.[3] At the time, William was unperturbed because he felt confident that he could bribe his way into the Commons. In fact, he already had his sights set elsewhere.

The prestigious seat Knight of the Shire of Wiltshire had become available because Robert Long (a relation of Catherine) had resigned his post. Wiltshire was one of the largest constituencies in England with an electorate of 5,000.[4] As Knight of the Shire was such a prominent position, it was customary to hold a borough seat for many years before getting promotion to the county. Wiltshire contained fifteen boroughs, the largest of which were Salisbury, Trowbridge, Westbury and Warminster. As each borough elected two MPs it would have been relatively easy for William to secure one of these seats, but in an ambitious, somewhat arrogant move, he put himself forward as an Independent candidate for the whole county.

Initially, Paul Methuen and Mr Long Wellesley were the only candidates declared, which meant that they would both gain automatic election to the two county seats. All this changed, however, when John Benett entered the race at the last minute. Three candidates were now fighting over two seats. With a proven record of accomplishment, Paul Methuen would almost certainly be re-elected. Benett was also a formidable opponent, as he came from a family that had represented Wiltshire in Parliament over several successive generations. One of the main advantages he exalted over William was that he had lived and worked in Wiltshire all his life and was highly respected throughout the county. The Bath and West of England Society awarded him a gold medal in 1814 for his campaign to abolish tithes imposed by the Church. An eloquent man of the people, he possessed a profound understanding of the problems faced by voters in Wiltshire – they knew he would fight their corner in Parliament.

Facing fierce competition, William had no option but to embark on an expensive campaign, resplendent with marching bands, campaign songs and parades. His electioneering had the feel of a country fete or pageant, drawing crowds of onlookers eager to enjoy the spectacle. Despite all the posturing, his position was tenuous because many influential people in Wiltshire did not support him, particularly as he had never lived in the county. Many believed that after the election he would return to his grand house in Essex, forgetting all about them and their concerns. In addition, because William was standing for a high-profile seat in Parliament, his integrity and private life were open to scrutiny. Rumours abounded about his substantial debts, his womanizing and his untrustworthiness.

Troubles started when John Cam Hobhouse published an addendum to his book *Travels through Albania and Greece to Constantinople*, highlighting the fact that William had caused the brief war against Turkey in 1806. Furious over the betrayal of their mutual friend Kinnaird, Hobhouse believed that exposing William's true character was in the public interest. However, William was adept at twisting facts and using the media to his own advantage. Issuing a press release of his own, he insisted that Hobhouse's addendum contained 'not one word of truth.'[5] Painting himself as some kind of saviour, William's version of events was truly inspired. He wrote, 'The negotiations I was involved in were for the purpose of *preventing* the war . . . and the result was the arresting of the devastation of the two provinces of Moldovia and Wallachia.'[6] A dubious witness stepped forward to publicly corroborate this story. Charles Thomson confirmed that Mr Long Wellesley had 'acted with the greatest energy and humanity, in rescuing not only British subjects, but likewise those of Russia, from the well-known power of the Turks.'[7]

Although William was not a popular candidate, he wielded

power over many of the electorate by virtue of the fact that he was a powerful landowner. Open ballots, along with published lists of all votes cast, ensured that men voted in accordance with instructions laid down by their superiors. Those who did not comply ran the risk of being turned out of their homes or dismissed from their jobs. Money changed hands in return for votes and those men who could not be bribed or blackmailed faced various forms of intimidation, including violence. Whatever methods William employed, ninety tenants from his estates were coerced into signing letters supporting his candidacy. They refuted reports that he was an oppressive landlord who set lethal mantraps, declaring that he was 'kind and generous . . . when times were bad for renters, he made us the most liberal allowances by abatements in our rents'.[8] It was true – rents had been reduced in Wiltshire – but this was entirely Catherine's doing.

Despite William's duress, polls indicated that Benett was still ahead. In an effort to boost his campaign, William left his heavily pregnant wife at Wanstead and moved to Salisbury, making it easier for him to drive about the county canvassing support. Impeccably dressed in his trademark black coat and brilliantly white shirt, he addressed crowds with his usual easy confidence and twinkling smile. He was well received in most areas, particularly as he often made speeches in taverns, with free food and drink provided for all those who took the trouble to attend.

William often encountered awkward questions from the floor, but he was well practised at fielding them. On one occasion, however, the verbal assault was sustained as gentlemen charged William with a succession of offences, including being an 'improvident waster', who treated his wife shamefully and misapplied his talents.[9] Mumblings of 'Hear, hear,' rose from the crowd, as men nodded their heads in agreement. The mob grew rowdy, shouting and jeering loudly. Objects were thrown at the podium, as the impeccable dandy was pelted with rotten vegetables and cow dung. Reeling from the assault, William had no option but to step down, smiling and waving graciously as he made a hasty retreat in his personalized carriage drawn by his Arabian greys.

The men who baited him were so well informed and articulate that William suspected that Benett had planted his own supporters among the crowd. They had made him look foolish and he was determined it would not happen again. From then onwards henchmen were employed to control crowds when he spoke, and to eject people when necessary. William also hired rabble-rousers to sabotage his opponent's meetings with hisses and jeers. Benett was an imposing gentleman, over six feet tall, with a wiry build. He was well able to take care of himself, but there was so much disruption he was forced to request protection from the mounted county yeomanry.

William's payroll for the election was increasing by the day, to such an extent that he could not keep track of his own expenditure. He was forced to put a notice in the newspapers: 'Professional gentlemen, and all tradesmen and others, who are engaged for Mr Long Wellesley in his present canvass, are requested to send their accounts to Mr George Butt, solicitor, Salisbury, that the same may be regularly discharged.'[10]

To the electorate, however, all this expenditure merely served to reinforce the fact that he was guilty as charged, an 'improvident waster of money'. Polls indicated that Benett was still ahead.

During his electioneering, William acquired the label 'Cock of the Walk', a nickname he embraced because it suited his swaggering cocksure image, while also perpetuating the legend that he was well-endowed. In order to promote himself, William ensured that various ditties were penned in tribute and wherever he went a marching band accompanied him, playing his theme song 'Cock of the Walk'. This catchy jingle was like an advertisement, announcing his arrival, while also conveying the key points of his manifesto.

Expert at self-publicity, William's next move was to harness the power of the press. On Friday 8 May, he invited in excess of three hundred voters to a splendid dinner at the Castle Inn public house in Marlborough. As expected, huge amounts of money had been spent organizing a hearty feast, with singers and bands to entertain.

Venison lovers had a treat, with many commenting that it was the best food and wine they had ever tasted. After dessert, the cloth was removed and the table reset with decanters of fine wine and port. Numerous toasts were drunk, first to 'Church and King', second to 'the Prince Regent' and the third to 'Field Marshall the Duke of Wellington'. The evening was a public relations coup for William, as it provided the perfect opportunity to reply to the objections raised against him in a convivial setting. To maximize the impact he hired a reporter to record his speeches, and these transcripts were intended to entertain and influence the voting public of the time. Preserved for posterity, they provide valuable insight into William's character, clearly demonstrating his considerable capacity for insincerity, deceit and self-delusion.[11]

The company was suitably merry when the toastmaster raised his glass to propose 'the health of Mrs Long Wellesley'. This was William's cue to stand up and return thanks: 'Gentlemen, thank you for drinking to the health of a lady to whom I owe so much, and who is so justly endeared to me.' His voice cracked with emotion as he spoke about his wife and he became so overcome with feeling that he could not proceed, while the cheering of the company showed that he had their sympathy. 'I apologize, gentlemen, if I betray anything like unmanly feelings, when speaking about my most beloved wife. Falsehoods have circulated about my marriage, which have made Mrs Long Wellesley thoroughly miserable. Gentlemen, I must be the most horrid monster on the face of the earth, if I were capable of treating with disrespect, a lady to whom I owe so much. I am under such great, such lasting, such binding obligations!' William's voice shook with indignation as he continued, 'Gentlemen, if my wife has suffered, it is due to the calumny of my opponents.'

The company cheered, 'Bravo! Bravo!'

William sat down heavily, to wipe away his tears and regain his composure. The chairman patted him on the back, as the crowd continued to cheer. A song followed, 'Here's a Health to All Good Lasses', sung with fine effect, after which the chairman gave the health of Mr Long Wellesley, which was drunk with enthusiasm.

When the din of affection had subsided, William rose to address the freeholders: 'Gentlemen, certain quarters have attempted to destroy my character with malicious gossip and falsehood. I am no Irishman. George the Third, our gracious Sovereign, is about as much a Hanoverian as I am an Irishman – born, bred, and educated in England . . . My enemies have also objected that I am not a native of this county. Why, gentlemen, I acknowledge, since I have travelled through your county – since I have seen you at your homes – since I see you here – I *do* regret that I am not a native of Wiltshire.'

'Hear! Hear!' The cheering grew even louder.

Warming to the task, William continued, 'Having resolved to make Wiltshire the place of my constant residence, I determined to offer myself for the county.'

'Hear, hear!'

'Gentlemen, I have been accused of sitting for a government borough, at St Ives, and of being a "government tool". This claim is entirely false! I opposed their foreign policy; I voted for the Corn Bill; I did not support Lord Castlereagh's General Treaty; and even spoke against my own father, a Cabinet minister, following his speech on the property tax. This transaction, at least, shows that I am Independent.'

While delivering this speech, Mr Long Wellesley was warmly cheered by the crowd, who were too inebriated to scrutinize his politics and recognize that he was probably motived by self-interest. In his role as Master of the Mint, William's father was lobbying for the introduction of a property tax to generate revenue for the greater good. William objected to these proposals since he owned many thousands of acres. Similarly, the 1815 Corn Bill was intended to protect farmers and the rural economy, by placing high tariffs on imported food. This benefited William and his numerous tenant farmers, but had disastrous short-term results for many others. Failed harvests in 1816 and 1817 meant that ordinary people could not afford the inflated prices and many were starving.

When the applause finally died down, the raucous company sang along to the hilarious glee 'Cock of the Walk':

Come muster my Lads, nor be under control
For 'Wellesley' and Freedom, we'll go to the Poll
Tho' Horsemen with Bludgeons, and Threats should appear,
A Plumper for 'Wellesley' we'll give without fear.

Chorus
So 'Benett' and 'Calley' may bluster and talk,
Be early and ready,
Good order and steady,
You'll make him at last the brave 'Cock of the Walk'.

Your Benett may boast he can plough and can sow;
Fat pigs; and Potatoes and Barley can grow;
With the Tenantry these! They are not worth a Souse
To a man you should send to the Parliament House.

Chorus
So 'Benett' and 'Calley' . . .(etc.)

Those Banners we saw at the Hustings display'd
To our minds such achievements of valour convey'd
That with true English hearts, as a compliment due,
We will readily vote for the Wellington blue.

Rising yet again, William continued to hold forth for at least another hour, bragging about his association with the Duke of Wellington. As the evening wore on, his claims grew more ludicrous as he declared, 'Gentlemen, my pride is, although I am rich, I have never abused wealth.' Even this was met with cheers and applause. Over the course of the evening more than twenty-five toasts were drunk, while the singing carried on until after the sun rose. Alcohol and entertainment induced a general sense of well-being; everyone left the party with the impression that Mr Long Wellesley was a mighty fine fellow, well worthy of their vote in the ensuing election.

The public dinner at the Castle Inn was a triumph for William. Transcripts of his speeches were widely circulated in Wiltshire newspapers and discussed in coffee houses throughout the county.

But his campaign lost momentum when he was forced to return to Wanstead for the birth of the couple's third child. Hoping for a daughter to dote on, he told Catherine that if the baby was a girl he intended to call her 'Victory'. Back home, William shut himself away in his study to concentrate on resolving his financial issues. Debts were mounting, the mortgage of £60,000 had fallen through and William needed to raise funds fast. Faithful Shawe was busy trying to fix the problem; he wrote with news that 'Lightfoot has £10,000 at your service on very moderate terms if you want it.'[12] Unfortunately, this amount was not nearly enough to cover the cost of his electioneering. In addition, he still needed to pay Dora and Emma their portion of inheritance, £30,000 in total. William tried to borrow money from all manner of sources; even the freeholders in Wiltshire heard rumours about his dire personal finances. This did not stop him continuing to spend money lavishly, and he hired an army of recruits to help with his election campaign.

Catherine gave birth to a daughter at Wanstead House on 29 May 1818. She did not approve of the name 'Victory' and a compromise was reached. Swaddled in the family's green and gold christening robe, Victoria Catherine Mary Pole Tylney Long Wellesley was baptized by Reverend William Gilly at a small private ceremony in St Mary's Church, Wanstead. Victoria was not a particularly popular name in the nineteenth century, but the Long Wellesleys made it fashionable. One year later, on 24 May 1819, another baby girl was born and her parents called her Victoria. Baptized in the Cupola Room of Kensington Place, Alexandrina Victoria was the daughter of the Duke of Kent and the only living, legitimate grandchild of George III. This tiny Victoria was extremely precious – she would one day be queen of England.

This must have resonated with Catherine. If she had chosen to marry the Duke of Clarence seven years earlier, her eldest child would now be an heir to the throne. But she had no regrets; although there had been ups and downs in her marriage, she still adored William and the excitement of their life together.

*

William returned to Wiltshire a few days after the birth of his daughter. With the election looming he needed to be there, canvassing support until the very last minute. As the election drew closer, streets in Wiltshire were hung with bunting and banners, imperial purple for Methuen, blue for Long Wellesley and red for Benett. The rainbow of colours on display suggested that it would be a close contest.[13] At great expense, William hired a cavalcade of carriages to transport his supporters to the ballot. A band of musicians followed him everywhere, announcing his arrival with rousing renditions of 'Cock of the Walk', as his supporters paraded behind singing along and waving banners of Wellesley blue.

With many years of dedicated service to the county, Paul Methuen was the clear leader, with second place being contested between William and John Benett. The first day of polling gave Mr Long Wellesley 162 votes and Mr Benett 85. The proceedings were severely disrupted by a mob that threatened and intimidated Benett's supporters. William made an insincere speech at the end of the day, as he tried his best to disassociate himself from the violence. People were not fooled: everyone was aware that the antagonists were on his payroll.

After the second day of polling, Long Wellesley had a comfortable lead over Mr Benett of 99 votes. But on the third day, William lost ground because his supporters were too drunk to make it to the polling station in time to vote. The mistake cost William a great deal of money, as he had to pay for transportation and hospitality again the following day. On the fourth day, he ensured that his voters arrived at nine o'clock sharp and the local inn did not serve free food and drink until after all 140 of his 'friends' had voted. By the close of the day, William had recovered a significant advantage over Benett.

During his speech on the fifth day, William unashamedly exploited his family connections, unfurling the Wellesley banner to explain its meaning: 'The first spot, the crest, was conferred for the salvation of India, the union flag for the capture of Seringapatam. On account of my family, there is no county in England that would be disgraced in returning me as their representative, though I don't build on this fact.'

After the sixth day, Mr Long Wellesley was almost 400 votes ahead of his rival. By now Benett was completely demoralized by all the skulduggery. He was unable to make speeches due to constant taunts and interruptions, his supporters were terrorized on their way to the polls, all the windows in the Wool Pack Inn were smashed, causing many injuries, and his solicitor had his head cracked open with a bludgeon. Overall, there was so much violence that the Sheriff of Wiltshire was forced to intervene and call order. His threats had little effect and after the eighth day Benett conceded defeat. He addressed a letter to the High Sheriff stating it was 'fruitless any longer to continue this contest'.

Mr Long Wellesley was elected as the second candidate for Wiltshire, behind Paul Methuen. William held a grand victory parade to the council chamber, complete with brass band, food and drink stalls plus entertainment. From the hustings, he made a speech dripping with insincerity: 'Gentlemen, before we part I must say a few words to you. Having assumed the name of Cock of the Walk with your most hearty approbation . . . I will maintain that character. You will find me sincere – you shall find me active – always where your wishes and my duties ought to see me.'

The following day, William climbed into his carriage and drove away without a backward glance.

22. Blind Man's Bluff

❧

1819

Victory in the Wiltshire elections came at a great price; William admitted that his campaign had cost 'an expense of not less than between £30,000 and £40,000', plunging him even further into debt.[1] Vast sums had been wasted on food, drink, entertainment, security, transport, posters, livery and brass bands. Conveniently forgetting his promise to become a resident of Wiltshire, the 'Cock of the Walk' returned to Wanstead House immediately after the elections, claiming that he was needed in the House of Commons. In reality, he spent several months trying to resolve his credit crisis.

During the election campaign Catherine had heard that her husband was spending copiously. She contacted her administrator, who confirmed that funds were low, and then she sent William a concerned note: 'I am very anxious to hear that you are well, but fear that you are sadly worried about the accounts.'[2] Despite all this, William continued to deceive her about the extent of his liabilities. By now he had reluctantly agreed to settle with the Miss Longs, but because he was already so heavily in debt, nobody would lend him money. Eventually he managed to raise £30,000 from a money-lender, the Earl de la Warr, at the extortionate repayment rate of ten per cent per annum. This additional loan crippled William. When the Miss Longs heard about his dire financial situation, they referred the matter to Lord Shaftesbury, stating that they would wait for their money. It was too late, however, as William had already signed up for the onerous deal. William was not qualified to manage estates or handle vast sums of money and he stumbled from one pecuniary crisis to another. Signing up for a new loan at an exorbitant rate was the latest in a long line of financial blunders. It would prove to be the catalyst for all the trouble that was to come.

William would later blame the Miss Longs for forcing him to take such drastic measures. In truth, however, this loan was probably used to fund his election campaign, and Dora and Emma never received a penny of it.[3] By now the Miss Longs were both approaching their late twenties and William's mean-mindedness had ruined their marriage prospects. Without their portions they could not afford to set themselves up in comfortable homes. Emma's chance of happiness evaporated when Mr Burke finally gave up and married someone else. His affections had been sincere; he had waited seven years. Naturally, poor Emma was distraught. The whole situation was a dreadful shame because both sisters adored children and longed for families of their own.

William's father, Mr Pole, was a well-respected politician who excelled in his roles as Cabinet minister and Master of the Mint. In 1816, he had helped to stabilize the economy by introducing a 'Great Re-coinage'. Currency reform was vital due to a shortage of silver and copper coins, which contributed to the culture of trade based on credit that could not be sustained. Displaying incredible organizational skills, Mr Pole directed the design process, oversaw the operation of the new steam-driven presses at the mint in Tower Hill, and completed distribution of £2,600,000 in new coins across Britain within fourteen days. Sir Joseph Banks proclaimed, 'The bold manner in which [Mr Pole] devised, and executed one of the most difficult works ... during the present Reign ... does honour to the name of Wellesley.'[4] The coinage was a lasting legacy that remained in circulation until decimalization in 1971.

With the Wellesleys at the forefront of government, William saw himself as a rising star in the political arena. When Parliament reconvened after the summer break he focused his attention on advancing his career, sitting on select committees and making several speeches in the Commons. In reality, however, William did not command respect among his fellow MPs because they remembered his diplomatic and military indiscretions. Ordinarily, this would not have been an issue; politicians have notoriously short memories. The problem was that William never learned from his mistakes. This was demonstrated when his loose talk at a dinner party came back to haunt him. Hell-bent on revenge, Hobhouse published an anonymous report about the cover-up at the Treasury, where William had been involved in falsifying official documents. This was a serious offence, implicating both William and the former foreign secretary, George Canning. Aside from the ensuing blackened reputations, the Wellesleys were furious with William for the needless betrayal of a close family friend.

As well as being untrustworthy, William was also hopelessly out of touch. The Peterloo Massacre, on 16 August 1819, had stunned the nation. A crowd of 60–80,000 men, women and children had gathered at St Peter's Fields in Manchester to rally for parliamentary reform. They carried garlands and banners calling for 'Vote by Ballot' and 'Suffrage Universal'. Troops with muskets and bayonets were sent in to break up the peaceful protest, storming through the crowd indiscriminately. In just ten minutes the battle was over. Eleven innocents were slaughtered; many had stab wounds from sabres, while others were crushed or trampled under horses' hooves. Over 500 wounded bodies lay strewn in the field, children included – a carnage that resembled the aftermath of Waterloo. Peterloo was one of the defining events of the era. It was the moment when the ruling elite was forced to acknowledge that repression of the masses could not continue for much longer. After years of biting hardship and periods of famine, the lower classes were dangerously close to rebellion and the government was in constant fear of a French-style revolution. It was clear that major issues needed to be addressed. Astute politicians searched for measures to ease poverty and pressed for parliamentary reform.

During debates in the Commons, William professed to sympathize with the poor, stating that adequate employment should be found for the whole labouring class.[5] Regarding Peterloo, however, he sided firmly with the government, stating that no 'advantage would be gained by carrying out a public enquiry',[6] while also defending the Sheriff of Wiltshire in suppressing protests in the county.[7] In response, his old rival John Benett declared, 'When men are in a state of want, and almost of starvation, their complaints ought surely to be heard.'[8]

A class war was raging but, typically, William was only interested in promoting his own concerns and gratification. Completely misjudging the mood of the nation, and dumbfounding the Commons, he started campaigning for amendments to the Game Laws. Poaching was one of William's pet hates, but it was a ridiculous topic to debate at a time when repression of the lower classes was being called into question. Amendments to the Game Laws would only inflame the situation, as it highlighted the divisions and inequality. Oblivious to his own folly, William spoke with zeal about the evils of poaching, advocating the severest penalties for people caught stealing from the estates of landed gentry. He pontificated so frequently on the subject, the whole House groaned whenever he stood up, heckling with cries of 'Spoke, spoke!' until he sat down.[9]

Aside from his torturous speeches about poachers, William was part of a select committee appointed to investigate the amount of money being paid to the Duke of York. With funds in such short supply, Parliament was clamouring for a reduction in payments set aside for the royal household. Considering his own extravagance, William was surprisingly severe about everyone else's spending. On 5 February 1819, *The Times* recorded that William was firmly in favour of cutting the duke's allowances. Preaching to the Commons, he moralized, 'I cannot refrain from expressing the need for urgent economy in every branch of government expenditure.' He went on to say, 'I have brought with me to this House, a little stock of common sense, but a large stock of common honesty.' On hearing this, everybody in the House fell about laughing and the hilarity did not die down for some considerable time.[10] Blind to his own shortcomings, William was so self-deluded and out of touch, he became an object of ridicule in Parliament.

*

During the season of 1819, entertainment at Wanstead House was constrained by the lack of finances. Catherine hosted a few select gatherings to impress William's political cronies, but there were no fetes or other major events. William stayed in town several evenings a week to conduct business or talk politics, and Catherine joined him occasionally to attend functions or visit the Drury Lane Theatre and Vauxhall Gardens. She continued to reside mainly at Wanstead, however, an arrangement that suited her well, as she could devote time to her children. Young Will and James were dark-haired like the Wellesleys, but one-year-old Victoria was more like Catherine with a halo of blonde curls, an angelic face and infectious giggle. Catherine was pleased when William agreed that her mother and sisters could visit over the summer. Lady Catherine, Dora and Emma accepted gratefully, delighted at the opportunity to spend time with the children. The spinster aunts spent an idyllic few weeks, chasing about on the lawns, playing blind man's bluff, enjoying treasure hunts, fishing in the streams or sailing in the pleasure boats.

When Parliament resumed after the summer break, William slipped back into his routine of living in London during the week. Catherine was perfectly happy with this arrangement, going out and about with her friends and spending time with her children. Whenever William returned to Wanstead at the weekend, he was the ideal husband, lavishing time on Catherine. He was so tender and attentive that she had no cause to suspect a single thing. Undoubtedly, she would have been devastated to discover that William was still leading a double life.

The previous year, Catherine had been very businesslike in her dealings with the mother of William's illegitimate son. The child should have been William's responsibility, but it was Catherine who undertook support from her own pin money. This was not entirely due to benevolence; she had agreed to provide Maria Kinnaird with an annuity strictly on the understanding that she stayed away from William. But Maria had returned from France and moved into a

house in Seymour Terrace, Edgware Road, where William paid
the bills and rent. Resuming their relationship, the couple hosted
intimate dinner parties where Maria was the only woman present
and she held court in exactly the same manner as when she had
been living with Douglas Kinnaird.[11] William carefully conducted
the affair behind closed doors for fear of Catherine's reprisals.
Some evenings his coachman took him to Seymour Terrace straight
from the House of Commons, but if he had another engagement
he arrived at about midnight and remained there until the next
morning. Every night the coachman and the butler Bicknell waited
outside the house for him, ostensibly to guard the carriage and
horses while he made a brief visit. But they had instructions to leave
without him at around 2 a.m., so that anyone watching the house
would believe that William had gone home.[12]

Despite his pecuniary embarrassments, William ran two separate establishments with his customary extravagance. Skilfully
dividing his time between his wife and his mistress, he grew accomplished at juggling two women and keeping both of them happy.
Unsurprisingly, unpaid bills mounted up as William's financial
crisis deepened. The prospect of debtors' prison did not worry
him because MPs were exempt from prosecution for debts. He
remained desperate to borrow money, however, because nobody
would advance him any more credit, not even the tallow chandler
supplying his candles.[13] He was in such a sorry financial state he
could no longer afford to light his house. Naturally, his old friend
Douglas Kinnaird refused to help, teaching William another valuable lesson – when facing fiscal difficulties the last woman on earth
you should seduce is your banker's mistress!

Early the following year, events overtook William. On 29 January
1820, George III died and the Prince Regent was pronounced
George IV. A general election was legally required due to the death
of the old king, and a constitutional crisis seemed inevitable with
the nation in a state of panic following Peterloo. Still in real fear of
a French-style revolution, the governing classes became even more

anxious when secret agents uncovered a plot to overthrow the establishment. The Cato Street Conspirators were planning an uprising, supported by various trade societies spread throughout England. But first they intended to burst in on a Cabinet dinner, murder everybody present and carry away their heads on pikes. At the time, both Wellington and Mr Pole were in the Cabinet. When Wellington heard about the plot, he proposed that all guests at the dinner should be armed with pistols, so that they could ambush the would-be assassins. This was a high-risk strategy and, needless to say, his colleagues were unwilling, even though Wellington reassured them that he would draft in reinforcements, in the form of soldiers disguised as servants. Fortunately, a gunfight involving Cabinet ministers was not necessary as the conspiracy was exposed well in advance and the plotters were captured, though not without a skirmish in which a Bow Street Runner was stabbed to death. Although the ringleaders of the gang were subsequently tried and hanged, the feeling of unease persisted.

The Cato Street Conspiracy should have struck a chord with William, particularly as members of his close family were prime targets. However, he was more interested in his own affairs than the state of the nation. In order to remain immune from prosecution for debt, he needed to retain his seat in Parliament. Paul Methuen had stepped down as Knight of the Shire of Wiltshire, but when Mr Astley and Mr Benett came forward to stand for the county, William realized that he could not afford the cost of another election campaign. On 7 March 1820, he reluctantly tendered his resignation, citing his reason as 'indefinite expense'. Addressing the freeholders of Wiltshire, he declared, 'In these difficult times, the duty I owe to my tenantry and family will not permit me to risk the injury of their interests.'[14] Following William's withdrawal, Astley and Benett gained automatic election as MPs for Wiltshire because they were the only two candidates remaining.[15]

Catherine was aware that her husband owed money all over town because tradesmen had been calling at Wanstead House demanding payment. As she was not a party to any of these transactions, she had no way of knowing just how much he had spent.

William continued to reassure her because he felt confident that another parliamentary seat could be acquired for him relatively easily. But in the meantime, the moment he relinquished his seat in the House of Commons he was at risk of being sent to debtors' prison. Within two weeks of resigning as MP for Wiltshire, William received a reliable tip-off that he would be arrested within the hour. Forced to flee abroad in great haste, he did not have time to pack a bag, or even send a note to his wife. Instead, he hopped aboard the first available vessel sailing to France and cruised swiftly away down the Thames. As one review recorded, 'He was compelled to escape from his unsatisfied creditors in an open boat down the Thames, thereby adding one stain more to his already tarnished name by leaving his poor wife and three children to shift for themselves as best they might.'[16]

23. France

❦

Debonair as ever, destitute Brummell was waiting to welcome William when his boat docked in Calais. Arriving at Beau's lodgings, shivering uncontrollably, William pulled a chair up to the fire. His old friend quipped, 'Why Wellesley you appear cold! It must have been devilishly *hot* in England, or we should never have seen you here.'[1] For almost a decade the two men had been 'in habits of intimacy', and they conversed candidly as they strolled arm-in-arm through the port.[2] William moved into lodgings, hoping that it would be purely on a temporary basis as he intended to return to England as soon as a parliamentary seat could be found for him.

Calais in April was dull, dismal and desolate. There were no sights worth visiting; for most travellers the town was simply a place to pass through on their way to other destinations. William was accustomed to being part of a celebrity couple, attending lavish dinners and balls. He hated being alone in France with no society apart from his old friend. Impoverished, Brummell would have been living on the streets if some of his old friends had not rallied around. The Marquess of Worcester had come to his rescue, exerting influence to secure a position at the consulate at Caen. As a result, Brummell earned a small wage and relied on the generosity of anyone prepared to invite him to supper. A renowned wit and raconteur, the exiled leader of the dandies had formerly been one of the most sought-after dinner guests in London. William was shocked to witness his pitiful lifestyle first-hand.

Hardship and isolation gave William time to reflect; he did not want to end up alone like Brummell. William was determined to return to England as soon as possible; much to his own surprise, he discovered that he missed his wife and children dreadfully. Letters flew backwards and forwards across the Channel as he consulted with advisors endeavouring to draw up an agreement that would satisfy his creditors. Mr Lightfoot, one of his solicitors, travelled to Calais and William executed the Wanstead House Deed on 11 May 1820. Under the terms of the agreement, £30,000-worth of goods from Wanstead House was to be held by creditors as security for a period of two years. If debts were not repaid within this timescale, assets would be seized.[3] Forever the optimist, William felt confident that all his debts would be settled within six months, and the charge over the contents at Wanstead House lifted. In the meantime, as soon as agreement was reached with his creditors, William intended to return to England and resume his role as lord of the manor at Wanstead.

At the meeting of creditors, it transpired that thirty people were owed a total of £25,000, and they were all willing to sign the Wanstead House Deed. Only one person, Mr Timberlake, attended with an attorney and refused to sign the agreement. He subsequently went to court and obtained a judgement for £3,000. Outraged by the turn of events, William insisted that his debt to Timberlake was only £100, but he was unable to attend court to refute the claim. The unsatisfied judgement registered against him meant that he could not return home in the foreseeable future.

William had already set the wheels in motion to dispose of assets such as his horses, carriages and valuable timber from the estates. Now that he was stuck in France, he needed a trustee to handle his affairs in England. His reliable fixer Shawe was the obvious choice and William was relieved when he agreed to take on the task. Documents were signed giving Shawe the power to act for William. It would prove to be an onerous undertaking. Although William's situation was dire, he was unrealistic, refusing to accept the cutbacks Shawe suggested. On one occasion William insisted, 'the idea of *one* carriage and *one* man-servant is all nonsense'.[4]

Desperately homesick, William often stood on the ramparts at Calais gazing across the Channel at England. On clear days he could see the white cliffs of Dover and their proximity made him even more frustrated. His wife had promised to follow him to France, but she had already postponed her departure several times and it was becoming apparent that she was simply finding excuses not to join him. William was aware that Catherine had the means to live very comfortably on her own; she could stay at Wanstead or take the children to live with her mother and sisters at Draycot. He was at her mercy; without her financial support, he was completely destitute. Fearing that he had been abandoned, William sent her a heartfelt note from Calais pleading, 'the sooner you can come here the better'.[5]

Catherine was in no hurry to follow her husband to France after he had run up such extortionate liabilities – she decided to let him stew for a while. Catherine was not liable for his debts as the marriage settlement had been specifically drawn up to protect her assets. Rents were still coming in from the estates, and she was entitled to draw her pin money of £7,000, which would now be paid to her direct. Anxious to get his hands on her income, William counselled his wife, 'I took very good care in the instructions I had drawn up, to give Shawe and Forbes power to settle my affairs, not to touch the [£7,000] per annum, which is yours; and of course you will sign no document to give them such power.'[6]

William was also entitled to his share of rents from the estates, but he was so deeply in debt that his income was immediately swallowed up into a vast black hole. Nobody would have blamed Catherine if she had decided to let her wayward husband rot in Calais. Dejected, William continued to plead with her: 'I have received a most gloomy letter from Shawe upon the subject of my affairs. A hint is thrown out to me to leave my children, the boys, in England for six months; if the thing is proposed to you, I beg you will say I have the most decided objection to it, and never will assent to such folly. I may give up my property to pay my debts, but I will not give up my children.'[7]

Catherine was considering her options and she needed reassurances. Yearning to be reunited with his family, William promised to curb his spending and live within his means. Loyal as ever, it did not take Catherine very long to concede. It was not easy to relocate to another country with three young children in tow, but she was a capable woman and the arrangements were made swiftly. It would have been inappropriate for her to travel without a male escort so she was relieved when Bicknell agreed to accompany her. The loyal butler had the manners and bearing of a gentleman and his help on the journey was invaluable. With all the upheaval the children had to endure, Catherine did not want to separate them from all the people they held dear; she took their nursemaids along with a small entourage of her most trustworthy staff.

Relieved to see his wife, William took Catherine in his arms and declared that he had been desolate without her and the children. Making light of the situation, she reminded him that she had always longed to travel across Europe and was excited about the adventures that lay ahead. Catherine had planned meticulously, working out a tight budget that included accommodation, staff and carriage costs. She calculated that for a family of five to spend twelve months in France, the total cost would be £888 10s 4d.[8] Perhaps this estimate was unrealistic, but Catherine wanted to live as moderately as possible so that William's debts could be repaid quickly. If they managed to live on £1,000, she would have £6,000 left over to pay to creditors.

William had other ideas; he lived in the moment, and convinced his wife that they should make the most of their sojourn in France. Within days of Catherine arriving, armed with her chequebook, the family travelled to Paris and acquired rooms at the fashionable Hôtel d'Aument, near the Champs-Élysées. The hotel held all the genteel trappings required for the Long Wellesleys to launch into Parisian high society. Their elegant apartments included spacious drawing rooms and an intimate dining room. Stables behind the courtyard comfortably accommodated William's precious horses and carriages, which had been transported from England, along with his expensive clothing and other prized possessions. As soon as the family were unpacked, William set about hiring more staff, including a superb French cook, a housemaid, a groom and a coachman called John Randall. Although William was generous when lavishing money on himself, he was less inclined to consider the needs of his children. Catherine wanted to hire a tutor for the boys, but William assured her that it was an unnecessary expense as they would be back at home within the year.

Paris was Europe's foremost city of fashion and gastronomy and the English elite flocked there in droves after the Napoleonic Wars had ended. Many had established themselves in Paris in a similar fashion to the Long Wellesleys, including the Marquess of Bristol, Lord and Lady Jersey, Lords Rancliffe, Thanet, Kensington, Berkeley Craven, Campbell, Irvine and Thomas Moore, to name but a few.[9] Within days the Long Wellesleys became part of the social elite. Catherine was a popular, well-connected woman with many friends in Paris, including her distant cousin Lord John Russell (the famous Whig politician and reformer who would become prime minister in 1846). Invitations also arrived from the French royal family who were keen to honour Wellington's nephew and pay their respects to their former landlady from their years in exile at Wanstead House.

Alone in Calais, William had been miserable without his wife and the comforts she afforded him. Catherine's pin money paid for his luxurious accommodation, his magnificent thoroughbreds and his dazzling lifestyle. He appreciated that he was nothing without Catherine; his lucrative marriage gave him the status he craved. True to his word, William was extremely indulgent towards his wife. The couple dined out together every evening, meeting friends at smart hotels or attending assembly rooms for supper and dancing. Paris was wonderfully romantic and Catherine basked in the blissful glow of a second honeymoon. William seemed to have fallen in love with her all over again; he was attentive in company and ardent in private. Before entering her bedchamber for a night of passion, he always gave her a signal by tapping his signature tattoo on her door, as if to announce the arrival of an important guest. Catherine had not seen much of her husband in the previous two years as he had been busy with elections and parliamentary duties and, though she did not know it, Mrs Kinnaird. She loved being with William every day and nestling in his arms every night.

Catherine's sweet, natural, engaging nature always drew people to her. Making friends easily, she quickly became part of a set of fashionable ladies who took afternoon tea together. Her constant companion was the cultured Englishwoman Countess Montalembert. The ladies often drove out together, along the Champs-Élysées, a wide tree-lined boulevard with lawns and ornamental gardens on each side. The beau monde paraded there every afternoon during the summer, just as they did during fashionable hour in Hyde Park. William tended to take his ride at the same time each day, hoping to glimpse his wife while she was out driving in her small open barouche. Whenever they met, it was always with delight and pleasure. They would both stop to chat, and then William would kiss his wife's hand extravagantly before she drove on. 'Your husband is most attentive,' commented the Countess of Montalembert one afternoon, as she studied her friend's rosy glow.

Smiling broadly, Catherine replied, 'I have never been happier in my entire life.'[10]

William also felt liberated; life in Paris was like a long holiday. With a team of experts managing his estates and no parliamentary responsibilities, he could indulge himself even more than usual, hunting during the day and revelling with friends every evening. His Paris set comprised many political figures, including Whigs, Liberals, Reformers and red-hot Tories. Discussions often became heated as the gentlemen debated the Corn Laws and other important issues over a glass of fine French wine. Most evenings, after Catherine had retired for the night, William went on to clubs for port, cigars and animated conversation. On these occasions, his frequent companion was Thomas Moore, the entertaining Irish poet, singer and songwriter. Lyrical Tom Moore, who was the same age as William, had earned a fortune from his popular ballads and writing. His extravagant lifestyle resulted in huge debts, and he was forced to flee England in 1819. As a good friend of Lord Byron, Moore shared the poet's opinion that William was a fool. However, he also found the Long Pole extremely amusing, appreciating his droll humour and endless supply of ridiculous anecdotes. The two gentlemen often stayed up until the early hours drinking, telling bawdy jokes or singing Irish ballads. On other nights, left to his own devices, William would slip away to pass a few pleasant hours in a brothel.[11]

The lively Paris set was always arranging parties and a big celebration was planned for St Patrick's Day. There was some debate about who should take the chair for the evening, with entertaining Tom Moore being the popular choice, although William held forth insisting that he deserved the honour. Lord Charlemont, who was proud of his Irish heritage, was quick to point out, 'Mr Long Wellesley is an Englishman born and bred. Surely an Irishman should have the Chair on this occasion.' Everyone agreed, and Moore was duly elected.[12] On 17 March, sixty people sat down to a sumptuous dinner at Cadran Bleu and Tom Moore performed folk songs and ballads as guests joined in. William stood at the head of the table, jigging and singing along at the top of his voice, prompting Moore to comment that it was impressive that an Englishman should know so many Irish songs. Taking the jibe with good grace, William faced his audience and took a bow. Despite all the hilarity, the evening ended badly and Tom Moore recorded in his diary, 'About six or seven drunken fools (Long Wellesley at their head) remained after the party broke up and disgraced it by quarrelling among themselves, which made it necessary to call in the *Gens-d'armes*.'[13] Clearly, William's days as a hellraiser were not over.

William convinced himself that everything would be resolved satisfactorily. Distanced from the reality of his problems, he put his credit crisis to the back of his mind and continued to be the life and soul of the party, revelling in the company of his friends until the early hours. Just a few days after Napoleon died in May 1821, a new yarn was doing the rounds. Lingering over port one evening, William and his friends were amused by the story. When news of Bonaparte's death reached England, Sir Edward Neagle was sent immediately to inform King George. He hurried in, bowed low and announced, 'I have the pleasure to tell Your Majesty that your bitterest enemy is dead.'

'No – is she, by Gad!' said the king. 'My wife is dead?'

Neagle cringed. 'Queen Caroline is quite well, Your Majesty. Napoleon is dead.'[14]

Catherine enjoyed sharing the many pleasures of Paris with her children. The family apartments were in the centre of town, so she often took them out for walks past the fashionable shops. Victoria had grown chubby due to her love of French patisseries. She insisted on going out every morning so that she could press her face up against the window of the local cake shop and choose from the mouth-watering array of chocolate éclairs, oozing fresh cream slices or round tarts bursting with fresh strawberries. Sometimes Catherine would sit drinking coffee while Victoria devoured her cake in a cafe. On other occasions, the patisserie was placed reverentially in a small white box and tied with a thin red ribbon to take away.

Like a true Englishwoman abroad, Catherine craved small luxuries from home, including Harvey's brown sauce, English cheese and tongue, and Windsor soap. British produce was available in Paris, plus her sisters regularly sent parcels containing her favourite food. Catherine ensured that Bicknell kept a book of household accounts, in which he meticulously listed daily expenses:[15]

		Francs	Sous
23 May	Mending a parasol for Mrs L.W.	2	10
	Paid for black and red sealing-wax	4	10
	Gave the young gentlemen	10	0
	Paid a locksmith	6	0
	Paid for English cheese	10	10
	Paid a bottle of Harvey's Sauce	6	0
	Paid for an umbrella for Mr L.W.	23	0
	Paid a bottle of red ink	2	0
	Paid for mending Mrs L. W.'s watch	5	0
	Paid for a Cabriolet & Fiacre for Mr L. W.	7	10

	Paid for common paper & visiting cards	5	0
	Paid for writing paper	8	0
	Paid for Windsor and common soap	6	10
	Paid 2 pair of galoshes for the young men	11	10
27 May	Paid for postage of a letter for Mrs L. W.	2	12
	Gave Mrs L. W.	8	0
	Paid for shoe brushes	4	10
	Paid for ivory counters	3	10
	Paid for cheese	2	10
	Paid for a silk handkerchief Mrs L. W.	7	0
	Paid for a parasol for Mrs L. W.	24	0
	Paid for a cake & sweetmeats for Miss	10	0
	Paid for a ribbon for Miss	10	0
	Frs	176	2

Conscious of expenditure, Catherine accounted for every franc and tried to keep a tight rein on finances. The Long Wellesleys still enjoyed luxuries such as horses and carriages, good food and wine, but on a less ostentatious scale. Living at Wanstead House had incurred enormous costs: the lavish parties, the stables and hounds, the heating and lighting, plus the numerous staff that tended the grounds and house. Residing in a rented apartment in Paris was cheap by comparison, particularly as they did not keep many servants, or entertain extravagantly at home. This meant that the family could live very comfortably on her income of £7,000, which arrived from England in quarterly instalments of £1,750.

Catherine had always been sensible about money. Although she had spent freely on her coming-of-age celebrations and on her wedding outfit, her expenditure had always been within her means. In contrast, William had run through the £300,000 in her bank account in around two years, and then continued to spend copiously. His extravagance was now curtailed. Nobody would extend him credit, so he had no choice but to survive on Catherine's income. Unfortunately, however, the damage had already been done.

24. Riches of Ages

❧

1821

Back in England, a team of experts had been working tirelessly for more than a year to resolve William's financial problems. Mr Blake, his attorney, audited the estates; Mr Yerbury collected overdue rents; Colonel Merrick Shawe, Colonel Forbes and Mr Wright did their utmost to dispose of assets. Despite these combined efforts, there had been little progress because the country was submerged in deep recession. Everyone was flat broke. Fixer Shawe was trying to broker various deals, including the sale of timber from the estates. On 22 December 1820, he had written to enlighten William on the distressed state of the market: 'Mr Tomlins called on me here, and he makes a favourable report for the negotiations for the public houses. He thinks he shall get £1,800 for the Green Man and has some hope that the houses may altogether yield £5,000.'[1]

William's thoroughbreds were an endless source of pride and joy, so it must have been a wrench to have to part with them. One week later, Shawe reported, 'Watts is in despair about the horses. There is no one in town and there is no cash in the country. He has only been offered £200 for the two and there is no chance upon a better market until after Christmas.'[2]

More bad news followed from William's friend Fitzroy Stanhope. Writing from London, he advised:

The carriages, horses and hounds are not arrived. I fear I shall have more difficulty in disposing of them than you are aware of, as there is no one in London, I never saw it half so empty in my life; there were only three horses sold at Tattershall's last Monday. Horses are about half the price they were two years since.[3]

Extravagance had undoubtedly played a major role in William's downfall, but some of his debt was due to circumstances beyond his control, including the fact that Catherine's estates had been neglected throughout her minority. As a result, significant sums were needed for improvements, and William had raised mortgages to invest in new machinery, mills and land drainage. Unfortunately, he did not have the money or the resolve to finish the works, which meant that productivity on his estates was low. With everyone struggling, many of William's tenants defaulted and his rent roll for the previous year was £4,220 13s 10d in arrears. His attorney informed him that he would never recover the bulk of this money. Cash flow was a huge problem; with his rental income diminished, William could not meet the interest payments due on his loans.

On 17 November 1820, an insolvency notice appeared in *The Times*:

All persons having any CLAIM or DEMAND on
WILLIAM POLE TYLNEY LONG WELLESLEY,
of Wanstead-House, in the County of Essex, esq.,
are requested to send the particulars thereof to
Messrs Robson, Lightfoot and Robson,
Castle Street, Leicester Square,
on or before 1 January next.

William was officially declared bankrupt. Following the announcement, more creditors came forward with claims. By early 1821, the charge over the contents at Wanstead House had risen from £30,000 to £60,000. The attorney, Mr Blake, kept William fully apprised of all these developments. Writing on 21 February 1821, Blake also supplied William with a breakdown of his assets and liabilities, which revealed the extent of his debts:[4]

Annual Income	£
Annual rent roll and composite tithes	36,420
Profit from manors and woodlands	2,000
Dividends on stock	333
Minus annual charges payable (incl. Mrs Wellesley's pin money)	(31,397)
Rents written-off (bad debts)	(3,256)
Considering the state of the times, the surplus to be reckoned upon	CR 4,100

Floating Debt	
Amount of debts claimed by creditors prior to notice in papers	29,210
Amount of bills delivered since notice in papers	27,847
Legal fees	648
Total due on simple contracts, including the law Bill, appears to be	57,705
Plus your bond to Messrs Goslings amounting to	12,300
TOTAL	DR £70,005

This was not pleasant reading for William. With his estates mortgaged to the hilt, his annual income just about covered his repayments and outgoings. Aside from these loans, he had accumulated an enormous debt of £70,000. Under the terms of the Wanstead Agreement, William's creditors had granted him two years in which to repay his debts. The period of grace had almost expired and William's representatives had been unable to raise the money because the amount owing was simply too vast. Drastic measures were needed. William realized there was no other option: the contents of Wanstead House would have to be sold at auction.

Naturally, Catherine was heartbroken to learn that all her precious family heirlooms would be sold off to the highest bidders. Nothing could be done; William had spent all her money, as well as his own. William could not evade her questions any longer because his bankruptcy was now a matter of public record, with a full statement of his affairs available. Nevertheless, he continued to deny the extent of his debts, telling his wife that the figures were hugely inflated because incorrect demands had been lodged against him. This may well have been true; creditors could have easily lumped up their bills, knowing that Mr Long Wellesley had no way of disproving their claims. As usual, Catherine chose to believe her husband, although it did not make the situation any less painful for her.

Announcements first appeared in the newspapers early in May: 'Auction Notice – Advertising first sale at Wanstead House, commencing 10 June for thirty-one days. Five shillings for a catalogue, which will admit three to view.'[5]

Throughout the summer of 1822, London was buzzing with gossip about the auction. The *Literary Chronicle* reported:

> The last 'nine days' wonder of the good people of the British metropolis has been the view of Wanstead House, with its magnificent furniture, gobelin tapestry, collection of paintings, etc., all of which are to be disposed of by the magic hammer of Mr Robins, of Regent Street, in the course of the ensuing six weeks.[6]

Scandal sold newspapers and the press were quick to capitalize. Capturing the public mood, reporters used emotive language to create a feeling of melancholy. The *Manchester Iris* lamented:

> We are at a loss for words to express our feelings on the sale of this mansion, and of its magnificent furniture. Indignation, pity, and astonishment, by turns take possession of our breasts . . . In no country in the world are fortunes made and unmade – won and lost – in so sudden and surprising a manner as our own.[7]

Catherine's predicament held a pitiful fascination for the public. Having followed her story for more than a decade, participating in the excitement of her courtship and early married life, they now shared her sense of loss. Caught up in the unfolding melodrama, people flocked to Wanstead House in droves to view the splendid contents and witness the tragic scene first-hand. With the doors thrown open to anyone who could pay the admittance fee, Wanstead became 'the most attractive resort of the fashionable world who deserted the west end of the town in shoals, and made Whitechapel more travelled than Whitehall'.[8] Princess Augusta, the Duchess of Gloucester and the Prince and Princess of Denmark were among the thousands who thronged the house, rubbing shoulders with all manner of lowly individuals. Editors of the *Literary Chronicle* were among those who 'could not resist the curiosity of mixing for once with the nobles and genteels at Wanstead House . . . taking the bird's eye view of everything'.[9]

Poignant caricatures appeared in print-shop windows capturing the public excitement mixed with empathy for all Catherine had lost.[10] An eyewitness report published in the *Literary Chronicle* continued in the same vein:

> No public sale ever perhaps excited so much interest as this, not merely on account of its magnitude, the splendour of the furniture, or the grandeur of the mansion; but there was a sort of melancholy feeling attending it, in recollecting this was part of the princely fortune of an English heiress, Miss Tylney Long, whose husband has, in some dozen years only, dissipated the accumulated riches of ages, without dignity, and sunk into comparative poverty, without pity.[11]

Gaining momentum, other newspapers continued in a melodramatic vein: 'The gifts of Sovereigns, and of the illustrious in arts, arms, dignity . . . even the last lingering bottle of what is costly or common in the cellars, are ALL to be swept away, under the hammer of the auctioneer.'[12]

Back at Draycot House in Wiltshire, Catherine's mother and sisters shrank from the public scandal, while lamenting the fact that family heirlooms, exhibits and treasures gathered so lovingly over several generations would all be lost. Before the sale, Dora and Emma approached Merrick Shawe with a list of items they would like to purchase at the auction. They asked him to speak to Mr Robins, the auctioneer, to ensure that all the family portraits were secured for them. William Hogarth's painting *Assembly at Wanstead House*, showing their ancestors gathered together in the Salon, was a priority. Nothing much escaped the attention of Merrick Shawe; he had already made arrangements. Writing to William, Shawe confirmed,

> We went over [Wanstead House] with old Molly who pointed out the family portraits. It would be wrong to suffer one of them to be sold, and they would not fetch anything worth considering... I dare say it will not make £100 difference, and you would be fairly blamed for letting them go.[13]

Lady Catherine was less concerned about worldly goods. She had been in poor health for some time and the continual stress of it all was hampering her recovery. Dora and Emma fussed over their mother, coaxing her to take a little food or drink, but they could do little to ease the upset. Lady Catherine had had misgivings about William from the start, but even she could never have anticipated just how badly it would all turn out. She could not help reflecting on how things might have been. By now George IV was in poor health, and there was a strong possibility that the Duke of Clarence would be the next king. If her daughter had married him, her eldest grandson would be an heir to the throne of England. Instead, the entire family were holed up in exile like criminals. In addition, Lady Catherine had heard reports that her grandchildren never went to church and that they were wild and untutored. Sick with worry, she confided in Dora that she suffered 'painful anxiety [regarding their] education as Christians . . . and a horror of them being brought up without principles'.[14]

Lady Catherine had been estranged from her daughter and grandchildren for many years, when William had refused to allow them to visit. Now broken-hearted, she missed them all terribly and feared she would never see them again.

*

The months leading up to the Wanstead sale were extremely stressful for the Long Wellesleys. Catherine was distraught at the thought of all her treasured family heirlooms going under the hammer. Hypocrisy was rife among the expatriates in Paris; although many of her acquaintances feigned sympathy to her face, she knew they secretly delighted in her misfortune. Unable to face the humiliation, the family retreated to Calais. Scouring the English newspapers, Catherine was upset by all the bad publicity. News of the scandal reached as far as the USA, where New York newspapers were unsympathetic, putting the saga into perspective by pointing out that Catherine was still earning more than the president of the United States. Their report drips irony:

> A gentleman by the name of [Long Wellesley] ... has unfortunately been so simple as to lose at sport the trifling estate of £60,000 per annum . . . Still more distressing, he has been obliged to retire to Paris, to struggle for a livelihood, on his wife's miserable jointure of £7,000 or $31,000 per annum – not above 6,000 dollars more than our President receives.[15]

The Long Wellesley family lived quietly in Calais for five months, where they moved into Dessin's Hotel, situated just off the Place d'Armes. It was a fairly smart establishment where guests were offered many pleasant diversions such as a large courtyard with gardens, commodious baths, a small theatre and a good restaurant.[16] Nevertheless, it was a comedown from their customary splendour; their lifestyle was modest compared with Paris, which meant they were able to economize and let go of most of their French staff. Shut away from high society, with no dinners to arrange or servants to supervise, Catherine enjoyed a type of simple freedom she had never known before. Spending quality time with her husband and children was a nice change from Paris; they provided pleasant distraction from the scandal back in England. Dining with them most evenings, Brummell observed that the couple lived together in 'great harmony and happiness'.[17] William's attitude towards his wife was 'attentive and indulgent'; most afternoons the couple strolled out arm-in-arm along the seafront promenade and Catherine said she was pleased to have 'so much of his society'.[18]

But Calais was too desolate for William; he was urbane, preferring to run with a smart set in a metropolis such as London or Paris. Forced to seek out new diversions, he discovered a novel pastime that was enjoyable and rewarding. William started to devote some time to his children – Will was nine years old, James seven and Victoria three. They all adored their father and were delighted to receive some attention from him. Children of landed gentry often had ponies when they were four or five years old, so that they could gallop about their estate. William was an accomplished horseman, but he had neglected to teach his boys to ride. Will and James were touchingly grateful as their father placed them on suitably docile mounts and led them slowly around the stable yard. As the boys grew more confident, they cantered out into soft open fields and learned how to jump over small obstacles. Wiry James was a fearless, natural sportsman like his father. In contrast, Will was a slow-witted, nervous child who struggled to keep up with his daring younger brother. Despite her angelic appearance, Victoria was a spirited toddler and she threw tantrums when she was not permitted to go out riding with her brothers. William did not have much time for his daughter and he was prone to reprimanding her for telling lies. Some years later he would instruct her tutor, 'of all things root out from her mind that proneness to dissimulation I have discovered in her – the curse of women'.[19]

The coachman Randall was one of the staff that remained, driving the family on their days out. Despite everything that was happening in England, Catherine counted her blessings as she watched her children laughing while they splashed about in streams or chased around. In an age when childhood mortality was common, she had seen many of her friends suffer sorely from bereavement, and she recognized that their loss was far greater than her own. Bricks and mortar could be replaced, and she had several other grand mansions at her disposal including Tylney Hall and Seagry House. Pragmatic as ever, Catherine insisted that she had no reason to complain while she had three healthy children.

Although Catherine remained relatively content in Calais, William was becoming bored of playing happy families. After his wife was safely tucked up in bed every night, he went out in search of excitement and found it in the arms of another woman. For the sake of convenience, William kept his latest conquest in lodgings nearby, in Rue Royale, paying for her rooms and board with his wife's pin money.[20] On nights when he visited his paramour, he took along a servant from his hotel to wait outside with his horses and carriage. He never prevailed upon Bicknell, however, because it was clear that the butler was devoted to Catherine and tired of being complicit in schemes to deceive her. For this reason, William wanted to dismiss the butler, but Catherine would not hear of it. Having left all her family and friends behind in England, Bicknell was one of the few people she felt able to rely on and trust; she could not part with him. It was rare for William to concede, but on this occasion he relented, perhaps because he knew his sordid secrets were safe. Although Bicknell's loyalty lay firmly with Catherine, the honourable butler would never hurt her by enlightening her with the truth.

William could not use Bicknell, and he did not trust the coachman Randall sufficiently to make him party to his secrets. Instead, William hired an amenable Anglo-Irish valet called John Meara to attend exclusively to his needs.[21] Around the same time, he moved his mistress into a hotel on the same street as his own, which enabled him to dispense with the bother of taking his carriage, thus facilitating his nocturnal wanderings.[22] William was taking huge risks, but he enjoyed living dangerously.

Throughout his time in Calais, William was in constant touch with his advisors. The auction was a painful process, but he fully expected that the proceeds would be sufficient to clear all his debts, which would be a huge relief. Having spent more than two years in exile, William was desperate to return to England. He planned to get on a boat as soon as the auction was over.

25. Sale of the Century

❧

JUNE 1822

The auctioneer appointed to the Wanstead sale was Mr George Robins of Regent Street, a swaggering forty-five-year-old cockney whose guttural vowels made him sound like an East End market trader.[1] This did not deter his fondness for flowery language, and his flamboyance on the rostrum made him a target for society wits.[2] The commission at Wanstead was so high profile, it would make him famous. It took Robins several months to catalogue all the splendid contents in the vast house and various specialists were called in to assess the library and wine cellars.[3] There was such an abundance of sculpture, tapestry, furniture and artwork that the auction would last for thirty-one days.[4]

Newspapers reported that many items were 'worthy of attention in this extraordinary sale, the mere inventory of which fills a catalogue of four hundred quarto pages, which is published in three parts of five shillings each.'[5] Bursting with superlatives, Robins used extravagant language to tantalize buyers with flowery descriptions. Everything was 'magnificent . . . superb . . . splendid . . . costly antique Buhl . . . ornately carved with Cupid Figures . . . inlaid with ivory and valuable gems'. Desirable items included sofas and pier tables designed by William Kent, plus some truly magnificent pieces of antique French buhl.

Thirty thousand people attended the first day of the auction on 10 June 1822. The swarming crowd had to be controlled by policemen and media interest was intense. One newspaper recorded: 'The out-houses are furnished with refreshments of every description, and the place has the appearance of a country fair. Numbers lately were disappointed from seeing the celebrated Grotto, as several persons that were permitted to view it . . . conveyed away fragments and did considerable mischief.'[6]

By the end of the first day, the contents of four bedchambers plus the Green Damask Velvet Sitting Room had been sold. One hundred and sixty-five lots raised a total of £656 13s. Over the following days, contents continued to be sold, room by room. The splendid Genoa velvet window curtains, bordered with costly gold lace and silk tassels, sold at around £45 a pair; sumptuous Grecian scroll-back and end sofas fetched somewhere between £50 to £100; silk Axminster carpets, bordered with the family crest and arms, raised between £30 to £55, depending on the size.

Corresponding regularly, Merrick Shawe kept William apprised of events. Shawe wrote:

> I went to Wanstead on Friday last but the crowd was so great that I could do nothing but give some directions for the security of the property in the house and also to protect the gardens and grotto from damage . . . we were obliged to apply for ten more police men in addition to the nine already there. Mr Bertram, Robins' man, assured me there were 30,000 to view the house on Saturday.[7]

At this stage, even saintly Shawe was losing patience. Having worked tirelessly for over two years, he was growing tired of William's unrealistic demands and expectations. He finished his letter on an unusually harsh note, saying:

> I wish you were here for a variety of reasons. The real pressure of affairs here would soon reduce your ideas within a moderate compass. All your notions, believe me, want paring down as much as ever. When you look at your means and your rental, etc., you look through a magnifying glass. When you look at the probable expense you look through a microscope. Now, your affairs require that you should do exactly the reverse.[8]

*

Paintings and sculptures were sold on the eighth, ninth and tenth days of the auction. It was no secret that the sixth Duke of Devonshire had always coveted the bronze statues recovered from Herculaneum, which stood in the Great Hall at Wanstead House. His agent, George Spencer Ridgeway, appeared with strict instructions to acquire specific items irrespective of the cost. The duke purchased a number of lots to adorn his residence at Chatsworth House, paying just £231 for the three ancient sculptures, a fraction of their actual worth. However, he paid handsomely for the two chandeliers that illuminated Kent's painted ceiling in the Great Hall. Described in the sale catalogue as 'magnificently carved, richly gilt and surmounted by a superb spread eagle destroying a snake', they sold for a total of £593 5s.

The contents of the Grand Salon were auctioned on the sixteenth day of the sale. The famous oriental ebony chairs, once owned by Elizabeth I, splendidly carved and inlaid with ivory, sold for between £31 and £38 a pair. They were 'knocked down at an enormous price. Graham of Waterloo Place, was the purchaser'.[9]

On the seventeenth day, the tasteful furniture in William's dressing room and study was up for grabs. His treasured rosewood and buhl library table fetched £93 9s; the ten-foot-tall rosewood bookcase, £52 10s; the flamboyant purple morocco sofa and chairs, £49 7s; his set of nine handsomely cut scent bottles, £1 11s; and his cherished marble and copper bath, £31 10s.

By the end of the third week, prices were dwindling miserably. Bargains were there for the taking, as the contents of Catherine's magnificent Blue Damask State Bedchamber went up for auction. Incredibly, the splendid antique French buhl Parisian armoire, inlaid with elaborate gilt and tortoiseshell mouldings and friezes, of arabesque design, raised just £19 19s.[10]

The cavernous wine cellars at Wanstead House were renowned and huge crowds reappeared on the twenty-sixth day to purchase the rare and fine wines. There was an abundance of stock, with hundreds of crates of Madeira, claret and port stacked from floor to ceiling. Each lot comprised three dozen bottles. Three cases of Superior Old Claret could be purchased for around £17; Old East

India Madeira sold for around £16; Curious Old Sherry fetched around £13. Wooden barrels filled with Old East Indian Madeira raised £130 each. The takings at the end of the day were an astounding £2,642 15s 6d.

Many of the heirlooms that held huge sentimental value for Catherine were sold for a pittance. The ancient sculptures went for the price of dinner at Grillion's; her precious buhl armoire was sold for the handful of gold sovereigns that William had scattered so liberally in the dust. The chandeliers with the family crest would now be displayed at Chatsworth House. The Earl of Pembroke had snapped up carpets and curtains for Wilton House, along with a set of William Kent sofas ornately carved with mermaids and seashells. Various items would go to Leeds Castle in Kent. Naturally, this was heart-breaking for the Tylney Long family, but William had the opportunity to make one small gesture by saving the family portraits, which held great sentimental value for Dora and Emma. These were the only items the sisters wanted and, as Merrick Shawe had pointed out, they were of no real worth to anyone outside the family. Rather than granting their wish, William instructed the auctioneer to withdraw the portraits from the sale, claiming that he would purchase them himself, as a gift for Catherine. True to form, however, he never actually got round to settling up with Robins. As a result, the paintings were put into storage and many of them went missing as the years went by. After Robins's death, they formed part of his estate and were eventually sold at auction in 1852. The portrait of Catherine painted by Alfred Edward Chalon on her coming of age was never recovered.

From William's point of view, the auction was a complete catastrophe because it took place at the worst possible time, when the country was in a deep recession and the market at its most depressed. The splendid contents of Wanstead were sold for a fraction of their value and worth. The sale raised a total of just £32,395 6s 6d, around half the amount William needed to repay his creditors. It would later come to light that the huge shortfall was in part due to underhand dealings by the crafty cockney auctioneer. Robins would become renowned for using every trick of the trade, drafting in 'well-placed accomplices or winking at dealers' rings which, while they defrauded the vendor, increased the auctioneer's business'.[11] Merrick Shawe had been wary, warning William,

> I do not like your plan of making Robins take £10,000 worth. Who is to pay the £500 interest? Your estate cannot pay, and you are adding a heavy weight to your encumbrances. The £6,000 agreed to by Mr Robins is too much if it can be avoided.[12]

It appeared that Robins had set his commission at a flat rate of somewhere between £6,000 and £10,000. If William had had any business acumen whatsoever, he should have paid the auctioneer a percentage of the sale value, as this would have given Robins an incentive to achieve the highest possible price. Instead, Robins sold off contents well below value to his own friends and associates – while squirrelling away items under the counter for himself.

In another masterstroke, Robins shrewdly kept all the money collected on the door – five shillings for a catalogue, which admitted three to view. This added up to a huge amount considering the crowds that flocked to Wanstead daily, over a period of two months. Even before the sale began, 20,000 copies of the catalogue were sold to people attending the viewings. Newspapers reported, 'We really envy Mr Robins the honour of being the author of a work of which twenty thousand copies have been sold, even though under the humble title of an auctioneer's catalogue.'[13] Added to this, 30,000 people attended the first day of the auction, plus thousands more over the following weeks. Taking everything into account, Robins would have earned around £10,000 simply from the sale of his catalogues. With all his dodgy dealings, Robins probably earned almost as much money from the auction as William did. If William had been more astute, the auction would not have been so calamitous for him. Still deeply in debt, he would have to remain in exile for the foreseeable future. Very little had been gained, despite all the heartache and loss.

26. Crisis at Calais

William was desperate to return to England, but this was not prudent while he was still so deeply in debt, as he would probably be arrested and thrown into debtors' prison. Catherine, however, was free to go home and she longed to visit her mother, who was seriously ill. She also had the welfare of her children to consider; although William had employed numerous staff to attend to his every comfort, he still had not bothered to hire a tutor for the boys. By law, men had ultimate control and Catherine held little sway over the education and upbringing of her own children. Despite her numerous entreaties, William had totally neglected the boys' schooling, insisting that mucking-out the stables was character-building. Although Will and James were nine and seven, they could barely read or write. Beau Brummell was among those who were shocked by the children's behaviour. The boys were like feral creatures, wild, uneducated and always filthy from the stables. Even the angelic Victoria had learned obscene language from the grooms, and she frequently uttered the most coarse and vulgar oaths in French. Whenever her brothers annoyed her, the tiny three-year-old would hiss, 'God damn you,' or 'Damn both your eyes.'[1]

One evening over dinner, Brummell was unusually tactful when he broached the subject with William, suggesting that Will and James should be mixing with genteel boys of their own age, rather than rough stable lads. Catherine agreed that the boys would benefit from a formal education and she suggested that she should take them back to England to get them settled in school. Speaking wistfully, she told William that the trip would also give her the opportunity to visit her family after an absence of over two years. This was not an unreasonable request, especially in light of everything Catherine had been through; it was natural for her to want to see her mother. William would not hear of it; he was afraid that if his wife left France with the children, she might be tempted to remain in England and abandon him.

With his exile abroad now prolonged indefinitely, William delegated yet another task to faithful Shawe, asking him to find a tutor for the boys. Having neglected the children's education thus far, William was characteristically deluded when he wrote to Shawe, gushing, 'I feel more alive to the good education of my children than I do to any other circumstances of my life.'[2]

Mr Pitman came with such glowing references and qualifications, William wrote and urged for him to be sent over as soon as possible:

> My Dear Shawe, your account of Mr Pitman . . . is so satisfactory I beg you to see him immediately, and make with him the following arrangement. That he shall live in my family, have a separate table for the two boys and himself, and his salary of £250 per annum . . . You must explain to him that they are young, wild, and quite uneducated; they know nothing, but I believe they have imbibed no ill principles.[3]

John Pitman was a kindly, spare, nervous man with grey hair and spectacles. Within days of taking up his post, he was already wary of his employer, Mr Long Wellesley, who could be charming in one instant and volatile the next. The tutor had been warned that the children were uneducated, but he was still appalled by their behaviour. Pitman was particularly 'surprised and shocked on hearing the boys use some very disgusting expressions . . . and vulgar oaths in French. When he reproved them, young Will told him that his father . . . liked it, and had always allowed him to do so.'[4] It seemed that Mr Wellesley believed it was 'manly' to educate his sons in the ways of the world and he fully intended to take his sons along to 'bull-baits, dog-fights, cock-fights and all other manly sports.'[5]

Although Mr Pitman was tempted to give up his position and return to England, the children had many endearing qualities and he grew attached to them very quickly. The younger boy, James, was a lot like his father: charming, athletic and completely wild. The older boy, Will, was slower and easily led astray by his forceful younger brother. Will was given to violent rages, but was always tearful and contrite afterwards, cuddling up to his tutor for comfort. The dedicated gentleman stayed because he felt he had a duty to them. Pitman believed that if he walked out at this delicate point in their development, they might become totally irredeemable.

As always, William's parents were supportive and they travelled to Calais immediately after the auction to console their son. By now, plain old Mr Pole had gained recognition for his achievements as Master of the Mint, and he was raised to the peerage in July 1821. He now deservedly held a title – Baron Maryborough.

Lord and Lady Maryborough were perfect role models. With a marriage that would span a period of sixty-two years, they were steady, reliable people, devoted to each other and their children. Unfortunately, William had never listened to their advice; he was reckless and headstrong from a young age, ignoring his father's many warnings about extravagance. This had already resulted in one exile when, aged sixteen, William had been sent on diplomatic postings to avoid prosecution for debts. At the time, his father explained the difficulties he experienced providing for William's expenses, pleading with him, 'I hope you will . . . confine your ideas and your expenses within the just bounds of propriety.'[6]

Despite this, William had continued to spend lavishly, particularly when he was working at the embassy in Constantinople, buying expensive gifts to impress people. His father had written affectionately and tactfully:

> It is with extreme pain that I am forced to place any limits to the natural generosity of your temper, which I will not call extravagance for I am sure it deserves a better name . . . You are very kind to think of sending presents to me and your Mother. But we beg you will not put yourself to one farthing expense on our accounts . . . The best present you can make us is such

a testimony of your good conduct and advancement as we have lately received ... all we wish for is a continuance of your celebrity.[7]

Ironically, William had declared war on Turkey shortly after this letter was written. Nevertheless, Lord and Lady Maryborough had continued to cajole and compliment their son to keep him on side, but William did not learn. Fifteen years on, he found himself in the same predicament, stranded abroad in order to avoid debtors' prison.

Prior to the auction, William had not asked his parents for help or advice, possibly because he was too proud. At this point, however, Lord Maryborough rallied in support, stepping in to try to obtain a mortgage against his own estate in Ballyfin. Unfortunately, Lord Maryborough was unable to raise any money, because the recession had drastically reduced the value of his land in Ireland. Master of the Mint for nine years, Lord Maryborough was renowned for his financial acumen, and he became one of the four trustees appointed to resolve William's affairs in England. William genuinely believed that his shrewd father would be able to work miracles and get him home within one year. However, on 16 August 1822, Lord Maryborough wrote to him with bad news: 'Upon the most painful examination of every document ... [the trustees] are unanimous in our opinion that there is not the most faint hope of effecting anything essential for you in a lesser period than *five years*.'[8]

William was devastated to learn that he would not be able to return to England for such a long period of time. His father also added, 'I hope you will seriously consider the absolute necessity of the strictest economy.'[9] For William, this sermon was an unwelcome reprise of his youth.

By now both William and Catherine had grown tired of France and they were desperate to move on. Naples seemed like a good option, particularly as Catherine had always longed to go on a Grand Tour of Italy, taking in the sights and the architecture. Before setting off on such a long trip, however, she would have appreciated the opportunity to cross the Channel to visit her sick mother. A more benevolent man may have relented, but William insisted they set off immediately, maintaining that they needed to cross the Alps before it snowed. On 16 September 1822, they left for Naples in a blaze of style and ceremony. A parade of equipages conveyed the family, their luggage and their servants. Their entourage included Henry Bicknell the butler, John Meara the valet and Mr Pitman the tutor. Streaming banners of Wellesley blue fluttered from all the carriage windows, with coachmen kitted out in matching liveries. The Long Wellesleys were embarking on a new adventure that would prove to be even more shocking than the last.

PART THREE

EXILE

'Mr and Mrs Long Wellesley, who were the charm of
every party in Naples, have left for Paris.'

Morning Chronicle, December 1823

27. Naples

❦

Nestling beside volcanic Mount Vesuvius, Naples overlooks a picturesque bay with golden beaches and azure waters. But the Long Wellesleys did not have the opportunity to enjoy the enchanting scenery as the weather was bitterly cold when they arrived. Paying little heed to Lord Maryborough's plea for strict economy, William rented a splendid suite of rooms at the Cappella Vecchia in Piazza dei Martiri, one of the most elegant locations in the town. Many English high rollers lived in Naples at the time, so naturally William wanted to set himself up in style. He hired cooks, maids, grooms and a family physician called Dr Thomas Bulkeley. The doctor was a tall, stout, well-groomed gentleman, who sported a jet-black beard styled with a sharp point at the end. His devilish appearance was deceiving – he was a mild, courteous, amiable man.[1] During the Peninsular War he had served as surgeon to the 9th Regiment, where he became renowned for his humanity, often rushing forward in battle to assist the wounded at great personal risk.[2]

The Long Wellesley family kept the good doctor busy. Young Will had contracted a severe chest infection after accidentally falling into Lake Geneva; James fell off a horse and broke his arm; little Victoria was severely run-down from the journey; Catherine was being treated for her nerves; and William was suffering from a troublesome eye infection. Bulkeley was very accommodating, attending to his patients at all hours of the day and night. In return, Mr Long Wellesley paid the doctor handsomely, rewarding him with gifts of fine cigars and wine.

Dr Bulkeley was full of admiration for Mrs Long Wellesley, who remained sweetly composed and dignified despite all her woes. In an age without antibiotics, every minor childhood illness induced fear and Catherine kept vigil at the bedsides of her children, nursing them through the day and night. She worried that a bout of measles or whooping cough might sweep through her household, claiming her three children in a matter of weeks. She knew many women who had watched helplessly as babes died in their arms, including all three of William's sisters. James's broken arm caused concern but she was especially anxious about Victoria who was so feverish and weak that her lovely blonde curls dropped out in clumps. Eventually her hair was so sparse that Catherine had no option but to shave it all off. Afterwards she tended it carefully, massaging balms into her daughter's scalp until her hair grew back thick and strong. Later in life, Victoria attributed her abundance of lustrous curls to her mother's care at this time.[3]

Catherine stayed in close contact with her sisters, her letters filled with news about her children. Her correspondence was that of a devoted wife and mother.[4] In return her sisters sent treats from home, with Dora writing, 'Here is Moore's Almanack. It must be very uncomfortable to be so long without an English almanac! We will get Peacock's and send it as soon as we can.'[5] Shortly after her arrival in Naples, Catherine's spirits lifted when she received promising news from her sister Dora concerning her mother's health:

> Dear Mamma is poorly. But I trust nothing that need alarm us at present. We think, however, she certainly has *rather* a tendency to dropsy, her legs being so swollen and weak. But she has *no pain anywhere*, the bile is quite recovered and she begins to eat again with more enjoyment and is in good spirits.[6]

Catherine was relieved to hear that her mother was getting better and she was touched by her sister's thoughtful gifts. Their parcels had grown even more frequent and Catherine found the little gestures very comforting. But just a few weeks later, her peace of mind was shattered yet again when she received bad news. Her beloved mother was no more – Lady Catherine was dead.

Lady Catherine had dedicated her life to benevolence and many grateful people mourned her loss. Stacks of condolences poured in for the Miss Longs, and numerous epitaphs appeared in the press. One newspaper recorded:

Lady Catherine Tylney Long may, assuredly, be considered to have been one of the highest ornaments of the age in which she lived. She was distinguished by her sweetness of temper, mildness of demeanour, her love of domestic life, and her almost unparalleled benevolence.[7]

In another paper the following notice appeared:

The loss of this excellent lady will long be deplored by all who had the honour of her acquaintance, but by none more than the poor of her neighbourhood, to whom she was a very munificent benefactress.[8]

It was a great pity that the final years of Lady Catherine's life had been filled with such sadness: the family fortune dissipated, her precious daughter living in exile and her grandchildren running around like wild animals. Dora and Emma were party to this grief, stoically caring for their mother and nursing her themselves. Catherine regretted deeply that she had not returned to England to visit her mother one last time. She wasted no time in writing to her sisters, expressing 'heartfelt pain at hearing the sad, sad news, that our excellent mother is no more. This is indeed a trial, but we must bear it with fortitude and resignation. It is the will of God, and we must submit.'[9]

In her letter, Catherine was full of praise for William, demonstrating that despite all that had happened, she was still mesmerized by him. She wrote:

I have received the greatest kindness and affection from Mr L. W. No human creature could have been so kind, or shown greater feeling upon the sad occasion, than he has done. I saw a most kind letter he wrote yesterday to Lord Maryborough, in which he desires him strictly to attend to *your* wishes in everything.[10]

This was rather naive on Catherine's part, considering the fact that William had such a long history of treating her sisters shabbily. He had never shown any inclination whatsoever of attending to their wishes. William was a convincing liar and the sisters protected her from the truth, so perhaps Catherine was not aware of the extent of the bad feeling between them. In this instance, William felt magnanimous in offering the sisters use of either Draycot House or Seagry House despite the fact that both of these properties belonged to Catherine.

Catherine mourned the loss of her mother sorely. On the surface, William appeared to be sympathetic to his wife and concerned for her sisters, who were now homeless. Secretly, he was elated because Lady Catherine's passing meant that her various annuities ceased. In addition, under the terms of the marriage settlement, part of Lady Catherine's allowance reverted to Catherine, who could now claim a further £3,500. Perhaps this was to reimburse Catherine for the annuities she had settled on Dora and Emma. As a result, Catherine's pin money was restored to the original amount of £11,000 (minus the £500 paid to Maria Kinnaird).[11] William was quick to write to his father and trustee, Lord Maryborough, to find out what financial benefit he could personally gain from the death. He hoped to be able to cut off the entail and get his hands on Draycot House. Efficient as ever, his father replied by return:

> Mr Wright will go to Draycot in a few days and he will take the Misses Long's pleasure as to Draycot House and Seagry. The Home Farm is, I believe, in very good order, and it is now in our possession, paying well – we shall have no difficulty in doing everything respecting Draycot, which you have deemed.[12]

Although Catherine was delighted by her husband's generosity and consideration for her sisters, Dora was suspicious and not so easily swayed. She sent William a cordial reply:

> My sister and I beg to offer you our best thanks for your kindness. But we decline your obliging proposals with a thousand

thanks, as it is our intention to be travelling about for some time. There are many places we have never seen & we think it, as yet, too early days to fix our residence anywhere.[13]

Dora did not trust William; she worried that he would intimidate Catherine, forcing her to sign over Draycot House. Once this was done, he could sell off all the Long family's heirlooms, just as he had disposed of the Tylney treasures at Wanstead. She wrote to Bartholomew Bouverie for clarification, and the charitable gentleman wrote back to her immediately to put her mind at rest:

> I do assure you . . . it is quite impossible that your sister can have cut off the entail of Draycot . . . All the Long Estates are in strict settlement on your sister's children, then on yourselves, and your children. This entail must continue till a son of your sister's comes of age, and then, they may together cut it off . . . Should your sister die before her husband, he has not even a life interest in Draycot, and those Estates. They pass immediately to his son.[14]

William's disregard for Lady Catherine was well known; his selfishness had deprived her of her final wish to see her grandchildren one last time. Unfailingly candid, Bouverie went on to criticize William for being two-faced: 'I hate all humbug, and it would have been far better, had Mr Long Wellesley, after all his inattention to your mother, avoided any empty profession of that sort.'[15]

The trustees were doing everything in their power to resolve William's affairs. Lord Maryborough was trying to find a tenant for Wanstead House but this was not a viable proposition because running costs were astronomical, well above the means of most people. In addition, the mansion was now just a vast, empty shell, stripped of all its treasures. Nobody could afford to move in and furnish the huge building; the curtains and carpets alone would cost an absolute fortune. Earl Tylney's pleasure palace was too big and ostentatious to maintain.

Merrick Shawe had more disappointing news for William: the deal to sell timber had fallen through due to clauses in the Tynley family wills. William already knew that Wanstead House was protected – according to his marriage settlement, it could not be sold. In addition, he discovered that Sir Josiah's walnut groves plus the magnificent avenues of elms and sweet chestnuts were safeguarded due to a legal clause stating that trees within sight of the house could not be felled.

Catherine had always owned Draycot House, but an agreement was in place allowing her mother to reside there throughout her lifetime. Now that Lady Catherine was dead, Draycot House reverted to Catherine. This meant that Wanstead House was surplus to William's requirements and he was prepared to sell it for whatever price he could get. A terrible plan formed in his head. Although he did not have the power to sell Wanstead House, there was a legal loophole. No document was in place to prevent him from simply knocking down the building. William decided he would demolish the beautifully crafted Palladian mansion and sell the bricks for scrap. Once the house was gone, all the ornamental timber could be disposed of too. Undoubtedly it would be desecration of the highest order, but he was determined to realize his assets at any cost. William instructed his trustees to proceed with this brutal course of action. Catherine was still mourning for her mother when William broke the bad news. He insisted there was no other option – Wanstead House would have to be razed to the ground.

28. Nothing Lasts Forever

࿊

1823

Back in England, on 12 May 1823, the materials of Wanstead House were sold to a consortium of builders for a paltry sum. Two days later, *The Times* reported:

> Wanstead House was sold by auction on Monday last, for £10,000: one of the conditions of the sale binds the purchaser to clear everything away, even to the foundation, by Lady-day 1825 . . . The purchasers are Messrs Stannard and Athow, of Norwich, in conjunction with three other townsmen. The auctioneer announced to the company, by their request, that they intended to sell the whole in lots, large or small, to suit buyers, and they absolutely sold a pair of marble chimney pieces for 300 guineas before they left the room. Thus is sacrificed, on the shrine of extravagance and gambling, a mansion, which cost in its erection more than £360,000, and which has no equal in the county of Essex.

Messrs Stannard and Athow, builders from Norwich, were professional gentlemen who possessed the skills required to break up the building and sell it off in bits. Mr Stannard, an experienced surveyor, lived at the house for several months and was always on hand to offer help or advice to prospective buyers. The splendid Palladian architecture at Wanstead House was renowned, and connoisseurs of art had a unique opportunity to purchase a piece of the magnificent palace at a knock-down price. The builders wasted no time, and notices were placed in the newspapers advertising the sale:[1]

Wanstead House Essex, Thirty Days Sale

*The materials of this magnificent and extensive
building are now selling by private contract; and
persons may be accommodated with every description of building material (from the Cottage to
the Palace) on the most reasonable terms, upon
application to Mr Joseph Stannard, on the Premises.*

Buyers had their pick of crafted stonework such as the grand
staircase, stately obelisks and decorative stone urns intricately
carved with ancient stories. The internal fixtures included the
ornate marble fireplace from the Salon, adorned with a spread
eagle; heavy wooden doors with gilt-edged frames; plus the beautifully hand-carved oak staircase. Colen Campbell's elegant portico,
supported by six Corinthian columns, drew a great deal of interest,
particularly as the stone relief at the top was exquisitely hand-
crafted. Notices announced that the portico would be sold at the
third sale, on 1 July, 'with delivery free to any place on the Thames
between Westminster and Woolwich, including carting to the
waterside'.[2]

Art lovers lamented the fact that the much-admired ceiling
frescos could not be saved. They had been painted on plaster and
were impossible to remove. William Kent's wonderful representa-
tions would soon be reduced to dust: *The Seasons* (in the Grand
Dining Room), *Morning, Noon, Evening and Night* (in the Great
Hall) and *Jupiter and Semele* (in the Grand Drawing Room).

Hundreds of people attended the sale. Lord Tankerville and the
Reverend Savill Ogle, of Newcastle, purchased four marble fire-
places for £426. Humble locals bought pieces of Wanstead House
to ornament their modest homes. Prices were extremely reasonable:
'The wainscot floors sold for about £5 per square foot; wainscot
doors, with locks and joints, 2s to 2s 6d.'[3]

It took several months for the interiors to be ripped out and
sold, by which time the company that had judiciously purchased
the building had already doubled their money. As soon as the fixtures were sold, the structure was demolished – all that remained of

the palatial palace was a pile of rubble. There were three million bricks in all, and Messrs Stannard and Athow managed to salvage everything. Anything they could not sell was taken to Norwich, where they could use it for their own building projects.

In keeping with the terms of the contract, every last stone was removed and, by Lady Day 1825, Wanstead House was entirely erased from the face of the earth. Even the foundations were excavated and bartered. All that was left of the gracious building was a hole in the ground. Once the house was obliterated, William could start hacking away at the pleasure grounds. Great swathes of ancient avenues would be chopped down and sold off as timber. Gardens that had once been compared to Versailles were trampled, torn and left in tatters. *Sic transit gloria mundi*, as one commentator noted – nothing lasts forever.

Back in Naples, Bulkeley was treating Catherine for depression. Despite all her troubles, the doctor found her to be 'a lady possessing the most amiable disposition and the sweetest manners'.[4] Catherine was a resilient woman, but she had endured too much and she shut herself away, mourning the loss of her mother. William was the model husband, staying at home with his wife and doing everything in his power to comfort her. As the months passed, Catherine's spirits lifted as she watched the sky above Naples turn a searing blue, the warm air scented with orange blossom. Whenever she drove to the coast, she was charmed by the sunlit shores and sweeping views across the Bay of Naples. Her postilion always stopped at the same spot on the brow of the hill so that the stunning panorama of sea and mountains could be taken in at a glance. Gently lapping azure waters were dotted with white sails and the enchanting island of Capri lay to the right, with Vesuvius on the left puffing plumes of blue smoke onto the cloudless horizon.

Dr Bulkeley noticed that Catherine found great comfort in her children – she was consumed with love for them. During the daytime little Victoria went everywhere with her, and she often took the boys out in the afternoon, when they had finished lessons with their tutor, Mr Pitman. Catherine strolled along golden beaches, while the children paddled in the sea, poking about in rock pools or hunting for starfish and shells. Greedy little Victoria missed the French patisseries, but quickly discovered the marvellous icehouses serving delicious Neapolitan ice cream. Catherine was managing her money very well, and the additional income generated by her mother's death enabled her to indulge in luxuries to make the most of her time in Naples. She loved taking boat trips and grew to enjoy sailing so much that she purchased her own pleasure barge.[5] The bay shimmered like a sea of diamonds and from the water only the rooftops of Naples were visible through the foliage. Colourful tiles, tall steeples and glinting cupolas gave the air of an Eastern city. Catherine always felt a rush of pleasure as the wind swept up her hair or a cool spray of refreshing seawater splashed her face.

Life was idyllic. The apartments at the Cappella Vecchia were beautifully furnished with a terrace running along the back, lined with fragrant orange trees and Spanish jasmine. Sultry evenings enabled the Long Wellesleys to host intimate dinner parties on their scented veranda. Serenaded by accomplished Italian musicians or opera singers, guests enjoyed local delicacies such as succulent wild boar, tender Sorrento veal and iced watermelon.

Naples abounded with scholarly English residents, keenly interested in the excavations at Pompeii and Herculaneum. The British ambassador, William Hamilton, was a renowned antiquarian who became famous for bringing the Rosetta Stone to Britain in 1801.[6] His minister, Sir William Drummond, was occupied with literary pursuits. Both academics had fastidious taste and refinement; they were ideal ambassadors, portraying a very favourable image of the English to the inhabitants of Naples. Hamilton, in particular, was such an enthusiast he could talk at length about the history of his vases and antiquities to anyone willing to listen for several hours.[7]

Hamilton and Drummond took a very studious approach to sightseeing and many newcomers preferred to seek out the droll Sir William Gell, an archaeologist of such renown that the government had granted him special facilities for sketching the excavations at Pompeii.[8] His wit shone most brilliantly at dinner parties, where

he enjoyed meeting distinguished visitors to Naples and recommending excursions for them. A comical gentleman, he had a
penchant for the ridiculous and his tours were always filled with
unlikely stories about ancient heroes. Catherine found his humour
irresistible, particularly as he always delivered his ludicrous tales
with such a grave expression. One evening, Catherine felt laughter
bubble up from some forgotten place deep inside her, spilling out
irrepressibly. The sound was strange to her ears and she realized,
with regret, that it had been a long time since she had laughed out
loud. What had become of the light-hearted, optimistic young
woman she had once been?

Gell suffered from such severe gout that he had to be transported everywhere in a sedan chair, carried by bearers. Nevertheless,
the painful malady never affected his good temper and he was
always pleasant company. Unfortunately, even Gell could not
cheer Catherine on the day she visited the Museo Borbonico,
which housed the treasures found at Herculaneum and Pompeii.
As people marvelled at the finest sculptures of antiquity, buried
for centuries amid the ruins, Catherine was reminded of all her
wonderful treasures at Wanstead House that had been sold off at
auction.

Melancholy, however, passed quickly in Naples. The noisy,
animated, friendly Neapolitan people enchanted Catherine.
Whenever she went out with her children, people greeted the
family warmly and there was always plenty to entertain them.
Impromptu theatres sprang up in the streets and squares as applauding audiences crowded round tightrope walkers, puppeteers,
musicians and dancers. Catherine's days were filled with sunshine
and laughter, but demons from the past still lingered beneath
the surface, coming back to haunt her in the dead of night. Although she mourned the loss of her mother and the destruction
of Wanstead House, she also felt strangely detached from it all.
Gloomy England seemed a long way away from the glorious, sun-
drenched world she had escaped to.

Catherine might well have passed a pleasant summer in Naples if her husband had not become embroiled in yet another scandal. On this occasion his behaviour was so outrageous, it resulted in a high-profile court case that would shock the British public and resonate throughout the nation for years to come.

29. Treading on a Volcano

❧

1823

Driven by his libido, William was impetuous, reckless and amoral. The illicit thrill was like a drug to him and it is possible that he had a sex addiction. During his entire stay on the continent – whether in Paris, Calais or Naples – he was in the habit of visiting prostitutes several times a week.[1] William enjoyed high society, but he also liked to move in the back alleys, mixing in the lowest circles. From the time of his arrival in Naples, he employed a man named Bordesi, ostensibly to teach him Italian, but in reality the man was his *ruffiano* or pimp, a thug brought in to source prostitutes for William or handle other dubious dealings.[2] Boasting to Bulkeley, William claimed that his man, Bordesi, 'was a consummate bravo, and had murdered nine persons'.[3]

Living dangerously was inherent in William. His wife had made it clear that she would never share him with another woman, so he could not afford to get caught out. Another episode like the Maria Kinnaird affair would be disastrous for him because he was completely reliant on his wife's money. Moreover, although he had not bothered to stay in touch with his former mistress, Catherine continued to maintain his illegitimate child by providing an annuity of £500, which served as a constant reminder of his past indiscretions. Nevertheless, the perils of adultery only served to make infidelities even more exciting for him.

The elite social circle in Naples revolved around the British ambassador, William Hamilton, who enjoyed hosting glittering functions at the embassy with the help of his wife and his sister, Mrs Maxwell. Mrs Maxwell had a long-standing acquaintance with the Wellesley family and had been part of Wellington's circle when he served in India. Having known William when he was a handsome young dandy, she was pleased to find that he was still a fine specimen of an Englishman. At the age of thirty-five William possessed the mesmerizing charm and good looks that characterized all the Wellesley men. His smiling eyes now crinkled attractively at the corners and slivers of silver streaked the dark hair at his temples, while audacious arrogance simply added to his allure. Mrs Maxwell was rather taken with him, but she was not the only one to be dazzled by his charm.

In April the expatriate community was abuzz with reports of two new arrivals and several of Catherine's acquaintances mentioned meeting 'the handsome Mrs Bligh'.[4] A few evenings later, during an embassy function, Catherine saw William talking to an exceptionally alluring young woman with alabaster skin and exquisitely chiselled features, reminiscent of delicate fine china. The pale translucency of her complexion had an ethereal quality, contrasting with her glossy dark hair and startling blue eyes. William must have noticed his wife's watchful gaze, because he went over to her shortly afterwards. When Catherine enquired who the lady was, William looked surprised and replied, 'It is impossible that you do not recollect her.'[5]

It transpired that Helena Bligh had lived at the Lake House in Wanstead for a number of years, with her parents Colonel and Mrs Paterson, attending balls and parties there in 1813 and 1814. Catherine had vague recollections of the family that had moved into the Lake House shortly after her marriage but she did not recognize Mrs Bligh, who had been just sixteen years old the last time they met. In contrast, however, the other woman had vivid memories of her visits to the great house, where she had been awestruck by the glittering entertainment, as well as the spellbinding host. Helena had been one of the throngs of young women harbouring a secret infatuation for the desirable Mr Long Wellesley, admiring him from afar. On being introduced to Mrs Bligh, Catherine found her to be 'an agreeable, quiet person'.[6]

From then onwards, whenever Catherine hosted large dinner

parties, she invited Captain and Mrs Bligh and gradually became friendlier with them. After some weeks, the Blighs went out sailing on Catherine's pleasure barge and were guests in William's box at the opera. Catherine had her own group of friends and was not particularly intimate with Mrs Bligh, but she could not help noticing that her husband paid Helena a great deal of attention.[7] William explained that Helena was a long-standing family acquaintance, so Catherine was unconcerned. When he started to call on Helena at her home, however, he needed a more concrete reason for the intimacy. Eventually, he confided in his wife and revealed a family secret – Helena was his cousin. Before long, William had made this claim in many quarters, saying to one friend, 'I will introduce you to a damn'd fine woman, the daughter of the Duke of Wellington, and my cousin.'[8]

William's story may well have been true. Helena was certainly a protégée of Wellington, and there was conjecture in many quarters that she was his natural daughter.[9] For a start, the family resemblance was striking. Added to this, Helena had been born in India during Wellington's campaign and rumour implied that he had been close to the beautiful Mrs Paterson, even sailing back with mother and child on the voyage home in 1805. On returning to England, Wellington continued to take a keen interest in the welfare of the child, which was one of the reasons William had granted the Paterson family a lease on the Lake House at Wanstead.

Catherine was among those who genuinely believed that Helena was William's first cousin. Owing to this, she was not alarmed by the amount of time her husband was spending with the ethereal beauty. The Wellesleys were a close family, so the relationship seemed perfectly natural to her. William claimed that Helena needed his help and advice because she 'lived very unhappily with her husband', who was prone to violent outbursts towards her. Having had some personal experience of domestic disharmony, Catherine empathized, feeling genuine concern for Helena's troubles.[10]

*

Dr Bulkeley was relieved that Catherine was finally emerging
from her melancholy. She continued to spend a lot of time with
her children, especially her little daughter, who was too young
to attend lessons with Pitman. Victoria was still weak from the
illness that had caused severe hair loss and Catherine fussed over
her, taking her out whenever she went on sailing trips and other
excursions. A popular lady, Catherine made friends easily and her
Naples set included Princess Rasimousky and Sir Richard Church.
Resourceful and capable, Catherine was a self-contained woman,
accustomed to pursuing her own interests independently of her
husband. Sailing became her greatest novelty.

Catherine had grown particularly close to Sir Richard Church,
an Anglo-Irish major general of around forty, decorated in 1815
for leading the campaign that drove the French out of Styria,
Croatia and Istria.[11] He was an immensely attractive man with
masses of unruly dark hair, a wide generous smile and a large
well-groomed moustache. As Sir Richard could not afford to
keep his own pleasure boat, he was only too delighted to be captain
of Mrs Long Wellesley's vessel whenever the opportunity arose.
Almost every day, Catherine and a small party of friends would
set sail, heading for the island of Capri or some other picturesque
spot where they could stop to soak up the scenery and enjoy a
picnic accompanied by a glass or two of chilled wine.

William preferred to hunt or to explore the stunning landscape
on horseback, so he was perfectly content to leave his wife in the
capable hands of the dashing military commander. With Catherine
suitably diverted, it was easier for him to go about his own business
undetected. Catherine's routine was leisurely; she took breakfast
on a tray in her room, spent time with her children and went out
sailing later in the day. Parasols protected the family from the sun
and a pleasant breeze from the water kept them cool. Enjoying
separate pursuits, the Long Wellesleys looked forward to meeting
up in the evenings when they entertained large parties on their
scented terrace, or went to the theatre, embassy functions or other
places of amusement, often staying out together until three or

four o'clock in the morning. This arrangement suited them both, and John Meara noted that 'they lived very happily together'.[12]

Naples and its environs offered many interesting sights, inspiring William to organize outings to amuse his friends. Helena Bligh was often included in his group, but her husband was not always able to join in due to delicate health. Suffering from an illness contracted during the Peninsular War, Captain Thomas Bligh had moved to southern Europe because his health benefited from the milder climate. Despite this precaution, he was not expected to live for very long. A large group expressed interest when William proposed a night-time excursion to Mount Vesuvius, when views of the volcanic eruptions were most spectacular. Too ill to participate, Captain Bligh objected to his wife being one of the party, because it would involve her staying out overnight, unaccompanied. On hearing this, Helena's temper became violent and she screamed angrily, 'I shall do as I please!' In a vicious tirade she made it clear that she had already sacrificed too much, reminding him that he was sadly lacking in every department, unable to consummate their union or father children. Captain Bligh was shocked by the bitter attack; his wife was usually quiet and sympathetic. Eventually he agreed that she could go on the excursion on the condition that his brother, Edward Bligh, accompanied her.[13]

The party left Naples at midnight and proceeded in carriages to a hermitage about halfway up the slopes. From there the ladies were taken up the mountain in palanquins carried by bearers, while the gentlemen followed behind on foot. On arriving at the meeting point, Mr Bligh discovered that Helena was not with the other ladies and Mr Long Wellesley could not be found either. Furious that they had somehow managed to slip away from him, Mr Bligh could not find his way back down the mountain without a guide, so he had to wait with the rest of the group. When he arrived back at the hermitage several hours later, he found his sister-in-law there with Long Wellesley. Helena claimed to have stayed behind because she had sprained her ankle.

Edward Bligh was not fooled by the charade and he gave his brother a full account of what had happened at Vesuvius. Captain

Bligh challenged his wife, telling her that she was prohibited from going out with Long Wellesley or accepting visits from him. Helena was more than a match for him, arguing savagely. Living in the same house, Edward Bligh, his wife and children witnessed many more bitter disputes over the following days.

Peace and harmony continued to reign in the Long Wellesley household. In the days following the trip to Mount Vesuvius, William became indisposed, causing him to retire to bed much earlier than usual, at around midnight.[14] In June 1823, the French ambassador, Monsieur Le Serres, sent an invitation requesting the company of Mr and Mrs Long Wellesley at a grand assembly. On the day of the function William took to his bed, telling his wife that he was too ill to go out. After supper, Catherine got dressed and went into her husband's bedchamber, where William had been asleep for some hours. Rousing him gently, she asked how he was feeling and tried to induce him to accompany her to the assembly, which promised to be a splendid affair. Catherine looked beautiful in a daringly low-cut gown, her cleavage ablaze with diamonds. After much good-humoured joking about her dress, William teased that she had become 'quite the dandy'. Nevertheless, he declined to accompany her to the ball because he was still feeling unwell.[15]

Catherine was confident in the society of her friends and she had no qualms about going out unaccompanied in Naples. Arriving home at around four o'clock in the morning, she tiptoed into William's bedchamber to check that he was comfortable and was surprised to find the covers pulled back and his bed empty. The sheets were cold to her touch, so it was obvious that William had been gone for some time. Worried that her husband had been taken ill suddenly, Catherine berated herself for going out and leaving him unattended. All her enquiries drew a blank and she was frantic by the time William returned home at around two o'clock the following afternoon. Waltzing in nonchalantly, William was completely unaware that his wife had been looking for him until he saw her worried face. Apologetic, he had a simple excuse for his absence, explaining that as he had slept most of the previous day, he woke up very early that morning and rode out to watch the sunrise over the bay.

From then onwards William seemed to have trouble sleeping and his routine changed considerably. Every evening he retired to bed before midnight and then, supposedly, rose before dawn to go out riding before the sun became too blistering. Rather conveniently, this new regime meant that Catherine never saw her husband between bedtime and two o'clock the following afternoon, when he arrived home from his long ride. The Long Wellesleys had adjoining bedchambers and William started to lock his door from the inside, ostensibly so the children would not disturb him. In reality, it was to prevent Catherine from discovering that he had sneaked out. His valet would help him escape, rousing the porter from his bed and saying 'a friend of Mr Wellesley needs to get out'.[16] This was effected without the porter knowing who was leaving, as William would conceal his face. William quickly discovered, however, that while it was relatively simple to escape from his own apartment, entering Helena's lodgings undetected was not easy. The problem was solved by his pimp, who arranged a lease on the house next door. From the balcony of his rented property, William could climb onto Helena's balcony and enter her bedroom through the window.[17]

Ludicrous as the plot of a French farce, servants in the Bligh household were not fooled by the elaborate charade. Highly titillated by all the carry-on, they delighted in the scandal, competing with each other to find evidence. Helena's room was at the top of the house but, as Captain Bligh was too infirm to share her bed, he slept on the ground floor. Maids were therefore intrigued to discover the muddy imprints of a man's top boot on Mrs Bligh's bedroom rug. They also noted that her plain nightdress had been substituted for luxurious silk robes, ornamented with lace. Then there was the matter of the pet pooch, an animal Helena was so attached to she carried him everywhere, tucked in the crook of her arm like a fashion accessory. The dog had always slept contentedly on her bed, until suddenly he was imprisoned in the stables at night. Even when the desolate dog barked and cried for his mistress, she paid him no heed. One enterprising maid laid a trap, fixing small pins to the shutters in Mrs Bligh's bedroom – invariably the pins were found on the floor the next morning. Naturally, all this caused much amusement below stairs, with servants gossiping about banished dogs, locked doors, open windows and mysterious footprints.[18]

Captain Bligh's physician advocated fresh air and exercise, so the sickly gentleman was in the habit of riding out every evening, at the most genial time of the day. Before long, people noticed that Mr Long Wellesley always called on Mrs Bligh while her husband was out and molten rumours quickly spread throughout Naples. Concerned about the scandal set to erupt within his expatriate community, the British ambassador promptly dispatched his sister to try to help. During her time in India, Mrs Maxwell had been intimately acquainted with the Paterson family and Helena had often been left in her care. As a close friend, Mrs Maxwell felt it her duty to call on the younger woman to warn her about all the gossip circulating. They were sitting in the drawing room drinking tea when Mrs Maxwell recommended that Helena should decline visits from Mr Long Wellesley for the sake of her reputation. Helena insisted that her relationship with William was of 'long-standing and entirely respectable', claiming that his visits were for 'the purpose of consulting him in the unhappy dissention which exists between me and my husband'.[19] Mrs Maxwell had never heard any previous complaints about Captain Bligh and could not imagine him harming Helena in any way. The ladies talked intimately for a while longer and the older woman left harbouring the belief that she had convinced Helena to behave with more prudence in future. Mrs Maxwell was sadly mistaken. Caught up in the most tantalizing adventure of her life, Helena had lost all sense of propriety and reason.

As a virginal seventeen-year-old, Helena had married her invalid husband in 1815. At the time she had felt fondness plus a strong sense of sympathy, which she mistook for love. By all accounts the couple lived together in harmony and Helena was a docile wife. This all changed, however, when she met the audacious Mr Long Wellesley, burnished by the Italian sunshine, glowing with health and vitality – the antithesis of her frail, sickly husband. Eight years into her marriage, aged twenty-five, Helena was only just beginning to understand the huge sacrifice she had made in tying herself to a man who never shared her bed. Unable to perform sexually, Captain Bligh would never be able to provide her with children or satisfy her sensual cravings. Bursting with pent-up carnal longing, Helena's attraction to William was so fierce it made her blood rush and pulse race. The master of seduction, William would have seen the signs and handled her with expertise. Brushing her cheek softly with his lips in a relatively innocent gesture, he waited for the occasion when she would tilt her head back, inviting him to explore further. Whatever techniques he employed, he certainly kept Helena enthralled.

William spent every night in Helena's bed. A man of many moods, he could be tender and loving, taking her slowly, sweetly and skilfully. On other occasions he was passionate and urgent. Snuggled together, the delicious thrill of flesh-on-flesh was overwhelming; inexperienced Helena had never felt such intimacy. As she lay in his arms, all her defences were down and she found herself telling secrets she had never spoken before. She talked about her loveless marriage and her aching loneliness. William kissed away her tears with such gentleness and understanding, Helena was shaken to the core.

Never able to stay out of trouble for long, William soon found himself ensnared in another intrigue that required delicate handling. Bulkeley was his most trusted confidant in Naples, but when William explained his predicament, the good doctor became highly indignant and refused to help. He insisted that he would not perform an illegal procedure, or act against his own scruples. William had asked the doctor to induce a miscarriage. Mrs Bligh wanted to terminate a pregnancy. As the discussion grew increasingly heated, Bulkeley asked William why he was even involved; surely this was a matter for Captain Bligh? The doctor had, of course, guessed the circumstances but, shifty as ever, William would not give him a straight answer. Persevering, the doctor suggested that Captain Bligh should be warned about the proposed termination of his unborn child. Baulking at the idea, William made it clear that Captain Bligh was not the father of Helena's child because he 'was not able to afford her gratifications she desired'.

'Who is the father?' asked Bulkeley, but William just shrugged. Speaking with candour, Bulkeley looked William in the eye and said, 'I heard that you had sexual intercourse with Mrs Bligh on Mount Vesuvius . . . and have boasted of the circumstance.'[20]

Dodging the issue yet again, William did not deny the accusation, but replied inanely, 'I hope you would not believe that I am capable of boasting of having had a lady's favours.'

On hearing this response Bulkeley gave up his questioning, but declined to visit Helena, stating, 'She is a most dangerous woman for a physician to have anything to do with . . . in advising her I will be treading on a volcano.'

Over the course of the week, William continued to pester Bulkeley, yapping at his heels. Eventually, after much persuasion, the doctor relented. When he visited Mrs Bligh, he found her in a state of great distress and she told him, 'If you do not give me something to cause a miscarriage, my ruin must be inevitable.'

Bulkeley refused, saying, 'My business is to preserve life, and not to destroy it.' When Mrs Bligh persisted, the doctor told her he would speak to Captain Bligh as he had the right to know her intentions towards his unborn child. Helena begged him not to tell her husband, saying that he was incapable of fathering a child. On hearing this yet again, the doctor demanded, 'Then how has this happened? There is only one Immaculate Conception that I believe in!'

Disgusted by everything he had heard, Bulkeley left Helena in tears, refusing categorically to help her abort the foetus. Outside the house, William was waiting with his carriage and he persuaded the doctor to climb in. Resuming the discussion, he informed the doctor that Mrs Bligh had been trying to induce a miscarriage herself. William said, 'She has been taking penny-royal tea, and has this day taken a bottle of laudanum as long as my finger.'

Feeling compromised for a number of reasons both professional and personal, Bulkeley reminded him that Mrs Long Wellesley 'is a most amiable person . . . if this should reach her ears . . . the news would destroy her peace of mind'.

When Bulkeley visited Helena a few days later, she informed him that she had effected a miscarriage and 'the discharge that was coming from her was abundant and as black as ink'.

Delighted with the outcome and hoping to buy his silence, William showered the good doctor with gifts, sending him expensive cigars, inviting him to his box at the opera and presenting him with a personalized snuffbox. He need not have worried; nobody was going to tell Catherine about his sordid affair. As Bulkeley pointed out, Catherine was 'a most amiable and excellent person' – her staff adored her. This included Meara, who felt guilty about aiding and abetting his master by sneaking him out of the house, but he had Catherine's best interests at heart. Pitman had also heard the rumours and did everything in his power to protect his gentle mistress and the children. Hoping to spare her feelings, everyone worked hard to keep Catherine in the dark. But it was only a matter of time; inevitably, the situation would come to a head.

30. *Always the Last to Know*

❦

William continued to be indiscreet, visiting the ravishing Mrs Bligh at every opportunity. Planning to leave Naples in the not too distant future, he felt confident that the affair would reach a natural conclusion and that when the time came he would be able to move on unscathed. William always ensured that his amours came and went with no lasting ties or repercussions. His obsession with Helena was similar to his passion for Mrs Kinnaird, but he had thought nothing of leaving Maria and his child behind in England without so much as a backward glance. On this occasion, Helena had other ideas and William was to get more than he bargained for.

With all the rumours circulating around Naples, Captain Bligh and his brother continued to demand that Helena stop all visits from Mr Long Wellesley. This was not unreasonable considering the circumstances but Helena became so violent and abusive that Edward took his wife and children and left the scene of the battle. He then went to fetch Mrs Maxwell, hoping that the sensible lady could offer counsel to his foolish sister-in-law. When Mrs Maxwell arrived at the Blighs' house, Helena told her that she was going to leave her husband because she would not stay in a house where her friends were refused admittance. When pressed on the matter, Helena admitted that her husband only objected to one person, Mr Long Wellesley, who she described as her 'best and only friend'. Mrs Maxwell pointed out that Captain Bligh's reaction was understandable given the vicious rumours circulating; he was simply trying to protect his wife's reputation.[1]

On 31 July, the very same evening as Mrs Maxwell's visit,

Helena left her house at six o'clock without consulting her husband or any other person. Two hours later, the minister William Drummond and other embassy staff spotted Helena at the gardens of Villa Reale, where an Austrian band played every evening. She was walking arm-in-arm with William in a secluded part of the shrubbery and although they kept their faces averted they were easily recognizable.

William was extremely anxious when he discovered that Helena had left her husband; his little fling had gone horribly wrong and she had put him in a terrible position. He'd had affairs in the past, but nobody had ever been foolish enough to decamp and cause a scandal. Most women had the sense to realize that he would never leave his wealthy wife and the comfortable lifestyle she provided, but Helena was naive enough to believe that he genuinely loved her. While they were walking, William made it clear that he disapproved of the step she had taken, saying it was 'rash and injudicious', while urging her in the most earnest manner to return to her husband's house.[2]

Mrs Maxwell was sent to the gardens to retrieve Helena. Arriving in Mr Hamilton's equipage, she tried to persuade Helena to get inside, assuring her that if she returned home she would be 'very kindly received'. Stubborn, Helena refused to budge; when Mrs Maxwell returned without her, Captain Bligh 'was much affected and wept'.[3]

William was also in a state of great agitation. On returning home he locked himself in his room with Meara, who noticed that his master looked very pale and dejected, white-lipped and with his mouth parched. Grabbing his valet by the arm, William said, 'Meara, they are going to play hell with me! Mrs Bligh has left her husband and I am afraid that the groom and lady's maid will bear witness against me. You must go to them at once, and pay them anything for their silence. The Blighs have not got a sous to offer them.'[4]

Not only was William's relationship with Catherine at stake, but English law stipulated that it was illegal to have sex with another man's wife. On returning to England, William could face

charges for criminal intercourse, more commonly referred to as
'criminal conversation'. Servants often provided vital evidence,
especially if they had witnessed the parties in bed together. If he
were found guilty, William would face severe penalties – Henry
Wellesley was awarded an enormous £20,000 when Lord Paget
eloped with his wife. Aside from the financial consequences, William did not want to face the social repercussions. He enjoyed
celebrity; he had no desire to live on the outskirts of society as a
penniless outcast.

With the dawning of a new day came fresh hope that Helena
would come to her senses and return to her husband. In cases such
as these it was common for family or friends to intervene, to try to
persuade a couple to reconcile. With this in mind, William called
on Helena at L'Isle Britannique Hôtel and recommended that she
send for the British minister and Mrs Maxwell, to act as appeasers
between her and Captain Bligh. For the sake of propriety, he also
suggested that Helena should seek protection under Mrs Maxwell's
roof, advocating, 'The more you are watched the better, and the
more public all your conduct is the better.'5

Prior to leaving her husband, Helena had written to the Duke
of Wellington asking for advice, but she had not waited for his reply
before acting. Wellington's marked commitment to Helena was
evident when he wrote to Mr Hamilton at the embassy, 'I am really
most concerned for poor Mrs Bligh. My own acquaintance with
her dates from the same period with that of your sister; and I felt a
great interest for her.'6 On the subject of the separation Wellington
wrote, 'I earnestly urged her obedience to conciliate and to be
reconciled to Captain Bligh; and I pointed out to her the uncomfortable situation in which she above all other women would find
herself when in a state of separation from her husband.'7

The general consensus was that Helena should return home but,
fighting off pressure from the highest quarters, she refused. Helena
was granted ample opportunity to reconsider, but when news of the
separation became generally known Captain Bligh did not want

people to think him a fool. On 2 August, he took 'legal measures to prevent trades people from giving her credit . . . and called at her hotel to inform them not to supply her with anything, for he would not be answerable for any debt she might contract'.[8]

Helena had left her husband in such haste she had not packed a bag or taken any of her belongings. Now she was also without credit, so in effect she was destitute in a foreign country far away from family and friends. When she appealed to Mrs Maxwell and Mr Hamilton, they told her to return to her husband. William also wanted Helena to go home, but he was concerned that if he did not comply with her wishes she would tell his wife everything. Helena had a passionate, unpredictable temperament that William usually found thrilling, but there was nothing enjoyable about the terrible scenes she was creating. Helena had shown herself to be stubborn, determined and deliberate – perhaps William had finally met his match. Appalled by the steps she had taken, William was in an intolerable position.

By now Naples was buzzing with the news that Mrs Bligh had *eloped* with Mr Long Wellesley. This was such a dangerous predicament for William that he felt the need to rush to a court to swear an affidavit in front of a judge proclaiming his innocence. The sworn statement was then posted to the Duke of Wellington in England because William believed that if criminal charges were ever brought against him it would help his case. Trying to vindicate himself further, William then scribbled a hasty note to Helena's mother, Mrs Paterson:

> Madam, I am sorry to write to you upon a subject, which must be painful to a mother. Most assuredly the step, which your daughter took of quitting her husband's house, was very precipitate and ill-advised; however, her provocation was great . . . The Duke of Wellington is furnished with the documents necessary to prove your daughter's innocence of crime.[9]

Blissfully unaware of all that had happened, Catherine went

about her business, appearing in public smiling serenely. Concerned for her health, Dr Bulkeley called on William, advising him 'in the strongest terms to be the first to break the news to his wife'.[10] Recent experience with wilful Helena had caused William to think fondly of his sweet-natured, amenable wife. Promising to do everything in his power to preserve her peace of mind, William told Bulkeley on more than one occasion that Catherine was 'a most excellent and amiable person'.[11] Not wanting to ruin his marriage or his relationship with his wife, William realized that he would have to spin a very convincing yarn this time. But that was his speciality.

Never one to throw tantrums, Catherine listened quietly as William explained that there was no truth in the rumours circulating. Persuasive as ever, it did not take him very long to convince Catherine of his innocence, particularly as she was so susceptible to believing him. The circumstance that swung it completely for her was the fact that William had sworn an affidavit in court – surely he would never compromise himself unnecessarily by committing perjury?

Producing the affidavit, William went through the points with Catherine, insisting that he had nothing to hide. Speaking calmly, he said, 'I have never visited Mrs Bligh *but* in an open manner. I have never seen her under any roof but her own, except in general society.'[12] He also stated categorically that when Mrs Bligh confided her intention to quit her husband's house, 'I used all the persuasion within my power to prevent her from adopting such a step.'[13] Nevertheless, he felt that she had endured immeasurable provocation, claiming, 'I found her one morning in a flood of tears,' because her husband had said she was 'a whore, a bitch at heat . . . and that all the Wellesley family were whores, that she was a bastard of the family, that the Duke of Wellington was a rascal'.[14] William even claimed that on one occasion Helena 'suffered severely from a blow, which her husband had given her'.[15]

This type of language and violence would have been abhorrent to Catherine. Having damaged Captain Bligh's reputation and made him look unhinged, William cunningly claimed that the allegations about his affair with Helena were entirely a figment of the captain's sick mind. Speaking with tears in his eyes, he told Catherine that he hoped she would not listen to a word spoken by the treacherous madman who had destroyed his own marriage and was now trying to ruin theirs.

Describing the violent altercations that took place in the Bligh household, William said that both the captain and his brother mistreated Helena. Yelling the most violent menaces and words, they chased her 'over two floors of the house to her bedroom, where she locked herself in, and from which she did not remove till they had left the house'. William went on to say that Mrs Bligh was so terrified she was resolved not to go home, although this would leave her penniless and ostracized from society.

William convinced her that Captain Bligh was a dangerous lunatic, a similar character to her stalker, Scott, who had harboured wild delusions, even attempting to murder William with a carving knife. Much of this story was a fabrication, but Catherine was horrified by all she had heard. Some time later she would comment, 'I placed implicit confidence in his word, believing . . . that both Mr Long Wellesley and Mrs Bligh were most unjustly accused.'[16] The part she found most shocking was that Helena had stated if she were forced to return to her husband, 'he would drive her to an act of desperation'. To think that her friend had contemplated suicide dismayed soft-hearted Catherine.

The factor that really swung it for Catherine, however, was that William had sworn in the affidavit that Helena was his cousin, and Wellington had been sent a copy of the declaration. Catherine felt it was her duty to look after a family member in her time of need. After giving the matter some consideration she decided to call on Helena. In her own account of the meeting Catherine stated:

> I called upon her at her lodgings, and found her in tears. She gave me a long account of the ill-usage she had received, and miseries she had endured under her husband's roof . . . I most foolishly believed all she said. I told her I was come to offer her my protection until she had received answers from her friends in England . . . She then expressed herself in terms of

the deepest gratitude to me, said, that after the unjust reports which had been circulated to her disadvantage, I was the last person in the world from whom she had any reason to expect to receive kindness.

Catherine was a charitable woman, always inclined to think the best of people. She hated to see Mrs Bligh destitute in a foreign country, far away from her family and friends. Without money or clothes, Helena desperately needed financial assistance and Catherine loaned her sufficient funds to cover immediate expenses. Offering protection to the other woman was characteristic of Catherine's compassion and artlessness. In a brief note, Sir Richard Church commended her actions: 'Your kind intentions towards [Mrs Bligh]; this act of kindness is equally creditable to your heart as to your judgement.'

By adopting this course it was Catherine's intention to declare to the outside world that she trusted in her husband's innocence. Polite but firm about how much protection she could extend, Catherine made it clear that the other woman could not reside under her roof, declaring, 'had she been my own sister, I never would ask her to live any length of time entirely with us'. A compromise was reached; Catherine paid for Helena to move into lodgings very near to the Long Wellesley family home at the Cappella Vecchia.

Some days after the alleged elopement, Catherine sent a note filled with generosity and genuine concern:

My Dear Mrs Bligh, I am afraid I shall not be enabled to call upon you today, but tomorrow I hope to have that pleasure, and that you will drive out with me. If you do not dislike dining at my late hours, I shall be delighted if you will dine with me (Mr Long Wellesley dines with Sir William Drummond), and afterwards go with me to the Opera. Pray send me word how you are today.[17]

When Catherine offered support to Helena she fully expected it to be short term, because Colonel Paterson intended to travel to the continent to collect his disgraced daughter. The Duke of Wellington had also written to say that he was in contact with Helena, stating: 'I will certainly advise her to go immediately to her father. This is the only step which can . . . put her in a respectable situation if separated, or can obtain for her any allowance from [Captain Bligh] or his family. Anything else must devote her to certain destruction.'[18]

With help on the way, Catherine felt duty-bound to protect Helena until her family arrived. In sharp contrast, Mrs Maxwell refused to have anything to do with Helena. True to form, William deemed Mrs Maxwell's conduct 'a singular instance of heartlessness and of her absolute abandonment of the Christian virtue, charity'.[19]

The British ambassador was among those to openly voice his disapproval, making it clear that Helena was not fit for decent society, having 'left her husband's house on the most frivolous pretences'.[20] When Helena stated her intention to appear at the embassy to be presented to the king of Naples, Mr Hamilton wrote to her in no uncertain terms: 'It is quite out of my power to present to his Majesty, a lady who only a few weeks ago thought fit publicly to leave her husband's house and protection.'[21] He warned that if she turned up on the night, 'I shall certainly not hesitate to desire the servants not to admit you.'[22]

Taking exception to the slur, William besieged the minister with letters, causing Hamilton to write, 'My dear Wellesley – it is really not worthwhile for you and me to carry on a paper war about trifles.'[23] Unwilling to let the matter rest, William threatened legal action, accusing the ambassador of casting aspersions, 'derogatory to the character of an English Gentleman . . . tending unjustly to criminate my character and conduct'. Full of bluster, William did not have a case because the ambassador had been careful not to implicate anyone else. Pointing this out, Hamilton observed, 'I had only to look to the person in question, not to any other individual.'

The situation was getting out of hand, with hot-headed William growing more abusive, even suggesting that he would possibly issue a challenge to defend his honour. Undeterred by William's bullying tactics, Hamilton refused to back down, asserting, 'I can in no way alter or excuse Mrs Bligh's conduct, and had I acted otherwise, I am confident that all the other English ladies who propose to go to Court on Tuesday next, would stay away.'

Hamilton had deduced why William was so zealous in his appeal – if Helena was admitted to the function it would be a public declaration that the British ambassador had excused her conduct. In turn, this would exonerate William. A man of principle, Hamilton was not prepared to compromise his values, determining in one final note, 'It is indeed, high time that our correspondence on this unfortunate subject should terminate.' True to his word, Hamilton could not be drawn into any further exchanges. Foolishly, however, William continued to slander the ambassador all over Naples until Hamilton eventually felt compelled to offer up evidence for public scrutiny. Some months later, the protracted exchanges that passed between them would be published in the press, vindicating the ambassador and damaging William's reputation even further.

Double standards prevailed. While Helena was shamed and shunned by all, William was permitted to go about his business as usual, even boasting of his prowess in some quarters. The irony was that although William was quick to defend Helena in public, his private opinion was very different. Speaking candidly and confidentially to Dr Bulkeley, William complained bitterly about his mistress, calling her, 'a lewd and abandoned woman, who had given herself up to the grossest gratification of her passion.'[24]

31. Acting in the Dark

Captain Bligh was in a terrible state. When he wasn't consumed with anger, he was overcome with misery, often breaking down in floods of tears. After his wife abandoned him, it took Captain Bligh less than two weeks to gather a strong body of evidence against her, including sworn testimonials from witnesses and servants. Distressed by all he discovered, he wrote to Helena, 'It can leave no longer any possible doubt of your criminality, of which it seems you did not hesitate to make even my house the theatre.'[1]

Helena remained stubbornly unrepentant. Confounded as to why Catherine would harbour her husband's mistress, Captain Bligh decided that she needed to be made aware of the facts. He wrote to Catherine, 'I have every reason to believe Mrs Bligh had been carrying on an intrigue for some time previous to her elopement from my house with Mr Long Wellesley, I therefore can now only look upon her as his mistress.'[2]

Offering to provide proof of the affair, Bligh suggested he call on Catherine. A more curious woman may well have permitted herself a quick look at the evidence uncovered. Catherine was an intelligent woman, but she was also very trusting, always ready to think the best of the man she loved. As far as she was concerned, William was merely doing his family duty to protect his cousin. Aside from this, she firmly believed that Bligh was a dangerous madman: violent, abusive and wildly deluded. Wanting nothing to do with him, Catherine's reply was brief but firm: 'I beg to state that I am by no means "acting in the dark". The line of conduct

I think proper to pursue towards Mrs Bligh is founded upon my firm conviction of her innocence.'[3]

With hopes dashed of acquiring an ally in Catherine, Captain Bligh tried a different approach. He went on the rampage, sending threatening letters to William and issuing several challenges. It was an age when men sometimes duelled to defend their honour, but eleven years had passed since William's infamous gunfight with Lord Kilworth and he now held his own mortality in greater esteem. Deftly refusing Bligh's challenges on the grounds that he was innocent of all charges, William stated that fighting in a duel would be construed as 'a confirmation of the malicious reports.'[4] On another occasion, William declared arrogantly that if he were ever convicted of criminal intercourse in court 'it would be time enough to fight, but till I am declared guilty I shall be presumed innocent'.[5]

Hell-bent on revenge, Captain Bligh and his brother took to following William's carriage with loaded pistols in their pockets, with the cuckold proclaiming, 'if I cannot have satisfaction in one way, I will in another'.[6]

Captain Bligh's reaction merely reinforced Catherine's opinion that he was a madman. As she often travelled in the same carriage as William, she was terrified that someone would in due course be shot and killed. Eventually she went to the police and asked them to place Captain Bligh under arrest. The police informed her that they would have to investigate the matter and, in the meantime, all parties involved would have to be taken into custody. Captain Bligh, Edward Bligh and William were imprisoned. While the brothers paced their cells like caged animals, raging furiously at their captors, William made the best of the situation by bribing the guards handsomely to provide him with a feast washed down with fine wine.

Catherine and Helena were placed under house arrest for their own protection. Catherine felt thoroughly humiliated, particularly when she was forced to send an appeal to Hamilton at the British embassy. The ambassador visited her the next day and arranged for all parties to be liberated, with William and Bligh bound over to keep the peace. Captain Bligh's excessive behaviour made Catherine even more convinced that Helena had been telling the truth about his violence and abuse, particularly when the spell in prison did not deter his pursuit of William.

William gave Catherine no cause for concern, treating her with affection and indulgence while not paying any undue attention to Helena. Once his wife was safely tucked up in bed, however, he locked his bedroom door, sneaked out of the house and strolled down the road to his mistress. It was a dangerous game to play, but the prospect of getting caught made it even more thrilling. On the odd night that William visited Catherine in her bedchamber, Helena was jealous and petulant until William soothed her with empty promises.

Skilfully juggling his women, William somehow managed to keep them both happy. In many respects the ladies in his life were very different. Passionate, demanding and unpredictable, Helena could explode in a jealous rage at any time. After a night with her, William was often relieved to be going home to his gentle, accommodating wife. Despite these contrasts, they did have one thing in common – they were both hopelessly in love with the same man.

Hunted by Captain Bligh, dogged by Mrs Bligh and involved in a legal dispute with the British ambassador, William was desperate to escape Naples. Unaware of the looming scandal, Lord Maryborough had written from England on 1 August 1823 with wonderful news concerning William's finances. Bursting with enthusiasm, William's father proclaimed:

> You may return at the end of three years with all your debts paid or secured – with all your conditions satisfied; with the Wardenship of the Forest restored to you and your family, with Mrs Wellesley's diamonds saved, with your farms on all your estates in perfect repair, and the future outgoings for repairs regulated upon an economical and certain footing,

without an arrear due to any person whatever, and a clear income of £13,000 a year!⁷

This was a remarkable achievement; Lord Maryborough had worked tirelessly to resolve his son's affairs. Utilizing his considerable experience in managing estates, Maryborough increased productivity and profitability in Wiltshire, Essex and Hampshire by finding prosperous new tenants, introducing new farming methods and restocking farms. As a result, business was thriving and William should have been delighted with the outcome. He would be able to move back to England and live in style at Draycot House, with a handsome income of £23,500 a year inclusive of his wife's pin money.

Nevertheless, William was not happy because he could not bear the prospect of living in exile for another three years. Thoroughly fed up with the untenable situation he had created for himself in Naples, he wanted to return to England immediately. From his perspective, his estates were now reaping sizeable profits so he did not see any reason why he should remain abroad – or even bother to repay his creditors. All he needed was parliamentary privilege to protect himself from prosecution for debts, and then he could take up residence at Draycot House and resume his former lifestyle. Rather than being grateful to his trustees for their enormous efforts, William had grown resentful and impatient with them. Irritated that nobody had managed to procure a seat in Parliament for him, he suggested that his trustees were not doing enough. He wrote to his father, 'I should conceive there could be little difficulty without fear, for a few hundred pounds, of purchasing me a seat in Parliament, before I return . . . it can be hardly necessary to [refuse] my resolution.'⁸

In an ungrateful letter filled with subtle recriminations, William went on to imply that he could have done a much better job of managing his affairs himself. Finishing on a note of self-pity, he lamented, 'My friends and acquaintances in England act as if I was *dead*.'⁹

William had benefited greatly from Lady Catherine's death, particularly as Draycot House had now passed to Catherine. Sir James Tylney Long had undertaken extensive remodelling, transforming his ancestral home into a stately mansion with an elegant Georgian facade of fourteen bays, plus wings to the east and west elevations.[10] The house stood on a sizeable estate of 4,000 acres, which meant that William could quite easily resume his role as lord of the manor. With Draycot House ready and waiting for him, he realized that he did not want to lose Catherine or the wealth and status his marriage afforded him. He resolved to dispose of his mistress, severing all ties when he quit Naples. With this in mind, William hired a carriage and made arrangements for Helena to travel to Paris, where her father had arranged to meet her. On discovering his intention, Helena became hysterical and threatened that she would 'inform his wife that there had been criminal intercourse between them'.[11]

By the end of September 1823, preparations were well under way for the Long Wellesleys to leave Naples. They planned to head straight for Paris, only stopping off for a few days to visit William's sister Priscilla, Lady Burghersh in Florence. Much to his regret, William was not able to abandon Mrs Bligh because she launched into such tirades, threatening to tell his wife about the abortion and generally 'conducted herself with great violence'.[12] Catherine reluctantly agreed that Mrs Bligh could travel with the family because she knew that Colonel Paterson was already en route to Paris to collect his daughter. Owing to this, she fully expected that Mrs Bligh would be safely returned to her own family within the month.

William and Catherine left Naples on 5 October 1823, chased away by Captain Bligh and his brother, who pursued them out of town with loaded pistols. This was not the last time they would encounter Bligh, who would resurface to inflict his revenge, but for now they had escaped relatively unscathed. On this journey the Long Wellesleys' entourage included Dr Bulkeley, Pitman the tutor, Bicknell and Meara, who would all continue to bear witness to the unfolding melodrama. Newspapers reported with a touch of irony,

'Mr and Mrs Long Wellesley, who were the charm of every party in Naples, have left for Paris.'[13]

En route to Florence, the party stopped at picturesque Albano, overlooking a volcanic lake close to Rome. Catherine decided to break their journey for a few days to explore and visit the sights in Rome. Helena was growing increasingly petulant and her presence was becoming burdensome. Keen to be rid of her, Catherine decided that it would be in everyone's best interests for Helena to head straight for Paris as planned, especially as her father had arranged to meet her there. Catherine asked William to make all the necessary travel arrangements, and she prevailed on Dr Bulkeley to accompany Helena, so that she would not have to travel alone. When Helena heard the news over dinner she flew into such an ungovernable frenzy that Catherine had to take her upstairs and summon Bulkeley to sedate her. Left alone at the table with Pitman, William remarked, 'I should not be surprised if Mrs Bligh in her rage shall tell my wife that there has been some intrigue between us, but I have one satisfaction, Mrs Long Wellesley will not believe it.'[14]

The doctor found Mrs Bligh in a state of extreme agitation. Becoming hysterical, she threatened suicide, saying, 'Mr Wellesley has ruined me . . . and now he wants to desert me, and I am determined I will tell his wife.'[15] Helena had given up a great deal to be with William: the sanctuary of her home and marriage as well as her reputation. What she did not seem to appreciate, however, was that William had never asked her to leave her husband – in fact, he had vehemently discouraged the move. Considerable remonstration continued between Bulkeley and Helena, until the despairing woman attempted to throw herself out of the window, but she was no match for the bulky eighteen-stone doctor, who restrained her easily. Hearing the commotion, Catherine walked into the room and after a lengthy discussion managed to persuade Helena to travel on to her family without further delay.

Setting off for Paris, it was a stressful journey for the good doctor because Mrs Bligh's conduct was 'most violent and improper' as she constantly baited him.[16] On one occasion she told him that William had promised to catch up with her carriage in Florence, vowing 'that they never more should part'. Remonstrating with her, Bulkeley pointed out the ruin this would cause to both William and his wife. However, Helena insisted that many men kept mistresses, mentioning one particular nobleman of high rank, saying, 'He always kept a mistress in the house, and his wife was not a bit the less happy.' She then proceeded to observe, 'No woman could resist such a fine fellow as Mr Long Wellesley,' going on to remark, 'Mrs Long Wellesley is not fit to be the wife of such a splendid fellow.'

32. Florence

CRANE

1823

Arriving in Florence on 21 October 1823, the Long Wellesleys were impressed by the architecturally beautiful city steeped in history, art, music and culture. William's brother-in-law, Lord Burghersh, had been the Minister Plenipotentiary for the past eight years, a job that suited him well because it enabled him to indulge his passion for Italian opera and cultivate his musical skills. A fine violinist and prolific composer, he had recently covered himself in glory by founding the Royal Academy of Music in London. His wife was an accomplished artist and painter, as well as being William's younger sister. Lord and Lady Burghersh were an interesting, glamorous couple, in their element in Florence.

Within days of arriving, William decided that his family would settle there for the winter, insisting that it was too treacherous to cross the Alps at that time of the year, particularly with young children in tow. Catherine was hugely disappointed because she had planned to meet her sisters in Paris and pass some months with them there. Still grieving for her mother, she longed for the comfort of Dora and Emma. She was also distraught because the lengthy correspondence between William and Mr Hamilton had recently been published in the English newspapers; she was mortified that the whole nation had been entertained with every last detail of the sordid episode in Naples. Dora sent an optimistic, affectionate note of reassurance:

> My dear Catherine, I think the scandal you alluded to seems
> quite forgotten . . . I own that I can hardly help lamenting that

the Paris scheme is for the present laid aside. I should so infinitely have preferred passing the winter with you there, to spending it anywhere, or with any lady.[1]

William had various motives for avoiding Paris, but primarily he wanted to keep Catherine separate from her family and friends. Despite Dora's reassurances, William was aware that the debacle in Naples was still fresh in everybody's minds. Catherine had many friends in Paris and he was worried that they would convince her to leave him and return to England. In Florence, however, Catherine was alone and vulnerable with nobody to take her side – William wanted to keep things that way. Another reason was the fact that he had caught up with Helena's carriage and he intended to pass a pleasant winter in Florence with his mistress.

On arriving in Florence, Catherine was surprised to find Helena comfortably settled in her own apartment; Bulkeley had been unable to shunt her on to Paris. Before long Helena moved into the same hotel as the family and resumed her habit of dining with them in the evenings. Whenever William hosted dinner parties he invited only gentlemen who would not take exception to her presence, but on one occasion Catherine invited several ladies, who all sent excuses. Scandal had followed them from Naples and the situation was becoming increasingly onerous for Catherine.

William was unconcerned because his sister was a woman of great influence, presiding over Florentine society in a similar manner to Hamilton in Naples. Expecting special dispensation, he was sorely disappointed when Priscilla proved to be highly proper – only the truly worthy were admitted into her elite circle. When William appeared at the opera with his wife and Helena in tow, Priscilla was outraged. It was one thing to keep a mistress discreetly and quietly, but it was totally unacceptable to steal another man's wife and parade her in public. Harbouring no illusions about her wayward brother, Priscilla thoroughly disapproved of his domestic arrangements and she promptly excluded Mrs Bligh from polite company. Taking Catherine under her wing, Priscilla introduced her to her closest friends and whenever the Long Wellesleys attended functions, the invitation was never extended to Mrs Bligh, who was left behind to sulk at her hotel.

Aside from all this, the talented ambassador had his own reasons for despising his brother-in-law. Lord Burghersh had been on board one of the Royal Navy ships sent into the Dardanelles when William declared war on Turkey, in 1807. It had been a minor event in history, but with major outcomes for those affected. Burghersh was disgusted by the way William had never shown any remorse, even though his arrogance had ruined many lives. Two hundred Englishmen had died needlessly, cut down in the prime of life – parents lost sons, wives lost husbands, and countless children grew up without their fathers. With the horror of the carnage still fresh in his mind, Burghersh had written to his father:

> You will hardly believe that in the four forts of the Dardanelles there are three hundred and odd pieces of cannon, firing marble shot, some of them the enormous weight of nine hundred pounds. One of this last calibre came across the quarter-deck near where I was standing, and smashed three men, so that there was only the legs of one, a part of the shoulder of another remaining.[2]

Less than two years after this incident, Burghersh had served alongside William in the Peninsula, witnessing the insubordination that led to his dismissal.

Within a week of arriving in Florence, William resumed his old habit of spending all his days and nights with his mistress, while neglecting his wife and only meeting up with her at dinner. Catherine had grown accustomed to William being out during the day, so initially she did not suspect anything. She would later remark about Helena,

> Her conduct before me all this time was perfectly correct; I had no reason to imagine she did not deserve the opinion I had formed of her. She appeared to be very fond of my chil-

dren; when the eldest boy met with an accident, she was very kind and attentive to him.[3]

While William enjoyed his ménage à trois, Bulkeley, Pitman and Meara were unwilling participants in the deception, maintaining an elaborate charade to protect Catherine's feelings.[4] Life was extremely stressful for the loyal employees, especially for Meara, who bore the brunt of the burden in helping to sneak William around the hotel undetected. On one particularly traumatic occasion, Mrs Bligh sent a hotel waiter to fetch Meara at about noon. When the valet arrived at the door of her sitting room, she demanded, 'What is to be done? Mr Wellesley's here. How shall we get him up?'[5] William then appeared, stark naked under his silk *robe de chambre*, a circumstance that made it virtually impossible for Meara to smuggle him unnoticed through hotel passages that were by now bustling with guests and servants employed in cleaning tasks. To add to the tension, Catherine was up and about and looking for William, so they could bump into her at any turn. Meara managed the task admirably, running on ahead and contriving to empty the corridors by using one excuse or another. As soon as the path was clear, he signalled for William to follow and the two men ducked and dived until William was safely back inside his own bedchamber.

Everyone venerated the good doctor, particularly William, who always treated him with the utmost respect and 'held him in a sort of awe'.[6] While Bulkeley remained a close friend and confidant of William, he was also deeply loyal to Catherine. When Pitman expressed surprise that the physician had left behind a thriving practice in Naples in order to accompany the family, Bulkeley told him that he had come along to protect Mrs Long Wellesley, saying that he was afraid that William would 'wipe the floor with her'. The stout doctor and spare tutor struck up a firm friendship, united in the common task of shielding Mrs Long Wellesley and her children.

*

Despite the valiant attempts of her staff to shield her from the truth, Catherine was growing increasingly suspicious. Not long afterwards, her eyes were finally opened to the true nature of her husband's relationship with Mrs Bligh. When she challenged William, she expected him to concede and apologize, as he had done with the Maria Kinnaird affair. But on this occasion he chose to ignore her protests; after all, what could she do to stop him? Tensions were high: Catherine continued to object, while William refused to relent.

Everything began to unravel alarmingly when William decided to teach Catherine a lesson and remind her who was in charge. He was not the type of man to administer a beating, but his methods were just as painful and humiliating. Dropping all pretence, he started to ignore his wife in public, while paying marked attention to his mistress. Handing Helena down from his carriage, he would offer his arm to her, leaving Catherine to be attended by Bulkeley or some other gentleman of the party. The doctor was one of the few respectable people prepared to go out with them, only tagging along to accompany Catherine and spare her embarrassment. One night at the opera William sat at the front of the box with Helena, flirting so shamelessly that Catherine felt obliged to issue a caution, asking him 'to be more circumspect in his behaviour, on account of the public opinion'.[7] Never one to take kindly to reproof, especially from his wife, William retaliated by rebuking her and paying even more attention to Helena. Catherine found his blatant disregard excruciating. Retreating into a dark corner, she began to cry silently until she was 'seized with strong hysterical fits', sobbing so intensely she could barely breathe. As she was always in control of her feelings, Pitman and Bulkeley were alarmed to see her in such a state, particularly in public. The tutor rushed away to fetch some water while the doctor stayed behind, coaxing her to breathe deeply. Clutching tightly to Bulkeley's arm, Catherine begged, 'Don't you leave me.'

William ignored his wife completely during the entire episode; it was left to Bulkeley to take Catherine home as she cried pitifully, hugging herself tightly to try to stop the grief pouring out of her in huge racking sobs. When the doctor asked her if she was in any pain, she replied along the lines, 'I have always thought that the term broken-hearted was just an expression, but I have such a pain in my chest it genuinely feels like my heart is breaking. I can barely breathe with the hurt of it all.' Half in love with the sweet woman, Bulkeley suppressed the urge to take her in his arms and comfort her. Instead he held her hand and promised, 'I will speak to Mr Long Wellesley tomorrow.'

At the earliest opportunity, Bulkeley tried his hardest to persuade William to send Mrs Bligh on her way to Paris, but he kept delaying or making up excuses to avoid doing so. In the meantime the doctor was often subjected to the uncomfortable chore of dining with the family in the evenings, sitting at the same table as William, his wife and his mistress. Pitman and the children were permitted to join them for dessert and afterwards they all retired to the drawing room, where the atmosphere was always tense because the lovers often drank too much and flirted outrageously. William was in the habit of reclining on a sofa near the fire and Helena would contrive to sit nearby, positioning a large screen to protect herself from the heat, but mainly to shield her from view.

On one particular evening, the couple were visible when Helena slipped off her shoe and placed her foot in William's lap, caressing the bulge in his breeches. All in a flurry, Pitman jumped up, grabbed a pack of cards and gathered the children around a table at the far end of the room, engaging them in a lively game that distracted them admirably. Having learned from past experience, Catherine did not rise to the provocation; she would not give William the satisfaction of seeing her break down. Her eyes did not stray from her needlepoint as she continued sewing, her tapestry box at her feet. Nevertheless, the doctor thought it prudent to move his chair closer to Catherine, manoeuvring his bulky frame into a position that obscured her view of the lovebirds. Opening up his newspaper as wide as possible, he made small observations to her as he turned the pages.

William needed to find new ways to provoke his wife. He was aware that while Catherine would suffer her own indignities with

quiet restraint, she would not tolerate him interfering with the
children. He started to use the boys as weapons, adopting various
tactics to alienate them from their mother. One evening he picked
up the decanter and poured each of the boys a large glass of claret.
They looked over at their mother, knowing she would disapprove,
but their father encouraged them to drink up, promptly refilling
their glasses when they were empty. Wanting to avoid a blazing
argument in front of the children, Catherine walked over to the
table and removed the wine without saying a word. She knew that
if she spoke, she would be on the receiving end of a barrage of
insults from her husband. William ordered her to put the wine
back, insisting that he knew what was best – after all, he had drunk
alcohol when he was their age. Locking eyes, Catherine returned
his glare, although she did not dare to utter the obvious retort,
'And look how well you turned out!'

Laughing malevolently, William ridiculed Catherine for being
stuffy and encouraged his children to follow suit. The boys snig-
gered at her and from then onwards they often joined their father
in taking a glass or two of wine in the evenings. Alcohol made them
belligerent and they argued with their mother whenever she
objected to their drinking or asked them to go to bed. Will was ten
and James eight when they suffered their first hangovers. During
this time William also encouraged the boys to use foul language,
entering into bawdy conversations with them and speaking about
women in the most obscene terms. He frequently advised them to
debauch whenever they could, stating, 'You should hunt women
young and old, at your full pleasure.'[8] On another occasion William
suggested that women in their thirties were dried up and withered,
remarking, 'A lady is worth nothing after the age of twenty-five.'[9]
The snipe was directed at Catherine, who would be thirty-five on
her next birthday. Angling for an argument, William continued,
'If I was twenty-one again I would know how to act!'

Keeping her eyes fixed on her needlepoint, Catherine observed
quietly, 'I wish that I was twenty-one again. Then I should know
how to act.'

'What do you mean by that?' demanded William roughly.

'I was merely agreeing with you,' replied Catherine. 'I wish that I was twenty-one again. Then I should know how to act.'

Bulkeley was pleased to hear Catherine's clever response, but he could tell that she was labouring under great emotion. Deciding to call a halt to the evening, the doctor stood up and bid a polite goodnight to Catherine, then walked contemptuously past Mrs Bligh without a word. Outraged by the blatant slight, Helena retorted, 'This is a pretty gentleman-like sort of doctor you have got! What terrible treatment of a lady, in her own drawing room.'

'Perhaps Doctor Bulkeley does not think that this drawing room belongs to you,' replied Catherine tartly. She then excused herself from the company, ushering the children out of the room. Sensing the shift in her attitude, the boys did not argue, but followed her obediently upstairs to bed.

After participating in this farce for three tiresome weeks, Bulkeley and Pitman were shocked to realize that William and Helena 'had formed a system to alienate the children's affections from their mother'.[10] By constantly undermining and ridiculing Catherine, the boys were growing increasingly dismissive of her. After discussing the matter, Pitman told the doctor, 'I cannot afford much aid in the drawing room, but in the school room you might rely on my powerful cooperation to prevent such a calamity.'[11] From this period onward the gentlemen generally contrived to keep the children grouped around their mother in the evenings, singing rhymes or playing games until it was time for them to go to bed.

Always fiercely loyal to her husband in public, Catherine maintained a dignified silence and did not confide her concerns until mid-December when Bulkeley accompanied her on a night visit to the nursery, as Victoria was ill. After receiving assurance that her daughter was in no danger, she burst into tears and said, 'Doctor Bulkeley, I am convinced you are my friend, and perceive how you have taken my part, and I feel satisfied that you will not desert me in the hour of my distress; for indeed I now want a friend.'[12] Soothing as ever, the doctor pledged his support.

Although Catherine had known about the affair for some time, she was powerless to act. She was stranded alone in a foreign country, with no family or friends to help her. If she left the marital home she would find herself in a similar situation to Helena, an outcast with a tarnished reputation. Never one to miss an opportunity, William would undoubtedly spread slander, saying that she had eloped with some man or other – maybe even citing Bulkeley. Worse still, she would be forced to leave her children behind.

Tentatively, Bulkeley suggested, 'You should throw yourself on the protection of your brother-in-law, the ambassador.' This was a good plan; it would mean that nobody could accuse Catherine of misconduct. But there was still the problem of leaving the children behind – this was something she would *never* consider. Why should she leave her home and her children? Catherine would stay and fight – it was the mistress who had to go.

Catherine remained steadfast, insisting, 'Nothing could induce me to quit my husband.' Fixing a brave smile on her face, she returned to the drawing room tranquil and composed. Her opportunity to finally exorcise the other woman came when she discovered that Mrs Bligh had received several letters from her parents, advising that it was highly improper for her to continue living in the same hotel as Mr and Mrs Long Wellesley. They insisted that she travel to Paris immediately and they had even sent £200 to pay the expense of her journey. The Duke of Wellington had also written to Helena in the strongest terms urging her to return to England. In view of this, Catherine told Helena that she should respect the wishes of her family and travel immediately to Paris where her father was waiting to meet her. On hearing her words, Helena flew into a terrible rage and became violently abusive. Shocked by her obscene language, Catherine told the irate woman that she had no choice but to withdraw her protection.

In no uncertain terms, Catherine told William to make arrangements for Mrs Bligh's immediate departure. After all, it was what her family demanded. Naturally, Helena raved and threatened suicide, but William had run out of excuses to keep her there. That same day, Catherine summoned Bulkeley after finding the lock on the medicine chest smashed open. Guileless as ever, Catherine worried that Mrs Bligh would take an overdose, but the doctor had

WILTSHIRE ELECTION.

Nomination at Devizes,

On the 18th of JUNE Instant,

THE GLORIOUS ANNIVERSARY

OF

THE BATTLE

OF

WATERLOO!

It is no less extraordinary than gratifying that the Day on which the illustrious

DUKE OF WELLINGTON

obtained his most splendid Titles should be commemorated in this great and Independent County by the

NOMINATION

OF HIS NEPHEW,

Wm. Long Wellesley, Esq.

To be one of our REPRESENTATIVES in PARLIAMENT.

We cannot err in supporting the Man who has fought with that gallant Hero in the midst of some of those Battles which have saved our Country from Perdition.
We surely shall do right in Electing this near Relative of the Noble Duke to be our Representative, who now nobly steps forward to rescue our County from Tyranny.

STICK CLOSE TO THE QUESTION!!

Wellesley & Independence

HEREAFTER FOR

YOUR CHILDREN'S CHILDREN,

OR THE

Disgraceful Slavery of Clubs and Quorum.

Let us then rally around him on the Day of Nomination, when it is earnestly hoped that the Friends of Mr. LONG WELLESLEY will convince the World of their Loyalty and Independence by appearing in his Favor.

Brodie and Dowding, Printers, Salisbury.

17. William produced posters for his election campaign in 1818.
He rarely missed an opportunity to exploit his connection
with the Duke of Wellington.

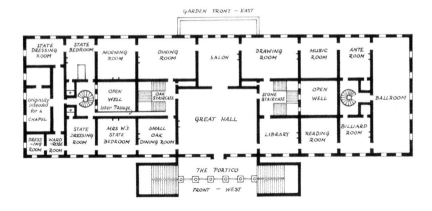

18. This floor plan shows that the Principal State Floor at Wanstead enjoyed panoramic views of the gardens. Harmoniously proportioned, the interconnecting rooms provided one huge area for entertainment.

19. The furniture at Wanstead House was magnificent. This buhl armoire was auctioned by Christies in December 2005, selling for £1,016,000.

WANSTEAD HOUSE, ESSEX.

Magnificent Furniture,
COLLECTION OF FINE PAINTINGS AND SCULPTURE,
MASSIVE SILVER & GILT PLATE,
SPLENDID LIBRARY OF CHOICE BOOKS,
THE VALUABLE
CELLARS OF FINE-FLAVOURED OLD WINES, ALES, &c. &c.

A CATALOGUE
OF THE MAGNIFICENT AND COSTLY

FURNITURE

OF THE PRINCELY MANSION,
WANSTEAD HOUSE,
CONSISTING OF GRAND

COSTLY STATE BEDSTEADS, WITH RICH VELVET, SILK, DAMASK, AND OTHER FURNITURES;
WINDOW CURTAINS AND HANGINGS; EXCELLENT BEDDING;

Splendid Suites of Drawing and Ball Room Curtains of Genoa Velvet, Damasks,
and Silks, trimmed with Gold Lace;

COUCHES, SOFAS, AND CHAIRS, TO CORRESPOND; BEAUTIFUL AXMINSTER CARPETS;
BRILLIANT PLATES OF GLASS; SET OF ORIENTAL EBONY CHAIRS AND SOFAS; SCREENS AND CABINETS;
RARE OLD CHINA, AND RICH CUT GLASS;
A Variety of Parisian and Buhl Cabinets and Bookcases; magnificent Library Tables; Cabinet Articles of every
Description; elegant Clocks; superb Chandeliers; full-sized Billiard Table;
SPLENDID SERVICES OF MASSIVE RICH CHASED AND GILT SILVER PLATE,
ABOUT 22,000 OUNCES,
IN USEFUL AND ORNAMENTAL ARTICLES;
Valuable Agate-Handle Knives and Forks; exquisite Carvings in Ivory, superbly mounted; magnificent Plateau, &c.
A VALUABLE
COLLECTION OF FINE PAINTINGS AND SCULPTURE,
BY ITALIAN, FLEMISH, AND ENGLISH MASTERS;
Bronzes, Casts from the Antique, splendid Gobelin Tapestry, Damask and Velvet Hangings, &c.

Library of Ancient and Modern Books,
Elegantly Bound, embracing many early Specimens of Typography, continued by every Work of Celebrity to the present
Day; also abounding in the GRAPHIC ART, with the most choice Impressions from the *Foreign* and *English Schools.*

The choice fine-flavoured OLD WINES, in Wood and Bottle;
CAPITAL HOME-BREWED ALE;
Fixtures; Two Fire Engines; Brewing and Dairy Utensils; Garden Lights and Tools; Green House Plants; Pleasure
Boats, Punts; capital Harness; and a Variety of other Articles,
The whole forming an Assemblage of the most valuable Property ever offered to the Public:

WHICH, BY ORDER OF THE TRUSTEES, WILL BE
SOLD BY AUCTION,

BY MR. ROBINS,
(OF WARWICK HOUSE, REGENT STREET,)
ON THE PREMISES, WANSTEAD HOUSE,
On MONDAY, 10th JUNE, 1822, and 31 following Days,
SATURDAYS AND SUNDAYS EXCEPTED, AT ELEVEN O'CLOCK.

To be viewed on WEDNESDAY, the 22nd of MAY, and every Day till the Time of Sale (Sunday excepted) by Catalogues,
at Five Shillings each Part, to admit Three Persons, which will be delivered at WANSTEAD HOUSE; at Messrs. ROBSON,
LIGHTFOOT, and ROBSON's Office, Castle Street, Leicester Square; at Messrs. BRUNDRETT, SPINKS, and REDDISH's,
Temple; and at Mr. ROBINS's Office, Regent Street.

Printed by J. BRETTELL, Rupert Street, Haymarket.

20. The frontispiece from the Wanstead House sale catalogue.

21. Rue Castiglione, Paris, c. 1829. William and Catherine rented apartments in this fashionable part of the city. Place de Vendôme is pictured in the distance.

22. When visiting Naples, Catherine often stopped her carriage on the brow of a hill to take in views of Mount Vesuvius.

THE HON.BLE

WILLIAM POLE TYLNEY LONG WELLESLEY.

23. An engraving of William Long Wellesley, c. 1827.

24. The idyllic Lake House in Wanstead Park was the childhood home of Helena Bligh.

25. *The effects of a Blithe W riding on a Long Pole* delights in innuendo as Mrs 'Blithe' sits astride an erect see-saw. In the background, Dora and Emma look on while the Lord Chancellor shields the children.

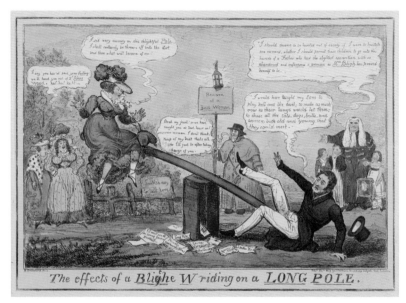

26. William created theatre in the courtroom, sitting in benches usually reserved for counsel and constantly disrupting the proceedings. Mrs Bligh is pictured behind him although she never actually attended the trial.

27. *Vice and Profligacy extinguished by Equity* indicates that *Wellesley v Beaufort* is seen a seminal moment in the fight for justice.

VICE and PROFLIGACY, Extinguished by EQUITY.

28. A portrait of Catherine by her friend Lady Parker (c. 1825).

29. *A Bright Thought* ridicules William's intellectual posturing through ironic book titles. His suggestive pose indicates that he remained attractive and virile well into his forties.

more sinister suspicions. William confirmed his fears, saying, 'I'll be damned if she would not poison Mrs Wellesley, if she could . . . we must get rid of this damned dangerous bitch!'

Four days before Christmas 1823, Catherine and the doctor watched from an upstairs window as a carriage bore Helena away to Paris.

33. *The Final Straw*

చ๛ๆ๛ว

1824

Catherine's attitude towards William's infidelity was fairly unusual for the time. Georgiana Spencer, Duchess of Devonshire,
had famously tolerated a ménage à trois under her own roof and
many other women (and men) elected to ignore marital infidelity.
Genuinely believing in his own blamelessness, William frequently
proclaimed, 'I'm not a quarrelsome man.'[1] He considered it perfectly acceptable for husbands to have affairs. Scrutinizing members
of his own family, he was aware that even the most scrupulous of
men enjoyed the occasional peccadillo.

The Duke of Wellington was a living legend, the epitome of a
knight in shining armour. By all accounts the lady by his side should
have been as bewitching as Guinevere or some other enchanting
heroine but, in reality, the gentle duchess was frail, pockmarked
and withdrawn. The situation was frustrating for Wellington, who
loved female company; over the course of his lifetime some of
his closest confidantes were women. These relationships were not
always platonic, but Wellington was never violently in love until
Marianne Patterson came along. When he first met the dark-haired
American beauty in 1816, he was captivated by her huge doe-like
eyes that were 'brilliant yet melting black'.[2] More than anything
else, he was struck by her endearing personality and onlookers
began to remark on his lover-like attendance of her. Although the
pair became close friends, Marianne's conduct was irreproachable
and there was never any question of a liaison while she was married.

When her husband died in 1823, Marianne was free to marry
again – but the duke was not. The great military commander was

utterly desolate. Marianne, in contrast, was not as heartbroken as he might have wished. Wellington was shocked when she fell straight into the arms of another man. The thing that hurt most was the fact that her admirer was his brother Richard, Marquess Wellesley. When Wellington heard news of the planned nuptials, he raged to his confidante Mrs Arbuthnot, stating that Richard had 'not a shilling in the world . . . no house to take her to . . . a most jealous disposition . . . a violent temper'.[3] The wedding went ahead at the Royal Lodge, Phoenix Park, in October 1823, causing another major rift between the two rival siblings. The marquess triumphed over the duke by plucking Marianne from under his nose and winning the affections of Wellington's most adored companion. Marrying a wealthy widow certainly eased Richard's financial embarrassments, plus his new wife was half his age and a great beauty. Nevertheless, the sixty-three-year-old Lothario still had a string of affairs, which the new marchioness found hurtful and difficult to tolerate. But just like the Duchess of Wellington, Marianne conformed to the custom of the time; she did not confront her husband.

Marital infidelity was not unusual, but there was a strict code of conduct. William had broken the golden rule – he humiliated his wife by parading his mistress in public. Aside from this, he should have known from experience that Catherine would not tolerate his adultery. Catherine conformed to the convention of the time in many respects – she was a dutiful wife, who supported her husband through many calamities – but she was also a strong, modern woman with a mind of her own. She had boldly challenged the lines of propriety on many occasions, becoming a lady of business, refusing to marry a man she did not love and standing firm against her family when they disapproved of William. Influenced by the bluestockings, Catherine believed in valuing herself. Owing to this, she would not compromise her principles – she would never share William with another woman.

Trusting that she had seen the last of Helena, Catherine hoped to regain intimacy in her marriage. Instead, William was furious with her for taking matters into her own hands, interfering in his business and ordering his mistress away. He firmly believed that she should behave like other wives and turn a blind eye. She had meddled in his affairs before, ordering Maria Kinnaird to move to France, and he was not prepared to tolerate it again. Abandoning all remaining civility, he treated Catherine with the utmost contempt, scarcely speaking to her without swearing and, when he did, it was usually to criticize her in the most obscene terms. He continued to undermine her in front of the children, and if she tried to engage him in conversation his stock reply was, 'What a damned fool you are.'[4]

More than anything, Catherine adored her children and William skilfully used them as a weapon to torment her. In November young Will was taking lessons at a riding school when he fell off a pony, fracturing his arm and completely dislocating his elbow joint. Consequently, Bulkeley recommended that he did not ride for several months, but William took him out again at the earliest opportunity. When Catherine and Bulkeley arrived on the scene, they saw that William was encouraging his sons to 'ride their ponies as hard as they could go'. The doctor was alarmed to see the boys galloping so recklessly and Catherine also cautioned them not to go so fast because Will's broken arm was still weak. On hearing this, William called her a 'damnation fool', telling her, 'drop your nonsense'. A few days later a similar occurrence took place when they visited Pisa and William was equally violent and insulting towards his wife.

Catherine's patience was reaching its limits. Meanwhile William was growing increasingly concerned that he could face criminal charges, and he tried his hardest to convince Bulkeley that he had never had sexual intercourse with Helena. Describing her as 'an abandoned and profligate woman', he said, 'She wished to intrigue with me, but I refused so to do.'[5] Knowing that Bulkeley had witnessed some inappropriate behaviour, he also complained, 'She has been constantly in the habit of pushing her feet between my legs as I sat at dinner.'[6] Although this did not fool the doctor, he was duped into believing that Mrs Bligh was on her way to Paris.

Within days of her departure, Helena managed to escape from

her keeper and double back to Florence. The hotel manager was able to provide her with secluded accommodation and William confided in Meara, 'Mr Schneiderff has let Mrs Bligh have apartments on the other side of the house; do not let anybody know anything about it.'[7] William kept his mistress in the same hotel as his wife for several months, slipping away for clandestine visits most days and nights. The situation grew increasingly nerve-racking for Meara, flitting undetected between the two apartments carrying clothes, medicines and other items. On several occasions he had to rouse his master in the early hours in order to sneak him back to his own bed before Bulkeley came to treat him for an eye infection.

Early in January the carnival at Florence commenced with a masked ball at one of the principal theatres. Lord and Lady Burghersh were present, along with the Long Wellesleys and a number of the English gentry. Shortly after arriving at the glitzy party, William left his wife and joined Helena in a carriage, where they both changed into costumes and masks procured for them by Meara. Cleverly disguised, they joined the masquerade undetected and danced the night away. For the entire evening, Catherine was left to trail along behind her sister-in-law, wondering what had become of her husband. William did not emerge from his bedchamber until three o'clock the following afternoon, courtesy of Meara's usual conjuring trick. The ruse had worked well for William, and he began to use disguises to avoid detection. This was not uncommon, and Sir Henry Mildmay was known to have smuggled himself into his mistress's house 'disguised with a beard and the dress of a sailor'.[8]

Subjected to such bizarre behaviour, it did not take Catherine very long to guess what was occurring. In a chilling prophecy she told Bulkeley, 'Mrs Bligh is hovering about me and the children like an evil spirit, and we are doomed to be dragged about as it might please.'[9] Although she never saw Helena, she felt the other woman's malevolent presence eating away at the fabric of her life. From this time onwards William treated Catherine with blatant disregard, refusing to accompany her to the opera or any other place. On several occasions Pitman noticed with regret the 'harsh, morose and unkind manner of Mr Wellesley towards his wife, who was of a meek and tender disposition, and appeared to suffer great pain and depression from the treatment she received'.[10]

Eventually Catherine's suspicions were confirmed when she spotted her arch rival at a window. Overwhelmed with despair, she sent for her good friend and demanded, 'So then, Doctor Bulkeley, Mrs Bligh has been in the very next apartments to mine ever since I withdrew from her my countenance and protection.'[11] The doctor implored Catherine not to act impulsively. Pledging to stand by her, he reasoned, 'You are now far from your relatives and friends, and I therefore entreat you to suppress your feelings and follow my counsel until you reach them.' Promising to follow his advice, Catherine adopted a dignified and reserved line of conduct towards her husband, biding her time.

The Long Wellesleys eventually arrived in Paris in May 1824, renting apartments at the elegant Hôtel de Londres in the fashionable Place de Vendôme. They quickly resumed their old habit of dining out with friends in the evenings. Thomas Moore and his set had moved on, replaced by a new wave of English elite intent on enjoying the frivolity of gay Paris. Catherine had high hopes, believing that Mrs Bligh would be reunited with her family and the affair would finally come to an end. However, when Helena stubbornly refused to meet her father, Colonel Paterson finally lost patience. Abandoning all hopes of saving her reputation, he publicly disowned his daughter and returned to England alone.

Popular as ever, Catherine had a strong network of friends in Paris. For the sake of appearances William always accompanied her out in the evenings, but he continued to slip away day and night to meet his mistress. Driving out one afternoon, Catherine saw William and Helena coming towards her in an open-top curricle. As the two carriages crossed alongside each other, the lovers ignored Catherine and continued to canoodle. This was the final straw for Catherine. Already at the lowest point in her life, she was a shadow of her former self and her husband's unfeeling conduct was driving her further into despair. A familiar stabbing pain seared Catherine's heart as she headed home, where the doctor attended her. True to his word, Bulkeley had accompanied her to Paris and would not leave her until she was safely with her family. The doctor had serious concerns because Catherine was suffering from seizures that gripped her chest so tightly they took her breath away.

Catherine realized that something had to be done. Her life was a charade; there were three people in her marriage and she was leading an utterly miserable existence. Strong beliefs in the sanctity of matrimony made her reluctant to leave. In addition, like so many other women in the same situation, her primary concern was for her children. English law decreed that men had full control of their children – women did not even have *any* rights to access. Playing his trump card, William made it clear that if she went, Catherine would have to leave her children behind. Arrogant as ever, it did not occur to him that he might be outmanoeuvred by his wife. Although Catherine had meekly stood by while he dissipated her fortune, she would put up a spectacular fight for her children. She needed to resurrect the bold and strong part of her nature. The time had come for her to act.

34. Catherine's Letter

❦

JUNE 1824

Letters played a major role in Georgian society; they were an important form of social networking and people eagerly awaited the penny-post deliveries that arrived three times a day in London.[1] News and gossip travelled fast as people dashed off replies by return, throwing in an amusing anecdote or clever turn of phrase. Numerous instructional books saw letter writing as an art form that should entertain and reflect the personality of the writer. Catherine's letters reveal her warmth as well as her open and honest nature. This was particularly apparent in a heart-wrenching appeal to her father-in-law, in which she poured out all her despair and misery. On 21 June 1824, Catherine sent the following letter to Lord Maryborough declaring her intention to separate from William:

> My Dear Lord Maryborough,
>
> Under a distress of mind which more than subdues me, it is with extreme reluctance I take up my pen to address you, aware that in the communication I am about to make, I must unavoidably increase the heavy affliction under which Lady Maryborough and yourself are at this moment suffering.
>
> You are, my dear Lord Maryborough, but too well acquainted with the miseries I have endured for many months past from the conduct of my husband, how I have borne them you are also acquainted with; and if I do not enlarge upon them here, it is only to spare your feelings and my own.

I had hoped by a silent submission to the wrongs I have experienced and conduct above reproach that I might yet reclaim my husband, and if possible, bring back to us both the happiness of which he had cruelly bereaved us. In this hope I have been painfully deceived, and I have reached the moment when a patient exercise of every measure calculated to produce such a result serves only to mark me out as a victim for further insult and degradation.

Under these distressing circumstances I am driven to feel that I was not created for such treatment and that the moment is arrived when, in justice to myself, my family and my children, I am called upon to take a most decided measure. Hitherto I have never considered *any* sacrifice too great to promote the happiness of my husband. I have shared with him the exile, the penalty of his imprudence, without a murmur still hoping, vainly hoping, that such devoted proof of affection might reclaim him, and that I should feel my reward in the returning affection of my husband. In this I have been disappointed . . .

You are unfortunately no stranger to the history of Mrs Bligh. I had hoped that Mr Long Wellesley had made an atoning sacrifice to myself and his family by a separation from this abandoned woman. This, I grieve to say, is not the case, and she is established at Paris, in the next street to myself, absorbing all the attentions, affections and society of my husband, and condemning me to the humiliating scene (in open day) of meeting him riding with her in the Bois de Boulogne, while I am taking there, my drive in my own carriage.

My dear Lord, this must end – my nerves, my health, my spirits and my happiness are the cost; I have borne it till I can bear it no longer. There is a point where submission becomes a weakness, and resistance is felt a duty. I have reached it and the sad alternative is mine to choose between living this wretched, with one who has (in conduct) cast me off, or mitigating my misery by separating myself from a husband, who no longer appears to value me. Every sentiment of just pride, of religious duty, binds me to prefer the latter sad alternative and under the harassed feelings of exhausted patience, I am unalterably determined (if Mr Long Wellesley will not give up Mrs Bligh) at every hazard and at every risk; to separate myself from a husband who already in conduct has abandoned me – preferring to live unhappy by myself to having under my eye the living cause of my misery. All I ask for is my children; do not let them be taken from me.

Under these feelings, and on this determination, I have thought it right to bring my situation under your Lordship's eye, in the hope that the voice of a father, combined with the influence of a heart like yours on him not yet (I trust) totally perverted, may still prevent a measure on which I am otherwise resolved. What it must cost me you must be well aware under the love I bear my children and the affection I yet retain for Mr Long Wellesley – alas! I can no longer rely on his promises while he is under a spell so fatal to our happiness. I have therefore determined on this appeal to your Lordship in the first instance, to my own family in the next, and failing either – to the laws of my country finally. This is my firm purpose, and if it can be arrested, it must be by the interference of friends, and by their becoming parties to the securities I require.

I demand the abandonment of Mrs Bligh, a solemn pledge of honour, on the part of Mr Long Wellesley to separate himself from her, never to revisit her and that she must be made to leave Paris and reside bearing her own name, in some known abode, distant from us. These are not hard terms to exact to reclaim him to my affection, to redeem him to himself, and to preserve him to my children! This is all I demand. In return, I offer, hard as it may be upon myself and my children, not merely to sacrifice any portion of my own fortune that may be deemed a liberal provision for Mrs Bligh, but I offer to forgive the wrongs he has heaped upon me, to banish them, if possible from my mind and still to cherish the expectation that when he is exported from the degrading thraldom which now surrounds him, conduct and happiness may once again become our mutual lot.

Failing this, I demand a separation from my husband, that it may be arranged for me, as early as possible, and that it may be conducted through the means of your Lordship's interference.

If this abandoned woman is to triumph, if my husband will not separate himself from her, it is time for me to look for a protector; and where can I so naturally expect to find one as in the father of my husband who, having witnessed the conduct of both, will be first to condemn his son and the last to refuse his protection to his unhappy wife.

It is my wish, my dear Lord Maryborough, that you should without loss of time have a communication with your son upon this melancholy subject. I have consulted our excellent and mutual friend, Sir George Dallas. He is of opinion with myself that the only person who can now have any proper influence over the mind of Mr Long Wellesley is yourself – it is vain for any person here to make the attempt again – it has been repeatedly tried, but alas! All have failed.

Pray remember me most kindly to Lady Maryborough and believe me my dear Lord,

Your affectionate & obliged,

Catherine Long Wellesley[2]

By any standards, this was a startlingly forthright letter to send to one's father-in-law but Lord Maryborough had always held Catherine in great esteem. During the early nineteenth century it was common for parents or friends to mediate when a couple was threatening to separate. Catherine had chosen her ally well; Lord Maryborough would prove to be a fair-minded man and one of the few people capable of standing up to William.

With endearing honesty, Catherine stated that her motive for writing was to 'reclaim the affections of my husband'. Despite all that had happened, she loved William and was hoping for reconciliation. She also set down generous 'terms', offering to pay off the mistress with 'any portion of my own fortune that may be deemed a liberal provision for Mrs Bligh'. This was precisely how she had handled the Maria Kinnaird affair, and she hoped it would have the desired effect on this occasion.

At face value, Catherine's letter seems to be an appeal straight from the heart. Barely mentioning the loss of her fortune, she talks of mental cruelty and desertion, insisting, 'I have borne it till I can bear it no longer.' On another level, however, it is a remarkably shrewd and calculated letter that hints at her future intentions. Lord Maryborough was an astute gentleman, with a sound knowledge of the law, so undoubtedly he understood the underlying message and implications.

Catherine was well aware that she was taking a serious step in challenging William. It was extremely rare for a wife to instigate a marital break-up, because women had no rights whatsoever regarding their offspring. English law decreed that children were entirely governed by their father, who could do as he wished, including denying access to the mother. If Catherine separated from her husband, the law compelled her to leave behind her children, and she faced the very real prospect of never being permitted to see them again.

Leaving children in the hands of a vengeful man sometimes had serious repercussions. When Lady Worsley eloped in 1781, she did not take her baby daughter with her because she felt certain that her husband would not want the child and would therefore hand her over at a later date. Just a short while afterwards, however, she received the dreadful news that her previously healthy infant was dead. Although she firmly believed that her husband had murdered the child in retribution, she could not prove it. Infant mortality was common and neither a coroner nor a magistrate investigated.[3]

Obviously this was an extreme case and there was no suggestion that William would have murdered his children. But he certainly had no qualms about causing them harm in other ways: by neglecting them; impairing their well-being with alcohol; or endangering them with reckless horse riding. A father had the right to do with his children as he saw fit, while a mother did not have the power to intervene. Unscrupulous men exploited this point of law to manipulate their wives, using their children as a weapon. This was highlighted by Byron, who remarked gleefully on the birth of his daughter, 'What an instrument of torture I have gained in you!'[4]

From experience Catherine knew that her husband was vindictive and she was genuinely fearful of what might happen next. In her letter to Lord Maryborough she expressed her greatest longing: 'All I ask is my children; do not let them be taken from me.'

35. Don't Forget Me

✦

JULY 1824

It took six days for Catherine's letter to reach Savile Row. Dropping everything, Lord and Lady Maryborough headed directly to France. Arriving in Paris late in the evening of 9 July, they immediately sent a note to their unsuspecting son. William was lounging in his hotel drawing room nursing a glass of port when the messenger arrived. On reading the communication from his parents, he roared so loudly he could be heard all around the Place de Vendôme. He burst into such an ungovernable fury, Bulkeley felt compelled to protect Catherine, so he stepped forward to place his considerable frame between the couple. Flinging his parents' note into the fireplace, William grabbed two heavy candlesticks and hurled them across the room. Picking up a book, he started to bang it on a table while screaming abuse at his wife, yelling, 'You damned bitch. You have set my own father and mother against me.'[1] He continued to rave in a most dreadful, menacing manner while Catherine stood silently, flinching at the abuse. Eventually William asked Bulkeley to leave the room, but the doctor refused to go because he believed that Catherine was in actual bodily danger and it was therefore his duty to stay with her. On hearing this, William turned his wrath upon the physician, unleashing a torrent of profanity. As Bulkeley delicately put it, '[Mr Long Wellesley] uttered every opprobrious epithet which language could furnish.'

Suspecting that his note would cause considerable disharmony, Lord Maryborough decided that it would be prudent to follow immediately behind it. Calling at the Hôtel de Londres, he heard the commotion in the drawing room and barged straight in. Lord

Maryborough did not need to speak even one word; William stopped dead in his tracks, disarmed by his father's steely blue glare. The air was heavy with disapproval, the patriarch standing firm, while his son squirmed like a small boy. Seized with irrational panic, William decided that the best course of action was to escape. Squealing like a pig, he grabbed a candlestick and bolted out through the French doors into the gardens. As Catherine watched her husband disappearing into the dark night, the flame from his candle fading into the distance, she could not have guessed that it would be the last time she ever saw William.

The following day Lord and Lady Maryborough attempted to see their son, but he refused to meet with them, insisting that he would not negotiate with his wife through a third party. As a result, a temporary agreement was reached through a series of curt notes. On 10 July, William wrote to Catherine, 'I will allow no one to interfere between me and my wife. Now write to me yourself and tell me what you want.'[2]

She replied:

> The treatment which I have endured from you for many months past has been such as I can no longer submit to . . . I have resolved to separate myself from a husband who already in conduct has abandoned me. It is horribly necessary for me to mention that I allude to your degrading connection with that abandoned woman, Mrs Bligh.

Although Catherine mentioned her intention 'to separate' she did not want to involve solicitors at this early stage. If anything, she simply wanted William to give up his mistress.

Trying to intimidate her, William countered, 'My lawyers as you well know are Messrs Lightfoot & Robson and they shall receive instructions from me to meet yours.'

Later that day he dashed off another note:

> I deny your ever having been treated by me in 'a degrading manner' or ever having been in conduct 'abandoned by me'.

I have only to end this communication between us, by praying to God you may not live, to repent every hour of your life your folly ... Whatever further communication you have to make to me had better be made through legal persons.

Unperturbed by his veiled threats, Catherine replied, 'It is my intention to go to England as early as possible ... and I request you will appoint a lawyer who may communicate with mine on my arrival there.'

In a magnanimous moment William wrote, 'It seems to me you may want money, I shall therefore request Daly to give you any you may require.'

Catherine's reply drips irony: 'I am very much obliged to you for your offer of money through Mr Daly. But as the command of a large sum is within my own power and entirely at my own disposal, I shall not have occasion to take advantage of your offer.'

Just five days after the arrival of her in-laws, travel plans had been made and Catherine was ready to leave for England. Her good friend Sir George Dallas had arrived to accompany her home. This sudden turn of events prompted William to attempt reconciliation, but Catherine kept the upper hand by refusing to see him before her departure. Filled with regret, William made frantic promises to his father, to Mr Daly and to Sir George Dallas, solemnly vowing that he would make amends to 'win back the affections of my wife'. Pledging on his honour, William resolved to immediately separate from Mrs Bligh, insisting he would never see her again. This was exactly what Catherine wanted to hear. On 14 July, she sent a conciliatory note to her husband:

I cannot leave Paris without expressing to you the great satisfaction I feel at my children being allowed to accompany me, nor without assuring you that as far as is in my power, I shall be happy to attend strictly to the wishes you have expressed and the instructions you have given in your letter for their management.[3]

William's tone was equally appeasing when he replied:

I received yesterday your note, in which you condescend to express your satisfaction, at being accompanied by your children. Their separation from me has broke my heart, but the interests of my family require the subjection of all feeling.[4]

Ending with a heartfelt postscript, underlined for emphasis, William implored, '*PS Don't let the children forget me.*'

Huge crowds were waiting at the docks when Catherine arrived back in England with her children. The throng recognized them and a cheer erupted as they stepped off the boat, leaving Catherine totally bemused until someone told her that they were waiting for the ship carrying the remains of Lord Byron. Life is fragile – Byron was merely thirty-six years old when he succumbed to a fever in Greece. William was the same age as the poet and Catherine felt a pang of regret as she remembered his recent ill health, including the debilitating eye infection he had been suffering for over a year. Despite all that had happened, Catherine did not relish returning to England alone.

Chivalrous Lord Maryborough had come to Catherine's rescue and worked wonders. Less than a month after writing to him, she was back living at Draycot House in Wiltshire. She was also pleased that William had behaved generously in the end, allowing the children to come home with her. It was a good sign. Lord Maryborough had also performed miracles in relation to William's financial affairs, settling debts much more quickly than anticipated. The arrangement with William's creditors was due to be completed on 29 September, which meant that he would soon be able to return to England. Two or three months apart would give them both time to reflect, and Catherine felt sure that he would give up his mistress and join her at Draycot very soon.

The media was unaware that William's intrigue with Mrs Bligh had continued after he left Naples, so there was no hint of a separation in the press. Newspapers confirmed Catherine's version of events, reporting, 'Mrs Long Wellesley and the three children are now at Draycot, where Mr Wellesley will join them on his return to England in September or October this year.'[5]

Everything seemed set for an amicable reconciliation. All William needed to do was to disentangle himself from his relationship with Mrs Bligh and win back Catherine's affections. But this would prove to be more difficult than he imagined.

36. A Monster Amongst Savages

JULY 1824

William was amazed by how much his wife had managed to accomplish in just one week. She had laid down terms for a temporary separation, organized travel arrangements and returned to England with her three children. Nevertheless, he too was heartened by the fact that they had parted on conciliatory terms and he fully expected to be back with his family at the end of September. As a gesture of goodwill, William had allowed Catherine to take the children with her, but there were stipulations. First, she had promised not to consult solicitors about a legal separation as this would jeopardize his creditors' agreement. She had also agreed to his terms regarding the upbringing and education of the children, who were to remain at Draycot at all times under the strict supervision of Mr Pitman. But money was the main inducement – William only agreed that the children could go home with Catherine after she offered him payment in the form of an alimony settlement. He would receive £4,000 a year, paid in quarterly instalments of £1,000.

William was a man of many contrasts with remarkable charisma. Aside from the many women that had fallen for him, the fact that he inspired great loyalty in men such as Bulkeley, Meara and Pitman paid testament to his considerable charm. Despite everything they had witnessed, all three of these men would continue to protect him at considerable cost to their own peace of mind. Going above and beyond the call of duty, they always had his best interests at heart and now they would work together to try to help him reconcile with his family. At his most beguiling, William was irresistible. Trying to make amends for his recent behaviour, a remorseful William apologized to his parents and even sent a contrite note to Bulkeley saying, 'You must forget all that has passed, excepting my regard for you: like Hamlet in the play, "I am somewhat choleric and rash."'[1]

After escorting Catherine to her boat, Lord and Lady Maryborough returned to Paris to counsel their son, making it clear that he needed to dispose of his mistress before he returned to England. William spun them convoluted yarns describing his previous attempts to escape from her. He told them that he had travelled hundreds of miles across the continent, stopping at many places with the express intention of losing her along the way. Despite his best endeavours, Helena was like a bloodhound, always managing to track him down. Constant suicide threats made it difficult for him to send her away. In fact, he believed she was so dangerously unstable that he had attempted to have her committed into a lunatic asylum just outside Paris, but she had managed to escape.[2]

Eventually Lord Maryborough enlisted the help of faithful Bulkeley, who agreed to accompany William on a tour of North America. This was a considerable undertaking for the doctor, but he believed that it would be the most effective way for William to become permanently detached from Mrs Bligh, while also convincing Catherine that he had commenced a line of reformation. The following day, William set off for The Hague while his parents stayed behind hoping they could persuade Helena to return to England with them. Instead they had to witness a terrible scene – Helena attempted suicide by taking laudanum, and she then slashed her wrists in front of them using sharp scissors. Horrified by what they had witnessed, Lord and Lady Maryborough called Dr Hyde to attend to her wounds. Lord Maryborough would later report to William, 'Doctor Hyde brought the Paris Mad Doctor to her, and, after staying two hours with her, he determined she was of sound mind, and would not take charge of her. In my own mind, I have no doubt but that all her attempts upon her life were pretended.'[3]

Although Lord and Lady Maryborough were unable to convince Helena to travel with them, they went home pleased with everything they had achieved: Catherine was home safely, and plans were well under way for William to sail to North America accompanied by trustworthy Bulkeley. They felt confident that within the space of a few months, William would be a reformed character ready to be reunited with his family at Draycot.

In order to make his escape, William made Helena various promises, feeding her another string of lies about his travelling arrangements. This was a regular occurrence and in the past she had always tracked him down. Just four months previously he had tried to lose her on the journey between Florence and Paris. From Genoa she had sent him a note in her childish handwriting:

> I am quite astonished to find that you have not yet made your appearance in this place. What am I to conjecture? I met a party on the road who had left Schneiderffs [the hotel in Florence] on Monday, and they told me you were still there. I cannot and will not believe this, as I am quite sure you would not deceive me, or break your word. It would indeed be cruel![4]

Emotional blackmail was Helena's speciality (very different from the forthright Catherine).

On this occasion, when William left Paris, it took Helena a few days to locate him at a hotel in The Hague. Showing him her slashed wrists, Helena threatened to open up her veins again. William had been determined to separate from her, but all his resolve evaporated. He was capable of being a complete brute, but somehow Helena had genuinely touched his heart. She infuriated him, but she also moved him in a way no other woman ever had. William could not turn her away.

Poor Meara could not suffer any more drama or intrigue. When the valet saw that Mrs Bligh was back in residence, he sent William an emotional letter of resignation:

> Honoured Sir, I am sorry from my heart and soul, to leave you.
> The return of Mrs Bligh has made me so unhappy that I am,

with tears in my eyes, driven to take this step both for the
safety of my health and future tranquillity of my mind.[5]

Meara was uncommonly loyal; he had only stayed on this long
through genuine affection for his master. He continued:

Never, Sir, has a person of my sphere of life taken such a lively
interest, or suffered more than I have, since this unfortunate
affair has occurred. Never was a man more circumspect in his
conduct than I have been on all occasions.

Asking for a good reference, Meara concluded, 'Sir, all my hopes
are placed in your generous heart . . . I have the honour to be your
faithful servant.'

When William received the resignation he sent for Meara in a
great rage and asked, 'Are you mad, would you leave me without
a soul!' Making it clear that he would not provide a good reference,
he insisted that the valet should stay for one more month, until he
left for North America. The devoted valet reluctantly agreed. At the
end of July they travelled to Ostend, where Bulkeley was waiting to
take William away on his trip. On seeing the doctor, Meara's eyes
filled with tears of relief, because he believed that his master would
be saved from his adulterous life and restored to his wife and children. Patting the valet on the back, Bulkeley said, 'Cheer up, Meara,
something will be done now.'

'You must stay out of sight,' warned the valet. 'If Mrs Bligh sees
you, she will know instantly that a scheme has been formed against
her.' The dreaded Mrs Bligh had taken to carrying a knife to slash
her own wrists, but Meara worried that she could just as easily
thrust the blade between his ribs.

The situation had become completely untenable for William.
When he left for Paris early that evening, accompanied by Bulkeley,
he intended to sever all ties with Helena. Poor Meara was left to
cope with the murderous Mrs Bligh on his own. The valet was given
the unenviable task of duping her into believing that William had
received a challenge from her father, and had set off immediately
for Calais. Meara assured her that they would follow on in a few

days. When they set off on the journey, Mrs Bligh abused him so savagely that he was obliged to sit outside the carriage. Deeply regretting his promise to stay on for one month, the valet's only inducement was the knowledge that Dr Gladstone was waiting at Calais to take Helena back to England. Somehow she discovered the scheme and took out all her fury on Meara, screaming and pummelling him with her fists. Then she turned round and headed straight for Paris.

Reaching William's hotel before Helena, Meara told his master what had happened. Sitting down heavily on a chair, William put his head in his hands, rubbed his temples and said, 'God help me!' Arriving shortly afterwards, Mrs Bligh blamed Meara for everything, accusing him of duping her and treating her roughly. Worn out by her theatrics, William became run-down and developed a high fever brought on by his recurring eye infection. This caused his doctors much concern. While he was delirious in bed, Mrs Bligh moved back into his hotel room to take care of him. William's chance to get away from her had evaporated and he did not have the energy for another theatrical escape.

Bulkeley realized it was pointless to continue hoping that William would reform his conduct. Prior to returning to his practice in Naples, he presented William with a bill for £467 for his medical attendance on the Long Wellesley family. Declining to pay the demand, William refused to have anything more to do with the good doctor.[6]

Bulkeley wrote to Lord Maryborough with news that William was back with the dreaded Mrs Bligh. An exchange of correspondence ensued and William's letters revealed his astonishing level of self-delusion. He had the audacity to tell his father that Catherine had caused the rift in their marriage – by making a fuss over nothing. Appalled at his son's mulishness, Lord Maryborough voiced his displeasure in a brutally candid letter. He lamented, 'Your greatest misfortune is, the vain self-delusion of supposing, that you are brought into your present melancholy . . . by others; and not by your own conduct.'[7] Talking of Catherine, he stated, 'Your wife is admired by all . . . her only fault has been bearing with your intolerable conduct for too long.' His assessment of Helena was particularly ferocious: 'That most horrible monster Mrs Bligh . . . is entirely void of every principle of morality . . . which civilised human beings have . . . She would be a monster amongst savages . . . If you do not separate yourself from this scandalous profligate witch, you must share her fate.' Finishing on a conciliatory note, Maryborough stated, 'My heart bleeds at what I have written. I call you to witness I have written it for your own good.'

In writing to William in such strong terms, Maryborough was following the conventions of the time – it was considered to be a father's duty to counsel his son and to show him the error of his ways. Now that William was on the verge of catastrophe, Maryborough tried his hardest to make him see sense by pointing out, 'The whole world approves of your wife's separating from you and were you now to come to England, and it were possible for you to remain out of jail, you would be driven out of society.' On seeing a copy of the letter, Catherine said that she hoped it would show her husband 'the true colours of his situation and make the deepest impression on his heart and mind'.[8]

For much of his life William had strived for recognition and approval in the highest echelons of society. His father was correct to say that if he did not rein himself in, he would be ostracized by the very people he had tried to impress. Scandal followed William wherever he went and his entire adult life had been a series of self-inflicted disasters. It seemed that he would never learn his lesson or redeem himself in any way. On this occasion he might have prevented absolute ruin if he had found the resolve to end his affair with Helena. But he chose to play with fire, and the worst tragedy of all was yet to come.

PART FOUR

JUDGEMENT

'If you expect happiness, you grasp at a shadow.'

Letter from William to Catherine, August 1824

37. Draycot House

❧

After all her trials on the continent, Catherine relished the tranquillity of Draycot, comforted with childhood memories of the years spent quietly with her mother and sisters. Lady Catherine had never been seduced by glamour; her priorities were always her charities and her children. Realizing that her mother's simple lifestyle had probably been much more rewarding than her own, Catherine found great solace in the company of her children. The terrible gripping pains in her chest had stopped; she felt relaxed and relieved to be home.

Driving out every day, Catherine renewed acquaintances with neighbours and tenants on her estate. Evidence of Lord Maryborough's endeavours could be seen everywhere in the prosperous new leaseholders, well-stocked farms and increased productivity throughout Draycot. Catherine soon discovered, however, that the growth in her income had come at a high price because some of her old friends had been evicted through non-payment of rents. Many working families had ended up in the workhouse where men, women and children lived apart. This meant that families could only meet up once a week on Sundays, which was their day off. Facing the prospect of being parted from her own children, Catherine felt great empathy and was sorry that she was no longer in a position to help them. She wrote to her aunt, Lady Sarah de Crespigny, 'Many sad changes have taken place, since I was last at dear Draycot. You will easily imagine what were my feelings upon reaching this place. It required all my fortitude to struggle against them.'[1]

Some of Catherine's old favourites were still at Draycot and they were pleased to see her. Receiving a warm welcome wherever she went, Catherine found the society of country folk refreshing, comforting and undemanding. Farmer Smyth gave her a bag of partridges to take home, and Farmer Lane let the boys taste his home-brewed ale.[2] The children also flourished in their new environment; they had more freedom in the country to go out riding or fishing on the estate. Separated from her husband, Catherine was not inclined to go out in the evenings, but her sisters provided all the society she desired. Supper at Draycot was an informal affair and the children were often permitted to eat in the dining room with the adults. Afterwards, Dora and Emma organized treasure hunts, card games, charades and blind man's buff; little Victoria would later recall that she had never been happier.

Now that she was back in Wiltshire, Catherine became actively involved in the running of her estates, writing letters and attending to business. She consulted with Merrick Shawe, who was a frequent visitor to Draycot, as he was responsible for calling on the farms to offer advice and ensure that everything was running smoothly. Lord Maryborough had also asked him to keep an eye on Catherine and the children. Although Shawe had always been a close associate of William, helping to fix his problems, he was not particularly well acquainted with his wife. After just a few afternoons in Catherine's company, Shawe was completely enchanted by the sad, sweet lady. Just as Dr Bulkeley and Mr Pitman before him, Shawe had fallen under her spell.

Catherine still did not have legal custody of the children – by law they were entirely under the control of their father. William had entrusted them to the care of Mr Pitman, strictly on the understanding that his orders were carried out rigidly, warning the tutor, 'I will never forgive you if you allow anyone but myself to interfere about them.'[3] He left strict instructions with Pitman regarding the education of his children. In order to prepare the boys for Eton, Pitman concentrated on Latin and classic literature. They were also taught French, arithmetic and how to write a good letter. Contemporary books advised that 'letter-writing is so manifestly the main object and design of all education . . . a truly important art'.[4] To demonstrate their progress, it was Pitman's duty to ensure that Will and James wrote to their father every Friday.

However, William's apparent interest in the boys' education was not entirely altruistic and he used their innocent snippets of information to undermine Catherine's authority at home by issuing unreasonable orders and demands. When he discovered that the boys often visited friends, he banned them from leaving Draycot or mixing with children of their own rank. William instructed Pitman:

> Do not allow the boys to ride in the towns, or junket about to the neighbours . . . I have a very great dread of their making acquaintances, especially with little masters; I would much rather they mixed with farmers' sons and peasantry.[5]

Two weeks later, William wrote to Pitman:

> If you can obtain a gentleman of the fancy . . . engage him to give [the boys] lessons in boxing; their amusements ought to consist now of cricket, bat and ball, quoits, &c. I hope they have entirely got rid of their nursery dress, and undress themselves, and are completely out of the control of female servants.[6]

A stalemate had developed between the couple. William wanted to return to the family home, but on his own terms. He was wielding his power, demonstrating that he was the master of the house and could do as he pleased. The constant badgering was typical of his methods; he was trying to make life as difficult as possible for his wife in the hope that she would concede. Catherine was equally resolute that she would only take him back on the condition that he left his mistress and showed some remorse for the hurt he had caused. Naturally, she needed assurances for the future. Growing to dread his weekly commandments, she complained that his letters contained 'matter calculated to annoy and distress me

and to make my children as much as possible independent of me'.[7]
Before long even this amount of control did not satisfy William; he
sent two of his stooges to work at Draycot and spy on Catherine.
Ostensibly Mr Langdon and Mr Wright were employed to take the
boys out hunting and teach them other manly sports, but in reality
their main purpose was to report back to William.[8]

Money was also a problem for Catherine – after paying William
his alimony she was left with just £1,625 a quarter to pay staff, run
a household, and support and educate her children. Knowing this,
William made demands about boxing lessons and other expensive
activities. The following month he wrote to Will:

> I am very much dissatisfied to find that my orders have not
> been attended, by procuring for yourself and brother a brace
> of greyhounds each. My intention was, and is, that you and
> your brother should each keep a brace of greyhounds [and a
> pack of harriers], which Mr Wright must procure for you.[9]

Blissfully happy at the prospect of coursing hares, the children
were completely unaware of the part they were playing in undermining their mother. Young Will wrote an excited note to his aunt
Dora:

> I hope you like Cheltenham but . . . we are very dull without
> you. We have had no blind man's buff since you left us, nor
> shall we until you return. What do you think, Aunt Dora, I
> have just received a letter from Papa who gives us permission
> to keep two grey hounds each, and when we get them we shall
> have good sport coursing, and there will be plenty of hares for
> your dinner when you return.

William's strategy to drive a wedge between mother and children was working. When Catherine tried to explain why the boys
could not keep greyhounds, they grew angry with her.

The rumours about William incarcerating his wife in the
Grotto were probably untrue, but the strategies he now employed
were almost as effective as lock and key. Catherine became a pris-
oner in her own home because the children were not permitted to

leave Draycot. This meant that she had to stay behind when Dora and Emma visited Cheltenham. Even though he was in another country hundreds of miles away, William found ways to manipulate his wife; he continued to undermine her and control her. Isolated from all society, even from the company of her sisters, Catherine was forlorn. The bad weather did not help as the boys were stuck indoors for much of October, running riot through the house and bringing back bittersweet memories of her own little brother. She wrote to her aunt Lady de Crespigny, 'The hall and passages have been (as in older times) very much resorted to during the wet weather.' Describing the monotony of her life at Draycot, she finished the letter on a gloomy note: 'I see nobody and hear no news, therefore mine must be a sad dull letter, and in charity to you I will end it.'[10]

Catherine also stayed in close contact with her loyal friend Bulkeley, writing regularly with news of the children and informing him proudly:

> Victoria reads French and English nearly as well as Will, and already takes an interest in geography and history . . . Will has conquered a great deal of that irritability of temper . . . James is in high good looks; he has become a much more courageous rider; they have been out once or twice with the Duke of Beaufort's hounds.[11]

With regards to her husband she confided sorrowfully:

> There is nothing like the smallest spark of good or proper feeling towards me expressed in any of his letters. Everything (even his own mother tells me) is going on in the most deplorable way at Dieppe . . . I have endeavoured to bring back my husband . . . given him every possible opportunity of redeeming his character, but all, alas! has failed.

Despite everything that had happened, Catherine still cared deeply for her husband, even remarking to Bulkeley, 'I am sorry to hear a bad account of Mr Long Wellesley's eye.' Hoping for reassurances, yearning for William to come to his senses, Catherine scoured his letters for just one glimmer of hope, but she found 'nothing but defiance'. She justly reasoned, 'How can I expect to receive courtesy and attention from him in future when he does not express one spark of kindness towards me, or even in the least regret for the many miseries which he has heaped upon me?'

Catherine had devoted most of her adult life to William. Some of her best memories were of times spent with him, as were many of her worst. She had probably laughed a thousand times in his company, but she had shed twice as many tears. It had reached a point where the pain far outweighed the pleasure. Having been a dutiful, virtuous wife Catherine felt deeply hurt by the fact that her husband preferred the 'vile witch' Helena. In the cold light of day she stood by her beliefs, assuring Bulkeley, 'There is no fear of my relaxing – I am firm; I feel it a duty which I owe to myself, and my children.'

38. Go to the Devil

❦

William was seriously ill. He had been bedridden for several months with a high temperature and an eye infection so severe he was in danger of losing his sight. In January 1825, Dr Southcote referred him to two specialists in Paris, both of whom confirmed that William was suffering from syphilis. A surgeon performed an operation to remove a tumour from his eye, and William was put on a regular course of mercury. Helena suspected that he had venereal disease, particularly due to this prescription, but when she confronted him, William denied it. He wrote to Helena insisting, 'I most positively do not have the disease [syphilis] . . . I will be damned if ever I had it . . . I perceive this eye of mine is a puzzling case.'[1]

William had travelled to Paris, leaving Helena behind in Dieppe. The roads had been so bad the journey had taken him more than three days. With so much distance between them, William decided that he now had the perfect opportunity to extricate himself once and for all from Helena and return to England. Slipping from place to place like a fugitive, he travelled incognito under the assumed name of Hyde, grew a bushy beard and swapped his crisply tailored clothes for a cloth cap and fisherman's coat. Heavily disguised, travelling in a common carriage, he hoped that Helena would be unable to track him down.

Industrious Lord Maryborough and faithful Shawe had worked determinedly to resolve William's pecuniary crisis. By January 1825, all debts under £200 had been settled in full and every other creditor had received fifteen shillings in the pound, with the remaining dividend of five shilling due within months.[2] Apart from all of this, they had completed the laborious task of modernizing and restocking his estates – 23,000 acres spread over six counties. As a result, business was thriving with rental income and yields substantially increased. The estates were turning over good profits and William's finances had never been in a better state.

William was desperate to return home, as he was hoping to persuade his amenable wife to take him back. Rather than being grateful to his trustees for all their hard work, William criticized them because the final payment to creditors had been delayed. In a long letter to his father, his accusations were so damning it caused an irrevocable breach between them. Deluded as ever, he blamed Lord Maryborough for the breakdown of his marriage, writing, 'You arrived in Paris, by me most unexpectedly; and not only unasked, but unknown to me, you engaged yourself in my most unpleasant and delicate domestic concerns.'[3]

Furthermore, William reasoned that Lord Maryborough's tardiness had prevented him from returning home to reconcile with Catherine. He wrote:

> The entire of my conduct since July last, has been governed by an unbounded confidence in your word that after 29 September 1824, the power of my being a free agent in England could not be disputed. This is the 22 January 1825, here I am, my affairs unsettled, and without means of going to England.

William then went on to dismiss his father from his role as trustee in a most ungrateful fashion, stating, 'I am resolved from this date, never with my free will to seek the benefit of your experience and abilities in my affairs, I will not unnecessarily occupy your time.'

Naturally, Lord Maryborough was extremely hurt by the contents of this letter, and vowed that he would not speak to his son until he reformed his conduct. He told Lady Maryborough, 'I must decline giving William any further advice or opinion. He knows my views and I have determined not to fret and vex myself by further lectures. They serve no purpose.'[4]

Setting aside his displeasure, Lord Maryborough did not abandon his role as trustee as he felt it his duty to honour the promises he had made to tenants and creditors. He continued his good work, specifically to safeguard the interests of Catherine and his grand-children. A few weeks later, William wrote to his father expecting to be forgiven for his outburst. But Lord Maryborough's patience had run out and he returned his son's letter unopened. The rift proved to be permanent and William would never see his father again.

Having alienated his father, William turned his full attention to terrorizing his unfortunate wife. His behaviour and reasoning were chaotic. He desired reconciliation with Catherine but was too stubborn to take the necessary steps. Similarly, he wanted rid of Helena but did not have the resolve to walk away. He seemed to believe that if he pushed his wife far enough she would relent and agree to his terms, allowing him to move back into the family home as if nothing had happened.

By April 1825, Catherine's life had become unbearable and William's most recent demands pushed her too far. In a letter to Pitman he objected to 'those aunts', and banned Dora and Emma from Draycot, while reiterating that the children could not stir from the estate. In the same letter, William played a trump card to demonstrate the extent of his control over the children. He advised, 'Doctor Gladstone has written to me about James going to sea.'[5] Not surprisingly, the prospect of her ten-year-old son being sent away to join the navy caused Catherine untold grief. Apart from the months of separation, mortality rates were high for boys under fourteen, due to the many diseases they could contract, and one in five did not return home from their first voyage.

Always an advocate of manly sports, William also wrote encouraging the boys to ride their horses at great speed. This alarmed Catherine because James was already too reckless, taking tumbles regularly, and he had recently broken his arm. Agitated, she wrote to her mother-in-law, 'My dearest children, are now, more than ever, my all upon Earth and what would become of me I know not if anything amiss were to happen to any of them.'[6]

*

Having failed to win back his wife through provocation and harassment, William tried a more direct approach. Proposing reconciliation, he wrote to Catherine suggesting a 'return to our former intercourse . . . for the permanent interests of your children'.[7] She was not tempted by this offer, particularly as he went on to reiterate, 'No promises will I ever again give you. I once gave you a promise which I most religiously kept – for four years, and never a week passed away, when you did not fail to let me know eitherby your words or your manner, that I was violating it.'[8] William was referring to the fact that he had kept his word and not accumulated further debts while living abroad.

Catherine did not bother to reply to her husband, but she wrote to Lord Maryborough, 'Can Mr Long Wellesley imagine that I will ever hold any communication with him until he has shown sincere contrition? He is much mistaken if he does.'[9]

Around the same time, events took another bad turn for William. Newspapers announced that Captain Bligh would be filing for divorce by reason of adultery, while also suing Mr Long Wellesley for 'criminal conversation', the legal euphemism for adultery. One paper recorded that while in Naples, 'Mrs Bligh eloped from her husband, and went to reside with Mr Long Wellesley, with whom she is alleged to have cohabited some time there, and afterwards in Paris . . . up to the present time.'[10]

The scandal had broken. Full details of William's affair with Mrs Bligh would soon be offered up for public scrutiny. This meant that time had run out for William, he had squandered his chance to reconcile with his wife. It had gone too far. No self-respecting woman would take him back once the full details of his affair were common knowledge.

Catherine had tried everything within her power to reconcile with her husband. Just a few months previously, she had made it clear that she desperately wanted him back, on the condition that he apologized and severed all ties with Mrs Bligh. William was equally resolute that he would not grovel or compromise. This stalemate could have continued indefinitely, but Catherine reached breaking point when William threatened to come to England to snatch the children.

At this point, the children were William's only bargaining tool. Writing to Pitman, he advised that he would be returning to England in the near future to seize custody – by force if necessary. With the law firmly on his side, William smugly told the tutor, 'A man and his children ought to be allowed to go to the devil in their own way, if he pleases. Rely upon it, neither God or the devil shall interfere between me and my children.'[11]

39. Strain Every Nerve

✧

Almost one year had passed since Catherine had separated from her husband but she was still living in fear, terrorized by his constant demands and menaces. Now he was planning to return to England to take away her children. William had already damaged her life beyond repair, destroying her health, happiness and peace of mind, not to mention her houses and her fortune. Catherine had suffered her fair share of heartache but there was nothing more excruciating than watching her children suffer; she refused to stand back and let William ruin their lives. His recent conduct had clearly demonstrated the type of father he would be: encouraging his young boys to ride their horses recklessly, utter obscene oaths, get drunk and debauch at every opportunity.

With the *Bligh v Wellesley* adultery case pending, Catherine knew that the salacious details of William's affair would soon be raked over by the press and she would lose credibility if she did not react. One of the perils of celebrity is judgement by the court of public opinion. She was aware that the eyes of the nation were on her and the public would adjudicate over her next move. She was part of a culture that for the most part accepted male superiority. Women's rights were sadly neglected, but faced with the prospect of losing her children, the unfairness of the system certainly hit home for Catherine. Filled with righteous indignation, she resolved to challenge the status quo and fight for custody. Aside from personal motivations, Catherine was conscious of her public image and mindful of the fact that other women looked up to her – what she did next would set the trend for wives in similar situations.

For all these reasons, both public and private, she felt compelled to make a stand. Writing to Dr Bulkeley, she stated her intention to fight the system: 'I have shown patience and forbearance enough, it is full time that I should assert my rights; I am resolved to do so, they will find me firm.'[1]

Catherine's insistence on asserting her 'rights' was part of a growing tide of rebellion among women, which we now recognize as the early stirrings of feminism. Post-Peterloo, ideals were changing rapidly and people were questioning traditional customs, morals and beliefs. In this climate, the issue of child custody loomed large. A valiant woman was needed to challenge the status quo, and it was Catherine Long Wellesley who took up the gauntlet. Prior to her marriage, she had been a resourceful and daring woman, involved at the sharp edge of business and well able to handle unpalatable situations when necessary. She was an innovator, who had pushed the boundaries of propriety on many occasions, dealing with problems involving blackmailers and mistresses. Now that she had regained her confidence, she was ready to publicly challenge her husband, instigating a court case that would shake the establishment to the core.

Catherine's philanthropic family included visionaries such as the seventh Earl of Shaftesbury and Lord John Russell, who would lead the fight for social reform. One of the biggest influences in her life was Bartholomew Bouverie, her father's nephew and best friend, who was a member of the Shaftesbury family. Sir James Tylney Long had thought so highly of Bouverie he had appointed him guardian to his children in his will.[2] Bouverie served as a father figure to Catherine, offering advice and protecting her interests. Perhaps it was his influence that encouraged her to proceed as she did. Urging Catherine to commence legal proceedings, he explained that as matters stood, her husband could move into Draycot at any time, even bringing along his mistress if he wished! To protect against any further molestation, Bouverie recommended that Catherine should 'resort to Parliament, where a Bill of Divorce would reinstate the entire possession of all your property'.[3] In the 1820s, however, it was virtually impossible for a woman to obtain a divorce, and Bouverie admitted, 'a Bill of Divorce, instituted at the suit of the wife, has been rarely granted'.[4]

Bouverie also held out little hope that Catherine would gain custody of the children and he warned, 'You would labour under great difficulty . . . interfering with a Father's authority.'[5] Henry Windsor, Catherine's uncle, was equally pessimistic about her chances and he informed her, 'There seems to be *only one* case on record, of it having succeeded, and that was one of a most atrocious nature.'[6]

Windsor was probably referring to the notorious custody battle that had involved the infamous Lord Byron. In 1816, Lady Byron had filed for legal separation along with custody of her baby daughter, after private communication with the Lord Chancellor. With the nature of her allegations shrouded in mystery, her supporters fuelled rumours of sodomy, incest and rape of a ten-year-old girl. As a result, the poet faced judgement by the court of public opinion. *Blackwood's Magazine* printed a particularly damning article:

> It appears in short, as if this miserable man, having exhausted every species of sensual gratification – having drained the cup of sin even to its bitterest dregs – were resolved to show us that he is no longer a human being in his frailties, but a cool, unconcerned fiend.[7]

Byron submitted to his wife's demands by signing a private agreement, and then he promptly left England for good.[8] From exile he wrote in his own defence, 'I was accused of every monstrous vice by public rumour and private rancour . . . I felt that England was unfit for me.'[9]

In retaliation, the poet's friends orchestrated a malicious backlash against Lady Byron, branding her 'the foulest slanderer . . . the vilest of criminals'.[10] By the time they had finished, her reputation was also in tatters and she was shunned by society.

The couple settled matters out of court by signing a private Deed of Separation that included a caveat relating to the child. Almost a decade had passed and no other woman had dared to instigate custody proceedings in Chancery. In view of Lady Byron's ordeal, it would take a great deal of courage for Catherine to commence proceedings against William. The timing could not have been worse because Lord Byron had recently returned from exile in a casket. Sympathy for him was at its height as the hearts of men were wrung with pity for his sorrows.

The Byron custody suit was never tested in a court of law. This meant that Catherine's action would be groundbreaking. Her advisors had informed her that a legal separation would not suffice; only a Bill of Divorce would protect her against 'further molestation . . . and reinstate her property'. An Act of Parliament was required in order to grant a divorce; from 1800 to 1830 there were around a hundred petitions, of which seventy-five were granted.[11] A vast proportion came from childless men desperate for an heir – only a handful were instituted by women.[12] Divorce, particularly one instigated by a woman, was more or less taboo and, if she decided to proceed, Catherine was in danger of suffering public disgrace. However, she had already stated her resolve to separate from William 'at every hazard and at every risk'.[13] Taking unprecedented steps, Catherine decided to file for divorce, petitioning at the same time for custody of her children. Knowing that William would avail himself of the best lawyers, she needed to arm herself with first-rate representation. She hired the services of Mr Julius Hutchinson, of Lincoln's Inn, whose practice was right beside the Courts of Chancery. Hutchinson held several long meetings with Catherine, during which he established the grounds for her case.

Various double standards enshrined in law made it difficult for women to leave their husbands. A man could divorce his spouse for adultery, but the law made it much harder for a woman, who had to prove cruelty and desertion in addition to her husband's infidelity. The epistle Catherine had sent to Lord Maryborough one year earlier proved invaluable. The letter was much more than a simple cry for help – it clearly laid out Catherine's grounds for divorce. Alluding to her husband's cruelty, she described the 'miseries . . . insult and degradation . . . and wrongs he has heaped upon me'.

Desertion was also suggested through continual repetition of the word 'abandon', particularly when she resolved to 'separate myself from a husband who already in conduct has abandoned me'. She also made it clear that she had tried everything in her power to 'reconcile' with her husband, while also laying down generous 'terms', offering to pay off the mistress.

This letter demonstrated that although Catherine was mild-mannered, she was not foolish or weak. Far from being the impassioned ramblings of a distraught woman, the narrative had been shrewdly calculated to record her position unequivocally. Catherine had even primed the perfect witness to collaborate her version of events – William's own father! Catherine made him complicit when she wrote, 'You are, my dear Lord Maryborough, but too well acquainted with the miseries I have endured for many months past from the conduct of my husband.'

Despite William's many attempts to escape from his mistress, however half-hearted they may have been, Catherine had heard from many sources that they were back together. On hearing that William was still living with Mrs Bligh, the solicitor gave Catherine some excellent advice regarding alimony payments. He told her that she must stop sending William money, as she could be accused of furnishing him with the means to continue his adultery. In effect, she was aiding and abetting his life of vice.

Hutchinson was impressed by the fact that Catherine had gathered together such a strong body of evidence to support her case, including witnesses plus many incriminating letters written by William. Although Hutchinson assured Catherine that she had grounds for divorce, he warned that it would be a long and difficult process.

An even greater hurdle to surmount was the fact that English law granted fathers ultimate parental control. With the odds stacked firmly against her, Catherine's decision to fight for custody of her children was unprecedented. Making her case, she told her solicitor that William would corrupt their minds and lead them along a path of self-destruction. Hutchinson was appalled when he heard the circumstances: William had neglected the boys' education for two years, allowing them to run wild in the stables and pick up foul language from the grooms. He had also encouraged his sons to drink and swear, while ridiculing their mother's values and beliefs. Hutchinson was particularly disgusted by William's inappropriate behaviour in front of the children, flaunting his mistress in the family home, even permitting her to caress him intimately, in full view. With steely determination Catherine told her solicitor, 'I earnestly trust, then, I shall be considered the fittest parent of the two to have the care of such treasures; I shall strain every nerve to obtain this desired object.'[14]

Despite all he had heard, Hutchinson informed Catherine that it was highly unlikely that she would get custody of the children. Frustrated, Catherine replied: 'My children are now uncontaminated by bad example! They are growing happier by the day, and acquiring habits of virtue. I shudder to think of the fatal consequences of their being placed under their father's roof, where they would hear and see vice upheld and admired, and religion and morality turned into ridicule every day.'[15]

This made no difference whatsoever. Hutchinson warned that she faced an impossible task – no woman had ever fought for custody of her children in a court of law. Nevertheless, she was determined to go ahead. Like other members of her family, she would join the fight for social justice. In order to succeed, however, Catherine would have to overturn the law of the land.

40. Siege at Clarges Street

❦

1825

In May 1825, Catherine moved to No. 41 Clarges Street in Piccadilly so that she could consult more easily with her solicitor. William had insisted that the children remain at Draycot at all times, but Catherine disobeyed his orders and took Victoria with her. She did not dare move the boys, as William wrote to them every week and expected a reply by return. It was his way of checking up on them.

One of the hardest tasks Catherine faced was breaking the news to William's parents. Lord and Lady Maryborough continued to be tremendously supportive and Catherine had already acknowledged, 'had I been your own daughter, I could not have received greater kindness and affection from you. My heart is too full to allow me to express even half the gratitude I feel.'[1]

Equitable as ever, Lady Maryborough had replied, 'What painful reflections I have when I consider . . . that something belonging to me should be the cause of all your woe – I wonder you don't hate us all!!!'[2]

In view of her close relationship with William's parents, Catherine did not wish to instigate legal proceedings behind their backs. Almost one year had passed since her first appeal to them and the situation had grown worse. Outlining her public and private motivations, Catherine's resolve was apparent when she wrote, 'My Dear Lord Maryborough . . . in justice to my character, my honour, my happiness, and above all, the interests of my dear children I am irrevocably *determined* . . . to separate myself forever from Mr Long Wellesley.'[3] Apologizing profusely for the anguish her news would inflict, she continued:

I think this painful communication . . . will sufficiently explain my motives for declining from your most kind invitation to Ascot & Fern Hill . . . I could not help feeling dread of appearing to act with duplicity . . . I need not say how highly I should prize your friendship . . . but the feelings of Nature may perhaps forbid you to continue those affectionate attentions, which you have hitherto shown me.[4]

Catherine need not have worried about becoming estranged from her in-laws. Lady Maryborough's note arrived the following day affirming,

I will not conceal that your letter has given me the bitterest pangs . . . But, I value you too highly and love you too sincerely . . . and will not alienate you from us . . . I can say no more at present, I really am too much overcome.[5]

Also replying by return, Lord Maryborough's response was more guarded and measured. While assuring Catherine of his continued affection and regard, he made it clear that he would never testify against William in court. He declared, 'I could not be party to any steps taken against my son.'[6] Maryborough was aware that he could be called as a key witness because of everything he had observed in Paris. Aside from this, he was in possession of letters that would incriminate his son if they were produced in court. In consequence, he told Catherine that he would 'withdraw altogether' from the affair and not take sides.[7]

Catherine would need as many allies as possible if she was going to take on her husband and challenge the law. She was well aware that William would go on a rampage as soon his alimony stopped, but as he was terrorizing her, she had no choice but to continue.

William was constantly in touch with his advisors in England and, early in June 1825, his solicitor Mr Griffith travelled to Passy, near Paris, to offer legal advice and to break the bad news in person. Shocked to discover that his wife was filing for a divorce, William was overcome with self-pity. He wrote to Merrick Shawe: 'Mrs

Wellesley is determined to separate herself from me. God knows this is a bitter sorrow to me. My great anxiety is beyond all that I can express.'[8] Adopting a dejected tone, William sent a pleading missive, which Shawe delivered to Catherine. William told his wife that he had always cared for her, complaining, 'I do not merit this blow from you ... I recall having acted towards you in the kindest and most affectionate manner and I have always treated you with respect and consideration.'[9]

In the past, Catherine may have relented, but too much had happened and William's shallow entreaties had no effect. In fact, she had grown so cold towards him that she told Shawe, 'I had intended not to take any notice of the letter.'[10] Although Catherine did not bother replying to William, she felt the need to refute some of his claims, especially with the divorce case pending. She wrote to Shawe:

> There have been some few times when [Mr Long Wellesley] has acted with a considerable degree of kindness and an appearance of affection towards me ... But I can with truth declare that this was not the general tenor of his conduct to me, and I must deny that he treated me either in public or private with that respect which a man ought to show his wife ... I am unalterably determined never to live with him again.[11]

Deeply perplexed that his feeble attempts at reconciliation were not having the desired effect, William asked Shawe to continue mediation on his behalf, but his faithful old friend refused. His allegiance now lay firmly with Catherine.

William was even more stunned when his quarterly alimony payment was not forthcoming. Rudely awakened, he realized that if Catherine was successful in her suit, she would take back possession of her estates and income, leaving him without a penny. Determined to stop the proceedings at all costs, William made one final attempt to abandon his mistress in France, but Helena was once again with child. Although she had successfully induced one termination, two years earlier, she was now heavily pregnant with another baby and she refused to stay behind.

If William was to salvage anything, he could not be seen with Mrs Bligh. The motley couple travelled in disguise and took up residence in lodgings at No. 9 Seymour Place, under the assumed names of Monsieur and Madam Roncee. Nobody knew that William was back in England; he did not leave his lodgings for two weeks while he concocted a devious plot to overturn Catherine's case against him. William needed to fabricate evidence to show that he was still on friendly terms with his wife, and possibly even living with her. The courts would not grant Catherine a divorce while there was still hope of reconciliation.

As soon as he had hatched a plan, William decided that he was ready to pay his wife a visit. He had various tricks up his sleeve, but ultimately he hoped to snatch Victoria. His daughter was the perfect bargaining tool – Catherine would agree to anything to get her child back.

Late in the evening on 7 July, there was an unexpected caller at Catherine's house in Clarges Street, Piccadilly. The door knocker tapped loudly and the under-butler opened up to a surly ruffian dressed in a shabby brown stuff coat with coarse trousers. His face was in shadow, obscured by a black chip hat and bushy black beard. The red handkerchief tied round his neck completed a look designed to inspire great alarm and terror. When the thug tried to push past him, the under-butler succeeded in blocking his path, stalling him for a short time.[12]

Just across the hallway, Catherine sat in the drawing room with her two sisters, chatting quietly as she picked at her needlepoint. By now she was living in seclusion from all public society, constantly in fear that the man at her door would come looking for her, intent on wreaking revenge.[13] Many sleepless nights had been spent imagining the worst. Most of all, Catherine was petrified that he would snatch her children and hold them to ransom. It was even possible that he would hire an armed gang to assist in the kidnap. After months of living on her nerves, there was something about the knock and tone of voice in the hallway that made the ever-vigilant

Catherine uneasy. As realization dawned on her, she rose quickly from her armchair and said, 'Hush, that knock on the door and that voice is very familiar. I am convinced that it must be [*him*].'[14]

'That cannot be!' remarked Dora.

Nevertheless, Catherine was sure that he had come. Retreating quickly into the back parlour, she had just left the room when the intruder burst in. 'Where is Catherine?' he demanded. When Dora and Emma did not answer, he smashed his fist into a side table and repeated, 'Where is Catherine?' His demeanour was frightening, but the sisters refused to cooperate. Rushing up the stairs, the ruffian stormed from room to room, searching for the children. Crashing about, he slammed doors and overturned furniture before realizing that he was wasting his time – the children were not there.

During the commotion, Catherine had wasted no time in gathering up Victoria, and she slipped quietly down the backstairs with her precious daughter cradled in her arms. The servants were at supper when she hurried in, begging them to help her. Terrified that her tormentor would find her child, she was in a state of great agitation and a ferocious spasm gripped her chest. Although she was bent over double with pain, she took control of the situation and had the foresight to dispatch a footman to summon officers of the police from Marlborough Street.

With all the noise and confusion above stairs, Catherine had no idea how many intruders were rampaging through her house, possibly brandishing weapons. She made a snap decision to flee. Clutching her daughter tightly, she escaped through the back door. Under the cover of darkness, she cautiously felt her way along the deserted yard until she came to the stable block. Crouching down in the shadows, shielding her child, she was overwhelmed with fear as all kinds of scenarios played out in her head. Eventually she heard the rumble of a carriage and saw that the lights were heading towards her. Catherine knew that her fate rested on a knife-edge; she could only pray that the carriage would contain her rescuer, not her pursuer.

*

Most of the household servants did not know the intruder, but Bicknell immediately recognized Mr Long Wellesley. William began to issue orders, reminding the butler that he was still master of the house. Bicknell's loyalties, however, were firmly with Catherine. Taking charge of the situation, Bicknell apprehended Mr Long Wellesley, coaxed him into the drawing room and kept him talking. The butler hoped that this would give Mrs Long Wellesley time to make her escape. After a few minutes, William made another attempt to go upstairs, but was prevented from leaving the room by two stocky servants posted outside the door. 'Do you know who I am?' he demanded, outraged. But they continued to block his exit, staring at him impassively, without saying a word.[15] William then started ringing the servant's bell continuously, with great violence, demanding to see his wife, but everyone ignored him.

After half an hour of shouts and threats, he realized that his bullying tactics were having no effect, so he tried another approach. Breaking down into floods of tears, he fell onto the sofa and begged Bicknell to bring Victoria to him, saying he hadn't seen his children in almost a year. Playing for time, the butler agreed and left the room. Sometime later, when there was still no sign of Victoria, it became apparent to William that he had been double-crossed. Once again he started shouting and ringing the bell, but this time the under-butler appeared. William asked for Bicknell and was informed, 'Mr Bicknell is not here.'[16]

'You are a liar!' shouted William. 'Do you know who I am?'

Staring at him blankly, the servant replied, 'I do not.'

'I believe my name is Long Wellesley,' said William sarcastically. 'Do as I say.' As far as William was concerned, the servants were there to do his bidding. The under-butler had other ideas; he left the room without another word. William kept shouting and ringing the bell, but it was too late, his wife and child had already left the building.

While William was contained in the drawing room, Catherine had found safety. The chief of the Marlborough Street police had arrived, along with an experienced officer called Schofield.[17] The chief bundled Catherine and Victoria into a carriage and escorted them to Harley Street, where Henry Windsor, Catherine's uncle, was residing. Dora and Emma followed closely behind in another carriage, accompanied by their footmen and lady's maid.

Although there had been chaos in the house when William arrived, Catherine had been prepared for him. She had employed a couple of burly servants for protection, and was ready to unleash her own ambush. A plan of action had been concocted with the help of her solicitor, who had warned that she should not entertain William or even stay under the same roof as him because it would prejudice her case for divorce.

Police officer Schofield stayed behind at Clarges Street to watch William's movements. Unaware that a law enforcer was in the house, William started to pull continuously on the bell rope, demanding a bed for the night. When the servants refused to oblige, he lay down on the sofa in the drawing room and fell asleep. Just after midnight a messenger knocked on the door and tried to deliver a letter addressed to Mr Long Wellesley. The canny police officer denied all knowledge of a person by that name and refused to take the letter.

The messenger returned two hours later with a letter stamped by a solicitor called Mr Hoper. The man insisted it was of the utmost importance and needed an urgent reply. Schofield sent him packing, affirming that nobody by the name of Mr Long Wellesley lived at that address.

William finally left Clarges Street at six o'clock the following morning, thoroughly disgruntled by the fact that all his ploys had failed. He had not managed to compromise Catherine nor snatch his daughter to use as a bargaining tool. In addition, the letter from his solicitor had not been delivered, so he could not claim to be living at the same address as his wife.

William was in such a hot rage as he walked back to his lodgings, he did not notice that the police officer Schofield was following him. Feeling that everyone had turned against him, faithful Shawe suddenly became the object of his anger. William stamped along Jermyn Street, searching for Shawe's house and shouting for the colonel to come out. Frustrated with the lack of response, he kicked furiously at people's front doors with his heavy boots as he walked away.

Halfway down Jermyn Street, William passed his wedding venue, St James's Church. It must surely have sparked memories of that happy day, when the bells rang and everybody smiled as the excited newlyweds raced out of the church, holding hands and laughing with joy. Thirteen years on, William was there in entirely different circumstances, dressed like a vagabond. It must have been a bitter reminder of all that was lost.

Once back at Seymour Place, William climbed the stairs wearily and sat down heavily on his bed. It was not until sometime later that he noticed the man loitering outside and recognized Schofield as one of the guards from Clarges Street. Jumping back from the window in shock, William could not believe that he had walked straight into a trap laid by his wife. He was no longer safe because Catherine and her legal team knew where he lived. If his creditors found out, he would be arrested for debt and thrown into prison.

It took William and Helena less than twenty minutes to pack up a few essentials. The officer watched them leave in a hackney carriage in a state of great confusion and alarm. Helena was so heavily pregnant, she could barely heave herself into the coach. As William trundled off, he was followed surreptitiously by a curricle containing another policeman, who watched him alight at a house in Marylebone. William had played right into Catherine's hands. A few hours later, Schofield arrived at the house in Marylebone with a warrant. On gaining entrance to the premises, he served William with a suit for divorce issued by Catherine. William had no option but to accept the citation.

William had underestimated his wife. Catherine had thoroughly outsmarted him, serving divorce papers and driving him back into exile. The only ammunition William had left was the children. Hiring a band of brigands, he armed them with loaded pistols and sent them to Draycot to seize his sons. Yet again, Catherine was one step ahead. On the very night that William forced his way into Clarges Street, she had dispatched bodyguards to remove the boys from Draycot. By the time William's pack of thugs arrived in Wiltshire, the boys were already safely in hiding.

Creditors would soon discover his whereabouts so William needed to get back to France as soon as possible. Gleefully, newspapers reported the siege on Clarges Street. Having followed the trials and triumphs of William's life with great interest, they were delighted that he was back in England treating the nation to another sensational scandal. The public eagerly awaited the next instalment of the Long Wellesley saga but even the most hardened cynics were shocked and appalled by what happened next.

Served with a writ for divorce, William sent his wife a sinister letter containing a chilling prediction: 'No divorcing woman has yet enjoyed [contentment]. If you believe you will place yourself in a position that will enable you to advance the interests of your children, you are under delusion . . . if you expect happiness, you grasp at a shadow.'[18]

41. The Paragon

❦

Grasp at a shadow – William's words rang true. Despite all her good fortune, true happiness was something Catherine had never quite attained; it was always lurking just beyond her reach. Her moments of joy had been fleeting. Her early years had been tainted by the loss of her father and brother, and the years of constant battle with William had taken their toll. Her life had been agonizingly stripped away bit by bit, and now she was in danger of losing her children. Living in constant fear, the terrifying pains that gripped her chest became more frequent and she believed that she would not survive another seizure. Forced into hiding, flitting from house to house, she wrote to Bulkeley, deeply distressed, '[Mr Long Wellesley] is following me with the most cruel persecution.'[1]

Before the debacle at Clarges Street, Catherine had endeavoured to make her children Wards of Chancery pending a custody trial, although Hutchinson had advised that this was unlikely to be granted.[2] On 28 August, she instructed her solicitor to approach the Lord Chancellor once again. Catherine insisted:

> Mr Long Wellesley declared to Colonel Shawe, in Boulogne, that if he could not obtain custody of the children by legal measures, he would resort to stratagem . . . [He] will likely make the attempt during the present recess . . . Would not this threat justify my application to the Lord Chancellor, without further delay?[3]

Catherine would not rest until she found a way to safeguard her children. Despite all her worries, she was always thinking about others and she made the time to send thoughtful gifts and messages to friends. 'My dear Lady Maryborough,' she wrote, 'I was sincerely grieved to hear of your illness . . . I have since made frequent enquiries [of Colonel Shawe] and was happy to find you were recovering.'[4]

Bartholomew Bouverie wrote to Catherine: 'I hope your sisters have already conveyed you my best thanks for the venison, of which we began to partake on Thursday.'[5]

'My dear Mrs Wellesley,' wrote Lady Clarendon, 'I cannot let your note pass unacknowledged without thanking you for your kind attention in writing it; at a time when I am sure you might well be excused for not thinking of *others*.'[6]

With her nerves in shreds, Catherine was barely sleeping and she could not return to Clarges Street because she was terrified that William would reappear to snatch her children at gunpoint. With her health deteriorating rapidly, she suffered severe spasms in her chest and her stomach churned constantly. Unable to keep down food, her weight plunged dramatically and purple crescents hollowed her eyes as she drifted about the house like a ghost.

Dora and Emma were towers of strength, deciding that it would be prudent to go into hiding. The family left London on 7 September, and moved to a tranquil house overlooking the river at No. 2 The Paragon, Richmond. But Catherine could not find peace in sleepy Surrey; just one day after she arrived there, she received a note from Henry Windsor enclosing a missive from William. The instant she received the letter, she ran to her sisters worried that it contained more threats to remove the children from her care. Catherine was seized by a severe attack that gripped her chest and squeezed all the breath from her body. Doubled over in pain, she felt too weak to encounter any agitating news.

Handing the unopened letter to Dora, Catherine said, 'Would you take charge of this for me? If it contains any threats respecting the children, I authorize you to communicate with my solicitor . . . Please send for Plank the police officer, to resist any attempt to remove the children and to take all the necessary steps for their security.'[7]

Assuring her that they would manage the task and accede to all her wishes, Catherine's sisters helped her upstairs and settled her into bed. Before they left, Catherine pleaded, 'Please avoid mentioning this distressing subject to me at present, as I feel persuaded that, if I were to attempt reading the letter, my spasms would return, and I might be dead in a few hours.'

Shortly afterwards, Dora and Emma sent word to Bartholomew Bouverie, who replied by return, 'I fear your sister's illness must be increased by reflecting into what wretched hands her poor children must fall.' The sisters also summoned Dr Julius, who stayed with Catherine all night as her fever increased and produced delirium. Details of her illness had been sent to Henry Windsor and the news somehow reached Wellington. The duke immediately dispatched his own physician, Sir Henry Halford, to attend at Catherine's sickbed.

Arriving the following morning, Halford was pleased to discover that Catherine's fever had subsided and both doctors felt sure that she would make a full recovery. Feeling completely wretched, however, Catherine truly believed that she would be dead within days. Unable to rest until she had settled her affairs, she told her sisters about the will she had signed in 1815, under duress from William, while she was heavily pregnant with James. Although she did not recollect the particulars, she suspected that it was detrimental to the interests of her children.[8]

Determined to rescind the will, Catherine prepared a brief document, which she executed in the presence of two independent witnesses, John Pitman and Henry Bicknell. Catherine wrote simply, 'I hereby revoke any former will I may have made. In this act I am not influenced by any hostility towards Mr Long Wellesley; but I consider it my first duty to secure the interests of my dear children.'[9]

Having taken care of legal matters, Catherine told her physicians that she wanted to see her children one last time. They thought she was being overdramatic, but she could feel a spasm building up inside her chest and knew it would not be much longer. Summoning all her remaining strength, Catherine called for her maid to help her dress and disguise her ravaged appearance – she did not want her children to see her looking like this. After pinning up Catherine's hair, the maid skilfully painted her face, casting off the dark shadows under her eyes and creating a rosy glow on her cheeks.

Catherine was sitting serenely in the garden when the children were sent out to her. Despite her heartache, she put on her bravest smile as she tried to reassure them. There are no records of what was said, but she hugged them tightly in turn, knowing that she would not be there to watch them as they grew, nor to offer reassurance in times of trouble or to celebrate their marriages. Thoroughly drained, struggling with the intensity of her emotions, she called for the doctors to help her back to bed.

The following morning Catherine suffered another terrible seizure that squeezed the life out of her. She had never been one to succumb to hysteria, but in those final agonizing minutes she wailed and wept pitifully. She was not grieving for herself – despite all the heartbreak she had endured. Her agony was for her children and the realization that she would not be there to protect them or watch over them. She cried out, begging God to spare her. Despite the efforts of the best doctors in England, Catherine died at eleven o'clock, on 12 September 1825, just one month short of her thirty-sixth birthday. Sir Henry Halford, who attended on her to the end, pronounced, 'Mrs Long Wellesley died entirely of a broken heart.'[10]

42. Our Sweet Angel

SEPTEMBER 1825

Entering the room where Catherine's body was laid out, Dora and Emma clung together and wept for their sister, so cruelly taken in the prime of her life. Dora held Catherine's hand, while Emma stroked her hair, whispering, 'I cannot believe that our sweet angel is dead.'[1] Catherine's cheek felt cold as Emma lovingly traced the fine blue lines showing though the pale translucency of her skin. All the tension of the past months had drained from her face; her forehead was not furrowed and her mouth not set in a grim line. She looked peaceful and serene, but the essence of her was gone forever. Overcome with grief, it was Emma who cried out again, 'Oh God! Why did you break a heart like this?'[2] Pragmatic as ever, Dora comforted her younger sister. Drawing on religion for consolation, she told Emma that Catherine was finally at peace, saying that she was such an angel she would surely already be in heaven.

Dora and Emma were not the only people to be devastated by the tragic death. Catherine's generous heart had inspired love in many people. Lord and Lady Maryborough were distraught, while Pitman was inconsolable. The tutor wrote immediately to the good doctor to break the bad news:

My Dear Bulkeley, how shall I communicate to you the heart-rending misfortune, which has befallen us? Our beloved and amiable friend, Mrs Long Wellesley is no more! She died this morning after an illness of eight days. Her complaint was in the bowels, which reduced her to a state of extreme debility; this produced a violent nervous excitation, which terminated

in delirium and death. I cannot give you all the details, my
heart is too full. Her poor sisters, children, and myself, are in
a most deplorable state.[3]

Deeply distressed on hearing the news, Bouverie was quick to
blame William for the tragedy, remonstrating, 'Oh! What remorse
must that wretch feel, or rather ought to feel when he learns about
what his perfidy and cruelty have effected! Alas! I fear, his heart is
so hardened, and his mind so completely depraved as to be alive
only to a very different impression.'[4]

Harsh as this sounded, it proved to be a fair appraisal. William
had returned to France but when he heard the news of Catherine's
death he tried to take charge of the situation, firing off instructions
in every direction. To his agent Charles Yerbury he wrote, 'I will
have no ostentation at the funeral, no unnecessary pomp and
show.'[5] William also sent demands to Pitman, ordering, 'My poor
children must be sent to me immediately – I shall be at Boulogne
to meet them.'[6] On referring the matter to solicitors, Pitman was
relieved to discover that he was not obliged to comply with this
request because the children were finally in the process of being
made Wards of Chancery.

The Miss Longs did not have time to mourn for their sister;
William's threats forced them to spring into action. Up until now
the spinster sisters had avoided confrontation with their brother-
in-law, as they endeavoured to keep the peace for Catherine's sake.
But this was not a sign of weakness and they would prove to be
formidable opponents against William. Their main concern was to
comply with Catherine's deathbed wish to protect her children,
and they had the necessary authorization to act on her behalf as
next of kin. Within days Hutchinson had managed to persuade
the Lord Chancellor to sanction Catherine's petition to make her
children Wards of Chancery. Her solicitor had police testimony
of William's violent behaviour at Clarges Street and so was able
to make a strong case. Now the children could not be removed
from the custody of their aunts without the permission of the
Lord Chancellor.

Another priority for Dora was to protect the Long family's ancestral home and other assets in Wiltshire. Bouverie reassured them that under the terms of past wills, Catherine's eldest son would inherit all her property. In theory, Mr Long Wellesley was not entitled to even one penny of her estate but everyone knew that William would terrorize the child, demanding money exactly as he had done with Catherine.

Apart from his overtures towards the children, William sent instructions on how the funeral should be conducted. In a display of immense hypocrisy, he assumed the role of bereaved widower, making it clear that he would be chief mourner at the funeral. He intended to lead the procession. Catherine was highly regarded throughout Wiltshire and feelings ran high among local people, who threatened violence if William had the audacity to show his face. Horrified by William's intentions, Dora sought the advice of his father. Maryborough replied:

> I am really too astounded, and shocked . . . Mr Long Wellesley's determination to appear at your sister's funeral is most embarrassing. I see at once . . . the *dreadful* scene caused by [his] presence amidst Mrs Long Wellesley's peasantry, and numerous Upper Class of Gentlemen agitated by the misfortunes which have fallen upon a family so long and so highly respected in their county.[7]

Maintaining pressure on the spinster sisters, William sent his goons to their house in Richmond. On arrival they produced a peremptory order, demanding that the children be handed over to them for conveyance to France where their father was waiting to receive them. Dora was well prepared; she had applied to the magistrate for a Peace Officer to remain at the house at all times. In addition, guards were in place to protect the children day and night. Added to this, the law was on her side – she produced a letter proving that the children were now Wards of Chancery. Standing her ground, Dora sent the men packing.

*

On the Monday before the funeral, Catherine's body was removed from the house in Richmond at nine o'clock in the morning. Her coffin was so small it might have contained a child. Catherine's desolate boys watched tearfully from an upstairs window, as their mother's casket was carried out and placed in a hearse drawn by six black horses. A rainbow of floral tributes had been laid at the gates of the house and their sweet scent filled the air, as a melancholy procession set off from Richmond on the long journey to the family crypt at Draycot. Four mourning coaches followed behind, containing the Miss Longs, Bicknell the butler and other close friends. Pitman stayed behind to comfort the children.

Crowds gathered along the roadside to watch the heiress's final journey. The British public had been captivated by Catherine's story from the very beginning. She had won the hearts of the people as they had watched the shy, awkward teenager blossom into the ultimate woman of fashion. Their outpouring of grief was genuine.

The Duke of Wellington joined the sombre procession on Tuesday at Chippenham. As the hearse neared Draycot, throngs of people poured out of the surrounding parishes and villages to line the route. Estate workers had benefited from the generosity of the Longs for generations, and they were accustomed to attending momentous family occasions. Many had toasted Catherine's health at her coming-of-age celebrations, when she'd had the world at her feet, and they felt sorrowful to be turning out for her funeral less than fifteen years later.

Thousands of workers dressed in dark mourning clothes followed the hearse in a sombre line. When the procession arrived at Draycot, close family and friends crammed into the church, while a huge crowd stood outside praying for the soul of their dear departed. After the ceremony, Catherine's body was placed inside the family crypt, beside her parents and brother. As the crypt was sealed shut, Emma and Dora felt comforted by the fact that Catherine was laid to rest among the people who had loved her most dearly.

*

In the end, William did not dare appear at the funeral, mainly because he would almost certainly have been arrested for debt before he had even reached Wiltshire.

Plunged into a state of shock, the nation mourned Catherine. The press were in uproar, enraged by the circumstances surrounding her death. Many blamed William for his relentless persecution, with one reporter declaring, 'grief had produced an aneurism of the heart . . . the slightest fright would produce death'.[8]

Epitaphs appeared up and down the country, as another newspaper lamented, 'A wife reduced in life from the loftiest pinnacle of fortune . . . to death'.[9] *The Age* described it as 'one of the most tragic catastrophes that ever happened in real life'.[10] The *Sunday Times* observed that Mr Long Wellesley, 'owed her everything; in exile, as in ruin, she still clung to him; and had he a human heart, he would have treasured her with a mother's care'.[11]

One report was particularly poignant, capturing the general public mood:

> Thirteen years ago this excellent lady . . . rejected the addresses of royalty . . . and bestowed her hand, her heart, and a princely fortune on a man who . . . squandered them with a prodigal's hand away . . . A few years saw her ample possessions the prey of swarming creditors: her palatial mansion gutted of its brilliant furniture, and taken to its foundation, herself in exile in a foreign land . . . and at length deserted by the man for whom she had made such sacrifices, and who, after ruining her fortune, broke her heart . . . deserting her for a demirep.[12]

But this was not the end of Catherine's story – William was in for a big shock.

43. Wellesley v Beaufort

❧

1826

Following the death of his wife, William dropped the use of her surname. The press and everyone else followed suit; from then onwards he would be known simply as Mr Wellesley. William was shocked to discover that his wife had left her affairs in such good order that the monumental custody battle would still go ahead. Even though she did not live to see the trial, she had succeeded in the first step of the process, making her three children Wards of Chancery pending the outcome of the hearing.

Catherine had stated her case very clearly in a series of statements and letters to her solicitor, secure in the knowledge that there were numerous witnesses to corroborate her story. She based her case on the grounds that her husband was an 'unfit parent', claiming that William 'had been guilty of the grossest adultery; that he had brought up his children in a course of swearing and blasphemy', and that he did not have finances to support them.[1]

The notion that a man could be an unfit parent was radical. The custody battle *Wellesley v Beaufort* provoked nationwide reflection and debate, exploring this concept for the first time. *Wellesley v Beaufort* was sufficiently high profile to capture the public imagination, divide opinion and challenge the status quo. All classes in society took an interest in public affairs, and newspapers represented 'a genuinely wide body of opinion which engaged in a vigorous and frequently polarised debate'.[2]

People talked about the court case in coffee houses, factories, shops and taprooms all over England. Illiteracy did not mean that people were ill-informed. Daily news bulletins spilt out into the streets through the media of newspapers, posters and the colourful caricatures that filled the print-shop windows. Consumption of newspapers was social rather than solitary, with audiences gathering in alehouses to be entertained by Cobbett's *Political Register* or other publications that were read aloud. Debating societies, lecture rooms and public meetings were also used to discuss issues of the day. Coffee houses and reading rooms offered a variety of newspapers and periodicals. In 1815, the proprietor of Crown Coffee-House in Haymarket served around 1,800 customers every day, attributing his success to his stock of forty-three dailies, 'five or six copies of some, eight of the *Morning Chronicle*'.[3] In the home, individuals often read aloud to family and guests after dinner, in grand salons as well as humble abodes. Such social consumption meant that the daily news reached a considerable proportion of the population and quite naturally led to comment and debate.

One week after Catherine's death, the *Evening Herald* stated, 'The premature death of an amiable lady . . . furnishes a lasting lesson to the heartlessness of too many of the men of the present age.'[4] The comment struck a chord and was quoted and reprinted in several other newspapers. For several decades national identity had been inexorably linked to liberty and freedom, with many impassioned speeches about the Rights of Freeborn English*men*. The most pertinent term here was the word 'men' – women were overlooked in the fight for reform. Catherine lived in an entirely patriarchal society where the rights of women were sadly neglected.

In 1826, William would face the charge of criminal conversation, filed by Captain Bligh, as well as the custody battle *Wellesley v Beaufort*. With two high-profile court cases pending, he needed to return to England to prepare his argument. Industrious as ever, his father had kept his word to creditors and settled outstanding debts, which enabled William to arrive back in London in December 1825. Somehow William managed to raise £6,000 to purchase a charming villa in Hall Place (now Hall Gate), adjoining Regent's Park. The large house was set in two acres, with a sunny glass

conservatory overlooking the gardens.[5] Having established a suitable family home, he felt confident that the Lord Chancellor would
look favourably on his application for custody of his children.

Facing judicial and public scrutiny, William could not risk
being seen with his mistress, so he had left Helena behind in
France with their newborn son, William Bligh-Wellesley. After his
departure, Helena frequently observed, 'If it was not for my infant
child, I would destroy myself, I am in such an unhappy state of
mind.'[6] Without any money and unable to support the child,
Helena soon followed William to London – leaving her son behind
in Calais in the care of a French nurse.[7] Helena barely knew the
woman and there was no guarantee that she would find the baby
alive and well when she returned.

A message arrived for William, and he was furious to discover
his mistress holed up at the Hyde Park Hotel. With her presence
drawing attention, he had no option but to set her up in a more
discreet residence at No. 50 York Street under the assumed name
of Mrs Thompson. The couple resumed their elaborate charade,
donning heavy disguises and meeting clandestinely.[8] Once she was
back with William and established in her own home, Helena sent
for her child. William had been sorely neglectful of his baby son,
leaving him behind in Calais with no money for support. He had
behaved in a similar fashion when he abandoned Maria Kinnaird
and his child in 1820. This did not bode well for a man about to
appear in court to attest that he was a good father.

The Lord Chancellor was sufficiently concerned for the welfare
of Will, James and Victoria to take them into care. This was unprecedented. As Wards of Chancery, the children needed a temporary
home pending the outcome of the custody hearing and the court
agreed that they could be left in the care of the Miss Longs. The
spinster sisters lived in constant fear that William would arrive in
the middle of the night and take the children by force. They needed
to find a guardian of some standing who would be willing to take
on William. They approached the Duke of Wellington, who was
reluctant to become entangled in the onerous affairs of his nephew
yet again. On reflection, he agreed to become guardian for the sake

of the children, promising to perform the task 'zealously, and to the best of my abilities'.[9] There was no doubt that whoever assumed this role would have to face the full force of William's wrath. Nevertheless, the great military commander would prove to be a powerful protector who could not be intimidated. With Wellington's consent, Victoria continued to live with the Miss Longs while the boys were sent to Eton under the care of their tutor, Mr Pitman.

Preliminary hearings for the *Wellesley v Beaufort* case commenced in November 1825. The presiding judge was the Lord Chancellor, Lord Eldon,[10] a conservative stickler, staunchly resistant to reform of Chancery. Having officiated over some of the longest-running cases, his peers dubbed him 'Lord Endless' and Dickens lampooned him in *Bleak House*. But even those who mocked recognized his strict adherence to considerations of principle and of constitutional law. As far as William was concerned, he had no case to answer for the children were legally and naturally his. In view of this, he tried to overturn the trial before it had even begun, instructing his counsel to argue, 'No court has the right to take children from under the care of their father, who was lawfully their natural guardian.'[11]

But Lord Eldon was more than a match for William, countering that, 'it was beyond dispute that [the court] had such power' in extreme circumstance.[12]

On 7 November 1825, *The Times* reported that William had demanded a private hearing. Once again, Eldon issued a rebuttal, stating, 'In cases of this anxious and delicate kind, a public hearing was preferable, because it was a guard to the conduct of the judge ... as well as of public justice.'[13] Eldon was conscious that the nation was following the case and that his judgement would be subject to scrutiny with widespread repercussions. Public feelings were high.

The historic custody trial *Wellesley v Beaufort* opened on 24 February 1826 at the Court of Chancery, Lincoln's Inn. The name of the trial was misleading, because the Duke of Beaufort had no actual involvement in the custody case. As Catherine was dead, William had been obliged to file his suit against the trustees of her estate, namely the Duke of Beaufort (and others). In real terms the battle was *William Wellesley v Catherine Long Wellesley*. Her legal team were now following through on her instructions, driven forward by her appointed next of kin, her sisters Dora and Emma, and supported by the Duke of Wellington.

Wellesley v Beaufort was the ultimate cause célèbre. Real-life melodramas staged in a courtroom with a celebrity cast were more gripping than Drury Lane productions. A landmark courtcase promising tales of the grossest adultery guaranteed front-page headlines. *Wellesley v Beaufort* provided the perfect vehicle for the press to turn private scandal into theatrical spectacle, satisfying the public's appetite for salacious trials. *The Times* reported that 'excited' crowds gathered at the courthouse,[14] with hordes of female admirers hoping to glimpse the delectable Mr Wellesley, remarking, 'The most anxious of the crowd were some women, without bonnets, whose eagerness knew no bounds.'[15] Despite the bad press, William still embodied male desirability.

In a society where sexual inequality was deeply ingrained, the odds were stacked firmly against Catherine. Reiterating her case, Mr Shadwell opened the proceedings by declaring that affidavits would demonstrate that Mr Wellesley was an unfit father. He stated, 'Mr Wellesley has been guilty of the grossest adultery . . . he has brought up his children in a course of swearing and blasphemy'; and he does not have finances to support them.[16]

In response, Mr Wellesley admitted that he had neglected his wife and dissipated her wealth with liberal extravagance; however – as he rightly pointed out – this was not illegal. As such, he stated, 'My conduct ought not to deprive me of the paternal care of my children.'[17] He denied completely the accusations relating to his parenting, adultery and finances.

The more titillating the evidence, the more extensive the newspaper coverage became. The courtroom was packed to the rafters to hear accounts from the family physician who had witnessed William's shenanigans first-hand. Bulkeley's testimony did not disappoint: he described the 'criminal intercourse' between William and Mrs Bligh on Mount Vesuvius; the miscarriage which was induced despite his determination 'to preserve not destroy life'; Mrs Bligh's frustration that her husband was too infirm to perform 'the gratifications she desired'; the depravity of the ménage à trois; William calling Mrs Bligh a 'damned dangerous bitch' and finally his callous treatment of Catherine, swearing, declining her company and saying 'he would be damned if he went anywhere with her'.[18]

Naturally, William denied everything and attempted to discredit the doctor by swearing endless counter-affidavits. However, the British ambassador in Naples and the upright Mr Pitman were among those who corroborated Bulkeley's version of events. Tourists on the Mount Vesuvius trip told how Mr Wellesley and Mrs Bligh had stayed a night in the hermitage instead of completing the journey up the mountain. Servants described how Mrs Bligh would fall into William's arms, the expensive lingerie and how she banished her favourite dog from her bedroom.[19] The court also heard how the invalid Captain Bligh had chased William around Naples with loaded pistols in his pocket, forcing him to retreat and head for Paris.

By October 1826, the Lord Chancellor was thoroughly fed up with William's ridiculous counter-allegations, as he attempted to deny his adultery and discredit witnesses. Eldon decided to halt the custody case, pending the outcome of the criminal conversation trial. Reluctant to recess, William demanded that the Lord Chancellor name an early day to give judgement. Unfazed, Eldon stated that he was in no hurry because the impending *Bligh v Wellesley* adultery case would give 'a singular turn' on the subject, while going far towards determining certain allegations in the custody suit.[20]

Captain Bligh intended to divorce his wife on the grounds of adultery, but as obtaining a divorce was notoriously difficult, a precursory criminal conversation trial often took place to prove the infidelity. Mrs Bligh was not permitted to appear in court or testify in her own defence. In many respects it was the legal equivalent of a duel, a dispute to be thrashed out between the two rival men, the husband and the lover. Matters of honour needed to be addressed. On 1 November 1826, William appeared at the Court of Common Pleas, Guildhall, facing charges of criminal conversation filed by Captain Bligh. The trial was based on the premise that a wife forms part of her husband's goods and chattels. By embarking on a sexual liaison with Mrs Bligh, William had defiled another man's property.[21] Captain Bligh had summed up his case perfectly when he wrote to William, 'Adultery is the deepest civil injury that can be inflicted on a man . . . you have robbed me of the affections of my wife . . . and committed an outrage upon my domestic happiness.'[22] The calibre of witnesses such as William Hamilton and Sir William Drummond made their testimonies beyond dispute. To put the final nail in the coffin, Captain Bligh was able to produce documentary evidence. In the tumultuous aftermath of the siege at Clarges Street, William had rushed from his lodgings in great haste, leaving behind a stack of private correspondence between himself and Helena. On calling at the lodgings some days later, Captain Bligh paid off the landlady and took away the letters. Their explosive contents irrevocably incriminated William. Although William continued to protest his innocence, the evidence against him was overwhelming. It took the jury less than fifteen minutes to find for the plaintiff. The adulterer was declared guilty as charged and Captain Bligh awarded damages of £6,000.[23] But in many respects the money was immaterial; the important point was that Captain Bligh had his 'satisfaction' and his honour restored. William had lost the duel.

When the custody trial reconvened in the Court of Chancery on 9 November 1826, William was unable to deny his adultery because this had already been categorically proved. It had also become clear that many of the affidavits filed by William contained blatant lies regarding his adultery, which meant he could face charges for perjury. At this point, however, the Lord Chancellor was keen to press on and focus on the burning question – was William an unfit parent?

One of the key witnesses was Catherine. Although William objected to her letters and statements being read aloud in court, the Lord Chancellor deemed them admissible.[24] As William feared, spectators broke down in tears as they heard Catherine's story, told in her own words. She had employed powerful rhetoric, vividly describing the 'miseries I have endured . . . the insult and degradation . . . I have borne it till I can bear it no longer'. Her statements were highly emotive, providing convincing evidence: 'Under their father's roof, [my children] would hear vice upheld and admired, and morality and religion scorned and ridiculed every day.'[25] There could be no doubt that Catherine had led a miserable existence at the hands of her husband, and no one wanted her children to suffer the same fate.

John Pitman was perfectly placed to observe how William treated his children and proved to be the most crucial witness. The mousy middle-aged tutor was devoted to his charges and Eldon described him as 'a person of unimpeachable character'. Even at this stage Pitman was torn, having 'experienced much personal civility, attention, and even kindness from Mr Wellesley'.[26] However, he had the interests of the children to consider. Pitman testified that when he joined the family in July 1822, he was appalled to find that the children were like feral creatures, wild and filthy from playing all day in the stables. Even little Victoria had learned obscene language from the grooms.[27] Pitman corroborated Bulkeley's evidence, testifying that after Mrs Bligh moved into the family home, she formed a system with William to 'alienate the children's affections from their mother'. Together they permitted the boys to drink wine after dinner, ridiculing Catherine when she objected, and encouraging the children to do likewise.

William had not been as shrewd as his wife. He had been unguarded in his correspondence to Pitman and the damning contents of his own letters were used against him. The court heard that he had instructed the boys to 'chase all the cats, dogs, bulls and women, both young and old'. William had also sent commands:

'I positively order that all *Story Books* be burnt . . . I forbid all *Religious Tracts*.'[28] When James suffered yet another serious fall from his horse, Lady Maryborough was suitably concerned, writing to Catherine, 'I am most grieved to think what torrents of misery you must have had on account of James' accident.'[29] In contrast, William wrote to his son, 'My Dear Mr Jemps . . . I write to you to congratulate you upon your fall a-hunting . . . a few more good thumps, and you will soon learn how to fall easy.'[30]

Although the adultery trial was over, William's transgressions continued to entertain. Quality newspapers such as *The Times*, *Morning Chronicle*, *The Age* and *Bell's Life in London* took their positions in the courtroom and produced lengthy reports to keep the public fully apprised of developments. London newspapers often quoted from affidavits verbatim. Picking up the story, provincial papers followed suit. Taprooms and coffee houses the length and breadth of England were buzzing, as everybody continued to debate the social and moral issues raised by this trial. On 22 November 1826, the *Morning Chronicle* capitalized on the nation's love of theatre and amateur dramatics by publishing a lengthy skit, laid out like the script of a melodrama, complete with theatricals and heated exchanges:

> Mr Wellesley: rose to address his Lordship in the utmost agitation . . . incessantly striking the bar with the greatest force. He said – 'I am now accused of perjury . . . As a man of honour and an English gentleman, I call on you to do me justice . . . take these affidavits, read them, weigh and digest them, but, in God's name, decide on them.'
>
> The Chancellor: 'I shall give my judgement in what way I please, whatever you, or any other Englishman may think of it . . . I will also tell you that in this court there is a propriety of countenance as well as speech to be observed.'
>
> Mr Shadwell [Catherine's counsel]: 'Mr Wellesley's epistles contained the elegant phrases "Hell and Tommy", and "Damn

their infernal souls to Hell" . . . Mr W had at the very least two systems of education, which were not consistent or well calculated to benefit the children.'

Such a style of reporting was an instant success and many other newspapers followed suit. On 19 January 1827, *The Times* published a 9,000-word scripted report recalling the 'adultery on Mount Vesuvius' and other choice episodes involving the doctor and the abortion. It proved so popular that yet more salacious dialogues were published in *The Times* on 25 and 26 January. It is easy to imagine how these would have entertained in taprooms, as people consumed pints of ale and acted out the bawdy scenes. These 'scripts' took the social consumption of newspapers to a new level, and the courtroom drama may well have been re-enacted in genteel drawing rooms, salons or private theatres across the country. They certainly provided some light relief. According to one discourse, William purportedly told his wife, 'I acknowledge your high merits, but I am a slave of a passion from which I cannot emancipate myself, and which bows me to the earth.'[31]

Satirists were also keen to have their say. Isaac Cruikshank's cartoon *The effects of a Blithe W riding on a Long Pole* resurrected the old innuendoes, and showed a see-saw shaft between William's legs probing beneath the skirt of Mrs 'Blithe'.[32] The Lord Chancellor appeared in the background shielding the forlorn children and gesturing towards the Miss Longs. Forceful Dora stood hands on hips, with Emma right behind her. Most importantly, however, the cartoon revealed that *Wellesley v Beaufort* was finely balanced, with the weight of public opinion swaying to and fro like a see-saw. According to this cartoonist, however, William was now floundering as a result of his indiscretions.

The public and press were fixated on the fact that William had been found guilty of adultery, and this was clouding the issue of child custody. Needing a new strategy, William came up with an argument so compelling that the tide of opinion began to turn in his favour.

44. The Court of Public Opinion

༄

1827

Attempting to overturn any law is a mammoth task. For hundreds of years, men had been granted ultimate control of their children. Was there any need to change this? At the start of the trial, emotions were running high and there had been a lot of sympathy for Catherine. But more than one year later, the shock of her death had faded. Cold, hard reasoning had come into play and the fact remained – the law was firmly on William's side. In this climate of shifting allegiances, he presented an ingenious new argument.

William admitted to the charge of adultery, but insisted that this did not make him an unfit parent. Appealing to Eldon's cautious tendencies, he warned that his case could set a precedent for a most 'alarming interference between father and child'.[1] Furthermore, William insisted, 'If adultery becomes a ground for disqualifying a father from having custody of his own children – NO MAN CAN BE SAFE! It will endanger the parental rights of some of the first men in the kingdom.'[2] This was powerful rhetoric. The words rang in the ears of men across the nation.

Journalists were 'Gentle*men* of the Press'. The establishment was entirely male – politicians, law-makers and voters. Many men quaked at the prospect of women becoming too powerful, or at having to face acrimonious custody battles themselves.

This new development polarized opinion even further. William treated the courthouse like a stage, and his use of theatrics was captured in court sketches. During the final weeks of the trial, the Court of Chancery was bursting to the rafters every day, with all classes of people anxious to catch even a momentary glimpse of the notorious Mr Wellesley. William put on a great show for the crowds, occupying centre stage beside his solicitor, Mr Hart, in benches usually reserved for counsel. Occasionally, while Hart was engaged in dissecting the affidavits of the opposing party, his client found it difficult to suppress symptoms of satisfaction, and he frequently communicated his suggestions to the learned leader and the junior counsel by whom he was surrounded. Mr Wellesley's demeanour during the speeches of the defendant's counsel was aggressive. On one particular day, he completely lost his composure, interrupting so frequently he received a warning from Lord Eldon. When court was adjourned, people scrambled for standing room near the exit. As Mr Wellesley walked through the court, spectators formed a line for him to pass. According to one newspaper, he was assailed with hisses and cries of 'shame'; 'Placing his hands upon his lips, he smiled a somewhat gay and good-natured defiance.'[3]

One year into the trial, the press was deeply divided. On 17 January 1827, one newspaper described angry crowds shouting abuse at Mr Wellesley, including the taunts, 'You murdered your wife!' and 'You ought to be hanged!'[4] In contrast, *The Times* seemed to favour William. The following day they issued a rebuttal to the above article, stating categorically, 'We heard no symptom of disapprobation expressed.' Instead they maintained that the crowds contained hordes of female admirers, keen to catch a glimpse of Mr Wellesley.[5]

The power of the press was evident as the epic courtroom drama reached its climax. Employing similar techniques to Voltaire, reporters used melodrama to manipulate the masses in a way that dry factual reasoning never could. One publication stated, 'It is nauseating to hear the Counsel for this hopeful scion of nobility talk about his "high honour" and "illustrious family".'[6] On 5 November 1826, the *Sunday Times* dredged up William's misconduct, stating that he owed everything to his amiable wife. 'But how did he repay her? By introducing an adulteress wanton beneath her roof, in Naples; by making his wife the unconscious pander to his base appetites and her own misery, and driving her broken-hearted to the grave.' The article was so defamatory that William successfully sued for libel. The *Sunday Times* was forced to print an apology, but the damage was done – their report was in the public domain and newspapers quoted from it, far and wide.

The English justice system was also under scrutiny in the USA. On 25 December 1826, the *Daily National Intelligencer*, Washington, recorded: 'The whole disgusting story is told in the trial . . . Mrs Wellesley is a much beloved . . . virtuous . . . high-minded . . . injured lady . . . He is detestable . . . profligate . . . despised.' The law did nothing to protect women, and when William had started mistreating his wife there was no means of escape for her. In America, the *New Hampshire Statesman* ran an article about Catherine's riches to rags story, declaring: 'Wealth, Prodigality, Poverty. Mrs Long Wellesley lately died in England, the victim of an unfortunate marriage . . . Is it right . . . ?'[7]

Nevertheless, the prospect that paternal custody might be taken away was so daunting that newsmen who had previously criticized William for his adultery now tried to swing opinion in his favour. The two newspapers with the widest circulations, *The Times* and *Morning Chronicle*, adopted a carefully cultivated, apparently neutral stance, but they were clearly against change. Even during the play-acting, *The Times* made sure to drive home one vital point: 'The Lord Chancellor recollected there were several contradictions . . . regarding the adultery on Mount Vesuvius. Mr Hart observed that the question before his Lordship was not whether adultery had been committed . . . but whether Mr Wellesley was an *unfit parent*.'[8]

On 11 December 1826, *The Times* published extracts of William's letters to his children, along with open appeals to the public inviting them to judge the case for themselves. They were careful, however, to select only extracts that displayed his parenting skills in a favourable light, portraying him as an indulgent father administering gifts and good advice: 'My dear Mr Jemps . . . I am glad you continue to ride, and pray cultivate manly exercises . . . I was very uneasy at your not receiving your watches . . . attend to your studies, and always to speak the truth.' Other newspapers printed the same extracts, proclaiming, 'the fashion seems to have been set to run down Mr Wellesley without either consideration or mercy . . . These letters show something of Mr Wellesley's *paternal character* – for which he is attacked legally.'[9]

Every angle was exploited, with some papers turning the case into a class issue. On 22 January 1827, *John Bull* condemned the lower classes for their hypocrisy, immorality and paternal tyranny, insisting that road sweepers and pickpockets were in no position to 'express their disapprobation of the morality and virtue of the said Honourable William Long Wellesley … the nephew of the man who *Saved this Country*, – *that* of itself should insure [him] the justice' he deserves.[10] The *Literary Magnet* replied on 31 January, 'So much for Mr Long Wellesley's character as a husband! As a father, he does not appear to much greater advantage.' This monthly publication castigated *John Bull* for their 'shameless audacity' in taking his cause, while condemning a 'certain popular journalist for … scurrility, falsehood, and base sycophancy', and for bringing their profession into disrepute.

The *Morning Chronicle* had a reputation for liberal attitudes and for tackling social issues. It was surprising, therefore, that they deemed that the Court of Chancery should not entertain enquiries of this kind. It pontificated, 'Nothing more monstrous can be conceived than inquiries into a man's whole life for the purposes of the Chancellor setting his virtues and vices against each other, and striking a balance.'[11]

The Gentlemen of the Press were accustomed to fighting for Rights of Freeborn Englishmen, but the concerns of women were not in their interests, nor on their agenda. Even the most liberal-minded objected to female involvement in public affairs, as demonstrated by William Hazlitt's outburst in 1821, when he wrote, 'I have an utter aversion to Bluestockings. I do not care a fig for any woman that knows even what *an author* means.'[12]

With the trial drawing to a conclusion, it was time for the Lord Chancellor to make a decision. While he had serious concerns about Mr Wellesley's parenting, he was reluctant to overturn the law of the land and set a controversial precedent. Eldon felt that a good compromise would be to seek the advice of William's father and to offer him guardianship of his grandchildren. Lord

Maryborough was renowned for his integrity and the Lord Chancellor trusted his judgement.

William had caused his parents endless heartache, but he was still their flesh and blood. Lord Maryborough had made it clear that he would not be party to any steps taken against his son in a court of law, but he also had the welfare of his grandchildren to consider. Faced with a painful decision, Maryborough sent his reply to Eldon just one day before the verdict, strictly on the understanding that his letter was never made public. He wrote:

> Unfortunately . . . I know [Mr Wellesley's] disposition, and habits, to be such, that I am convinced, were I to become the Guardian of his children, I should have constant protests . . . and remonstrances without end. My whole life would be passed in a succession of quarrels . . . which might materially affect the welfare of the children.[13]

Instead, Maryborough confirmed his support for an alternative guardian, stating:

> The Duke of Wellington would not be liable to the distressing scenes at which I have hinted . . . the children would be brought up in the most becoming manner, and I should feel perfectly easy as to their morals and education.[14]

This summation made it clear that even William's closest family were 'desirous that the children should not fall into his hands'.[15]

The Lord Chancellor's judgement was heard on 1 February 1827. A huge crowd queued for hours outside the courtroom, before the doors even opened. Packed tightly into the courthouse, the hisses and complaints of the spectators were so audible that Eldon threatened to clear the room. When the noise dissipated, Eldon admitted, 'This case has cost me the greatest pain and many sleepless hours.'[16]

In his summing up, the Lord Chancellor stated that under the laws of the land, an authority over the actions of a father should exist somewhere. Eldon proclaimed that he was 'deeply shocked at Mr Wellesley's continued adultery and his curious ideas about bringing up children', which could endanger their principles and lead to debauchery. Eldon finished by pronouncing, 'I should deserve to be hunted out of society if . . . I should permit these children to go to their father.'

The Duke of Wellington was declared guardian and William was the first man in British legal history to be deprived of his children on the grounds that he was an unfit parent. As Eldon left the bench, a smothered expression of approval rippled through the crowd.

Naturally, this ruling was not popular in every quarter. The public and the courts would continue to debate the issue of child custody for many years. But this verdict was the first breakthrough in Chancery, paving the way for other women in child custody disputes. *Wellesley v Beaufort* had set a new legal precedent.

At the turn of the nineteenth century, the issue of child custody loomed large and women like Catherine were compelled to stay with cruel husbands for the sake of their offspring. In his definitive book on the subject, Lawrence Stone identifies *Wellesley v Beaufort* as the 'turning point' in Chancery.[17] Danaya Wright agrees that *Wellesley v Beaufort* 'became the precedent of choice', cited in subsequent child custody cases.[18] The impact of *Wellesley v Beaufort* was far-reaching, because it also addressed the important issue of child protection. In effect, William was the first parent in England to have his children taken into the care of the state because he was deemed to be unfit to have custody of them. The case was also hugely influential in the USA, where its ruling formed the basis of the Juvenile Court system.[19]

Catherine's legacy lives on. She made the ultimate sacrifice to gain the first breakthrough in Chancery, setting a new precedent regarding women's rights in child custody, which eventually resulted in a major change to the statute law in 1839. The Custody of Infants Act gave mothers of 'unblemished character' rights of access to their children in the event of separation or divorce. Women also gained custody of their children under seven years old. It became the first piece of feminist legislation passed into English law.[20]

45. The Frolicsome Companion

Shattered by the outcome of the trial, William withdrew into privacy for some time. The knocker on his door was muffled, and he did not receive any visitors, apart from the physicians who visited him daily. Laid up in bed, he had plenty of time to grow bitter. Disgusted by the fact that his own family had not supported him, William blamed Wellington for his misfortune, because the duke had openly opposed him and stood as guardian.

After lodging an appeal against the Lord Chancellor's judgement, William decided that he needed to convince his family to come out in support of him before the next hearing. Bribery and intimidation had worked well during his election campaign, so he tried this approach again. William claimed to have information that would ruin his father and uncles, and threatened to expose the whole family in the press. Naturally, the Wellesleys were appalled, but they refused to cooperate. When this ploy did not work, William came up with a more sinister plan.

At the time, Colonel James Grant was one of the few people who would suffer William's company. One evening at dinner William burst out with an account of what he would do if the Duke of Wellington interfered in his court appeal.[1]

'By God, I will shoot him,' declared William.

Grant could not believe his ears. 'Do you know what you are saying? You must be mad!'

William replied calmly, 'I am fully aware of what I am saying and I will expiate the Crime on the Scaffold.'

The next morning Grant met William again and saw by the sullen earnestness of his manner that his words had been no idle menace. News of the assassination plot reached the Duke of Wellington, and fixer Merrick Shawe was called on yet again to counsel the would-be assassin. But the prospect of the gallows had already dissuaded William.

Instead of killing his uncle, William decided that he would try to ruin his career by blackening his name with slander. His accusations appeared in the *Frolicsome Companion*, which promised to deliver more 'Amorous Scenes' and 'Voluptuous Anecdotes' than any other publication. The sordid account of the duke's love life contained many choice lies. Numerous women were named and shamed, including the highly proper Marianne, Marchioness Wellesley. William was proud of the fact that he had succeeded in discrediting two members of his own family in one fell swoop. Wellington was on the verge of becoming prime minister and the article might well have damaged his prospects. Wellington remained remarkably restrained under the circumstances; he wrote a courteous letter to William explaining that the threat to shoot him plus the libellous pamphlet put him in a rather awkward position, to say the least. He might have to prosecute, particularly if the accusations were published in a paper with a wider circulation than the *Frolicsome Companion*.

Having slandered members of his own family, William launched an attack on the Miss Longs, claiming that he did not want to leave his children in their care because the spinster sisters were conducting a sexual union of an unnatural and incestuous nature. The affidavit William produced for Lord Chancellor Eldon was a string of invented horrors. He claimed that: Dora and Emma were having sexual relations with each other, as well as sexual intercourse with the various young boys who played with his children; Victoria's governess was a prostitute; Emma had committed incest with her uncle; all the rest of the Long family were drunken blasphemers . . . and so on. No credence was given to the ludicrous accusations, particularly as everyone knew that the Long family were upstanding Evangelicals.

Similarly, William made vicious and ludicrous allegations against Mr Pitman and Dr Bulkeley. He falsely claimed that it had been Bulkeley who helped Helena abort her baby in Naples, and the public were scandalized. The reputations of both Pitman and Bulkeley were dragged through the mud and the good doctor's career was completely destroyed.

The mad ingenuity of William's mind made him believe that if he discredited all the people caring for his children, the Lord Chancellor would have to grant him custody. His plan did not work and William lost his appeal in 1828. Bombarding Eldon with letters, William continued to rage and lodge petitions. In fact, he considered himself such an expert on certain points of law that he felt qualified to publish a book – *A View of the Court of Chancery* (1830).

William's intellectual posturing was ridiculed in the cartoon *A Bright Thought*.[2] At first glance the satirical sketch seems to present William as he saw himself – a great thinker, a man of learning, surrounded by books and stacks of legal papers, with pen in hand. The caption above his head says, 'I'll be revenged and write a faithful history of the Court of Chancery.' On closer inspection, however, the titles of the books around him are ironic – *Affidavit*, *Petition* (both several times), *Answer*, *Bills of Costs 5000*. The lithograph also shows that William, in his early forties, was an attractive man, virile and athletic. The pose with his legs splayed is highly suggestive and sexual.

Catherine's priority had been to protect her children, but she had not been as meticulous about safeguarding her assets and William managed to gain a major victory over her. In 1815, she had been harassed into signing a will granting him £50,000 in the event of her death. On her deathbed, she had revoked this in the deed witnessed by John Pitman and Henry Bicknell. William attempted to overturn this document by making various claims and allegations, including that it was a forgery created by Dora Long. He filed a suit to this effect against Catherine's trustees, and the case was heard in the Prerogative Court on 24 February 1826. Astonishingly, William won the case – it was deemed that he was entitled to £50,000 from Catherine's estate.[3] The court ruling gave William the leverage he needed to pester Catherine's trustees for money; he even went around seizing assets and selling them. In effect, he was plundering his own sons' trust fund.

When it came to money, William was characteristically slippery. The task of managing him proved to be extremely onerous for the trustees, giving them a taste of the pressures Catherine had contended with. William also continued to harass the Miss Longs, insisting that they hand over all Catherine's worldly goods, including her private letters. In theory, as her widower he was entitled to these possessions. But it was a grey area because Catherine had been separated from him and trying to obtain a divorce. Arguments continued until Catherine's entire archive of papers was destroyed in a fire – Dora and Emma did not care to comment on whether the blaze had been started deliberately. However, they could not prevent William taking possession of Catherine's famous diamonds which she had set aside for Victoria. The jewels were auctioned at Christie's in London on 18 May 1827. The lot was described as 'a casket of jewels of extraordinary splendour and value', comprising of a magnificent necklace composed of thirty uncommonly large and fine brilliants, a sumptuous tiara, a pair of earrings with drops of great beauty and size, plus a pair of bracelets of thirty-six brilliant collets.[4] The hoard fetched an enormous £5,898, around the same price as the detached villa William had purchased at Regent's Park. Nevertheless, it was a huge loss from the £25,000 guineas paid in 1812. In no time, William ran through the cash he obtained from the sale of the diamonds, and found other ways to squeeze money from Catherine's estate.

Despite Catherine's efforts to safeguard her children, they went on to lead tragic lives, overshadowed by the loss of their beloved mother and the constant misdeeds of their depraved father. William continued to corrupt the boys with his malicious influence, encouraging them to abscond from boarding school and generally make life difficult for their guardian. They ran riot at Wellington's estate in Stratfield Saye, damaging furniture and smashing windows. To his great credit, Wellington remained true to his word and never relinquished custody, despite all the trouble they caused.

*

William continued to hound the Lord Chancellor, but although he lodged endless appeals he never gained custody of his children. Popularity, status and wealth meant everything to William, but he had lost public respect and become an outcast from society. Even his own father would have nothing to do with him. William wrote to his mother: 'I implore, I beg of you on my knees to see me. I am most anxious to have an interview with you and my father, to request you will both do me the favour to accept the guardianship of my children.'[5]

The letter had no effect, although his mother did grant him a short interview. When his mother advised that Lord Maryborough had no desire to be reconciled with him, William cried pitifully and asked, 'What justification can a father have for abandoning his son thus?'[6]

'What justification did you have when you abandoned your sweet, amiable wife?' was her reply.

Whenever William went out riding in Rotten Row, his former friends and associates ignored him completely. One afternoon a female relative stopped her carriage to speak with him. With affectionate remonstration, she urged William to withdraw from public life for a short while longer.[7] Deluded as ever, he replied jovially, 'Nonsense, this business will soon be forgotten; I will regain my true place in society.'

Just as he uttered these words he spotted a man of the cloth, with a shining bald head, advancing towards him on a spruce cob. He immediately recognized the dishonest clergyman who had counterfeited his cheque some years previously, during the golden years at Wanstead House. William had gallantly spared the man's life, saving him from the hangman's noose. Smiling over at the cleric, William said confidently to his companion, 'Well here comes one at any rate, who will not turn his back upon an old friend.'

Cantering up, the clergyman stared William full in the face and rode straight past. Even the dishonest cleric wanted nothing to do with him. In polite circles this was known as 'A Complete Cut'.

*

William went on to lead a long and villainous life, cementing his nickname 'Wicked William'. Stories of his scandalous exploits could fill volumes. In the two years following the custody battle, William focused entirely on revenge, vowing he would ruin everyone who had testified against him. As a young man he had been charming, and possessed of many redeeming qualities, but when his life spiralled out of control he became deluded, blaming everyone else for his misfortune. Spurred on by a sense of entitlement, he grew increasingly vindictive if anyone crossed him; even his own children did not escape his wrath.

In July 1831, the public were gripped when William carried out his threat to kidnap Victoria and convey her to France.[8] While the Miss Longs were out for the day, he turned up at their house in Unstead Wood, accompanied by four armed thugs, and forcibly removed Victoria from the servants minding her. Returning from their trip, Dora and Emma passed the carriage racing away, with the poor little girl inside. They could see that Victoria was in great distress, sitting between her father and another ruffian.[9] Naturally, Dora and Emma were frantic as they appealed for help, petitioning law agents as well as the Lord Chancellor. Close family blasted William for the 'brutal violence used to kidnap the unfortunate child', lamenting, 'If [Victoria] is not very promptly recovered she will be irretrievably ruined in mind … it is a most melancholy proof of Mr Wellesley's depravity and villainy.'[10] Thankfully, the Lord Chancellor intervened and William was thrown into the Fleet Prison for contempt of court. Some residual sympathy for William was evident as he was sent gifts in prison, while prominent tavern keepers kept him well fed and watered during his detention by supplying his 'table *gratis* with choicest wines and viands'.[11] But in the main, public interest in this story revolved around Victoria's safe return to England. After a two-week spell in captivity, William conceded and told the court where he was hiding Victoria. When she was reunited with the Miss Longs, one month after her abduction, the nation breathed a sigh of relief. William was released from prison without further repercussions and the matter was considered closed.[12] Unbeknown to the court, however, Victoria had only

been released after the Miss Longs had paid over a ransom to Mrs
Bligh, who was holding the child in France.

Until her death, Catherine had honoured her commitment to
Mrs Kinnaird and continued to support William's illegitimate
child. At the first opportunity, however, William stopped the payments, insisting that he was not liable for allowances granted by his
wife. Legally speaking this was true, but it was morally cruel. Maria
Kinnaird resorted to sending begging letters to William's family,
and eventually took him to court, where he was ordered to pay
her an annuity of £300 – much less than the £500 Catherine had
provided.[13]

In 1845, the cherished hereditary title automatically devolved
to Wicked William and, much to the embarrassment of the
Wellesley family, he became the fourth Earl of Mornington. The
newspapers described it as 'making a mockery of heraldry'.[14]
Numerous caricatures and newspaper reports bear witness to
the fact that he was a celebrity in his own lifetime, but with the
dawning of the upright Victorian era he became marginalized
for symbolizing everything that was wrong with the old order.
Contemporaries disowned him as a friend, omitted him from their
memoirs and played down their association with him. In effect,
William received the ultimate social 'cut' and he was written out of
history.

William finally passed away in 1857, in his seventieth year. His
funeral was a small affair conducted without pomp or ceremony,
paid for by his cousin, the second Duke of Wellington. A dozen
or so close family members stood in the rain as William's remains
were deposited in the catacombs at Kensal Green Cemetery. It
was a suitably dismal ending for a deplorable man. More than any
other newspaper, the *Morning Chronicle* had catalogued William's
escapades with humour and interest. On his death they supplied a
fittingly scathing epitaph: 'Redeemed by no single virtue – adorned
by no single grace – his life has gone out, even without a flicker of
repentance – his "retirement" was that of one who was deservedly
avoided by all men.'[15]

Epilogue

Catherine gave up her life to protect her children. On her death, her entire estate devolved to her elder son, a nervous child who was mercilessly bullied and beaten by his peers at Eton. The inheritance was a mixed blessing for Will, because he was no match for his devious father, who pursued him relentlessly for money, misappropriating huge sums by various means such as begging, cajoling or even terrorizing with violent threats.

James was a bright, handsome boy with a reckless streak. As the younger son he had to earn his living and he did this by joining the army for a spell and later becoming a prizefighter. Regrettably, the damage done by his father proved to be enduring. In his early years, James had not received the education of a young gentleman, exposed instead to working in stables and attending cockfights. As a result, the life he chose to follow was a coarse one, travelling from town to town, often living rough and boxing for his supper. Although he was fairly successful at his chosen career, the constant beatings took their toll and James died relatively young.

Victoria lived very happily with her aunts, who doted on her as if she were their own child. Guided by their example, Victoria always endeavoured 'to do good and to show kindness to all'.[1] As an eighteen-year-old debutante she was a great beauty, with lustrous blonde curls cascading down her back and her mother's gentle expression discernible in her startling blue eyes. When she was presented at court William IV took a keen interest, saying he 'wished to watch the little fairy dance'.[2] The king had been genuinely fond of Catherine and when her daughter appeared at the palace it struck a chord, bringing back bittersweet memories. Having never produced a legitimate heir, the sight of Victoria Long Wellesley reminded him of what could have been – she might have been his child and successor.

The Miss Longs provided a loving home for Victoria for fifty years, and her presence encouraged them to rent a town house in London each season, to enjoy the theatres, suppers and abundance of entertainment on offer. Living well into their eighties, Dora and Emma settled contentedly together, enjoying the same pursuits, even writing letters at the same table. The annuities settled on them by Catherine enabled their comfort and independence, but they upheld the thriftiness of their early years and 'thought fires in the bedroom self-indulgent'.[3] The economy they exercised on themselves was never practised on others and they were benevolent to the last degree. No tale of distress ever reached their ears without immediate assistance. Travelling was one of their greatest pleasures; most years they went to London for the season, arriving in town in April to attend the drawing-room celebrations of Queen Victoria's birthday.[4] In the hotter months they headed to one of the fashionable coastal resorts, staying at the Royal Crescent in Brighton, at the Marina in St Leonards-on-Sea, or wherever took their fancy.

Dora and Emma never married, their prospects ruined by William's refusal to pay over their portions. Victoria also remained single. Will and James never married, discouraged perhaps by memories of their parents' turbulent marriage and its disastrous consequences. As none of Catherine's children produced heirs, it marked the end of the industrious Tylneys. Not only had William ruined Sir Josiah's estates, he also succeeded in extinguishing his family line.

Mr Pitman was among the employees who suffered reprisals. Wicked William cast aspersions and raised various objections to the boys' tutor accompanying them to Eton. When this failed, he sent henchmen to intimidate Pitman at the school. Loyal as ever, the tutor stayed on for the sake of the boys who had already lost much and were now struggling to adapt. Sadly, William's threats took their toll and gentle Pitman died in January 1828, just a few months after settling the boys at Eton.

Dr Bulkeley returned to Italy and got married. He continued to keep in touch with Catherine's children, sending letters and small gifts, and when Victoria was kidnapped it was Bulkeley who travelled to Paris to track her down and accompany her back to England. William, however, spread such vicious slander that the doctor became notorious. Eventually, he appealed to Dora and Emma, writing, 'I implore you all to come forward and shield me from his infamous attacks by stating the particulars which your deceased Sister must have often dwelt upon.'[5] Despite their best endeavours, Bulkeley was no match for the bad publicity William engineered. The good doctor's medical practice was ruined and he barely earned a living.

Left without a reference, the valet Meara also struggled to find work. Friends of the family were well aware of his tremendous loyalty, but everyone declined his services because they could not face William's wrath. Mary Bagot was among those who refused, saying, 'It might make a quarrel between me and my brother.'[6] Nevertheless, Meara remained devoted to the children and more than twenty years after he left their service, he was still writing to enquire after them.

Sickly Captain Bligh did not receive one penny of the £6,000 in damages he had been awarded in court. Even before he could sue for the money, malady overtook him and he died in 1828.

Helena married William in 1828 and they had at least one more child together. William's second wife suffered even worse treatment than his first; he continued to squander money without sparing a thought for the welfare of his young family. Eventually he abandoned Helena, leaving her destitute and running off with her maid. Helena resorted to begging on the streets of London and she ended up living in the workhouse at Wanstead, where she applied for aid using her official title, Countess of Mornington. When Wellington learned of her plight, he came to her rescue, setting her up in a comfortable home and paying her a small pension.

In the final battle of the Wellesley brothers, the Duke of Wellington became prime minister in 1828. His greatest achievement in this role was ushering the Roman Catholic Relief Act through Parliament in 1829. His magnificent home at Apsley House still stands at No. 1 London, overlooking Hyde Park, and has changed very little since the Iron Duke was in residence. Open to the public, the museum boasts one of the finest art collections in London, with paintings by Velázquez and Rubens as well as displays of silver and hand-painted china. Apsley House pays testament to the fact that the Duke of Wellington has made his mark in history.

Richard, Marquess Wellesley watched from the sidelines as his younger brother became prime minister and attained everything he had ever dreamed of. By now, however, Richard had given up on political ambition and deep contentment had settled over him. Married to the lovely Marianne, the final decades of his long life were filled with peace. Richard Wellesley is the great-great-great-grandfather of Queen Elizabeth II and a huge portrait of him occupies pride of place in the staterooms at Buckingham Palace.

After serving the Wellesleys for more than half a century, faithful Shawe retired with a small pension, sufficient to allow him to indulge his pleasure in fine food and wine. Late in his life, he enjoyed nothing more than to sit in an armchair with a glass of claret, regaling his nephew with reminiscences of the Wellesley family, whom he held in great affection. Fortuitously, his nephew happened to be William Makepeace Thackeray. Armed with intimate first-hand accounts of one of the most sensational marriages of the Regency, Thackeray used his uncle's memories to enrich his writing. His tour de force, *Vanity Fair*, contains many veiled references to the Long Wellesleys and the events at Wanstead House.

In a low-key ceremony, the Duke of Clarence was crowned William IV in 1830. A benevolent monarch with no taste for grandeur, he greatly reduced the costs run up by George IV. King William's 'wish to spread happiness round him was genuine' and on his birthday he gave a banquet to 3,000 of the town's poorer inhabitants.[7] This was a far cry from the excesses of the Regency fete hosted by his older brother. William IV successfully bridged the gap between the decadence of the previous age and the staunch

Victorians. During his reign, the Great Reform Act was finally introduced, in 1832, implementing far-reaching changes to the electoral system of England and Wales, while laying the foundations for further reforms during the Victorian era.

Despite her great triumphs, history has been unkind to Catherine. In the main, stories about her are tragic, ending with her downfall and untimely death. She is often depicted as a faceless character, the cowering victim of a tyrannical husband; or else she is portrayed as a foolish woman who squandered the chance of becoming queen of England and ended her life in ruin. Until now, nobody has scratched beneath the surface of her story or identified her as the remarkable woman who successfully challenged the legal system in England.

Prior to the trial, William terrorized Catherine and, in the face of such abuse, most women would have given up the cause. In an age when women had very few rights, she showed remarkable courage. In many respects, the Lord Chancellor's verdict was a compromise, because the children went to a male guardian in William's family. Would Catherine have gained custody if she had lived? Could Eldon have handed over the children to a woman? Judging by the mood in the press, it seems unlikely. Even the social reformer Jeremy Bentham considered William to be the 'victim of plunderage, [warning that] a single precedent made by a single judge suffices to make law'.[8] The verdict was only achieved because influential men in William's family supported Catherine's application – namely the Duke of Wellington and Lord Maryborough. Without their help, the outcome may not have gone in her favour.

Catherine's story reveals a society on the cusp of change, at a time when attitudes to love, marriage and the role of women were being redefined and Regency decadence gave way to Victorian virtues. *Wellesley v Beaufort* came at the end of a pivotal era that influenced many aspects of modern life. As Lawrence Stone has argued, women's causes began to be heard and addressed in the

1830s, when well-born, well-connected women began to lobby for them. Catherine was one of these women.

Catherine was a popular celebrity, portrayed in the press as the ideal wife and mother. When she challenged the legal system, she was aware that her actions would influence other women, and that the nation would be watching. Acknowledging that her motivations were public as well as private, she resolved to protect her children 'at every hazard and at every risk',[9] stating, 'I feel that my own character demands, and that my beloved children's best interests require, that I should take the step on which I am determined.'[10]

Wanstead Park is all that remains of the Tylney legacy. For centuries it has been a much-treasured local amenity, a sanctuary where ordinary people can escape for an hour or two, taking a scenic stroll or enjoying a family picnic. Remnants of the old park remain. The original stone gateposts still stand at the top of Overton Drive, at the intersection with Blake Hall Road. If you walk through the gateposts and follow the curve of the road, it will take you past many of the features that once formed the approach to Wanstead House: Sir Josiah's octagonal lake; Grade I-listed St Mary's Church, which houses the Tylney family crypt along with a huge monument to Sir Josiah; and William's famous stables which now form part of the clubhouse at Wanstead Golf Club.

Follow the line of the old scenic walk down to the River Roding and you will come to the tranquil bluebell wood which continues to thrive, as does the heron pond, richly swathed with lily pads and dragonflies in the summer. Some of the winding avenues still lead to follies, including the Temple and derelict Grotto. For those who know Catherine's story, parts of the park retain an air of hushed tragedy. Probably the most poignant feature is a bunker near the eighteenth green at Wanstead golf course – the huge hole in the ground is where Wanstead House once stood, before it was removed from the face of the earth.

Despite all that was lost, Wanstead Park has survived to form part of Britain's first public open space, with the Corporation of London acting as conservators. On 6 May 1882, half a million Londoners turned out for the official opening of Epping Forest at which Queen Victoria declared, 'It gives me the greatest satisfaction to dedicate this beautiful Forest to the use and enjoyment of my people for all time.'[11]

Acknowledgements

Works of historical non-fiction invariably rely on the efforts of all those who have helped to lay the groundwork, through the cataloguing of archival resources, or the digitalization of material such as the vast array of nineteenth-century newspapers in the British Library. I must therefore thank staff at the many record offices I visited, most particularly my local archives at Redbridge and Newham. I am indebted to historian Tim Couzens for sharing his expertise on the Long family, for providing family trees and transcripts of wills, and for meticulously answering my many questions. Historian Georgina Green has also been hugely generous with her time, knowledge and friendship.

Heartfelt thanks to my agent Sallyanne Sweeney, of Mulcahy Associates, for having faith in me and helping to shape this book. Thanks also to everyone at Macmillan, especially my brilliantly insightful editors George Morley and Zennor Compton, my scrupulous editorial manager Nicholas Blake, the design team for creating the exquisite front cover, plus Philippa McEwan and her team for an amazing publicity campaign. My professors at Queen Mary, University of London, have been inspirational: Lisa Jardine, Amanda Vickery, Peter Hennessy, Mark Glancy, Virginia Davis and my mentor Colin Jones. I must express thanks to everyone who critiqued early drafts of this book: Georgina Green, Elizabeth Fremantle, Marisa Verazzo, Jan and Ian Thompson, Linda Foster, Mia Lampshire, Lorraine Hart, Laura Spencer, plus my daughters Sophie and Izzie Roberts. Numerous friends have spurred me on – thank you all – especially Helen Burnett, Matthew Gaughan and my siblings Rob and Susan Jason. Although many people have contributed to this book, errors are all my own.

Undoubtedly, my biggest debt of gratitude is owed to my

husband, Greg Roberts, who is currently a part-time Ph.D. candidate at Queen Mary, University of London, working on the scandalous life of Wicked William Wellesley. He has been my sounding board throughout and we have spent many hours discussing and researching together. In fact, it was Greg who got me started on this project by cataloguing and transcribing letters held at Redbridge Archives. His initial research laid the foundation for this book, which would never have been written without his encouragement, perseverance and generosity.

Finally, I must thank my wonderful parents, Roy and Rita Jason, who made many sacrifices without complaint and continue to provide much love and support.

To find out more about the writing of this book, including further information about characters and Wanstead House, please visit my website: www.geraldineroberts.com.

Bibliography

List of Abbreviations

BL	British Library
BM	British Museum
BMS	British Museum Satires
ERO	Essex Record Office
Stead	Hiram Stead Collection
TNA	National Archives, Kew
ODNB	*Oxford Dictionary of National Biography*
W v B	*Wellesley v Beaufort* – trial transcripts

Main Primary Sources

British Library Newspaper Archive
Newham Heritage and Archives, East London – Hiram Stead Collection
Parliamentary Archives: – HL/PO/JO/10/8/758 *Wellesley v Wellesley*, which
   incorporates trial transcripts and affidavits from *Wellesley v Beaufort*
Redbridge Information and Heritage (Redbridge)

Other Primary Sources

Author's own collection of prints and images
Beinecke Rare Book and Manuscript Library, Yale University
Bligh v Wellesley – trial transcripts taken from Hiram Stead Collection
Bodleian Library at Oxford University
British Library
British Museum
British Museum Satires
Christie's Auctioneers, Archives Department
City of Westminster Local Studies Department
Cornwall Record Office

Cumbria Record Office
De Montford University and University of Glasgow (Internet resource for
    William Fox-Talbot letters)
Duke of Wellington Museum, Apsley House, Hyde Park
Essex Record Office
Hansard Parliamentary Archive: http://hansard.millbanksystems.com/
Hartley Library, University of Southampton (Carver Papers and Wellington
    Archive)
Kent History and Library Centre
National Archives, Kew
National Library of Ireland
National Library of Scotland, Aberdeen
National Maritime Museum
Oxford Dictionary of National Biography, courtesy Senate House Library,
    University of London
Raglan MSS, Newport County Archive, Gwent
Senate House Library, University of London
Stratfield Saye Preservation Trust
University of Keele Library, Staffordshire
Wanstead House Sale Catalogue, 1822 (author's own copy)
Wiltshire and Swindon History Centre

SECONDARY SOURCES

Addison, William, *Wanstead Park* (Corporation of London Publication, 1973)
Anderson, Patricia, *The Printed Image and the Transformation of Popular
    Culture 1790–1860* (Oxford: Clarendon Press, 1991)
Anonymous, *Kaleidoscopiana Wiltoniensia; or, A Literary, Political and Moral
    View of the County of Wilts During the Contested Election [...] in June
    1818* (London: Brettell, 1818)
Anonymous, *Letters from an Irish Student to his Father*, vol. 1 (London:
    Lewis, 1809)
Anonymous, *Regency Etiquette: The Mirror of Graces (1811) by a Lady of
    Distinction* (London: Swan & Son, 1811)
Anonymous miscellaneous authors, *The Ambulator or A Pocket Companion for
    the Tour of London and its Environs* (London: Scatcherd & Letterman,
    1811)
Aspinall, Arthur, *Mrs Jordan & her Family* (London: Barker, 1951)
——, *Politics and the Press c.1780–1850* (London: Home & Van Thal,
    1949)

Austen, Jane, *Mansfield Park* (England: Wordsworth, 1992)
——, *Northanger Abbey* (England: Wordsworth, 1992)
——, *Pride and Prejudice* (England: Wordsworth, 1992)

Bagot, Josceline, *Canning and Friends* (London: John Murray, 1909)
Bagot, Sophia, *Links with the Past* (London: Edward Arnold, 1901)
Baker, J. H., *An Introduction to English Legal History* (London: LexisNexis, 2002)
Bamford, Francis, *The Journal of Mrs Arbuthnot*, vol. I (London: Macmillan, 1950)
Barchas, Janine, *Matters of Fact in Jane Austen: History, Location and Celebrity* (Baltimore: Johns Hopkins University Press, 2012)
Barker, Hannah, *Newspapers, Politics, and Public Opinion in late Eighteenth-Century England* (Oxford: Clarendon Press, 1998)
Barry, Octavia, *Lady Victoria Long Wellesley: A Memoir by her Eldest God-Daughter* (London: Skeffington & Son, 1899)
Beerbohm, Max, *Collected Works of Max Beerbohm* (USA: BiblioBazaar, 2007)
Bentham, Jeremy, *Works of Jeremy Bentham*, vol. 3 (Edinburgh: William Tait, 1843)
Berenson, Edward, *The Trial of Madame Caillaux* (Oxford: University of California Press, 1992)
Beresford, Philip, and William D. Rubenstein, *The Sunday Times Richest of the Rich* (Hampshire: Harriman, 2007)
Black, Jeremy, *The English Press in the Eighteenth Century* (London: Croom Helm, 1987)
Brown, Susan, Patricia Clements and Isobel Grundy (eds), 'Mary, Lady Champion de Crespigny', *Orlando: Women's Writing in the British Isles from the Beginnings to the Present* (Cambridge University Press Online, 2006)
Bryant, Arthur, *The Age of Elegance* (Britain: William Collins, Sons & Co., 1954)
Burnett, T. A. J., *The Rise and Fall of a Regency Dandy* (Oxford University Press, 1983)
Bury, Lady Charlotte, *The Diary of a Lady in Waiting*, vol. I (London: Bodley Head, 1908)
Butler, Iris, *The Eldest Brother* (London: Hodder and Stoughton, 1973)

Campbell, Colen, *Vitruvius Britannicus: The Classic of Eighteenth-Century British Architecture* (USA: Dover, 2007; originally published by the author in London in 1715)

Clay, Edith, *Lady Blessington at Naples* (London: Hamish Hamilton, 1979)

Colquhoun, Patrick, *A Treatise on the Wealth, Power, and Resources of the British Empire* (London: J. Mawman, 1814), pp. 124–5

Couzens, Tim, *Hand of Fate: The History of the Longs, Wellesleys and the Draycot Estate in Wiltshire* (Bradford on Avon: ELSP, 2001)

Darnton, Robert, 'The High Enlightenment and the Low-Life of Literature in Pre-revolutionary France', *Past and Present*, 51 (May 1971), pp. 81–115; www.jstor.org/stable/650404

Dawson, Oliver, *The Story of Wanstead Park* (London: Thomas Hood Memorial Press, 1995)

Dowden, Wilfred, *Journal of Thomas Moore* (London: AUP, 1983)

Dugdale, James, *The New British Traveller*, vol. 2 (London: J. Robins, 1819)

Eger, Elizabeth, and Lucy Peltz, *Brilliant Women: 18th-Century Bluestockings* (London: National Portrait Gallery, 2008)

Ehrman, Edwina, *The Wedding Dress: 300 Years of Bridal Fashions* (London: V&A Publishing, 2014), pp. 43–59

Elsdon Tuffs, Jack, *Wanstead House* (London: Wanstead Historical Society, 1983)

Evelyn, John, *The Diary of John Evelyn*, ed. by Guy de la Bédoyère (Woodbridge: Boydell, 1995)

Fane, John, *The Correspondence of Lord Burghersh 1808–1840* (London: John Murray, 1912)

Foreman, Amanda, *Georgiana Duchess of Devonshire* (London: HarperCollins, 1999)

Frye, Major W. E., edited by Salomon Reinach, *After Waterloo: Reminiscences of European Travel 1815–1819* (London, 1908)

Gash, N., untitled review of *Politics and the Press c.1780–1850*, by Arthur Aspinall, from *The English Historical Review*, vol. 65, 255 (Oxford University Press: April 1950), pp. 269–271; www.jstor.org/stable/554950

Gatrell, Vic, *City of Laughter: Sex and Satire in Eighteenth-century London* (Great Britain: Atlantic Books, 2006)

Gore, J. (ed.), *The Creevey Papers* (London: Batsford, 1963)

Green, Georgina, *Epping Forest Through the Ages* (London: Kingfisher, 1982)

Gronow, R. H., *Captain Gronow's Guide to Life in London and Paris* (reprinted London: Grolier, 2006)

——, *Days of the Dandies* (London: Edinburgh Press, 1909)

Hardie, James, *The Epistolary Guide* (New York: S. Marks, 1817), p. v

Harris, John, *The Palladian Revival: Lord Burlington, His Villa and Garden at Chiswick* (London: Royal Academy of Arts, 1994)

Hobhouse, John Cam, *Journey Through Albania* (London: Cawthorn, 1818)

——, *Recollections of a Long Life* (London: John Murray, 1910)

Hope, Thomas, *Costume of the Ancients* (London: W. Bulmer, 1812)

Inglis, Fred, *A Short History of Celebrity* (New Jersey: Princeton University Press, 2010)

Jackson, Sir George, *The Bath Archives*, vol. 1 (London, 1873)

Jeffery, Sally, *The Gardens of Wanstead House* (London Parks and Gardens Trust, 2003)

Jervis, Simon, and Maurice Tomlin, *Apsley House Wellington Museum* (London: Victoria & Albert Museum, 2001)

Jesse, Captain, *The Life of Beau Brummell* (London: Navarre Society, 1927)

Johnson, Joan, *Princely Chandos: James Brydges 1674–1744* (New Hampshire: Sutton, 1989)

Jones, Steven, *The Satirical Eye: Forms of Satire in the Romantic Period* (New York: Palgrave Macmillan, 2003)

Keeling, Denis F., *Wanstead House and Chatsworth* (Tylney Press, 1997)

Kelly, Ian, *Beau Brummell: The Ultimate Man of Style* (London: Hodder and Stoughton, 2005)

Kilvert, Francis, and William Plomer, *Kilvert's Diary: Selections from the Diary of Rev. Francis Kilvert*, vol. 1, 1 January 1870–19 August 1871 (London: Jonathan Cape, 1960)

Longford, Elizabeth, *Wellington: Pillar of State* (London: Weidenfeld & Nicolson, 1972)

——, *Wellington: Years of the Sword* (London: Weidenfeld & Nicolson, 1971)

Lunden, Walter, *Systematic Source Book in Juvenile Delinquency* (University of Pittsburgh, 1938)

Mason, Haydn, *The Darnton Debate: Books and Revolution in the Eighteenth Century* (Oxford: Voltaire Foundation, 1998)

Maza, Sarah, *Private Lives and Public Affairs: The Causes Célèbres of Prerevolutionary France* (London: University of California Press, 1993)

Moore, Wendy, *Wedlock: How Georgian Britain's Worst Husband Met His Match* (London: Phoenix, 2010)

Morris Cloak, Margaret (ed.), *A Persian at the Court of King George 1809–10: The Journal of Mirza Abul Hassan Khan* (London: Barrie & Jenkins, 1998)

Mowl, Timothy, *William Kent: Architect, Designer, Opportunist* (London: Pimlico, 2006)

Murray, Venetia, *High Society in the Regency Period 1788–1830* (London: Penguin, 1998)

Ogborn, Jane, and Peter Buckroyd, *Satire: Contexts in Literature* (Cambridge University Press, 2001)

Phillips, Nicola, *The Profligate Son: Or, a True Story of Family Conflict, Fashionable Vice, and Financial Ruin in Regency England* (Oxford University Press, 2013)

Porter, Roy, *English Society in the Eighteenth Century* (London: Penguin, 2001)

Postle, Martin (ed.), *Joshua Reynolds: The Creation of Celebrity* (London: Tate Gallery, 2005)

Priestley, J. B., *English Humour* (London: Longmans, Green, 1929)

Read, Donald, untitled review of *Newspapers, Politics, and Public Opinion in Late Eighteenth Century England* by Hannah Barker, from *The English Historical Review*, vol. 114, 459 (Oxford University Press, November 1999), p. 1336; www.jstor.org/stable/580316

Rendell, Jane, *The Pursuit of Pleasure* (London: Athlone Press, 2002)

Richardson, Ethel, *The Lion & the Rose* (Essex: The Anchor Press, 1922)

Roberts, Greg, *The Closure of Wanstead Park 1813*, unpublished article

——, *The Forgotten Brother*, unpublished MA dissertation

——, *The Scandalous Life of a Regency Rake*, unpublished PhD thesis

Robinson, John, and Hunter Robinson, *The Life of Robert Coates: Better Known as 'Romeo' and 'Diamond' Coates* (London: Low, Marsten, 1891)

Rubenhold, Hallie, *Lady Worsley's Whim* (London: Chatto & Windus, 2008)

Shelley, Frances, *The Diary of Frances Lady Shelley* (London: John Murray, 1912)

Sitwell, Edith, *English Eccentrics* (London: Folio, 1958)

Smollett, Tobias George, *The Adventures of Roderick Random* (London: Miller, 1768)

Stone, Lawrence, *Road to Divorce: England 1530 to 1987* (Guildford: Biddles, 1990)

Stowe, Harriet Beecher, *Lady Byron Vindicated* (Boston: Fields, Osgood, & Co., 1870)

Sweetman, John, *Raglan: From the Peninsula to the Crimea* (London: Arms & Armour, 1993)

Tanner, Tony, *Jane Austen* (Harvard University Press, 1986)

Thompson, E. P., *The Making of the English Working Class* (London: Penguin, 1991)

Thompson, E. P., and Eileen Yeo, *The Unknown Mayhew: Selections from the Morning Chronicle 1849–50* (London: Penguin, 1984)

Thorne, R. G., *The History of Parliament: House of Commons 1790–1820*, vol. 5 (London: Secker, 1986)

Timbs, John, *English Eccentrics and Eccentricities* (London: Chatto, 1875)

Tomalin, Claire, *Mrs Jordan's Profession: The Story of a Great Actress and a Future King* (London: Penguin, 1994)

Turner, R., *The Parlour Letter Writer* (Philadelphia: Cowperthwait, 1858)

Vickery, Amanda, *Behind Closed Doors: At Home in Georgian England* (London: Yale University Press, 2009)

———, *The Gentleman's Daughter: Women's Lives in Georgian England* (London: Yale University Press, 2003)

Wake, Jehanne, *Sisters of Fortune: The First American Heiresses to Take Europe by Storm* (London: Chatto & Windus, 2010)

Walpole, Horace, *Correspondence*, vol. 35, with John Chute, Richard Bentley, Earl of Strafford, Sir William Hamilton, Earl and Countess Harcourt and George Hardinge (Yale University Press, 1973)

Webster, Sir Charles (ed.), *Some Letters of the Duke of Wellington to his Brother, William Wellesley-Pole*, Camden Miscellany, vol. XVIII (London: Royal Historical Society, 1948)

Wellesley, William, *Two Letters to Earl Eldon* (London: Millar, 1827)

———, *A View of the Court of Chancery* (London: Ridgway, 1830)

Wilson, Ben, *Decency and Disorder 1789–1837* (London: Faber and Faber, 2007)

Wilson, Harriette, *Harriette Wilson's Memoirs: The Memoirs of the Reigning Courtesan of Regency London* (London: Weidenfeld & Nicolson, 2003)

Wilson, John, *A Soldier's Wife: Wellington's Marriage* (London: Weidenfield & Nicolson, 1987)

Wood, Marcus, *Radical Satire and Print Culture 1790–1822* (Oxford: Clarendon, 1994)

Wright, Danaya C., 'Policing Sexual Morality: Percy Shelley and the Expansive Scope of the *Parens Patriae* in the Law of Custody of Children', *Nineteenth-century Gender Studies*, issue 8.2 (summer 2012); www.ncgsjournal.com/issue82/wright.htm

Young, Arthur, *A Six Weeks Tour, Through the Southern Counties of England and Wales* (London: Nicholl, 1768)

Ziegler, Philip, *King William IV* (Great Britain: Redwood Press, 1973)

Notes

Introduction

1 Officially, the Regency lasted for nine years, from 1811 to 1820. Broadly speaking, however, the Regency period can be defined as the years when George III descended into madness and his son ruled Britain, first as Prince Regent and then as George IV.

2 Patrick Colquhoun, *A Treatise on the Wealth, Power, and Resources of the British Empire* (London: J. Mawman, 1814), pp. 124–5.

Prologue

1 Parliamentary Archives, HL/PO/JO/10/8/758 *Wellesley v Wellesley*, which incorporates *Wellesley v Beaufort (W v B)* affidavits of Dora Tylney Long, William Herbert, Benjamin Schofield.

2 *The Times*, 12 July 1825.

3 *W v B*, affidavit 5, Dora Tylney Long.

1. The Richest Heiress in the Kingdom

1 Jane Austen, *Pride and Prejudice* (Ware: Wordsworth Editions, 1992).

2 Newham Heritage and Archives, Hiram Stead Collection of memorabilia, large volume, p. 56. There are three ledgers in the Hiram Stead Collection – a large volume with numbered pages, a small volume and one labelled 'Materials on Wanstead'. References have been taken from the large volume unless otherwise specified.

3 Tony Tanner, *Jane Austen* (Harvard University Press, 1986), p. 105.

4 From author's collection, Catherine Tylney Long aged around twenty-one, engraving published by Edward Churton, after Alfred Edward Chalon (1780–1860).

5 Tim Couzens, *Hand of Fate: The History of the Longs, Wellesleys and the Draycot Estate in Wiltshire* (Bradford on Avon: ELSP, 2001), family trees pp. 181–8.

6 Lady Catherine Sydney Windsor was the daughter of the 4th Earl of Plymouth.

7 Couzens, *Hand of Fate*, p. 70.

8 Harriet Bouverie was the sister of the 1st Earl of Radnor and aunt of the 6th Earl of Shaftesbury.

9 Octavia Barry, *The Lady Victoria Long-Wellesley: A Memoir by her Eldest God-Daughter* (London: Skeffington and Son, 1899), pp. 24–5. Victoria Long-Wellesley was Catherine's daughter.

10 Ibid.

11 Sir James Tylney Long's will, TNA PROB/11/1253/199 – transcript courtesy Tim Couzens.

12 Barry, *Lady Victoria*, pp. 26–7.

13 Ibid.; and also ERO, D/DGn/443, letter, 8 November 1813, from Mr Bullock to John Barry relating to charitable trusts.

14 *Metropolitan Magazine*, vol. 14, p. 311.

15 Amanda Vickery, *Behind Closed Doors: At Home in Georgian England* (London: Yale University Press, 2009), p. 82.

16 Four million pounds – multiply by 100 for rough twenty-first-century equivalents. See 'Notes on the Text' for an explanation of currency conversions.

17 ODNB, Josiah Child.

18 Philip Beresford and William D. Rubenstein, *The Sunday Times Richest of the Rich* (Hampshire: Harriman, 2007), p. 187.

19 ODNB, Henry Somerset, 2nd Duke of Beaufort (1684–1714).

20 2nd Duke of Bedford (1680–1711); ODNB Lord John Russell, 4th Duke of Bedford (1710–71).

21 Diary entry 14 May 1665.

22 John Evelyn and Guy de la Boyodere, *The Diary of John Evelyn* (Woodbridge: Boydell, 1995), p. 258.

23 Richard Child was created Viscount Castlemaine in 1718 and Earl Tylney in 1731.

24 ODNB, Colen Campbell (1676–1729); *Vitruvius Britannicus*, vol. 1, drawing of Wanstead House is signed by Campbell and dated 1813.

25 *Vitruvius Britannicus*, vols 1 and 2 feature Wanstead House prominently, with Campbell claiming that the use of the antique form of temple was 'the first yet practised in this manner in the kingdom'.

26 *Horace Walpole's Correspondence* (vol. 35) with John Chute, Richard Bentley, Earl of Strafford, Sir William Hamilton, Earl and Countess Harcourt and George Hardinge (Yale University Press, 1973), letter to Richard Bentley, Thursday 17 July 1755.

27 Tim Mowl, *William Kent: Architect, Designer, Opportunist* (London: Jonathan Cape, 2006), p. 87.

28 Detailed descriptions of the interior of the house can be found in: Arthur Young, *A Six Weeks Tour, Through the Southern Counties of England and*

Wales (London: Nicholl, 1768), pp. 242–6; and *The Ambulator* (London: Scatcherd & Letterman, 1811), pp. 278–81.

29 Tylney's activities are recounted in chapter 51 of Tobias Smollett's *Roderick Random* (1748) through the character of Lord Strutwell – one of the first examples in English fiction of a man said to be 'notorious for a passion for his own sex'.

30 James Dugdale, *The New British Traveller*, vol. 2 (London: J. Robins, 1819), p. 410.

31 Stead, p. 75 and p. 78 – c. May 1822, *Literary Chronicle* extracts.

32 Joan Johnson, *Princely Chandos: James Brydges 1674–1744* (New Hampshire: Sutton, 1989), p. 168.

33 *Derby Mercury*, 4 March 1802. The future Louis XVIII's residence at Wanstead House was recorded several times by the *Morning Chronicle* (late 1807).

2. In Training

1 Redbridge Information and Heritage, 20130 (f.27).

2 *Lady's Monthly Museum*, vol. 1 (1806), p. 244.

3 Stead, p. 61.

4 As early as February 1806, newspapers identified sixteen-year-old Catherine as 'by far the richest female commoner in England', *Caledonian Mercury* (15 February 1806). See also: Janine Barchas, *Matters of Fact in Jane Austen: History, Location, and Celebrity* (Baltimore: Johns Hopkins University Press, 2012), p. 117.

5 *Lady's Monthly Museum*, vol. 1 (1806), p. 244.

6 *Morning Post*, 24 March 1807.

7 Susan Brown, Patricia Clements and Isobel Grundy (eds), 'Mary, Lady Champion de Crespigny', *Orlando: Women's Writing in the British Isles from the Beginnings to the Present* (Cambridge University Press Online, 2006); http://orlando.cambridge.org; 26 August 2014.

8 ODNB, Alfred Edward Chalon (1780–1860).

9 www.britishfineart.com/Cox01.htm; accessed 8 July 2004.

10 Ethel Richardson, *The Lion & the Rose* (Essex: The Anchor Press Limited, 1922), p. 549.

11 Ibid.

12 Wanstead House sale catalogue (1822) pp. 291–312 lists hundreds of popular novels purchased by Catherine. These include first editions of all Jane Austen's novels, plus the fifty-volume collection *British Novelists*, with prefaces by Mrs Barbauld, published in 1810. At Stratfield Saye there is an entire bookcase of Catherine's travel books.

13 William Wellesley, *Two Letters to Earl Eldon* (London: Millar, 1827), letter, 2 October 1809, from John Barry to Catherine, p. 98.

14 Ibid., p. 97.

15 Ibid.

16 Ibid., letter, 2 October 1809, pp. 94–5.

17 Ibid., letter, 14 September 1810, from John Barry to Catherine, p. 90.

18 Stead, p. 40; *The Times*, 5 and 12 October 1810; *Morning Post*, 8 October 1810.

19 Redbridge, 90/96 (E11), accounts dated January 1811.

20 Francis Kilvert and William Plomer, *Kilvert's Diary: Selections from the Diary of the Rev. Francis Kilvert*, vol. 1, 1 January 1870–19 August 1871, new and corrected ed. (London: Jonathan Cape, 1960), pp. 245–6.

3. London

1 Stead, p. 82; Edith Sitwell, *English Eccentrics* (London: Folio, 1958), p. 98.

2 *Metropolitan Magazine*, vol. 14 (London: Saunders and Otley, 1835), pp. 311–12.

3 Ibid.

4 Ibid.

5 Thomas Hope, *Costume of the Ancients* (London: W. Bulmer and Co., 1812).

6 *Metropolitan Magazine*, vol. 14, p. 311.

7 Stead, p. 25, quote taken from the diary of Lady Charlotte Bury.

8 *Morning Chronicle*, 4 June 1812; Stead, p. 59.

9 Redbridge, 20135 – the lock of hair is still folded inside the letter.

10 ODNB, Robert Coates (1772–1848).

11 Sitwell, *Eccentrics*, p. 93.

12 Ibid.

13 Ibid., p. 94.

14 Max Beerbohm, *Collected Works of Max Beerbohm* (London: BiblioBazaar, 2007), p. 161.

15 Richardson, *The Lion & the Rose*, p. 548.

16 Thomas Swymmer Champneys (1769–1839).

17 Redbridge, 20130 (f. 30 and f. 34), c. June 1811.

18 Ibid.

19 Sir George Jackson, *The Bath Archives*, vol. 1 (London, 1873), entry 9 May 1811, pp. 244–5.

20 Charlotte Bury, *Diary of a Lady in Waiting*, vol. I (London: Bodley Head, 1908), p. 71.

21 Arthur Aspinall, *Mrs Jordan & her Family* (London: Barker, 1951), pp. 207–8, letter, 19 October 1811, from the Duke of Clarence to Lady de Crespigny.

22 Stead, p. 82.

4. The Prince's Ball

1 Venetia Murray, *High Society in the Regency Period* (London: Penguin, 1999), p. 211.

2 *Morning Chronicle*, 21 June 1811.

3 *The Times*, 21 June 1811.

4 *Morning Chronicle*, 21 June 1811.

5 Claire Tomalin, *Mrs Jordan's Profession: The Story of a Great Actress and a Future King* (London: Penguin, 1994), p. 239.

6 Roy Porter, *English Society in the Eighteenth Century* (London: Penguin, 2001), p. 15.

7 Ibid.

8 E. P. Thompson and Eileen Yeo, *The Unknown Mayhew* (Middlesex: Penguin, 1973), p. 20.

9 Ibid., p. 137.

10 E. P. Thompson, *The Making of the English Working Class* (London: Penguin, 1991).

11 Vic Gatrell, *City of Laughter: Sex and Satire in Eighteenth-Century London* (Great Britain: Atlantic Books, 2006).

12 Print freely available on the Internet.

13 Aspinall, *Mrs Jordan*, pp. 210–11, letter, 22 October 1811, from Duke of Clarence to Lady de Crespigny.

5. A Lady of Business

1 BMS, 11744.

2 ERO D/DGn 433–40, group of letters recording actions of William Bullock as he conducted an audit for Catherine. One document dated 24 September 1811 shows the wording to be appended to the completed maps: 'Property of Miss Tylney Long (Richardson, Lowfield and Whitton)'.

3 Ibid., D/DB F116/1–4 – 1810–32.

4 Redbridge, 90/96 (E20) letter, 4 May 1811; and (E13) letter, 13 April 1811.

5 Wellesley, *Letters to Eldon*, letter, 2 October 1809, from John Barry to Catherine, p. 94.

6 Ibid.

7 TNA PROB 11/1253/199.

8 Wellesley, *Letters to Eldon*, p. 95.

9 ERO, D/DB F116/1–4 – 1810–32, letter, 18 October 1810.

10 Ibid.

11 BL, Add MS 52483, f. 112, letter, 2 February 1811, from Bullock to Catherine – sent to Draycot House.

12 Ibid.

13 Redbridge, 20130 (f. 47), letter, 1 March 1811.

14 Ibid.

15 *Morning Chronicle*, 2 July 1811.

16 *Morning Post*, 14 July 1811.

17 *Morning Post*, 15 July 1811.

18 *Morning Post*, 8 June 1811.

19 'Miss Tilney Long's Waltz' was performed at the Jane Austen Festival in 2013.

20 *Morning Post*, 15 July 1811.

21 Tomalin, *Mrs Jordan*, pp. 244–5.

6. The Finest Young Dandy

1 *La Boudoir*, 1 April 1837.

2 Arthur Wellesley did not become Lord Wellington until after the Battle of Talavera in 1809, but for the purposes of continuity he will be referred to as Wellington throughout.

3 Barry, *Lady Victoria*, p. 28.

4 Stead, p. 40.

5 Numerous theories exist for how the name 'polo' was derived and this is one theory.

6 *Fun Magazine*, 3 August 1872.

7 Ian Kelly, *Beau Brummell: The Ultimate Man of Style* (London: Hodder & Stoughton, 2005), p. 214.

8 Ibid.

9 Ben Wilson, *Decency and Disorder 1789–1837* (London: Faber and Faber, 2007).

10 Jackson, *Bath Archives*, entry 9 May 1811, pp. 244–5.

11 Stead, p. 25.

12 *The Times*, 16 July 1816.

13 Mirza Abul Hassan Khan (edited by Margaret Morris Cloake), *A Persian at the Court of King George 1809–10: The Journal of Mirza Abul Hassan Khan* (London: Barrie & Jenkins, 1988), pp. 235–6.

14 Anon., *Letters from an Irish Student to his Father*, vol. 1 (London: Lewis, 1809), p. 197.

15 Ibid., p. 201; Greg Roberts, unpublished PhD thesis.
16 *Morning Chronicle*, 16 August 1811. Poem attributed to the Cocoa-Tree Club; one of the authors was probably Lord Byron.
17 Stead, p. 67; Redbridge 20135 (f. 38–39).
18 Stead, p. 67, 14 August 1811.
19 *Morning Chronicle*, 17 August 1811.
20 Redbridge, 20135 (f. 36), 9 August 1811.

7. *The Royal Lover*

1 Philip Ziegler, *King William IV* (Great Britain: Redwood Press, 1973), p. 104.
2 Aspinall, *Mrs Jordan*, p. 208, letter from Duke of Clarence dated 11 October 1811.
3 Ibid., p. 210, letter, 22 October 1811.
4 Ibid.
5 Ibid., p. 211, letter, 27 October 1811.
6 Tomalin, *Mrs Jordan*, p. 247.
7 BMS, 11844.
8 Aspinall, *Mrs Jordan*, p. 208, letter, 19 October 1811.
9 Ibid.
10 Ibid.
11 Ibid., p. 211, letter, 22 October 1811.
12 Barry, *Lady Victoria*, p. 28.
13 BMS, 11747.
14 Kilvert, *Diary*, pp. 245–6.
15 *Morning Chronicle*, 3 January 1812.
16 *The Times*, 1 January 1812; *Morning Chronicle*, 3 January 1812.
17 BMS, 11947.
18 Aspinall, *Mrs Jordan*, p. 214, letter, 9 November 1811.
19 Redbridge 20126 (f. 10) and 20127 (f. 19), letter, 20 November 1811, Mr Pole to Catherine.
20 Ziegler, *William IV*, p. 106.
21 Stead, p. 66, c. November 1811.
22 Redbridge, 20135 (f. 11).

8. *A Dynamic Family*

1 Elizabeth Longford, *Wellington: Years of the Sword* (London: Weidenfeld & Nicolson, 1971), p. 163.
2 Ibid.
3 Greg Roberts, *The Forgotten Brother*, unpublished MA dissertation.

4 Greg Roberts, unpublished Ph.D. thesis. According to the baptismal records now held at Westminster Archives, Sophia Dubochet was baptised at St George's, Hanover Square on the same day as William (19 July 1788). Sophia was a well-known courtesan; sister to the notorious Harriette Wilson (1786–1845).

5 Greg Roberts, unpublished MA dissertation.

6 Redbridge 20130 (f. 49), letter 2 December 1817, from Mary Bagot to William.

7 Ibid., (f. 18), letter 19 January 1807 from Reverend Gilly to William.

8 Ibid., (f. 41).

9 Elizabeth Longford, *Wellington: Pillar of State* (London: Weidenfeld & Nicolson, 1972), p. 251.

10 Painted in Vienna when William was sixteen years old, courtesy Stratfield Saye Preservation Trust.

11 BL, Add MS 47234, John Cam Hobhouse, *Diary*, entry dated 17 June 1810.

12 John Cam Hobhouse, *Journey through Albania* (London: Cawthorn, 1813), with addendum added 1818.

13 *The Daily Advertiser, Oracle, and True Briton*, 16 September 1808.

14 Redbridge, 20135 (f. 36), letter, 17 September 1808, from Mary Bagot to William.

15 'Some Letters of the Duke of Wellington to his brother William Wellesley-Pole, edited by Sir Charles Webster', Camden Miscellany, vol. XVIII (London: Royal Historical Society, 1948), pp. 8–9, letter, 6 September 1808.

16 *The Daily Advertiser, Oracle, and True Briton*, 16 September 1808.

17 *The Times*, 13 October 1809.

18 Josceline Bagot, *Canning and Friends* (London: Murray, 1909), p. 338, letter, 30 October 1809.

9. Engagement

1 Redbridge, 20135 (f. 16), letter, 25 November 1811.

2 Ibid. (f. 10), letter, 20 November 1811.

3 Ibid.

4 Ibid. (f. 62), an anonymous letter, c. late November 1811.

5 Redbridge, 20130 (f. 27), letter, 2 March 1812 from J. Scott to Catherine.

6 Redbridge, 90/96 (E8), letter, 13 October 1825, from Bouverie to Dora Tylney Long.

7 Stead, p. 64.

8 Redbridge, 20127 (f. 24), 1 February 1812.

9 Edwina Ehrman, *The Wedding Dress: 300 Years of Bridal Fashions* (London: V&A Publishing, 2014), pp. 43–59.

10 Redbridge, 90/96 (E19) and (E20).

11 Table adapted from Couzens, *Hand of Fate*, p. 74.

12 *W v B*, affidavit 44, Julius Hutchinson (Catherine's solicitor).

13 Redbridge, 90/96 (E20), Marriage Settlement dated 13 March 1812.

14 Ibid.

15 Redbridge, 90/96 (E10), letter, 16 October 1823.

16 Redbridge, 20135 (f. 12), letter, 8 January 1812.

17 Redbridge, 20135 (passim).

18 Redbridge, 20127 (f. 19), letter, 20 November 1811, from Mr Pole to Catherine.

19 Ibid.

20 Ibid.

10. A Celebrity Wedding

1 *Bell's Court and Fashionable Magazine*, March 1812.

2 *Morning Chronicle*, 17 March 1812.

3 Ibid.

4 Ehrman, *The Wedding Dress*, pp. 43–59.

5 Ibid.

6 Ibid.

7 Christie's sale catalogue, dated 18 May 1827.

8 *Hull Packet*, 24 March 1812.

9 Ibid.

10 *Lancashire Gazette*, 18 January 1812.

11 Stead, p. 65, c. 14 March 1812.

12 Ibid.

13 *Morning Chronicle*, 3 April 1812; and also in Catherine's private papers at Redbridge Archives.

14 Ibid.

15 *Lancashire Gazette*, 15 January 1812.

16 Barchas, *Matters of Fact in Jane Austen: History, Location and Celebrity*.

17 Redbridge, 20135 (f. 13), letter, 24 November 1811, from Shawe to William.

11. Lord of the Manor

1 *Morning Chronicle*, 11 July 1812.

2 *Morning Chronicle*, 1 August 1812.

3 ERO, 22 June 1822.

4 *Baily's Monthly Magazine*, 1 March 1893.

5 William Addison, *Wanstead Park* (London: Corporation of London, 1973), p. 11.
6 *Baily's Monthly Magazine*, 1 March 1893.
7 Stead, p. 71, Easter Monday 1813.
8 ERO D/DCw F1, Lease Document, dated 9 October 1812.
9 Outbuildings specified in Sale Catalogue.

12. Tenderly She Loved Him

1 Barry, *Lady Victoria*, p. 32.
2 Redbridge, 90/96 (E16), letter, 14 September 1825.
3 Ibid.
4 Stead, p. 71, 2 February 1813.
5 Ibid., 9 February 1813.
6 *Morning Post*, 15 July 1814.
7 Amanda Foreman, *Georgiana Duchess of Devonshire* (London: Harper Collins, 1999), p. 3.
8 *Leeds Mercury*, 14 March 1812.
9 *Bell's Court and Fashionable Magazine*, 14 March 1812.
10 *Hull Packet*, 7 April 1812.
11 Longford, *Pillar of State*, p. 122.
12 *Morning Chronicle*, 7 August 1812.
13 *La Belle Assemblée*, London, April 1808.
14 Richardson, *The Lion & the Rose*, pp. 471–2.

13. Member of Parliament

1 ODNB, Richard Brinsley Sheridan (1751–1816), playwright and politician.
2 Sheridan once lived close to Wanstead House, in a building now called Sheridan Mews, at the top of Wanstead High Street.
3 ERO, *Chelmsford Chronicle*, 24 July 1812.
4 *Baily's Monthly Magazine of Sports & Pastimes*, 1 October 1863.
5 Ibid.
6 *London Daily Advertiser*, 5 April 1753.
7 *Old England*, 5 September 1749.
8 *The Public Advertiser*, 26 March 1788.
9 *Morning Post*, 28 March 1796.
10 *London Chronicle*, 26 March 1785.
11 Stead, p. 71, Easter Monday 1813.
12 Ibid.

13 ODNB, Lady Caroline Scott (1784–1857). Her novel *A Marriage in High Life* (London: Colburn, 1828) is based on Catherine's life, with a thinly veiled reference to her in its opening preface.
14 *Morning Post*, 14 June 1809.
15 *Morning Post*, 27 June 1811.
16 http://collections.britishart.yale.edu/vufind/Record/2038414/ Description; accessed 9 September 2014.

14. Joy and Pain

1 Redbridge, 90/96 (E11), letter, 7 January 1813.
2 Ibid., letter, 11 January 1813.
3 Ibid.
4 Ibid., letter, 12 January 1813.
5 ERO D/DB F116 1–4 – documents outlining accounts for the year 1811 upon which William has added comments.
6 Ibid.
7 ERO, *Chelmsford Chronicle*, 14 May 1813.
8 Amanda Vickery, *The Gentleman's Daughter: Women's Lives in Georgian England* (London: Yale University Press, 2003), p. 97.
9 Kent County Archives (U1371), letter, 8 October 1813, from Emily to Priscilla.
10 Vickery, *Gentleman's Daughter*, p. 103.
11 Stead, p. 71.
12 Ibid.
13 Kent County Archives (U1371 C9), letter, 9 October 1813.
14 Ibid., letter, 23 October 1813, from Emily to Priscilla.

15. A Consumer Society

1 Kelly, *Brummell*, p. 194.
2 Meyer & Mortimer Tailors, No. 6 Sackville Street, Mayfair, London W1.
3 Kelly, *Brummell*, p. 203.
4 John Harris, *The Palladian Revival* (London: Royal Academy of Arts, 1995) p. 14.
5 ODNB, Colen Campbell.
6 *Examiner*, 9 January 1814.
7 Modification of floor plan in the architect's drawings (author's collection).
8 Christie's believe that the French buhl at Wanstead was purchased by William.
9 All descriptions of furniture and interiors taken from sale catalogue.

10 *Examiner*, 9 January 1814.
11 Author's calculation in accordance with floor plans and items listed in sale catalogue.
12 Stead, report c. May 1822, p. 68.

16. Festivities at Wanstead House

1 Stead, p. 72.
2 Stead, p. 72, 27 June 1814.
3 *Baily's Monthly Magazine*, 1 October 1863.
4 Ibid.
5 Stead, p. 68, 21 August 1814.
6 Ibid.
7 *Ipswich Journal*, 6 August 1814.
8 Frances Shelley, *The Diary of Frances Lady Shelley* (London: John Murray, 1912), p. 68.
9 Ibid.
10 Stead, p. 68, 3 July 1814.
11 Ibid., p. 69.
12 *Chelmsford Chronicle*, 16 August 1816.
13 Ibid.
14 Ibid.
15 *Examiner*, 9 January 1814.
16 Foreman, *Georgiana*, p. 213.
17 Murray, *High Society*, pp. 231–2.
18 Ibid.
19 Descriptions of interiors in this chapter taken from sale catalogue.
20 Foreman, *Georgiana*, p. 134.
21 ODNB, George Bryan Brummell (1778–1840), dandy and socialite.
22 *Sunday Times*, 5 November 1826.
23 Stead, p. 107, 27 November 1826, reporting on Libel Action *The King v John Chapman*.
24 *Sunday Times*, 27 November 1826.
25 Redbridge, 90/96 (E1), letter, 22 September 1825.
26 Kent County Archives, U1371, letter, 15 December 1811.
27 Ibid., letter, 8 October 1813.
28 Redbridge, 20130 (f. 36).
29 Kent County Archives, U1371 C10, letter, 3 March 1814.
30 ERO, TB/39/1, trial transcript *The King v Long Wellesley*.
31 Greg Roberts, *The Closure of Wanstead Park, 1813* (2012), unpublished article.

17. Waterloo

1 Sophia Bagot, *Links with the Past* (London: Edward Arnold, 1901), pp. 103–4.
2 Ibid., p. 110.
3 Ibid., p. 114.
4 Ibid., p. 113.
5 J. Gore (ed.), *The Creevey Papers* (London: Batsford, 1963), p. 152.
6 Ibid., pp. 150–52.
7 ODNB, Arthur Wellesley.
8 Shelley, *Diary*, p. 102.
9 Longford, *Pillar of State*, p. 16.
10 ODNB, Arthur Wellesley.

18. Money Wars

1 Wellesley, *Letters to Eldon*, letter, 2 October 1809, from John Barry to Catherine, p. 94.
2 John Wilson, *A Soldier's Wife: Wellington's Marriage* (London: Weidenfield & Nicolson, 1987), p. 128.
3 *W v B*, affidavit 44, Julius Hutchinson.
4 Ibid.
5 Stead, p. 65.
6 *Morning Chronicle*, 13 April 1819.
7 John and Hunter Robinson, *The Life of Robert Coates: Better Known as 'Romeo' and 'Diamond' Coates* (London: Low, Marsten, 1891), p. 37.
8 Wellesley, *Letters to Eldon*, p. 5.
9 Ibid.
10 *W v B*, affidavit 7, John Meara, cites letter c. Feb 1825, from William to Helena Bligh.
11 Author has received private correspondence from more than one source, from various people claiming to be a descendant of William via illegitimate birth.
12 Stead, c. October 1815.
13 Jeffery, *Gardens*, p. 33.
14 Oliver Dawson, *The Story of Wanstead Park* (London: Thomas Hood Memorial Press, 1995).
15 Stead, book extract, *The Essex Review*, pp. 224–7.
16 *W v B*, affidavit 44, Julius Hutchinson.
17 Ibid.

19. *The Dishonest Cleric and Other Anecdotes*

1 Raglan MS, D.3135.
2 Austen, *Pride & Prejudice*, p. 14.
3 *W v B*, letter, 1 March 1825.

20. *The Bastard*

1 T. A. J. Burnett, *The Rise and Fall of a Regency Dandy* (Oxford University Press, 1983), p. 143.
2 Ibid., p. 40.
3 BL, Add MS 47234, and John Cam Hobhouse, *Recollections of a Long Life* (London: John Murray, 1910), diary entry 5 February 1818.
4 Ibid.
5 Redbridge, 20135 (f. 19), undated letter, c. early 1818.
6 Burnett, *Regency Dandy*, pp. 39–40.
7 BL, Add MS 47234, Hobhouse, *Journal*, diary entry 1 March 1818.
8 BL, Add MS 42093 f. 80 and f. 82, *Byron Collection*, diary entry 26 March 1818.
9 Ibid.
10 Barry, *Lady Victoria*, p. 100.
11 *W v B*, affidavit 2, Henry Bicknell.
12 R. Turner, *The Parlour Letter Writer* (Philadelphia: Cowperthwait, 1858).
13 Hartley Library, University of Southampton, Wellington Papers WP1/1185/33, letter, 28 July 1831, from Maria Kinnaird to the Duke of Wellington.
14 Ibid.
15 Iris Butler, *The Eldest Brother* (London: Hodder & Stoughton, 1973), p. 493.
16 Apsley House still stands at Hyde Park Corner (149 Piccadilly) overlooking Rotten Row. It is now the Wellington Museum, open to the public and containing all the trophies mentioned in this chapter.
17 ERO, D/DB F116/1-4 – 1810–1832, letter 21 January 1818.
18 Ibid.
19 Correspondence of John Fremantle, courtesy of Charles Fremantle, letter, 1 September 1817.
20 Ibid., letter, 18 July 1817.
21 Ibid., letter, 3 March 1818.
22 Anonymous, *Kaleidoscopiana Wiltoniensia* (London: Brettell, 1818), p. 3; entry dated 25 February 1818. Much of the information in the next chapter is taken from *Kaleidoscopiana Wiltoniensia*, a comprehensive 406-page publication printed shortly after the 1818 election. The book

contains a miscellany of newspaper articles, campaign letters, colourful first-hand accounts of William's electioneering, plus transcripts of his speeches.

23 Ibid., p. 342.

21. Cock of the Walk

1   Thompson, *The Making of the English Working Class*, p. 119.
2   Anon., *Kaleidoscopiana Wiltoniensia*, p. 342.
3   BL, Add MS 52483, f. 118/9, letter from Shawe to William dated 27 September 1817.
4   See entry for Wiltshire County in R. G. Thorne, *The History of Parliament: House of Commons 1790–1820*, vol. 5 (London: Secker, 1986).
5   Anon., *Kaleidoscopiana Wiltoniensia*, pp. 10–15, taken from *Salisbury and Winchester Journal*, 16 March 1818.
6   Ibid.
7   Ibid., pp. 17–18.
8   Ibid., pp. 40–43.
9   Ibid., pp. 19–21.
10 Ibid., p. 31.
11 Anon., *Kaleidoscopiana Wiltoniensia*, all quotes attributed to William in this chapter are his own as represented in transcripts of his speeches.
12 Redbridge, 20135 (f. 2), letter, 6 June 1818.
13 Unless otherwise specified, all information and quotes in this chapter taken from *Kaleidoscopiana Wiltoniensia*, pp. 294–365.

22. Blind Man's Bluff

1   Wellesley, *Letters to Eldon*, p. 6.
2   ERO, D/DB F116/1–4 – 1810–32, letter from Catherine to William, c. April 1818.
3   Redbridge, 90/96 (E17), letters, 15 November 1819 from Chartree and Bidwell solicitors.
4   TNA, MINT 1/56, Banks to Wellesley Pole, 21 June 1817.
5   *The Times*, 10 February 1819.
6   Ibid., 1 December 1819.
7   Ibid., 2 December 1819.
8   Ibid., 30 November 1819.
9   Ibid., 5 February 1819.
10 Ibid.
11 Wilfred Dowden, *Journal of Thomas Moore* (London: AUP, 1983), entry 12 May 1819.
12 *W v B*, affidavit 2, Bicknell.

13 Ibid.

14 *The Courier*, 17 March 1820.

15 Ibid., 16 March 1820.

16 Stead, book extract, *The Essex Review*, p. 227.

23. France

1 Captain Jesse, *The Life of Beau Brummell* (London: Navarre, 1927), vol. 1, p. 292.

2 *W v B*, affidavit 11, George Brummell.

3 Stead, small volume, 11 May 1820.

4 *W v B*, affidavit 21, William cites letter c. September 1822.

5 Ibid.

6 Ibid.

7 Ibid.

8 Redbridge, 90/96 (E20).

9 Dowden, *Moore's Journal*.

10 *W v B*, affidavit 69, John Randall.

11 *W v B*, affidavit 3, Bicknell.

12 Dowden, *Moore's Journal*, entry 28 February 1821.

13 Ibid., entry 19 March 1821.

14 Ibid., entry 23 August 1821.

15 *W v B*, supplementary evidence cited by Bicknell, Paris, May 1824.

24. Riches of Ages

1 BL, Add MS 52483 pp. 121–2, letter, 15 December 1820.

2 ERO, D/DB F116/1–4 – 1810–32, letter, 22 December 1820.

3 Redbridge, 20135 (f. 2), letter, 22 February 1821.

4 ERO, D/DB F116/1–4 – 1810–32, document dated 21 February 1821.

5 Stead, p. 76, c. May 1822.

6 Ibid., pp. 75, 78, extract from *Literary Chronicle*.

7 Ibid., extract from *Manchester Iris*.

8 Ibid.

9 Ibid., pp. 75, 78, extract from *Literary Chronicle*.

10 BMS, 14669.

11 Stead, pp. 75, 78, extract from *Literary Chronicle*.

12 Ibid., extract from *Manchester Iris*.

13 ERO, D/DB F116/4, letter, c. 22 June 1822.

14 Redbridge, 90/96 (E15), letter, 27 November 1823.

15 Stead, p. 60, c. August 1822, *Jeu d'Esprit*, New York.

16 Kelly, *Brummell*, p. 340.

17 *W v B*, affidavit 11, Brummell.

18 Ibid.
19 *W v B*, letter from William to Pitman dated 16 November 1824.
20 *W v B*, affidavit 3, Bicknell; and affidavit 4, Meara.
21 *W v B*, affidavit 95, Bicknell.
22 *W v B*, affidavit 4, Meara.

25. Sale of the Century

1 ODNB, George Henry Robins (1777–1847).
2 Robins is lampooned as Mr Hammerdown in Thackeray's *Vanity Fair*.
3 ERO, D/DB F116/4, letter, 22 June 1822, from Shawe to William.
4 Many of the details in this chapter are taken from the *Wanstead House Sale Catalogue* – author's own copy – which was used by the administrators and as such contains full details of the final sale price of each item.
5 Stead, p. 76.
6 Ibid., p. 18, report of opening day of the sale, 22 June 1822.
7 ERO, D/DB F116/4, letter from Shawe to William c. 22 June 1822.
8 Ibid.
9 *Morning Chronicle*, 8 July 1822.
10 The Parisian armoire sold for £1,016,000 at Christie's in London on 15 December 2005, revealing the quality of the furnishings at Wanstead House, as well as the ridiculously low auction prices.
11 ODNB, George Henry Robins.
12 ERO, D/DB F116/4, letter, 22 June 1822.
13 Stead, p. 78.

26. Crisis at Calais

1 *W v B*, affidavit 4, Meara.
2 *W v B*, affidavit 76, William, cites letter 27 June 1822.
3 Ibid.
4 *W v B*, affidavit 47, Pitman.
5 *W v B*, affidavit 52, Robert Southcote.
6 Redbridge, 20135 (f. 24), letter, 2 February 1807.
7 Ibid.
8 Redbridge, 20127 (f. 20), letter, 16 August 1822.
9 Ibid.

27. Naples

1 *W v B*, affidavit 60, Pitman.
2 *W v B*, affidavit 42, David Holmes.
3 Barry, *Lady Victoria*, p. 35.

4 Ibid., p. 34.

5 Redbridge, 90/96 (E13), letter, 25 November 1822.

6 Ibid.

7 Barry, *Lady Victoria*, p. 35.

8 Ibid.

9 Ibid., p. 23, letter, 4 February 1823.

10 Ibid., pp. 35–6, letter, 4 February 1823.

11 Redbridge, 90/96 (E20), Marriage Settlement dated 13 March 1812.

12 Redbridge, 20127 (f. 14), letter, 25 February 1823.

13 Ibid., 90/96 (E8), letter, 27 February 1823.

14 Ibid., letter, 26 February 1823.

15 Ibid.

28. Nothing Lasts Forever

1 Stead, *Materials on Wanstead*, c. May 1823.

2 Ibid.

3 Stead, p. 78, c. July 1823.

4 *W v B*, affidavit 39, Bulkeley.

5 *W v B*, affidavit 54, Helena Bligh.

6 ODNB, William Richard Hamilton (1777–1859), antiquary and diplomatist. Primary source material refers to William Hamilton as the British ambassador; his official title was envoy extraordinary and minister plenipotentiary.

7 Edith Clay, *Lady Blessington at Naples* (London: Hamish Hamilton Ltd, 1979); Lady Charlotte Bury, *Diary*.

8 ODNB, Sir William Gell (1777–1836), classical archaeologist and traveller.

29. Treading on a Volcano

1 *W v B*, affidavit 3, Bicknell.

2 *W v B*, affidavit 4, Meara.

3 *W v B*, affidavit 1, Bulkeley.

4 *W v B*, affidavit 35, Julius Hutchinson, cites statement from Catherine.

5 Ibid.

6 Ibid.

7 Ibid.

8 *W v B*, affidavit 4, Meara.

9 History of Parliament Online, entry for William Pole Tylney Long Wellesley.

10 Details in this chapter are taken from *W v B*, affidavit 35, Hutchinson, which cites statements from Catherine.

11 ODNB, Sir Richard Church (1784–1873), soldier and philhellene.

12 *W v B*, affidavit 4, Meara.

13 *Bligh v Wellesley* (1826), testimony of Edward Bligh.

14 *W v B*, affidavit 4, Meara.

15 *W v B*, affidivit 53, William.

16 *W v* B, affidavit 4, Meara.

17 Ibid.

18 *Bligh v Wellesley*, testimonies of Deborah Stephens and Mary Milton, maids at the Bligh household.

19 *W v B*, affidavit 35, Hutchinson.

20 Quotes in following section taken from *W v B*, affidavit 5, Bulkeley.

30. Always the Last to Know

1 *Bligh v Wellesley*, testimony of Mrs Maxwell.

2 *W v B*, affidavit 54, Helena Bligh; 76, William.

3 *Bligh v Wellesley*, testimony of Mrs Maxwell.

4 *W v B*, affidavit 4, Meara.

5 *W v B*, affidavit 54, Helena Bligh.

6 Yale University, Beinecke Rare Book and Manuscript Library, letter, 3 September 1823, from Wellington to William Hamilton.

7 Ibid.

8 *W v B*, affidavit 54, Helena Bligh.

9 *W v B*, affidavit 76, William.

10 *W v B*, affidavit 1, Bulkeley.

11 Ibid.

12 *W v B*, affidavit 8, James Nixon – enclosing a copy of the affidavit William swore in Naples.

13 Ibid.

14 Ibid.

15 Ibid.

16 Quotes in following section taken from *W v B*, affidavit 35, Hutchinson, which cites statement from Catherine.

17 *W v B*, affidavit 76, William.

18 Yale, Beinecke Library, letter, 3 September 1823, from Wellington to William Hamilton.

19 *W v B*, affidavit 76, William.

20 *Bligh v Wellesley*, testimony of Mr Hamilton, British consul at Naples.

21 Ibid.

22 Ibid.

23 The following exchange is taken from the testimony of Mr Hamilton, British consul at Naples – which included copies of letters between

himself and William in August 1823. These letters were published in the English newspapers that autumn.

24 *W v B*, affidavit 1, Bulkeley.

31. Acting in the Dark

1 *W v B*, affidavit 76, William, cites letters.
2 Ibid.
3 Ibid.
4 *W v B*, statement made by Catherine.
5 *Correspondence of William Henry Fox Talbot* internet resource http://foxtalbot.dmu.ac.uk/index.html, De Montford University and University of Glasgow, entry 29 October 1823.
6 *W v B*, statement made by Catherine.
7 Redbridge, 20127 (f. 16).
8 ERO D/DB F116/1–4 – 1810–32, c. 20 September 1825.
9 Ibid.
10 Couzens, *Hand of Fate*, p. 70.
11 *W v B*, affidavit 39, Bulkeley.
12 *W v B*, statement made by Catherine.
13 *Morning Chronicle*, 16 December 1823.
14 *W v B*, affidavit 47, Pitman.
15 *W v B*, affidavit 1, Bulkeley.
16 Ibid., for all quotes in this paragraph.

32. Florence

1 Redbridge, 90/96 (E15), letter, 27 November 1823.
2 John Fane, *The Correspondence of Lord Burghersh 1808–1840* (London: John Murray, 1912), pp. 9–10.
3 *W v B*, statement made by Catherine.
4 Events in this chapter are taken from *W v B*, testimonies of Bulkeley, Pitman and Meara – which support and collaborate with each other and also tie in with Catherine's statement. Naturally, William's version of events is very different, but his testimony was notoriously unreliable, especially because it was later proven in court that he had committed perjury.
5 W v B, affidavit 4, Meara.
6 Quotes in following section taken from *W v B*, affidavit 60, Pitman.
7 Quotes in following section taken from *W v B*, affidavit 1, Bulkeley.
8 Stead, p. 98.
9 Quotes in following section taken from *W v B*, affidavit 39, Bulkeley.

10 *W v B*, affidavit 60, Pitman.
11 Ibid.
12 Quotes in following section taken from *W v B*, affidavits 1 and 39, Bulkeley.

33. The Final Straw

1 Anon., *Kaleidoscopiana Wiltoniensia*, speech made by William on 8 May 1818.
2 Jehanne Wake, *Sisters of Fortune: The First American Heiresses to Take Europe by Storm* (London: Chatto & Windus), p. 140.
3 Francis Bamford, *The Journal of Mrs Arbuthnot*, vol. I (London: Macmillan, 1950), p. 421.
4 Quotes in following section taken from *W v B*, affidavits 9 and 10, Bulkeley.
5 *W v B*, affidavit 1, Bulkeley.
6 Ibid.
7 Quotes in following section taken from *W v B*, affidavit 40, Meara.
8 Lawrence Stone, *Road to Divorce: England 1530 to 1987* (Guildford: Biddles, 1990), p. 240.
9 *W v B*, affidavit 39, Bulkeley.
10 *W v B*, affidavit 47, Pitman.
11 Quotes in following section taken from *W v B*, affidavit 39, Bulkeley.

34. Catherine's Letter

1 In 1801 the rate was increased to the London Twopenny Post.
2 Redbridge, 90/96 (E10), letter, 21 June 1824; also in *W v B*, letters submitted in evidence, and cited in several contemporary newspapers.
3 Hallie Rubenhold, *Lady Worsley's Whim* (London: Chatto & Windus, 2008), p. 104.
4 Harriett Beecher Stowe, *Lady Byron Vindicated* (Boston: Fields, Osgood, & Co., 1870), p. 33.

35. Don't Forget Me

1 Quotes in following section taken from *W v B*, affidavit 10, Bulkeley.
2 Quotes in following section taken from Redbridge (E10), letters dated 10–11 July 1824; and *W v B*, letters submitted in evidence.
3 Redbridge, 90/96 (E10); *W v B*, letters submitted in evidence.
4 Ibid., letter, 15 July 1824; *W v B*, letters submitted in evidence.
5 Stead, p. 78, c. July 1824, *Devizes Gazette* press cutting.

36. A Monster Amongst Savages

1 *W v B*, affidavit 10, Bulkeley, cites letter 19 July 1824.
2 *The Age*, 4 February 1827.
3 Redbridge, 20135 (f. 21), letter, 2 August 1824.
4 *Morning Chronicle*, 2 November 1826, printed letter, 4 April 1824.
5 Quotes in following section taken from *W v B*, affidavit 40, Meara.
6 *W v B*, affidavit 21, William.
7 Quotes in this section from Redbridge, 20135 (21), letter, 2 August 1824.
8 *W v B*, affidavit 39, Bulkeley, cites letter from Catherine dated 2 September 1824.

37. Draycot House

1 Redbridge, 90/96 (E3), letter, 28 October 1824.
2 *W v B*, letter, 3 September 1824, from William to James.
3 *W v B*, letter, 15 September 1824, from William to Pitman.
4 A. M. Hardie, *The Epistolary Guide* (New York: S. Marks, 1817) p. v.
5 *W v B*, letter, 10 October 1824, from William to Pitman.
6 Ibid., letter, 21 October 1824.
7 Redbridge, 90/96 (E10), fragment of letter, c. late 1824.
8 *W v B*, affidavit 99, Gilbert Langdon.
9 *W v B*, letter, 30 November 1824, from William to his son Will.
10 Redbridge, 90/96 (E3), letter, October 28 1824.
11 Quotes in this section taken from *W v B*, affidavit 39, Bulkeley, cites letter 10 February 1825 from Catherine to Bulkeley.

38. Go to the Devil

1 *W v B*, affidavit 7, Meara, cites note from William to Helena Bligh.
2 Stead, p. 80, c. October 1824.
3 Quotes in this section taken from William Wellesley's *Letters to Lord Eldon*, p. 103, containing a letter, 22 January 1825, from William to Maryborough.
4 Redbridge, 90/96 (E17), letter, 29 August 1824.
5 *W v B*, letter, 25 April 1825, from William to Pitman.
6 Redbridge, 90/96 (E23), letter, 6 March 1825.
7 Redbridge, 20127 (f. 23), 20 August 1824.
8 Ibid.
9 Redbridge, 90/06 (E2), 23 August 1824.
10 Stead, p. 81, c. 1825.
11 *W v B*, letter, 16 November 1824, from William to Pitman.

39. Strain Every Nerve

1 *W v B*, affidavit 39, Bulkeley, attached letter from Catherine dated 20 May 1825.
2 Bouverie was named guardian to Catherine and her siblings if Lady Catherine should die during their minority.
3 Redbridge, 90/96 (E8), letter, 21 May 1825.
4 Ibid.
5 Ibid., letter, early August 1825.
6 Ibid., letter, 21 May 1825. Windsor may have been alluding to the poet Percy Shelley, who lost custody of his children in 1817. This custody suit, however, was not instigated by his wife. Shelley had abandoned her and his children in 1814, but he tried to gain custody following his wife's suicide in 1816. The maternal grandparents retained guardianship, however, citing various grounds including the allegation that Shelley was insane.
7 Stowe, *Lady Byron Vindicated*, p. 38.
8 Ibid.
9 Ibid., p. 37.
10 Ibid., p. 6.
11 Stone, *Road to Divorce*, p. 325.
12 Ibid., p. 326.
13 Redbridge, 90/96 (E10).
14 *W v B*, affidavit 39, Bulkeley.
15 Ibid.

40. Siege at Clarges Street

1 Redbridge, 90/96 (E17), letter, 19 August 1824.
2 Ibid. (E24) letter, 22 February 1825.
3 Ibid. (E22), letter, 4 June 1825; also *W v B*, affidavit 33, Dora Tylney Long.
4 Ibid.
5 Ibid. (E3), letter, 5 June 1825.
6 Ibid., letter, 8 June 1825.
7 Ibid.
8 *W v B*, affidavit 21, William, cites letter 15 June 1825.
9 Redbridge, 09/96 (E24) letter, 3 July 1825; *W v B*, affidavit 44, Julius Hutchinson.
10 Ibid.
11 Ibid.
12 *W v B*, affidavits of Dora Tylney Long, William Herbert, Benjamin Schofield.

13 *The Times*, 12 July 1825.
14 *W v B*, affidavit 5, Dora Tylney Long.
15 Quotes in following section taken from *W v B*, affidavit 30, Bicknell.
16 Quotes in following section taken from *W v B*, affidavit 92, William Herbert, under butler.
17 Quotes in following section taken from *W v B*, affidavit 50, Benjamin Schofield, police officer.
18 Redbridge, 20127 (f. 23), letter, 20 August 1824.

41. The Paragon

1 *W v B*, affidavit 44, Hutchinson cites letter 20 August 1825.
2 *W v B*, affidavit 63, Hutchinson.
3 *W v B*, affidavit 44, Hutchinson cites letter from Catherine dated 28 August 1825.
4 Redbridge, 90/96 (E13), letter, 27 July 1825.
5 Ibid. (E8), letter, early August 1825.
6 Ibid. (E2), letter, 31 July 1825.
7 Quotes in following section taken from *W v B*, affidavit 5, Dora Tylney Long.
8 Barry, *Lady Victoria*, pp. 41–2.
9 Stead, p. 89.
10 Redbridge, 90/96 (E28).

42. Our Sweet Angel

1 Redbridge, 90/96 (E16), letter, 14 September 1825.
2 Ibid.
3 *W v B*, affidavit 62, Bulkeley, cites letter 12 September 1825.
4 Redbridge, 90/96 (E8), letter, 13 September 1825.
5 *W v B*, affidavit 53, William, cites letter to Yerbury dated 15 September 1825.
6 Ibid., cites letter to Pitman dated 15 September 1825.
7 Redbridge, 90/96 (loose letter), 17 September 1825.
8 Stead, p. 92.
9 Ibid., p. 82, c. September 1825.
10 *The Age*, 2 February 1827.
11 5 November 1826.
12 Stead, p. 82, c. September 1825.

43. Wellesley v Beaufort

1 *The Times*, 25 February 1826.
2 Hannah Barker, *Newspapers, Politics, and Public Opinion in late Eighteenth-Century England* (Oxford: Clarendon Press, 1998), p. 4.
3 Arthur Aspinall, *Politics and the Press c. 1780–1850* (London: Home & Van Thal, 1949), p. 28.
4 *Evening Herald*, 14 September 1825.
5 ERO, D/DB F116/1–4 – 1810–32, 5 January 1826; Redbridge, 15 February 1826, from Bouverie to Dora Long.
6 *W v B*, affidavit 36, James Nixon.
7 Ibid.
8 *W v B*, affidavit 64, Susannah Scott.
9 Barry, *Lady Victoria*, p. 32, 2 December 1825.
10 ODNB, John Scott (1751–1838), Lord Chancellor and first Earl Eldon.
11 *The Times*, 5 November 1825.
12 Ibid.
13 Ibid., 7 November 1825.
14 Ibid., 5 November 1825.
15 Ibid., 18 January 1827.
16 Ibid., 25 February 1826.
17 Stead, p. 89, 24 February 1826.
18 Ibid., *The Times*, 18 March 1826.
19 *The Times*, 2 November 1826.
20 Stead, p. 88, c. October 1826.
21 J. H. Baker, *An Introduction to English Legal History* (London: LexisNexis, 2002), pp. 456–7.
22 *The Times*, 2 November 1826.
23 Ibid.
24 *The Times*, 17 January 1827.
25 *The Times*, 30 January 1827; *The Age*, 4 February 1827.
26 *W v B*, affidavit 47, Pitman.
27 Ibid.
28 *W v B*, letter, 25 April 1825.
29 Redbridge, 90/96 (E17), letter, 22 February 1825.
30 *W v B*, letter, 1 March 1825.
31 *The Times*, 24 January 1827.
32 BMS, 15443, an extract from *The Effects of a Blithe W riding on a Long Pole*, hand-coloured etching by Isaac Robert Cruikshank. Published in London by John Fairburn of Ludgate Hill, 1827.

44. The Court of Public Opinion

1 Wellesley, *Letters to Eldon*, p. 2.
2 Ibid.
3 Stead, small volume, 17 January 1827.
4 Ibid.
5 *The Times*, 17 January 1827.
6 Stead, small volume, c. January 1827.
7 Ibid., 21 January 1826.
8 19 January 1827.
9 Stead, p. 83, c. December 1826.
10 22 January 1827.
11 *Evening Paper*, 1 February 1827, quotes *Morning Chronicle*.
12 Elizabeth Eger and Lucy Peltz, *Brilliant Women: 18th-Century Bluestockings* (London: National Portrait Gallery, 2008), p. 130.
13 Redbridge, 90/96 (E3), letter, 31 January 1827.
14 Ibid.
15 *Evening Paper*, 1 February 1827.
16 Details and quotes in the following section taken from *Evening Paper*, 1 February 1827.
17 Stone, *Road to Divorce*, p. 177.
18 Danaya C. Wright, 'Policing Sexual Morality: Percy Shelley and the Expansive Scope of the *Parens Patriae* in the Law of Custody of Children', *Nineteenth-century Gender Studies*, issue 8.2 (summer 2012), www.ncgsjournal.com/issue82/wright.htm.
19 Walter Lunden, *Systematic Source Book in Juvenile Deliquency* (University of Pittsburgh, 1938), pp. 63–81.
20 Stone, *Divorce*, pp. 177–8.

45. The Frolicsome Companion

1 Details and quotes in the following section taken from Longford, *Pillar of State*, pp. 252–3.
2 BMS, 15929, 1829 lithograph.
3 *Ipswich Journal*, 4 March 1826.
4 Christie's, sale catalogue dated 18 May 1827.
5 Wellesley, *Letters to Eldon*, appendix D pp. 116–17, 29 April 1827.
6 Ibid.
7 Details and quotes in the following section taken from *Baily's Monthly Magazine*, October 1863.
8 *The Times*, 18 July 1831.
9 Barry, *Lady Victoria*, p. 40.

10 Redbridge, 90/96 (E11), letter, 18 July 1831, from Maria Downshire to Dora Tylney Long.

11 Greg Roberts, unpublished Ph.D. thesis.

12 Ibid.

13 University of Southampton, Wellington Papers WP1/1185/33, letter, 28 July 1831, from Maria Kinnaird to the Duke of Wellington.

14 *Morning Chronicle*, 4 July 1857.

15 Ibid.

Epilogue

1 Barry, *Lady Victoria*, p. 71.

2 Ibid., p. 77.

3 Ibid., p. 76.

4 *Morning Chronicle*, 26 April 1839, 26 April 1843.

5 Redbridge, 90/96 (E4), letter, 19 February 1826.

6 Redbridge, 90/96 (E17), letter, 22 February 1825.

7 ODNB, William IV; Ziegler, *William IV*, pp. 150–55.

8 Jeremy Bentham, *Works of Jeremy Bentham*, vol. 3 (Edinburgh: William Tait, 1843), p. 27.

9 Redbridge, 90/96 (E10).

10 Ibid. (E11), letter, 14 January 1825.

11 Georgina Green, *Epping Forest through the Ages* (London: Kingfisher, 1982), p. 49. Officially, Wanstead Park did not form part of this open space until 1 August 1882.

Index